# Silver Threads

# SILVER THREADS

## 25 Years of Parapsychology Research

*edited by* BEVERLEY KANE,
JEAN MILLAY, AND DEAN BROWN

*Foreword by* Willis Harman

PRAEGER

Westport, Connecticut
London

**Library of Congress Cataloging-in-Publication Data**

Silver threads : 25 years of parapsychology research / edited by
  Beverley Kane, Jean Millay, and Dean Brown ; foreword by Willis
  Harman.
      p.    cm.
  Includes bibliographical references and index.
  ISBN 0–275–94161–2 (alk. paper)
  1. Parapsychology.   I. Kane, Beverley.   II. Millay, Jean.
  III. Brown, Dean (Harold Dean)
  BF1031.S49   1993
  133—dc20        92–28551

British Library Cataloguing in Publication Data is available.

Library of Congress Catalog Card Number: 92–28551
ISBN: 0–275–94161–2

First published in 1993

Praeger Publishers, 88 Post Road West, Westport, CT 06881
An imprint of Greenwood Publishing Group, Inc.

Printed in the United States of America

The paper used in this book complies with the Permanent
Paper Standard issued by the National Information Standards
Organization (Z39.48–1984).

10 9 8 7 6 5 4 3 2 1

**Copyright Acknowledgments**

The authors and publisher gratefully acknowledge permission to use the following materials.

M. Persinger and S. Krippner. Dream and ESP and geomagnetic activity. *JASPR* 1989; 83:101–116.

Panel discussion on increasing psychic reliability. *Journal of Parapsychology* 1991; 55.

K. Ring. Near-death experiences. *Revision* 1986; 8, no.2:75–86. Reprinted with permission of the Helen Dwight Reid Educational Foundation. Published by Heidref Publications, 1319 18th Street N.W., Washington, D.C. 20036–1802. Copyright 1986.

E. Rauscher and B. Rubik. Human volitional effects on a model bacterial system. *PSI Research Journal* 1983; 2, no.1.

*To Our Founders and Our Finders*

*This work is dedicated to those who
founded the Parapsychology Research Group
and to those who will find this book
where and when
it is most meaningful to them.*

## The Brightest Star

Ten billion years ago, at the heart of the universe,
  an explosion occurred that we call the beginning of time.
The fragments from that explosion fled their quintessential origin and
  raced in every direction at almost the speed of light.
We, of course, you and I, are the condensation of these star-born
    fragments:
Matter aware of itself.
Star children with brains and consciousness, who can look back across
  all of space and time,
To reexperience and almost comprehend the moment of our birth.

Russell Targ

# Contents

# Contents

# Figures and Tables

**FIGURES**

## TABLES

# Foreword: Shifting Assumptions

*Willis Harman*

A recent cartoon shows a woman driver attempting to deal with a police officer who has accosted her for driving the wrong way down a one-way street. "Officer," she says, "did it ever occur to you that maybe the sign is wrong?"

It seems clear in retrospect that the relatively unfriendly reception of the scientific and medical communities to research in psi phenomena, dissociative states, altered states of consciousness, and other areas related to consciousness in some of its nonnormal forms has been mainly because the meaning and significance people attach to these experiences seem to clash so directly with prevailing assumptions about the nature of scientific reality. But perhaps, like the one-way street sign, it is our "official" concept of reality that is wrong.

The basic subject material of this book is phenomena and experiences that are considered "paranormal." Most of these are common in or have been reported by a variety of cultures throughout human history. They would, on that account, seem to have a certain face validity. They are, however, considered "paranormal" or their genuineness is disputed because they have seemed to most scientists not to be amenable to explanation in any conceivable conceptual framework compatible with modern scientific knowledge. That is one puzzle.

A second puzzle is why competent researchers such as the authors of these essays should put so much dedication, energy, and time into the investigations herein reported when their work is so little appreciated by their scientific colleagues—indeed is more likely than not to bring them disapprobation. Their passion is more than one would expect from mere excitement of exploring unfamiliar phenomena.

One clue toward understanding this latter puzzle comes from the fact that these phenomena and experiences have in so many cultures been embedded in some sort of spiritual tradition. In other words, they seem linked to those experiences and insights that humankind has always considered most highly valued and meaningful. They are not necessarily in the same realm as the spiritual, but the two appear somehow related.

The editors, in their introduction, speak of how these explorations into the paranormal not only appear to transcend the boundaries of discovered knowledge; they "push the envelope of epistemology." They comprise "a challenge to the most entrenched theories about the nature of reality" and invite a "rethinking, refinement, and revolutionizing of the very philosophy of science." This is heady stuff. If the editors are not exaggerating, this amounts to a scientific revolution surpassing in its breadth and fundamental nature the Darwinian or quantum revolutions.

One needs to place this claim in the context of a reassessment that is already taking place within science. The extreme positivism and reductionism of science at midcentury have given way to more relaxed attitudes. Scientists exhibit growing appreciation of the need for more holistic and organismic models in the biological sciences and for a more participative methodology. Many scientists are seeking appropriate ways to include subjective experience as relevant data in the creation of our pictures of reality; others, including Nobel laureate neuroscientist Roger Sperry, argue that a complete science must include consciousness as agency.

The phenomena and experiences that are the stuff of parapsychological research occupy a crucial position in this contemporary reevaluation of the scientific method. They are of interest to scientists because they challenge accepted paradigms; at the same time, these experiences are, in the main, familiar in the contexts of diverse spiritual traditions—and comprise a conspicuous focus of interest in the contemporary "New Age" subcultures that in some sense seem to be a modern surrogate for religion.

Because science and religion perform different functions in modern society, they are not expected to be identical. Nonetheless, there are areas of overlapping interest, and in those areas, a mature science and a mature religion should agree or have compatible interpretations. Three of these overlap areas stand out as of particular significance: (1) the origin of the universe and the evolution or creation of humankind; (2) altered states of consciousness, including near-death and other transcendent experiences; and (3) the area of "meaningful coincidences," as will be discussed.

Thus it would seem that one of the reasons the paranormal commands from some people such a strong allegiance is because its subject matter so clearly falls in this overlap region, and hence it seems to hold a key to the centuries-old tension between science and religion.

But the first puzzle remains: Why do these experiences and phenomena seem to be so incongruous with the view of reality given us by mainstream science? One possibility is that the reports can all be dismissed as illusions, laboratory artifacts, or deliberate deceptions. Another is that the phenomena exist but are not really "paranormal"; that is, they will in good time turn out to be explainable through the normal concepts of science, including those mysterious concepts of quantum physics. A third possibility is that there has been something wrong with science that precluded acceptance of these phenomena. As noted above, a few scientists are seriously considering this last possibility in ways and to an extent that would have been unthinkable even a couple of decades ago.

## THE PRESENT CHALLENGE TO SCIENCE

It has not only been people's other-states-of-consciousness and paranormal experiences that challenge the worldview of modern science. Among the areas in which there are major failures of the prevailing scientific worldview to accommodate well-established evidence are the following.

1. The fundamental inquiry within physics into the ultimate nature of things does not appear to be convergent. The search for fundamental particles seems to lead to still more fundamental particles; the search for the ultimate reductionist explanation seems to point to a wholeness. It is a fundamental initial assumption of physics, which has influenced every other area of science, that ultimate reality consists of fundamental particles, separate from one another and interacting through mechanisms (especially fields) that can be discovered and specified. But with Bell's theorem, quantum physics now displays an inherent contradiction; particles originally assumed separate turn out, apparently, to be connected.

2. There appears to be evidence for a fundamental self-organizing force in living systems, from the smallest to the largest known organisms, that remains unexplained by physical principles. Living systems exhibit a tendency toward self-organization (e.g., homeostasis; intricate patterns in flowers and butterfly wings), toward preservation of integrity (e.g., healing and regeneration; ontogenesis from a single fertilized egg to an adult organism), and toward survival of the organism and the species (e.g., complex instinctual patterns for protection and reproduction). The evidences of a cumulative effect, over time, of this self-organizing tendency in evolution cast doubt on the adequacy of the neo-Darwinist orthodox view.

3. There is a persistent puzzle of "action at a distance" or nonlocal causality. This shows up, as we have already observed, in the far reaches of quantum physics. It also appears in the area that John Beloff calls "meaningful coincidences," referring to two or more events in which there appears to be a *meaningful* connection although there is no physical connection.[1] Here "meaningful" may refer either to the subjective judgment of the observer or to a judgment

based in historical data (as in the case of astrology or the I Ching). The term meaningful coincidences includes Carl Jung's "synchronicity" and most of the range of the paranormal.[2] Examples include apparently telepathic communication, seemingly clairvoyant remote viewing, and the coincidence between the act of prayer and the occurrence of the prayed-for, such as healing. Another example is the feeling of having a guardian angel when a person feels warned about a danger or provided with a particularly fortuitous circumstance in life. A host of historical and anecdotal examples fall into the categories of "miracles" and "psi phenomena."

4. Our scientific knowledge about the universe appears to be incomplete in that there is no place in it for the consciousness of the observer—nor, in general, for volition (free will) or any of the other attributes of consciousness. Sperry insists that no science can be complete that does not include downward causation, from the higher level of consciousness to the lower, physicochemical level.[3]

5. One of the most perplexing aspects of consciousness' challenge to science is the concept of the self. The conscious self is ineluctably involved in observation; yet the science constructed from those observations contains no place for the self. Psychologist Gordon Allport wrote in 1955, in a little volume entitled *Becoming* (New Haven, Ct: Yale University Press), "For two generations, psychologists have tried every conceivable way of accounting for the integration, organization and striving of the human person without having recourse to the postulate of a self." The battle is still going on.

6. Related, but worthy of separate mention, is the area of altered states of consciousness, including particularly those states traditionally sought out in a spiritual or mystical context.

## REVIEWING THE NATURE OF SCIENTIFIC INQUIRY

To understand what it means for science to be presented with such a broad challenge, we need to review some basic aspects of scientific inquiry.

### Quine's "Theoretical Network" Argument

W.V.O. Quine, a major figure in recent philosophy of science, argued that the scientific explanation for any phenomenon is embedded in a theoretical network that involves multitudinous assumptions, including:[4]

1. assumptions involved in "observations" of the phenomenon;
2. hypotheses about the context of the phenomenon;
3. underlying theoretical hypotheses;
4. basic laws of the pertinent area of science;
5. the accepted nature of scientific methodology;

6. epistemological assumptions that underlie scientific inquiry; and

7. ontological assumptions about the basic nature of reality.

When there is an anomaly, or a failure of observations to conform to scientific expectations, it means that *somewhere* in that network there is a falsity. There is no way to tell just where in the theoretical network the falsity lies. Thus, in the face of an anomaly, we must consider revising any or all elements of the network. There ultimately is no such thing as a crucial experiment to prove a scientific hypothesis. Hypotheses and conceptual models are useful or not useful—not true or false.

When experience contradicts scientific theory, the theory must be changed, but there is no infallible logic for determining what to change. Karl Popper's insistence that theories are never proved, but only falsified or not, seemed at one point an important insight; in today's science, to talk of verification or falsification of theory sounds naive and simplistic. We must, says Quine, give up any idea that we can use experience either *to confirm or to falsify* particular scientific hypotheses. A consequence of Quine's view is that even our epistemological convictions about how we acquire knowledge and about the nature of explanation, justification, and confirmation are subject to revision and correction.

It is precisely to that point that present-day scientific paradoxes have brought us. Most scientists today would assert that science has moved away from the strict determinism, reductionism, positivism, and behaviorism of a half century ago. But it appears that subtler forms of "isms" remain, and it is not clear what scientists are moving *toward*.

## THREE ASPECTS OF SCIENTIFIC INQUIRY

In arguing that the areas of human experience listed above constitute a fundamental challenge to the adequacy of modern science, we are in no way attacking the fundamental spirit of scientific inquiry. We are, rather, suggesting that it is time for science to take a major step in its own evolution.

This point can be made more clear by considering the three basic aspects of scientific inquiry:[5]

1. *The activity of constructing, testing, and using conceptual models.* Creating, testing, and applying conceptual models make up the chief *activity* of scientists. It is not unique to science; the main way little children learn about their environment is to create mental models and test them by experience. The uniqueness of scientific inquiry lies in the other two aspects.

2. *The distinguishing values of science.* Chief among these are openness of inquiry, healthy skepticism, and public validation of knowledge.

3. *Adopted assumptions.* Modern science is characterized by certain basic ontological and epistemological assumptions that are the result of both the long-standing characteristics of Western culture and the tension between science and

the Church around the seventeenth century. It is in these basic assumptions that the current form of science is most vulnerable to challenge.

## THE METAPHYSICAL FOUNDATIONS OF MODERN SCIENCE

As a result of both the long-standing characteristics of Western culture and the tension between science and the Church around the seventeenth century, Western science by the eighteenth century had adopted an *ontological assumption of separateness:* separability of observer from observed, of man from nature, of mind from matter, of science from religion; separateness of fundamental particles from one another, separability of the parts of a system or organism to understand how it really works; separateness of scientific disciplines, of investigators competing over who was first discoverer.

The assumption of separateness leads to the hubris that we as humans can pursue our own objectives as though the earth and the other creatures are here for our benefit, to the myth of the objective observer, to reductionist explanations, and to the ethic of competition. It implies the locality of causes; that is, it precludes action at a distance, in either space or time. It implies the *epistemological assumption* that our sole empirical basis for constructing a science is the data from our physical senses.

From these two metaphysical assumptions follow others that have been assumed intrinsic to modern science; perhaps the most important of these are *objectivism,* the assumption of an objective world that the observer can hold at a distance and study separately from himself; *positivism,* the assumption that the real world is what is physically measurable; and *reductionism,* the assumption that we come to really understand a phenomenon through studying the behavior of its elemental parts (e.g., fundamental particles).

These are essentially the assumptions of *logical empiricism.* By the middle of this century, there was almost complete consensus that these are the proper foundation assumptions for science. They amount to the premise that the basic stuff of the universe is what physicists study: matter and physical energy—ultimately, fundamental particles and their associated fields and interrelations.

Scientists typically assume (or behave as though they do) that the philosophical premises that underlie science are not at issue—that they are part of the definition of science. And indeed, the traditional root assumptions are agreed to have served the physical sciences well. (To be sure, these foundation assumptions have been modified with the advent of quantum physics, particularly by the indeterminacy principle and the inherent statistical nature of measurement of the very small.) They have not served the biological sciences so well, however, despite the prevailing faith that ultimately everything in biology will be explained through molecular biology. And they have been a disaster when the human and social sciences have attempted to ape the science of physics. It is in these basic assumptions that the current form of science is most vulnerable to challenge.

Having started with a limiting set of assumptions, science has then found it necessary to deny the validity and even the possibility of a host of reported phenomena that don't fit within those limits. A tremendous amount of effort has gone on within science to defend the barricades against or to explain away these outcasts, such as miraculous healings and psi phenomena, as well as more ordinary experiences, such as volition, selective attention, and the hunger for meaning. If there is validity to the subject matter of this collection of essays, we are talking now about far more fundamental change—actual replacement of these underlying assumptions by dramatically different assumptions.

## TOWARD A MORE HOLISTIC SCIENCE

There is increasingly widespread agreement that science must develop the ability to look at things holistically. In a holistic view, everything, including physical and mental, is connected to everything, and a change in any part affects the whole. From this perspective, it is only when a part of the whole can be sufficiently isolated from the rest that reductionistic causes *appear* to adequately describe why things behave as they do. In the old view, the ordinary concepts of scientific causation apply, but in the wholeness view, *causes are limited explanations that depend on context.*

The mistake of modern society has been to assume that reductionistic scientific causes ultimately can explain everything. One should not expect reductionistic science to constitute an adequate worldview. The context of reductionistic science is the desire to gain control through manipulation of the physical environment. Within that context, its description of causes works amazingly well. Our problems arise when we change the context and attempt to elevate that kind of science to the level of a worldview. That is when we generate conflicts like free will versus determinism and science versus religion.

One of the main implications of a science based on oneness is the epistemological assumption that *we contact reality in not one, but two ways.* One of these is through physical sense data, which form the basis of normal science. The other is through being ourselves part of the oneness—through a deep, intuitive "inner knowing." In other words, the epistemological issue involved is whether our encountering of reality is limited to being aware of and giving meaning to the messages from our physical senses (sometimes referred to as objective) or whether it also includes a subjective aspect in an intuitive, aesthetic, spiritual, noetic, and mystical sense. (In this connection, an intuitive and aesthetic factor already enters into normal science in various ways—for example, the aesthetic principle of elegance; the principle of parsimony in choosing between alternative explanations.)

There is much to be said in favor of this proposition that science be restructured on the basis of an *ontological assumption of oneness and wholeness* and an *epistemological choice to include as input both physical sense data and subjective experience,* in particular the experience of such trained "inner explorers" as are found in the various esoteric and spiritual traditions.

Such an extended science would meet many of the criteria of the current attempts to reform science. It would not invalidate any of the physical and biological science we now have; it would, rather, be more inclusive.

It would favor more holistic and organismic models in the biological sciences; it would not be reductionist in any dogmatic sense. The biological sciences involve holistic concepts (e.g., organism, function of an organ) that have no counterparts at and are not reducible to the physical sciences level. Similarly, there is no reason to assume that the characteristics of consciousness are reducible to biology. In other words, although theory reduction (as, for example, the laws of optics explained through electromagnetic theory) will be welcomed whenever it proves to be possible, it is not a dogma of this science that it must be possible.

Such a science implies the appropriateness of finding ways to include subjective experience as relevant data in the creation of our pictures of reality; it also implies the inclusion of consciousness as agency.

It would include and emphasize more participative kinds of methodologies; it would assume that whereas we learn certain kinds of things by distancing ourselves from the subject studied, we get another kind of knowledge from intuitively becoming one with the subject. In such research, the experience of observing brings about sensitization and other changes in the observer. A *willingness to be transformed* himself or herself is an essential characteristic of the participatory scientist. The anthropologist who truly wants to understand a culture other than her own must allow that experience to change her so that the new culture is seen through new eyes, not eyes conditioned by her own culture. The psychotherapist who would perceive his client without distortion must have worked through his own neuroses that otherwise would warp perception. The social scientist who uses a participative approach to understanding and guiding organizational arrangements and processes will almost certainly be changed through his or her involvement. So the scientist who wants to study meditative processes and the transcendent experiences discussed in Section V of this book (let alone those "other states of consciousness" so treasured in the various spiritual traditions) has to be willing to go through the deep changes that will make him or her a competent observer.

This extended science would be concerned with downward causation, including causation from consciousness, as well as the reductionistic upward causation that currently dominates the scientific world. In such a science, conscious awareness, unconscious processes, volition, and the concept of the self do not present any fundamental contradiction. Nor does the recommendation, in the perennial wisdom of the world's spiritual traditions, of an inner search involving some sort of meditative or yogic discipline and the discovery of and identification with a higher or true Self that is beyond the physical realm but is nevertheless real.

Openness to alternative theories and explanations as well as healthy skepticism would be at least as important in this extended science as they are in modern science. Consensual validation of findings also would remain of central importance, but it would be accomplished in a different way.

Rather than having to defend against the anomalous, wholeness science permits the assumption that any class of inner experiences that have been reported or of phenomena that have been observed through the ages and across cultures apparently in some sense exist and have a face validity that cannot be denied. We seek, in other words, a science that can accommodate all that exists. (There are many subtleties. Whole societies can perceive things that observers from other societies do not, so it is necessary to be cautious about claiming that some class of experiences is universal, even in potential. There is a tendency among some people to regard it as a mark of New Age distinction to be willing to believe almost anything. Total gullibility is not a useful objective.)

The phenomena and experiences that are the stuff of parapsychological research, which are considered paranormal with respect to modern science, would fit comfortably in such a restructured science. That fact is brought out most clearly by a comparison of the sorts of questions one is led to ask in the two frameworks.

The combination of an ontological assumption of separateness, together with a positivistic assumption that what science deals with are ultimately quantifiable aspects of physical reality, has led scientists to be interested in certain types of questions, such as the following:

- If things are apparently separate and yet interact, what is the mechanism of the interaction? How to explain the interaction between two fundamental particles? Two celestial bodies? Two remotely located human beings? Action at a distance is a major puzzle; attempts to deal with it have centered around concepts of fields (gravitational, electromagnetic, morphogenetic) and particle exchange.

- Extrapolating backward to the big bang theory or to other theories about the origin of the universe in its current form, what have been the chief mechanisms of evolution of the physical world and the world of living organisms?

- How does the appearance of purpose arise in the world of living organisms and human experience? That is, how can it be explained in terms of such mechanisms as chance and natural selection?

- How can the experience of conscious awareness, selective attention, and so on be explained in terms of brain functioning and other mechanisms?

- What is the physical explanation for such meaningful coincidences or anomalous phenomena as apparently clairvoyant remote viewing or seeming psychokinesis?

If science were to be reconstituted on the basis of the ontological assumption of oneness and the epistemological assumption that in addition to the "outer" way of interacting with the universe, through the physical senses, there is an "inner" way through one's own consciousness and intuition, the questions of interest might appear quite differently. For example:

- What has been the evolution of the whole system (including the evolution of so-called scientific laws, since the constancy and inviolability of these cannot be taken for granted)? What has been the role of consciousness in evolution?
- If all is one, how does the appearance of separateness arise?
- If individual human minds are parts of a oneness, how do we avoid total confusion because of all the potential communication? Does the brain, then, function as a filter or as a reducing valve?
- Because I experience meaning and purpose in my own life and I am part of the intercommunicating whole, it is not surprising to find evidence of purpose in the universe. What can be said about this that may serve as a guide to individual and societal development?

Many of the questions about a wholeness science have been discussed in the literature under the definition of naturalistic inquiry.[6] The purpose of naturalistic inquiry is *understanding,* not prediction and control. It emphasizes the human as instrument, tacit knowledge, and qualitative inquiry.

Goodwin has described aspects of a "science of qualities."[7] It shares many of the aspects we have been considering. He urges that we "return to the vision of the Renaissance magi, in which subject and object, known and unknown, can relate and participate in an appropriate unity, made possible by the fact that reality is a single coordinated domain."

Some of the more radical implications of a wholeness science are not immediately apparent. Imagine starting from the holistic assumption that everything—not only physical things, but all things experienced, including sensations, emotions, feelings, motivations, thoughts—is really part of a single unity. If things are so interconnected that a change in any one can affect all, then *any accounting for cause is within a specific context, for a specific purpose.* In the broadest sense, *there are not cause and effect, but only a whole system evolving.* What normal science does, in this view, is to study relatively isolable systems in which causal factors can be considered limited and, in particular, in which no volitional factors need be taken into account. (To recall how special this is, note that the judicial setting comprises another special case, wherein volition and motivation are considered central.) Starting from the holistic assumption, there is no ultimate separation of observer from observed. Action at a distance does not pose a particular problem; we don't even have to hypothesize fields or particle exchanges to account for it. We don't find volition, other states of consciousness, teleological influences, meaningful coincidences, and so forth to be anomalous. To reemphasize the point, none of modern science is invalidated in the limited domains in which it was generated. However, some of the common extrapolations of scientific findings into the larger area of human affairs become questionable.

## SUMMARY

The point of all this discussion is that what is paranormal is a function of choice of the foundation assumptions of science. If the current metaphysical foundations are retained, it appears likely that the sorts of phenomena described in this book will remain paranormal and more or less ostracized from the halls of science. But there is another path: to recognize that the problem is not with the paranormal, but with our concept of science—more specifically with the metaphysical foundations adopted in the course of modern science's evolution.

If science were to be recast by building on the oneness assumption rather than on separability, it would appear not only to accommodate the paranormal, but also to respond to other complaints. For one thing, although the reductionistic science would still be available for the purposes to which it is suited, it would no longer have the authority to insist that we are here, solely through random causes, in a meaningless universe or that our consciousness is merely the chemical and physical processes of the brain. Lynn Margulis, professor of botany at the University of Massachusetts Amherst, told an audience at the 1991 annual meeting of the American Association for the Advancement of Science that bacteria and other one-celled animals react as though they involve something akin to consciousness in the human being. If something like consciousness is to be found in all living organisms, is it utterly preposterous to postulate a substratum of consciousness that pervades the entire physical universe? Or, for that matter, a superstratum?

The time is ripe to insist on a reexamination of the metaphysical foundations of modern science. Until this is done, research on consciousness will continue to miss the mark because it will continue to be distorted by the misguided attempt to fit it into a basically reductionistic and positivistic framework. We cannot let legitimate experimental results be excluded by the tyranny of founding assumptions that masquerade as ineluctable axioms or valid scientific findings.

The true significance of the subject matter of this collections of essays is that it points to this paradox of experience that doesn't fit in, and thus hastens the day when we may have a more adequate science: one that includes all the findings and powers of reductionistic science but puts them in a different context in which everything in human experience is validated and affirmed.

## NOTES

1. Beloff J. Psi phenomena: causal versus acausal interpretation. *Journal of the Society for Psychical Research.* 1977;49:773.

2. Peat FD. *Synchronicity: The Bridge Between Matter and Mind.* New York: Bantam; 1987.

3. Sperry RW. Structure and significance of the consciousness revolution. *Journal of Mind and Behavior.* 1987;8:1.

4. Quine WVO. *From a Logical Point of View.* 2nd ed. Cambridge, MA: Harvard University Press; 1962.

5. Rubenstein RA, Laughlin CD, Jr., McManus J. *Science as Cognitive Process: Toward an Empirical Philosophy of Science.* Philadelphia: University of Pennsylvania Press; 1984.

6. Lincoln YS, Guba ES. *Naturalistic Inquiry.* Troy, NY: Sage Publications; 1985.

7. Goodwin B. A science of qualities. In: Hilary BT, Peat FD, eds. *Quantum Implications: Festschrift for David Bohm.* London: Routledge & Kegan Paul; 1987.

# Acknowledgments

On behalf of the Parapsychology Research Group, we thank our founders, members, and benefactors for their visionary support of psi research. We are honored to have had Russell Targ followed by Charles Tart as our first two presidents. Tart was succeeded by Barbara Honegger, Elizabeth Rauscher, Saul-Paul Sirag, and Jean Millay. We gratefully acknowledge those who have hosted our meetings throughout the past quarter century: Jeffrey Smith, Nancy Keisling, and, later, Henry Dakin and his staff at the Washington Research Institute. They have generously provided comfort, hospitality, and inspiration through many long and lively meetings. Henry Dakin deserves additional gratitude for providing closed-circuit television monitors during meetings and audio and video recordings of our speakers. We thank our many distinguished visitors from around the world who have shared their research and their perspectives with us at our meetings. Ginger Ashworth has skillfully produced and distributed our monthly meeting notices, often at short notice. We additionally thank the many people who have served on the board of directors over the years, especially our current directors, who have spirited the book along with technical, historical, and creative assistance: Jean Burns, Henry Dakin, Ruth-Inge Heinze, Bryan McRae, Elizabeth Rauscher, Russell Targ, and Shelley Thomson.

On behalf of ourselves as editors, we thank those who spent tireless hours helping to prepare the book for publication: Ginger Ashworth, Jean Burns, Stephan Fuelling, and Carol Guion. Sola Patricia and Mary-Minn Peet-Sirag, the latter at her solar-powered, generator-run Macintosh-in-the-mountains, helped in the tedious process of tape transcription. Jane Oros of the Apple Computer Library Laboratory and Gary Hom helped to boldly scan where no one has scanned before. To Gary goes major credit for digitizing and enhancing the figures in the remote-viewing section. We also give appreciation for assistance from Charles Brush.

On behalf of ourselves as our selves, we acknowledge the unconditional support of our spouses, Rubén Kleiman-Kane and Wendy Wiegand.

# Introduction

## CONSCIOUSNESS

The science of consciousness—mind as process and mind in its states of being—has fascinated thoughtful people since the dawn of psychological time. In these times, our times, remarkable strides in science and technology and the flowering of creativity reflect the evolution of contemporary awareness. Those who have ventured to the frontiers of art and science confront mysteries in which the unexplained and the unexpressed push the envelope of epistemology. In the dialectics of change, quantitatively small discoveries produce a qualitatively different worldview. Each qualitative change reflects a small revolution in consciousness. In the formative years before such revolutions, pioneers set out, first tentatively and then boldly, guided by experience and intuition as much as by the traditional tools of the rational mind.

## THE PARAPSYCHOLOGY RESEARCH GROUP

Twenty-five years ago, a remarkable group of pioneers began organizing new discoveries into a rethinking, an updating, a refinement, a modernizing of the traditional concepts of the structures of consciousness. The past quarter century has brought together doctors of philosophy, medicine, physics, biochemistry, anthropology, education, and psychology, both researchers and clinical practitioners. Among the group also are computer scientists, engineers, artists, writers, poets, shamans, and spiritual healers. All have experienced unexplained events that do not properly fit within the scope of religion or science. The anomalous events typically occur in the context of one's professional field. For instance, a psychologist discovers that in his experience with his multiple-personality patients: "I have spoken to 'spirit voices' who have come through [patients with] multiple [personalities] who have told me things about my childhood. Specifics, like things that hung in the house. There's some undeniable evidence that something happens, something we don't understand and can't measure."[1]

The significance of these curiosities is a matter of perception and interpretation and personal choice. One chooses either to examine the small deviations or to shrug them off. In the PRG, the common thread running through the ineffable in each person's experiences has been the suspicion that at stake is a challenge to the most entrenched theories about the nature of reality. Our common goal has thus become an exploration of the nature of brain, mind, perception, and the physical and metaphysical universe.

We call ourselves the Parapsychology Research Group. The title is perhaps a misnomer, if one adheres to a strict definition of research as consisting of experimental activities and of parapsychology as consisting of the study of telepathy, clairvoyance, precognition, and psychokinesis. Although many members of the PRG are indeed internationally respected experimental parapsychologists, the PRG as an organization is a forum for ideas.

PRG membership has undergone many combinations and permutations over the years, but a stable core of the original group has met continuously since its inception. The format of the meetings is didactic, with an occasional meeting given to experiential (visualization, psychokinesis) or demonstrative (computer applications, shamanistic drumming) agendas.

Over the years, we have insisted that it is the duty of any avowed scientist to maintain open-mindedness about all human experiences. Twentieth-century natural laws reflect not merely the absolute limits of our measuring instruments, but, as throughout history, prevailing politics and popular psychology.

The concepts of scientific law and scientific method are continually being refined and deepened. The laws of the universe, as expressed in the many sciences, can be applied to the study of mind. Conversely, it has been fruitful to apply the laws of the mind to the laws that govern the other sciences. In physics, as Herbert discusses in Chapter 8, the role of the observer in measurement bred new philosophies of reality. In other sciences as well, it becomes imperative to consider the psychological factors that introduce observer bias into experiments. After all, it is impossible to contemplate or to observe any object of science except through the instrument of the mind.

Despite the generally liberal milieu of the San Francisco Bay Area and its Silicon Valley, and often despite their high professional standing, PRG members frequently face a harsh climate of intellectual dogmatism. So we have given one another the permission and the conviction and the stamina to assail outdated conventions and patterns of thought, while maintaining our own flexibility. We must have the courage to restructure, when necessary, our own secure deep habits, beliefs, values, and realities.

Why do we do it? Because the subtle clues about the universe that we receive through experience compel us to investigate as scientists; because to reject these gifts, these glimpses, is to fragment our own psyches; because the study of mind is the consummate metascience, providing the ultimate road map for the attainment of a richer humanity.

## THE BOOK

*Silver Threads* is an anthology of worldviews expressed from different perspectives and in different idioms. Some of the chapters consist of monographs derived from transcripts of PRG meetings; others are previously published works by PRG members and speakers; most chapters are original to this book. Some material has been edited for space considerations, but nowhere has there been an attempt to referee or unify the ideological content.

The essays are arranged somewhat arbitrarily into six sections, mapping out the broad parapsychological domain. Organized another way, the areas in which we present our findings and hypotheses are as follows:

1. Remote-viewing
2. Psychokinesis
3. Anagogies of physics and other sciences
4. States of consciousness and state-dependent processes
5. Methodology and experimental design
6. Medicine and healing

We suspect that in fact there is no difference between psi phenomena and those considered to be normal psychological processes. We predict that paranormal functions eventually will be identified as normative as more evidence accumulates and more sophisticated paradigms are worked out. In any case, the only way to proceed is to solicit and sift through more data and to strive for more comprehensive models.

In anticipation of such enlightened models, we begin with a basic theory section intended to cleanse us of some overwrought preconceptions about reality. We critically examine the foundations of scientific traditions and presage some new methodologies within science itself.

An excellent, definitive textbook, *Foundations of Parapsychology*,[2] rigorously and systematically details the historical, experimental, and theoretical bases of the subject. In our volume, we are saying, "We are the PRG. Here are some of the ideas we have entertained over the years. We trust that our book will synchronistically arrive in the hands of those for whom it will have meaning and value."

## THE TITLE

*Remember also your Creator in the days of your youth . . . before the silver cord is snapped . . . and the dust returns to the earth as it was, and the spirit returns to God who gave it.*

Ecclesiastes 12:1, 6, 7

On our Silver Anniversary, we evoke the image of the thread that, according to the Bible, connects the soul to the body. At death, the silver thread is severed, allowing the soul to float free to where all knowledge is available to it.

Research means exploration of new territories in an adventuresome, nonjudgmental manner. As the survey in the Appendix reveals, the beliefs and experiences of the PRG membership are heterogeneous. The editors are ourselves of diverse minds and abilities. Nevertheless, we accord the utmost respect to each author's viewpoint and to the sincerity and integrity of his or her pursuit of truth.

It is to those who seek to understand their own personal psychic experiences and to those who, even on purely rational grounds, suspect that "there must be something else out there" that this book is dedicated. It is for those who have ever dreamed about something that happened later and those who suddenly knew about an important event without being told. We show that these experiences are common around the world, from tribespeople to technocrats. Most important, we show that it is possible to nurture a permissive yet scholarly collegial structure in which to test the waters of reality without prejudice about allowable outcomes.

*Silver Threads* is the celebration of twenty-five years of open discussions about the nature of the psyche and its role in the universe. The evidence we present for the supernormal abilities of the mind is neither conclusive nor complete. However, as we entwine our threads together, we weave the fabric of a new consciousness.

## NOTES

1. New York psychologist Armand DiMele, in Klimo J. *Channeling: Investigations on Receiving Information from Paranormal Sources.* Los Angeles: Tarcher; 1987.

2. Edge HL, Morris RL, Rush JH, and Palmer J. *Foundations of Parapsychology.* Boston: Routledge & Kegan Paul; 1986.

*Silver Threads*

# I ————————————————

# FOUNDATIONS

*We begin with a basic theory section intended to cleanse us of some over-wrought preconceptions.*

from the Introduction

The cleansing process began in Willis Harman's foreword. ''Shifting Assumptions'' connotes a change in progress, the active transition from an old perspective to a new one. At this writing, another, analogous process has defined a new art genre: digital ''morphing''—from ''metamorphosis''—used in cinematography (and epitomized in *Terminator II* and Michael Jackson's *Black or White*) to create startling visual transformations of one object or person into another. In essence, our foreword and our Foundations section are morphing old beliefs into new at three complementary levels.

At the most general level, Harman reviewed the philosophy of science and initiated the reevaluation of our most fundamental concepts of science, philosophy, and the mind.

At the next, more solidified level, William Kautz delves further into the elements of scientific praxis. Kautz' most valuable contribution is to demystify terms like paranormal and psychic. By reframing and expanding these concepts to the more familiar notion of *intuition,* Kautz orients us to the unusual concepts in subsequent chapters.

At ground level, Beverley Kane focuses the broader discussion of philosophy, science, and society in an examination of the individual's everyday experience. Her thesis is that although the scientific method is and will continue to be appropriate to some types of formal investigations, it was never intended to disqualify the personal events that it cannot contain.

*Silver Threads* is about the science of the possible. In a colorful, fluid melting of images, Harman has morphed the dominant conservative philosophy into a liberal and visionary one; Kautz will morph skepticism about the paranormal into certainty about the intuitive; Kane will morph overreliance on formal proof systems into validation of personal experience. As basic theoretical *Foundations,* these two chapters reveal the *fundamental* nature of the perspectives and values in *Silver Threads*.

1 —————————————————————————————

# Parapsychology, Science, and Intuition

*William H. Kautz*

## THE FOUNDATION OF SCIENTIFIC INQUIRY

What is science, really? It is a number of things.[1] First, science is a collection of individuals—people who have defined themselves as scientists by orientation, education, or career. When we remark that "science says this" or "science says that," we usually are speaking about this collection of people.

Science also is a body of knowledge. Its accepted role in Western society is to generate information and authoritative answers to selected questions. Science is, therefore, a way of interpreting reality. When something new occurs in the world that is not understood, such as AIDS or an earthquake or acid rain, public officials and the media turn to scientists for an explanation. Reporters call the universities and expect that these institutions harbor the answer. In trusting such authorities, we often miss other dimensions of the issue at hand. For example, by focusing on a causative virus or other external agent to explain AIDS, we initially missed the important role played by the mind in controlling the body's immunity as well as the human caring side of the epidemic: how to live one's final moments on earth with dignity, be they forty days or forty years in the future.[2]

More than either of these aspects, science is a methodology for growing new knowledge from old. Modern science emerged a few hundred years ago out of a kind of deal with religion.[3] Up to that time, the church and its hierarchy of authorities (yes, the parallels are ominous!) held the final word on the interpretation and meaning of the world as it was then perceived. In effect, science said, "All right, we're now going to take charge of the material world. You church folks can keep the rest of reality." A new method, the scientific method, along with sophisticated tools, was gradually devised for exploring the physical world, creating thereby a collection of systematic information about it. In time, a great body of solid knowledge was built up about physical energy and matter, large and small, visible and invisible, in its many forms. A burgeoning technology was fed by this knowledge with profound social consequences.

Other fields of human endeavor, like anthropology, biology, and psychology, which lay on the fringes of the material world, tried to copy this amazing new methodology with various results.

To take this grand step, the budding science made a few simple assumptions—and then proceeded to almost forget them. We need to look at these assumptions.[4]

Surely the most crucial assumption is that there exists an objective reality, essentially separate from the human mind and simply present to be observed by humans. This assumption sounds fairly reasonable, especially now that we have been living with it for a few hundred years. It has worked well for understanding virtually all of the material world examined so far. When scientific methodology has been applied to human beings, including the experimenter doing the observing, it has been less successful. Related difficulties have arisen in fundamental particle physics as the finest components of matter were probed: certain observations were found to unavoidably affect the process under observation.[5]

Another assumption is the reductionist one: the way to understand anything is to break it down into its simpler components, understand these components, and then reassemble the simpler understandings into a whole. Again, this sounds reasonable and seems to have served well in the material world, but the farther one moves into personal and social situations, the more it is found that a reductionist approach is sorely inadequate. The many forms of life appear to be highly interconnected, and the essence of their functioning lies more in the nature of these interconnections than in the separate components.

The positivist assumption says, in effect, if you can't measure something, then it is not real. This, then, excludes from study anything that is not measurable. The physical world as we know it is certainly measurable: energy, mass, movement, properties of materials. But how much of the total human experience are we missing? The most important aspects of our lives cannot be measured, and therefore cannot be part of scientific knowledge.

There is one more assumption, actually more of a convention: the requirement for verification. When research is used to convert private experience to public knowledge, the principle of reproducibility requires that experiments be designed so that they can be repeated by anyone who has the appropriate equipment and skills. This practice allows findings to be verified independently—

historically a fine idea, especially in comparison with the unilateral way in which religion had been establishing knowledge.

Despite its virtues, this convention excludes from examination almost all one-time events, especially unexpected events, unless one is fortunate enough to have adequate instrumentation focused on the event at the moment it occurs. In particular, the replication requirement excludes many cosmic events, most earthquakes, alleged UFOs, and a host of spontaneous occurrences in what we have defined as biology, sociology, and psychology. Most seriously, it excludes the richest personal mind experiences, including those of special interest to parapsychologists.

By making these assumptions, science effectively excluded a large segment of knowledge that it might otherwise have generated over the centuries. As we approach the end of the twentieth century, we are discovering more and more aspects of life that science has not only excluded, but can never include because of these restrictive assumptions. We also are realizing more and more strongly the heavy price we are paying for this omission.

These basic assumptions have a number of practical implications.[6] First, it is presumed in science that all knowledge arises from sensual perception; there is no other way to generate knowledge. Second, the positivist assumption is taken to imply that everything currently regarded as qualitative will ultimately be found to be quantitative if we just work on it hard enough. Subjective experience may be valuable for the individual, but it doesn't lead to publicly verifiable information, so it is not of much use. Moreover, consciousness, or whatever we call consciousness, arises from matter, out of our brains, and not the other way around: whatever awareness we have of the world is fundamentally based on the principles of physics, chemistry, and biology. In addition, our only access to the future is through an analytical process.

The net effect of these centuries of research is that science has built a mammoth tower of knowledge, solid as a rock, about the physical world. This tower is a wonderful accomplishment, with many positive benefits to humankind. It is narrow, however, since it leaves out much of reality as we know it. As already noted, science has almost nothing to say about those personal and social events that are the high points or the turning points of our lives. This is not to say that material reality is invalid or unimportant, but rather that it is pitifully incomplete. It is simply all that can be effectively inquired about through present-day science.

## IS SCIENCE TOTALLY RATIONAL? WELL, NOT QUITE

Most of the stages of scientific discovery are completely systematic and rational, but two of these stages appear to depend strongly on another faculty of the human mind. Let us examine these.

The scientific method is essentially cyclic. It consists of a sequence of steps moving in a circle, but each time the circle is traversed, a little more is learned, so the circle is actually more like a spiral. At one point of each cycle a hypothesis is formed, a statement that *might* be true. Some kind of experiment or a plan of observation is then devised in an attempt to substantiate or refute the hypothesis. The experiment and observations are carried out; the data are collected, processed, and analyzed; and deductions are then drawn, using the tools of logic and mathematics. These deductions then permit the formulation of a new and better hypothesis. The cyclic process continues. Eventually a chain of validated hypotheses combine to create a theory, which is a kind of model that expresses how the natural world appears to be working.

Every step of this process is perfectly linear and logical—except one: within the methodology of science there is no fully systematic way to formulate the next hypothesis. At this step, the human being has to make an *arational* leap to generate the next one. He or she is aided by the rest of the cycle, but a totally mechanistic method of hypothesis generation is impossible. The scientific method, therefore, relies critically on another part of the human mind besides the cognitive, reasoning part.

The second way in which science is arational occurs in the selection of which problems are to be investigated in the first place. There are so many interesting matters to investigate that if trouble is encountered in one area, another problem can be attacked that appears to be more solvable. This factor has driven scientific research in the direction of problems that are tractable with available methods and tools. Scientific endeavors are further biased toward questions that are interesting to scientists, often irrespective of social needs and to the exclusion of areas that appear unusually fuzzy, apparently beyond available mathematics, or rife with unpredictable elements.

Scientists do not talk much about these limitations. They have a quiet fascination for the hidden essence of creativity, which they regard respectfully as a kind of spontaneous magic not to be tampered with. On the whole, they behave as if all their work is entirely systematic and logical, even though they know very well that it is not so.

## SCIENCE IN SOCIETY

As physical science grew and was so successful in material things, other fields began to imitate it. Biology was hooked and proceeded to classify, categorize, and analyze all forms of life. Only later did biologists discover that there is much more to living creatures than taxonomy—the strong interconnections among different life forms, for example.

Similar reversals have recently taken place in the social sciences, such as anthropology and linguistics, but the most profound transformations are being experienced in psychology. Following the path taken by physics, psychologists spent more than fifty years analyzing and classifying human behavior. They regarded the human mind as a sophisticated outgrowth of the body and tried to understand it through stimulus–response (cause–effect) experiments, especially with animals, using mechanistic models. As a result, psychologists developed little comprehension of what was transpiring within the human mind or psyche—the very province they had chosen to investigate. Nowadays much is being learned from the integral, humanistic, and transpersonal branches of psychology, particularly through psychotherapy and with a boost from Eastern philosophy. Leading-edge psychologists are finally beginning to regard mind, body, and spirit as an integrated, interdependent whole and are reorienting the discipline of psychology accordingly.[7,8]

Science's impact in public affairs is immense, for in the civilized world, it is the accepted authority on which many political decisions are based. The fact that scientific knowledge is limited to the material world has largely escaped attention. Indeed, scientific knowledge enjoys a high degree of credibility and has become an integral element in modern society. Science has set the social standard for sufficient proof and evidence, for factual correctness, for credible forecasts, and, in many ways, for moral right and wrong.[6,9] As citizens of the modern world, we are now caught up in this delusion, largely because the resultant technology has made life so comfortable. In fact, we eagerly look forward to the further benefits of science's probing of the physical world without asking whether we might have sold ourselves out under the banner of free inquiry and social progress.

Science has become our eyes and ears on the universe, and we have come to trust it greatly—perhaps too much—so that our mode of living is out of balance with the natural world. There remains to be publicly explored an immense domain of human experience, a domain in which we humans are still ignorant and in which science has not been able to help us. Yet the pretense that the power lies in the scientific approach remains strong, and this arrogance and lack of discrimination are holding us back.

## SCIENTIFIC DISCOVERY

The history of science itself provides abundant evidence that its great breakthroughs did not occur as a result of rational thinking alone. Science could not have moved forward as it did were it not for great insights that went beyond the reasoning process. In fact, these insights were the essential factor responsible for many important discoveries.[10–13]

This observation is supported in the biographies of many great scientists, who revealed (often late in life, when they cared little for what their peers thought of them) just how they obtained their breakthroughs. The story of Archimedes jumping out of the bathtub with his cry of "Eureka!" is familiar and typical (although it may not be true). Many know of Flemish chemist Friedrich August von Kekulé, who, dozing before the fire, saw a snake biting its own tail. From this insight, he conceived the benzene ring, opening the door to modern organic chemistry.[14]

The great mathematician Karl Friedrich Gauss wrote a letter to a friend about how he had proved an important theorem after four years of unsuccessful work. "At last, two days ago, I succeeded, not by dint of painful effort but, so to speak, by the grace of God. As a sudden flash of light, the enigma was solved. . . . For my part, I was unable to name the nature of the thread which connected what I previously knew with that which made my success possible."

Poincaré, another famous mathematician, reported: "For fifteen days I strove to prove that there could not be any functions like those I have since called Fuchsian functions. Every day I seated myself at my work table, stayed an hour or two, tried a great number of combinations and reached no results. One evening, contrary to my custom, I drank black coffee and could not sleep. Ideas arose in crowds. I felt them collide until pairs interlocked, so to speak, making a stable combination. By the next morning, . . . I had only to write out the results, which took a few hours." [15]

Einstein spoke about his own process, saying, "The intellect has little to do on the road to discovery. There comes a leap in consciousness, call it intuition or what you will, and the solution comes to you." And later, "The really valuable factor is intuition." [16,17]

In these and dozens of similar accounts, we see operating a different kind of mind process than the customary intellectual one. The discoverers typically have attributed their success not to careful reasoning and analysis, but to a sudden impulse, a quantum of new knowledge that entered their minds. The result might be attributed to unconscious reasoning were it not for the fact that in many cases, their discovery did not follow logically from what preceded it. Clearly, then, there must be a process in the human mind whereby totally new information can enter under the right conditions.

The name for this process is *intuition*.

## THE INTUITIVE PROCESS

Intuition is the mind process of direct apperception of knowledge, as distinct from knowledge acquisition by the senses, from reasoning, or even from memory in the usual sense. [18–20] Intuitive perception is an inner process, not something one deliberately does. Like reasoning, it is not a type of *behavior*, but it underlies behavior. Both intuition and reasoning are principal components of what we call thinking; almost all thinking involves both. We do not often observe intuition and reasoning in total isolation of each other, but it can and does happen.

Belief in the capacity of the mind to *directly* acquire new knowledge is the crucial credibility gap to be transcended. A number of basic questions arise. For instance, if the mind can produce new knowledge spontaneously, where is the information coming from? Why is the availability of such knowledge not more obvious? What governs its entry into the conscious mind? The absence of clear answers to these and other key questions has been the major stumbling

**Figure 1.1**
**Model of Consciousness Showing Intuition as the Communicative Link between the Superconscious Mind and the Conscious Mind**

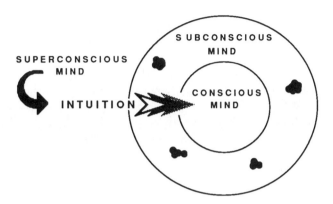

block to broad acceptance of direct knowing as an active component of thought, even though such subtle revelations are an intimate part of everyone's daily experience.

The source of direct knowledge may not have a where or even a when, but may be simply omnipresent—a property of reality, like the force fields of physics or like other abstract qualities of human life, such as love, which we accept without question. Is it such a stretch of faith to believe that all knowledge— past, present, and potential—already exists, ready to be accessed by the human mind?

My coworkers and I at the Center for Applied Intuition (CAI) near San Francisco have postulated a simple model of the mind, one that has evolved from our experience and research (Figure 1.1). In Figure 1.1, the concentric circles differentiate among three parts of the human mind. The center circle represents the *conscious* mind; roughly speaking, it represents that part of all reality we are aware of. By implication, we are not aware of anything outside the inner circle—the unconscious. The conscious mind is largely an attention focuser; it manages much of our sensory input and motor output and draws as needed from memory banks within the unconscious. It appears to have little or no memory of its own.

The ring just outside this conscious core represents the *subconscious* mind. This is the part of the unconscious that contains the personal record of one's experiences earlier in life. Most of these memories are irrelevant to conscious life most of the time; they simply reside in the subconscious. Most appear to be available through hypnosis and can be probed when there is a need to do so.[21] Some of the experiences stored in the subconscious, however, have been pushed (repressed) there because they were frightening or just irrelevant when they occurred and could not readily be dealt with at that time. These lapses, shown in Figure 1.1 as dark shapes, are scattered throughout the subconscious. In this incomplete state, they tend to fester over the days, months, and years that follow. As such, they constitute blocks to full mental functioning. After a while, it is difficult to retrieve them, yet they exert their influence on thought and feeling and particularly on one's emotional life. If sufficiently serious, they can adversely affect mental and physical health. They can be returned to consciousness for completion, either deliberately through psychotherapy, hypnosis, certain meditative exercises, or drugs or incidentally through peak experiences, "accidents," life-threatening illnesses, and similar personal crises.

Beyond the subconscious ring, there is the *superconscious* mind. One finds various names for this portion in many of the world's religious and spiritual traditions: the Great Book, the Book of God's Remembrance, the Akashic Records, and so on. The great psychologist Carl Jung called it the *collective unconscious.*[22] Here lies a reservoir of the whole domain of human experience, past and potential. It is not solely personal, but shared by all humanity. We may think of it as a bank of unlimited knowledge, although it is much more than that. Here lies the knowledge of who we are, where we are going in life, individually and collectively, and why: the answers to all our questions.

In these terms, the superconscious mind is the source of intuitive knowledge. Intuition is the process by which information or knowledge passes from the superconscious, through the subconscious, to the conscious mind. Intuition may be thought of as the communication channel that allows the conscious mind access to the superconscious.

## DEVELOPMENT OF INTUITIVE SKILL

Intuition is not the rare gift of a few people. Everyone has the basic ability or capacity to function intuitively. We all use our intuition continually, even though we may be unaware of doing so and credit the results of our thoughts to a rational process. Few people choose to deliberately develop this native capacity into a useful skill.

Young children are strong intuitives, but with disapproving parental and societal responses, they quickly learn to distrust their insights and push them into the background. The situation is quite different in some non-Western cultures, in which a direct-knowing capacity is taken for granted and even encouraged.

It is possible for adults to develop intuitive skills, even if the capacity has been repressed in earlier years. But learning intuition is different from learning most things encountered in school, such as memorizing multiplication tables, speaking French, or playing the piano. In these instances, the learner is acquiring something: facts, information, manual or mental skills, coordination. With intuition, it is just the opposite; it is a matter of undoing prior conditioning and getting rid of blocks, such as inappropriate beliefs and fears, that are impeding a natural development that is trying to take place. Thus learning intuition is really a kind of *un*learning.

To develop one's native intuitive ability into a useful skill, one must first dissolve out a sufficient number of the subconscious blocks (the dark shapes in Figure 1.1) to permit a clear transmission from the superconscious mind to the conscious mind, since these blocks can impede or distort the intuitive flow of information.

The second task is to learn to *listen* in the language of the superconscious. It does not communicate in English or even in pictures, although the intuitive message normally is clothed in these sense forms as it surfaces and also may be screened through a rational filter as it transits the subconscious mind. If it reaches consciousness without excessive distortion, it can then be understood and relayed to others. Most intuitive trainees receive intuitive information through one of their senses—certainly the most familiar way we all receive information—although with practice, the communication may bypass the senses and just manifest in the mind as a fragment of new knowledge.

The third task in developing one's intuition is to learn to distinguish between information arising from the superconscious mind and that coming from the subconscious mind. As most people try to quiet their mind, subconscious information bubbles up into consciousness in a steady stream. At first, the information from these two sources looks much the same. With practice, they can be distinguished, so that the personal, emotionally loaded memories can be quieted down and identified as such. The superconscious information can then be received clearly. The practice is one of learning to discriminate and trust that inner voice, which knows a great deal more than the outer one and is really running the show.

As one starts to develop intuitive faculties, personal issues that need attention (often with an emotional burden) typically arise, so it is helpful to work through these with a teacher, an informed therapist, or a support group of others involved in the same process.

Surely the single most important practice for aiding intuition development is meditation. Although this term as popularly used covers a great variety of mind activities, the choice among them is not critical to the beginner. What is most important is to find a form of meditation that is comfortable and fun; an arduous discipline is not likely to be effective or maintained over the time required to make it a habit. Active dreamwork also is a useful regular practice.

Finally, intuitive exercises work best when there is a good, human reason why the information is needed and not merely for the sake of curiosity, an experiment, or a demonstration to others.

## EXPERT INTUITIVES

At CAI, we work with a staff of *expert intuitives,* people who have successfully made the effort to develop their intuitive faculties to such a high level that they can consciously and deliberately provide totally new information on demand, independent of what they already consciously know from their earlier life experience.

Expert intuitives function in various modes. For some, the intuitively received information is communicated in an ordinary conversational manner and from a fully conscious state. Others appear to go to sleep but speak clearly and coherently from this state; when they "wake up" later, they have little or no recollection of what has transpired. This latter mode is called *mediumship* in traditional parapsychology, or *channeling* in modern parlance.[23-25] Sometimes the voice quality of the intuitive changes while asleep, and what seems to be another personality may emerge, but these features do not always occur. Most expert intuitives function somewhere between these two extremes. These various modes appear to arise as individual means for shifting the intuitive's conscious mind and personality out of the path of intuitive reception, so that clear information can flow through.

In more than fifteen years of work with many expert intuitives, I have not been able to detect any consistent differences in performance that would favor one mode over another. This experience contradicts two common and contradictory beliefs: that the highest accuracy and clarity can be obtained from an intuitive who is totally unconscious and, conversely, that the best results arise from an intuitive who is fully conscious. The state of the conscious mind of an intuitive, including the presence or absence of another entity, appears to be a personal preference of no general significance.

My experience at CAI also indicates that there is no limit to the depth and breadth of the information received. This claim includes information that is highly technical or deeply personal, explanatory or inspirational, factual or mystical, historical or contemporary, and even part of the future. With few exceptions, the information requested has been provided fully and accurately, as long as a few simple rules are followed.

## ACHIEVING SUCCESS IN INTUITIVE INQUIRIES

A number of conditions must be satisfied if the intuitive process is to work smoothly and effectively. The most important of these conditions is the motivation for conducting the inquiry. If one seeks information that is harmful to someone or that may reduce someone's freedom of thought or action in some way, the reception probably will be blocked. If information is sought that is already known or could easily be found by conventional means, the flow is weakened: the material tends to be vague, the process slows down, and sometimes the reception may stop entirely.

A second important requirement is that the questions for the inquiry need to be stated clearly and unambiguously. CAI began its intuitive inquiries in science to generate new hypotheses for research in areas that had stubbornly resisted progress by conventional means.[26,27] The formulation of the questions turned out to be critically important. Unlike ordinary discourse, the questions must be specific, unambiguous, and free of biases. When these qualities are present, then accurate, complete, and relevant answers are forthcoming.

For inquiries on scientific and technical topics, a procedure called *intuitive consensus* was developed.[26,28,29] Intuitive consensus is a kind of multi–psychic inquiry technique in which the carefully formulated questions are posed to several intuitives independently. The answers are then combined into a common response. After early experimentation, this technique now yields excellent agreement among the sources. It has been applied to more than a dozen scientific, parascientific, and social problem areas, chosen because they were totally unexplored or because they appeared to have resisted the quest for solutions by traditional means. For example, an investigation was undertaken into the triggering of earthquakes: what is happening in the ground just hours or days before an earthquake occurs? The goal in this study was not to predict specific earthquakes, but to understand the physical process underlying earthquakes sufficiently well to permit the intelligent development of an earthquake prediction technology. The resulting consensus was excellent and contained many surprises. Some of the particular results were later verified through experiment, some conducted by CAI staff and some incidentally by others in ignorance of our findings.

Other areas similarly explored using intuitive consensus are crib death, manic depression, human fertility, the detoxification of nuclear waste, levitation, the biographies of certain historical figures, and topics in archeology.

Intuition also can be used to investigate the future, not strictly as prediction, although some prediction is included, but rather as prophecy in the biblical sense: understanding the personal and social processes in progress so that one may improve the future by making better decisions in the present. Projections often are in the form of if-then statements: "If you do not cut back on your use of chlorofluorocarbons, then the temperature of the earth's atmosphere will rise and coastal cities will be flooded!" Although much of the course of human history can be predicted once the laws of social development are understood, other portions cannot be reliably predicted because they depend critically on human decisions. Thus responsible intuitive prophecy consists almost entirely of identifying decision points and issues, describing the consequences of the various options, and then leaving the decision up to the user of the information. In this way, the user can make a conscious and responsible choice instead of fatalistically accepting a predicted outcome as inevitable or blindly following orders. Two large and several small prophecy studies have been completed.[30]

To date, about 25 companies have enlisted CAI expert intuitives for business consulting. In a typical scenario, the intuitive meets with the company president, board of directors, or a project team for a half day or full day. Company representatives pose their questions with little or no explanation of background details. The expert intuitive provides the answers. It is immediately apparent to those present that the intuitive process is tapping a deep and broad source of information, well beyond what normally is accessed by most people and certainly beyond the personal knowledge and experience of the intuitive. Opportunities for follow-up and confirmation are not always possible in business consulting, but in no case has the information provided ever been found to be downright wrong.

## INTUITION AND PARAPSYCHOLOGY

What does the intuitive process say about parapsychology and the way parapsychologists function?

Most of the phenomena studied in parapsychology consist of the reception of novel information. This obviously is the case for clairvoyance, clairaudience, precognition, psychometry, and telepathy, all of which are situations in which the subject receives information not presumed to be accessible according to the ordinary ground rules of life as given to us by science.

We suggest that this psi-reception process is a manifestation of intuition.

Most of the categories just named refer to the various ways in which information appears to be received: through sight or hearing from an object or another person. We have already noted that these forms appear to be an artifact of the individual psychic and not in themselves significant. In the case of psychometry, for instance, it commonly is assumed that the information provided is somehow carried by the object through some kind of non–physical energy field and that the sensitive is somehow reading this field. There is no separate evidence for the existence of such a field, and contrary evidence is provided by experiments in clairvoyance and remote viewing that use no such objects.[31] In present terms, the information can be drawn directly from the superconscious, the object simply serving as a pointer or trigger. Thus the need for the object to be present is doubtful, although if the psychic *believes* its presence is essential, he may make it so.

Similarly, as already noted, whether the novel information appears to be received through inner seeing, inner hearing, or one of the other senses is a personal difference not essential to the reception. CAI's experience with expert intuitives and many psychics suggests that artifacts such as candles, incense, or crystals also are not fundamentally necessary, although an individual intuitive may believe that they are for him or her. We are not dealing here with a rare phenomenon that requires special conditions, but with a natural human capacity.

Apparitions, near-death experiences, and out-of-body travel may be included as manifestations of intuition, but models for these are lacking, and existing explanations are surely stretching the intuitive hypothesis too far at this point. Faith healing (except the diagnostic component), firewalking, and psychokinesis apparently cannot be explained as instances of intuition, but we can legitimately ask here how all these phenomena came to be included in parapsychology in the first place. Indeed, the field has come to be a catch-all for unexplained events—including cattle mutilations, crop circles, UFOs, yetis/sasquatches, and many others. It is surely a mistake to presume that all such phenomena have a common explanation. Perhaps the receptive sensory areas of parapsychology should be regarded as separate from the active motor areas.

In summary, the foregoing indicates that the human awareness process taking place in many parapsychological phenomena can be explained (if I may use that term) as an instance of intuition. Intuition thus emerges as the larger concept: the mind process that underlies and is responsible for receptive parapsychological performance. Moreover, intuition opens the doorway to an even greater range of knowledge and human experience than typically has been investigated within the narrow confines of parapsychology.

In establishing this explanation, are we just replacing one unknown with another? In a way, this is so because intuition is no better understood in scientific terms than parapsychology. But we have already noted the limitations of science for such studies. Moreover, intuition is offered here as the more fundamental process and the one more directly connected to everyday experience. Finally, intuition is a much more acceptable and plausible concept to the informed public and even to the scientific community. Thus the research needed to enable us to understand intuition better may be less unfamiliar and less formidable, and therefore more readily supported.

## A CHANGING SCIENCE, A CHANGING WORLDVIEW

There is a growing realization that present-day science is approaching a dead end. This trend has been most widely acknowledged in quantum physics, where fundamental paradoxes have arisen in the attempt to explore the ultimate microreality of matter and energy.[32] Impasses also are being encountered, to a lesser degree, in biology and astronomy. In addition, a reaction against science is mounting as society comes to realize the terrible price it is paying for technological progress.

To accommodate the changes presaged for science and necessitated for and by parapsychology as well, we must somehow transcend the established scientific method. We are being forced beyond the models we have been using and must create new ones. What one might call the nonlinearization of science is taking place. Willis Harman, president of the Institute of Noetic Sciences, has written and spoken eloquently on these matters. He reminds us that what we most need is a new science of subjective experience—in other words, a science that honors a fuller range of human activity, including the workings of consciousness; a science that is integrative and all-encompassing; a science that embraces the intimate part played by the mind in the external world, not just the mind that orthodox psychology defines, but also the greater mind that includes the superconscious.[6]

One of the immediate consequences of the new science is that a number of human potentials are being revealed, ones we did not know we had or were at least not acknowledged. More and more people are accomplishing feats, both physical and mental, previously assumed to be impossible. Athletic records are continually being broken. Public credulity of "savant"-type arithmetic calculation, super strength, and "psychic" feats, such as firewalking, is increasing every year.[33–36] Perhaps most important, we are discovering unrecognized mental capacities, including intuitive knowing.

In effect, we are now in the midst of evolving a broader definition of what it means to be a human being—a grander model than our predecessors assumed. Naturally, this new definition affects how we interface with our physical and social realities. It leads us to what some call the spiritual side of life—a loaded term, to be sure, because it means such different things to different people. But it is a way of acknowledging that there is more to life than what can be seen, heard, and figured out and that this unacknowledged part is behind everything else, hence crucially important in all we think and do.

We are saying, among other things, that a human being is not so much a body and a brain that has evolved to the point of generating consciousness, but by nature an evolving consciousness that has embodied itself in a body and a brain. This alternative view implies a greater human purpose. It points to our past ignorance of this purpose, an ignorance that has blinded us to the real meaning of life and has led us toward destruction of one another and our planetary home. This position does not necessarily imply that concepts such as spirit beings, the afterlife, reincarnation, and the like are literally valid, at least as they have been espoused. It does imply that consciousness transcends the body, and the essence of who or what we are lies beyond the materialist model.

We are gradually realizing that we are more than our bodies and our brains. The next question is: What is that more? Each of us needs to inquire seriously into this matter. Intuition is a means for this inquiry. It is proffered as the communicative link in the process of understanding who we really are and what in the world we are doing here. Intuition can provide information, knowledge, understanding, and even direct experience that we can readily utilize in our personal lives, in our professional activities, and in our comprehension of the world.

**NOTES**

1. Kuhn TS. *The Structure of Scientific Revolutions.* 2nd ed. Chicago: University of Chicago Press; 1970. For a more readable account, see the first three chapters of Willis Harman's *Global Mind Change* (see note 3 below).

2. Shilts R. *And the Band Played On: Politics, People, and the AIDS Epidemic.* New York: St. Martin's Press; 1987.

3. I am indebted to Willis Harman for his eloquent description of this piece of history and the assumptions to follow. See, for example, Harman W. *Global Mind Change: The Promise of the Last Years of the Twentieth Century.* Indianapolis: Knowledge Systems, Inc; 1988.

4. Harman. *Global Mind Change,* chs 1–3 and pp. 89–90.

5. The Heisenberg uncertainty principle. See, for example, Herbert N. *Quantum Reality: Beyond the New Physics*. New York: Doubleday; 1985.

6. Harman. *Global Mind Change*.

7. Grof S. *Beyond the Brain: Birth, Death and Transcendence in Psychotherapy*. Albany: State University of New York; 1985.

8. Vaughn F. *The Inward Arc: Healing and Wholeness in Psychotherapy and Spirituality*. Boston: Shambhala; 1986.

9. Harman W, Reingold H. *Higher Creativity: Liberating the Unconscious for Breakthrough Insights*. Los Angeles: Tarcher, Inc; 1984.

10. Brewster G. *The Creative Process*. New York: Mentor/New American Library; 1937, 1952.

11. Koestler A. *The Act of Creation*. New York: Dell; 1964:ch 5.

12. Hadamard J. *The Psychology of Invention in the Mathematical Field*. Princeton, NJ: Princeton University Press; 1949.

13. Shapiro G. *A Skeleton in the Darkroom: Stories of Serendipity in Science*. San Francisco: Harper & Row; 1986.

14. Findlay A. *A Hundred Years of Chemistry*. 2nd ed. London: Duckworth; 1948:36–38.

15. Poincaré H. Halstead G, trans. Mathematical creation. In: *The Foundation of Science*. Lancaster, PA: Science Press; 1946:26.

16. Vallentin A. *The Drama of Albert Einstein*. Garden City, NY: Doubleday; 1954.

17. Moszkowski A. Brose HL, trans. *Conversations with Einstein*. New York: Horizon Press; 1970:96.

18. Vaughn FE. *Awakening Intuition*. New York: Anchor/Doubleday; 1979.

19. Goldberg P. *The Intuitive Edge: Understanding and Developing Intuition*. Los Angeles: Tarcher; 1983.

20. Nadel L. *Sixth Sense: The Whole-Brain Book of Intuition, Hunches, Gut Feelings, and Their Place in Your Everyday Life*. Englewood Cliffs, NJ: Prentice-Hall; 1990.

21. See any standard text on hypnosis, for example, Hilgard E. *Divided Consciousness, Multiple Controls in Human Thought and Action*. New York: Wiley & Sons; 1986.

22. Jung CG. Winston R, Winston C, trans. *Memories, Dreams and Reflections*. New York: Random House; 1973.

23. Kautz W, Branon M. *Channeling: The Intuitive Connection*. San Francisco: Harper & Row; 1987.

24. Hastings A. *With the Tongues of Men and Angels: A Study of Channeling*. Fort Worth, TX: Holt, Rinehart & Winston; 1991.

25. Klimo J. *Channeling: Investigations on Receiving Information from Paranormal Sources*. Los Angeles: Tarcher; 1987.

26. Kautz WH, Branon M. *Intuiting the Future: A New Age Vision of the 1990s*. San Francisco: Harper & Row; 1989:37–39.

27. Most of work at CAI now takes the form of personal intuitive counseling for individuals.

28. Kautz WH. Earthquake triggering: a psychic exploration. *Psi Research*. 1982;3:117–112 and 4:101–116.

29. Kautz WH, Kodera M. *The Future of Japan: An Intuitive Scenario* (in Japanese). Tokyo: Tama Publishing Co.; 1985.

30. Records on file at the Center for Applied Intuition, Fairfax, CA.

31. Targ R, Putoff H. *Mind Reach: Scientists Look at Psychic Ability*. New York: Dell Publishing Co; 1977.

32. Capra F. *The Tao of Physics*. Berkeley: Shambhala; 1973.

33. Smith SB. *The Great Mental Calculators: The Psychology, Methods, and Lives of Calculating Prodigies, Past and Present*. New York: Columbia University Press; 1983.

34. Danforth LM. *Firewalking and Religious Healing: The Anastenaria of Greece and the American Firewalking Movement*. Princeton, NJ: Princeton University Press; 1989.

35. Licauco JT. *The Magicians of God: The Amazing Stories of Philippine Faith Healers*. Manila: National Bookstore, Inc; 1982.

36. Inglis B. *Trance: A Natural History of Altered States of Mind*. London: Paladin/ Grafton Books; 1989: chs 6 and 7.

**2** _____

# The Nature of Personal
# Belief Systems

*Beverley Kane*

*Is psi more like physics or more like love?*

Russell Targ

## PRECONDITIONS

*The proof of the pudding is in the eating.*

Old English Proverb

Immanuel Kant would arise in the morning, seat himself in his study and ask, "[Does] the simple but empirically determined Consciousness of my own existence [prove] the existence of objects in space outside myself?"[1] From this inner dialogue, Kant arrived at his theory on the nature of perception, a critique of idealism, speculation on the nature of space and time: in short his theory of reality.

Today's thoughtful person wakes up and merely asks, "Black socks or brown?"

For thousands of years, philosophers have speculated on, debated, and offered "axiomatic" proofs for the true nature of the universe. From Plato to Peirce,

Adapted from the Panel Discussion on the Nature of Reality, Parapsychology Research Group General Meeting, May 1988.

from dualism to deconstructionism, the "ists" and the "isms" have all stren-uously pitched tiles into the mosaic of reality. Most such philosophies, both Eastern and Western, are abstract and impersonal. They prescribe broadly for-mulated generalities in an abstruse, technical language. Philosophers seldom speak of their own anecdotal experiences or appeal to the everyday reality of the common person.

The premise of this chapter is that if psi phenomena can be proved to exist, "the proof is in the pudding"—personal experience. They cannot be wholly validated or, in Karl Popper's construction,[2] falsified with either the present laws of science or the formalisms of speculative philosophies. Since the 1930s, a number of scrupulously performed psi experiments have yielded highly sig-nificant positive results.[3] An intellectual appreciation of this data must be cor-roborated by personal experience for belief in psi to occur.

Despite the popular insistence that all "scientific" phenomena be objectively verified, we pursue most of life's activities in the realm of subjective experi-ence. Our mental machinations are predominantly trivial (compared with, say, Kant's elaborate ontology) and derive largely from unconscious elements. Yet the reflex nature of our decisions leaves little uncertainty about what we know: long division, our political views, and whether black socks or brown go with a blue suit.

Harvard psychologist-philosopher William James criticized philosophy for its departure from common experience. He exposed the fundamentally subjective nature of philosophical "logic":

The history of philosophy is to a great extent that of a certain clash of human tempera-ments. . . . Of whatever temperament a professional philosopher is, he tries, when philosophizing, to sink the fact of his temperament. Temperament is no conventionally recognized reason, so he urges impersonal reasons only for his conclusions. Yet his temperament really gives him a stronger bias than any of his more strictly objective premises. It loads the evidence for him one way or the other, making for a more senti-mental or a more hard-hearted view of the universe, just as this fact or that principle would. He *trusts* his temperament. Wanting a universe that suits it, he believes in any representation of the universe that does suit it (p. 19).[4]

James' philosophy of *pragmatism,* which revived the dormant theories of Charles Peirce, was predicated on the idea that Truth systems must be evalu-ated on the basis of their *utility* in the physical world. As physical beings, we rely on feedback from the material world to confirm the legitimacy of our ideas. James adopted Schiller's view that *"ideas (which themselves are but parts of our experience) become true just in so far as they help us to get into satisfactory relations with other parts of our experience. . . . This is the 'in-strumental' view of truth, the view that truth in our ideas means their power to 'work' "* (p. 49, James' italics).[4,5]

Psychologist Lawrence LeShan confirms the pragmatic view by stating, in effect, that the benchmark of a reality program is how well it meets the specified goals of the organism.[6] In particular, the system must be self-consistent and must answer the reasonable questions it has posed for itself. Its validity is established only when we *act* in terms of the beliefs it has engendered.

No one has yet stipulated—nor shall I—the definitive algorithm for a reality test. In the sections that follow, I make explicit some of the steps in an otherwise occult process.

## REALITY TESTING: A NEO-JUNGIAN PERSPECTIVE

*Logic is the beginning of reason, not the end.*
Commander Spock, *Star Trek VI*, Paramount Pictures, 1991

Reality testing is the process of evaluating feedback from the results of our accomplishments in the observable world. With that stated, we may still ask, how do we arrive at a methodology for knowing what we know? How do we admit or reject new truths into our set of beliefs? We are largely unconscious of the implicit rules we have established for deciding what to believe. Do we rely heavily on rational processes? Do we trust our own irretrievable experiences, either literally or symbolically? Do we trust the unreproducible experiences of others? What is the process by which we revise our beliefs? People who convert to a different religion, change political parties, or "come out" in a new sexual orientation conduct a conscious dialogue with their beliefs, but the key ingredient in the ultimate decision may remain elusive.

Twentieth-century Western philosophical and scientific thinking is anchored in a rational materialistic value system. In this system, logic is the primary lens through which we are conditioned to view truth. Chief among the reasons for exalting the intellectual function is that it provides the apparent basis for scientific understanding, which in turn yields our technological achievements. Although we value subjective experience for the sense of aesthetics, we usually do not accord it the privilege of arbitrating scientific truths. In business, politics, and academia we are expected to fortify subjective opinions with rational arguments.

One of the first modern scientists to elucidate the balance of rational and nonrational functions in the human psyche was the Swiss psychiatrist Carl Jung. The foundation of Jung's psychology is the concept of *individuation*—the means by which a person achieves psychological wholeness to become a fulfilled and balanced individual. One way that Jung characterized the process of individuation was by classifying the primary forces in the psyche that contribute to an individual's character. In his paper on psychological types, Jung established two personality types (introvert and extrovert) and four character functions: [7]

intellect—the rational, analytic function

sensation—sensory input from touch, taste, smell, sight, hearing

feeling—emotional stirrings

intuition—imagination, hunches, dreams

Jung did not originate this scheme; its antecedents are found in the legends of the Druids, in the records of the early Greeks, and in the writings of the alchemists in the Middle Ages. These earlier philosophers, astrologers, scientists, and physicians associated the elements earth, fire, air, and water—and later, the respective elemental humors: black bile, yellow bile, blood, and phlegm—with psychological states and traits.

The functions, according to Nichols, represent "the four characteristic potentials for apprehending raw experience and sorting it out in order to deal with it." [8] In other words, they supply the construction set of personal reality.

The following example illustrates the elements of belief formation based on the four Jungian functions. We will, with some caricature, consider an issue that has not been scientifically established, in that there are conflicting results from various medical studies. Our hypothesis is that vitamin C is effective in preventing viral infections such as colds. The type of evidence that is necessary and sufficient for a person to decide this point is stereotypical of the dominant function in his or her character.

If you are fundamentally an intellectual person who relies on objective proof, then what you would require to believe that vitamin C prevents colds is a large-scale, prospective, randomized, double-blind, drug-placebo trial published in the *New England Journal of Medicine*. This must be corroborated by additional researchers adhering to the methodology in the original study. You may or may not end up with a truth, since some experiments prove to be flawed, and many accepted notions in medical science have been abandoned when errors in methodology have been detected. [9] (And medical studies do not control for the *intent bias* of the investigators as parapsychological experiments do.)

If you are most attuned to your own sensory experience, you would take vitamin C for a year. You might even do your own crossover study in which you *didn't* take vitamin C for the subsequent year. If it was evident to you that in the first year you had fewer colds, then that would constitute proof for you that vitamin C is efficacious. Yet, the conclusions reached from some sensory experiences have been called into question in drug-placebo trials. In these studies, many participants randomized to the placebo groups report the primary effects or the side effects of the active drug. Only many months later, when the study is "unblinded," is it revealed to the subjects (and to the researchers) that they were responding to the placebo all along. [10]

If you are more inclined to an emotional or empathic validation of truth, then what would be necessary and sufficient for you to accept the efficacy of vitamin C is to have a number of friends testify that vitamin C has always prevented them from getting colds. In this case, empathy is defined as the ability to feel what another person feels. People who act on the testimonials in health magazines might be classified as empathic, since these articles, on the whole, don't pretend to appeal to logic by citing orthodox scientific studies.[11] Much of folk medicine is used on the basis of empathy. This approach also may prove faulty, in that preparations that heal some people are toxic to others.

If you primarily accept proof—or direct knowledge—from a psychic or an intuitional source, you might sit in a quiet place and meditate or read tarot cards. You would then receive an inner voice (or the Queen of Pentacles) saying, "Vitamin C prevents colds!" Alternatively, you would hold a tablet of vitamin C and try to divine its properties—a type of *psychometry*. Intuition seldom contributes all the information necessary to test a truth. As Targ and his coworkers discuss in Chapter 25, the greatest challenge in psychic research is how to show that an intuition is *correct*, how to increase psychic reliability. Many intuitive guesses are wrong, and there is little or no subjective sense of certainty that the information is valid.[12]

Clearly there is potential for validation and for error in each of the four approaches. In practice, all four functions contribute to reality testing to some extent within each person and within the scope of each experience. To illustrate this syncretism, here is a short exercise you can do right now.[13]

Consider the garment you are wearing.

First, what is it made of? Is it cotton or wool, polyester or silk? How many buttons or snaps or zippers does it have? Does it have long sleeves, or short? What is its color and pattern? Is it woven, or knit? Is it dirty, or clean? These questions are answered with the analytical, intellectual function.

Second, what sensations does it give your body? Does it feel soft, or scratchy? Is it tight, or loose? Does it keep your body warm, or cool? Does it smell of perfume, or of perspiration? These questions are answered with the sensation function.

Now, how does the garment make you feel emotionally? Does it make you feel cozy, or exposed? Does it make you feel sexy, or prim? Attractive, or unattractive? Do you feel casual, or formal? Does the color make you feel happy and energetic, or sluggish and depressed? These questions are answered with the emotional function.

Last, close your eyes and imagine that the garment can answer a question. What do you ask? What does it answer? How long can you keep up a dialogue? The information that comes from dialoguing with an object, such as a dream symbol, comes from the intuitive function, sometimes called the subconscious or unconscious.

As near as we can define an ultimate truth, it is one that is consistent in all four modes of knowledge acquisition.[14]

## THE NEED TO BELIEVE

Apart from the personality factors and cultural prejudices that influence judgment, belief systems are rooted in psychological and physical needs. Conclusions based on the need to believe are not necessarily incorrect. In fact, the logical extension of James' pragmatism and LeShan's goal-attainment criterion is that the confirmation of a valid belief lies in whether it helps us meet our needs. In Abraham Maslow's hierarchy of drives for self-actualization are survival, emotional satisfaction, meaning, and transcendence.[15] In its most general form, Maslow's principle amounts to the need to increase one's sense of personal power.[16] From that perspective, we can reframe the primary needs: to promote physical and emotional pleasure and fulfillment, to minimize cognitive dissonance, and to remove fear (especially of death).

Basic needs lend themselves to classification in the Jungian typology. Our societal and personal institutions and practices can be assigned to the respective need categories they seem to fill. Table 2.1 is a simplified scheme that illustrates this principle. The middle two columns are examples of traditional and nontraditional behaviors and institutions that provide need gratification. At the far right are forms of expression that we may consider self-deceptive, pathological, antisocial, or self-destructive.[17] The most extreme expression of a pathologically incoherent belief system is psychosis, which is by definition a break with reality. Although designating a person as psychotic can be extremely misguided,[18] characteristics of psychosis are that (1) *functioning* or goal-attainment in the physical world is severely impaired or ceases and (2) the person is subjectively unhappy.

Note that the table is not an array of truth values: it cannot confirm or deny that beliefs, which are implied by behaviors, which are in turn instigated by needs, are true. The point is precisely that some beliefs born of needs are true and some are not. Feelings of personal power—or in the current vernacular, self-esteem—obtain from the ability to gratify the four derivative types of needs. But how do we prove that this has occurred? The measure of success is ultimately subjective; it subordinates the logical function to our discretionary sense of direct knowing.[19]

In the New Age manifesto, *The Aquarian Conspiracy,* Marilyn Ferguson identifies power as ''a central issue in social and personal transformation.''[20] Ferguson contrasts the old power-seeking paradigm, with its politics of competition, fear, and denial, with the new emergent paradigm. The new value system is more closely aligned with Gandhi's principle of *satyagraha,* soul force or truth force, and extols cooperation among self-actualized individuals.

We must now examine how our current system—the dominant paradigm—orders our perceptions and contributes to or detracts from the individual's sense of power.

## CHOOSING TO RECOGNIZE ANOMALIES: THE ARTIFACT OF STATISTICAL REALITY

A major aim of science is to empower humankind through mastery over the physical environment—cozy homes, jet travel, Gore-Tex. Yet the individual often feels overwhelmed and depersonalized by the complexities of a technological society. She feels herself at least partially at the mercy of social and scientific trends (or megatrends, to use John Nesbitt's term).

One of the most denaturing perversities of our intellectual orthodoxy is our reliance on statistics. Our insurance risk, marriage prospects, and future health seem to be determined by a probability system that, by design, ignores the variables that make us unique and uniquely qualified to master our fate.

Statistical reality works well up to a point. It is comforting to know that, statistically, every time one drops a heavy object, it should indeed fall *down,* or that because the sun has risen 100% of our time on earth, the probability is high that it will do so tomorrow. Most applications of statistics, however, give probabilities far from unity. And out past the 95% confidence interval lies the power of the individual.

Medical science in particular overemphasizes statistical reasoning, yet we in medicine talk out of both sides of our mouths. When we test a drug or new therapy, a large majority of people must respond or the therapy will never come to market. On the other hand, when we try to prevent a disease, it is necessary only that a small population be at risk. In the first case, many people will be denied a treatment because they are in the minority for whom the therapy might work. In the second case, our screening and prevention programs coerce the many into fearing the fate of the few.

Statistically, one out of nine women will get breast cancer. Therefore, the other eight out of nine must be X-rayed regularly (but not too regularly, or the expense would be too great and there is a statistically non-zero risk of getting cancer from the mammography itself). Recommendations for virtually all such preventive measures are calculated arbitrarily on a cost-benefit basis: the cost of screening versus the social cost of the disease. On the one hand, we may believe that it is worth any number of screening tests to save one life. On the other hand, the growing number of mass screening tests creates disease anxiety, which paradoxically diminishes the individual's unique capacity to stay healthy. As Barrett discusses in Chapter 12, research in psychoneuroimmunology provides evidence that what we believe profoundly influences our health.

By focusing on the reproducible and statistically most likely outcomes in our experiments, we often ignore valuable clues to human potential. A major criticism of psi research is that much of the phenomena it purports to study, such as poltergeists and peak experiences, cannot be duplicated, much less reproduced a statistically significant number of times. Even individuals who want to recapitulate an anomalous experience may face the impossibility of being able to do so.

Table 2.1
Categories of Human Need and Their Resulting Activities

| Type of Need | Traditional Gratification | Nontraditional Gratification | Pathological Gratification |
|---|---|---|---|
| Generalized Power/ Control | science & technology[1] | shamanic & other rituals psychokinesis astrology, superstition | delusional schemes[2] assault crimes Tarot, I Ching[3] |
| Emotional Love | marriage & family support groups | seances[4] | autism[5] |
| Fears (avoiding) | police & legal system | reincarnation[6] multiple personality disorder | vigilante groups[7] racial supremacy groups projection[8] |
| Physical/ Sensory | exercise and athletics television, reading | biofeedback Transcendental Meditation[9] | severe disabling illness eating disorders[10] |
| Spiritual/ Intuitive | traditional religions[11] transcendent philosophies[12] art, music, etc. dreams | "New Age" organizations extrasensory perception[13] channeling | cults paranoia |

**Reducing
Cognitive
Dissonance**     rationalization     magical thinking     schizophrenia

1. These pursuits are considered primarily intellectual, and the intellect is the predominant medium of power in Western society.
2. Such as the belief that one is Jesus Christ or the Devil.
3. Forms of divination.
4. Specifically, attempting to contact deceased loved ones.
5. In some forms amounting to complete emotional withdrawal.
6. Counteracts, to some extent, the fear of death.
7. These may also be called "hate" groups, however hate may be construed as an aspect of fear.
8. Seeing one's own real or feared, often "negative" qualities, in another person.
9. Although many meditative practices are also considered spiritual pursuits, most simple forms of meditation, including TM, have primary physiological effects. TM has been extensively studied by Herbert Benson, MD and others for, e.g., its beneficial effect on blood pressure.
10. Actually an emotional need expressed through a physical malfunction.
11. Both Eastern and Western are traditional in their own contexts.
12. E.g., Emerson, Berkeley, Kant.
13. Loosely defined as telepathy and clairvoyance, with or without precognition or retrocognition.

Ironically, the most valued human abilities are those that, like psi events, show incomplete penetrance in the general population and are statistically most improbable. For instance, most people can run a few stodgy laps around the track. Only a few can capture gold medals in the Olympic 800-meter. Like a world-class athlete, gifted (and practiced) psychics can repeatedly demonstrate superior abilities. Others, including animals, exhibit less dramatic, but observable, evidence of intuitive ability. Hundreds of athletes are now performing at the level that won gold medals in the past. Only one anomalous performance is necessary to show what is possible for the human race.[21]

Medicine also has much to learn from its statistical anomalies. For instance, health scientists expect that virtually 100% of those who currently test positive for the AIDS virus, or human immunodeficiency virus (HIV), will eventually get AIDS and die. However, as of this writing, there are seven documented cases of HIV seroreversion (changing from HIV positive to negative).[22,23] What are the characteristics of the seroreverters and the interventions that were performed? What are the characteristics of those who have a spontaneous remission from cancer, who walk again despite little chance of neurological recovery, or who survive an airline crash? Such people are not evaluated scientifically because their numbers are small and their homeostatic mechanisms are subtle.[24]

A thorny example of statistical disempowerment is the aggressive campaign to reduce cholesterol. Long-term studies estimate that 12.6% of men with cholesterol levels over 220 will have a heart attack within 12 years of screening.[25] Presumably, more than 75% will not, and no one can predict for any *specific* man with a cholesterol level over 220, even given other predictors such as smoking, whether or not *he* will have a heart attack. What are the characteristics of the people who will not have heart attacks, who will live to a ripe old age despite strong cardiac risk factors? If we limit ourselves to the ritual of statistical, algorithmic medicine, we may sabotage the patient's anomalous self-healing factors that *may already be at work for him* and that may be unrecognized in any system except that of his own reality construction.[26]

In the science fiction book *Time Storms,* Gordon R. Dickson (Bantam Books, 1979) introduces the term *statistical immunes*—people who are spared against the losing odds of impending disaster. This concept, akin to the common notion of a charmed existence, is just the sort of thing that we might expect parapsychology to characterize.

Statistical reasoning (and even the idea of statistical immunity) promotes the fallacy that a certain number of people *must* suffer if others are to flourish, that there must be a certain percentage of poor versus rich, winners versus losers. This erroneous presumption that we live in a zero-sum universe is not a natural law, but one that is man-made from a pessimism (itself a *choice* of belief) that can be traced to myths of original sin and of good and evil.

In a like manner, beliefs about illness are inextricably linked to metaphors about reward and punishment, karma, demons, and other cultural and religious idiosyncrasies. The parapsychological approach to healing, and, in effect, to all reality, encourages people to assert *individual* strengths and abilities to over-come both statistical and religious determinism. Psychokinetic manipulation of one's own body, fate, and fortune is the most empowering consequence of recognizing and using psi abilities. When we seek to go beyond our limitations and have exhausted the repertoire of old truths, we become open to new ideas.

## THE NEED TO CHANGE BELIEFS

Reprinted with special permission of King Features Syndicate, Inc.

In achieving wholeness and maintaining sanity, we seek to meet all our needs without creating conflicting beliefs and values. For instance, material needs do not prompt most people to believe that it is ethical to steal. Resolving contra-dictions between old and new beliefs and between one's individuality and one's social conformity is the foundation of psychological growth. The most divisive conflict is the contradiction between logic and sensory (or extrasensory) expe-rience.

LeShan's *Alternative Realities: The Search for the Full Human Being* pro-vides an eloquent analysis of how beliefs are formed and what instigates new beliefs in individuals and in societies. His most important observation, arising in the context of his belief in extrasensory perception, concerns the two ways we begin to realize that a thought system is no longer adequate.

The first clue is when social problems, such as nuclear weapons, threaten to overwhelm us.

The second set of ways in which we are informed that a change is imminent are the small discrepancies, the little things that do not fit in that tell us there is something wrong with a large system of explanation. These discrepancies are not important in themselves—we can always adapt to them, individually argue them away—but they are the clues, the signposts that tell us that something is not right, that the system of expla-nation does not quite fit reality. . . . When the exceptions, things that cannot be ex-plained in the system, grow to be too many and too clear, the cultural picture of reality begins to break down and make room for the next picture to be developed and accepted (p. 98).[6]

The "little things that do not fit in" are invariably events in personal experience. The conflict between objectivity and subjectivity is intensified as we are forced to either integrate an anomalous experience or deceive ourselves that nothing out of the ordinary has happened. It can seem less nerve-racking to dismiss a few experiences than to topple a whole logical framework.

In the classic Victorian satire *Flatland,* the two Square brothers in a two-dimensional world glimpse a Sphere descending from three-dimensional reality.[27] One brother, secure in the validity of his sensorium, proclaims to fellow Flatlanders his new belief in the third dimension, a crime punishable by life imprisonment. The second brother cannot bring himself to attest to the phenomenon of higher dimensionality and, like Peter denying Christ, refutes his own experience. James tempers harsh judgment of such denials by reminding us to "observe particularly . . . the part played by older truths. . . . Their influence is absolutely controlling. Loyalty to them is the first principle—in most cases it is the only principle, for by far the most usual way of handling phenomena so novel that they would make for a serious re-arrangement of our preconception is to ignore them altogether, or to abuse those who bear witness for them" (p. 51).[4]

Although experience offers the most tangible influence for liberalization of beliefs, much of what we believe is taken on faith. We believe that physicists have detected atoms; although most of us have never seen one, the evidence for atoms seems logical to us. In the realm of psi, also, some things are taken on faith, by appeal either to logic or to empathy. In the Appendix, the Belief System Survey graph shows that the people in our sample believe in more things than they have experienced.

No one believes that we live, pragmatically speaking, in an anything-goes universe. We all have limits to our credulity through some process of elimination. LeShan says: "The perceptions we have are not entirely up to us. . . . Whatever is 'out there' plays a part in our perception and response. The way we perceive the outside world is determined by a combination of 'us' and 'it'; no explanation that is either all one or all the other will stand up very long. I can perceive Beethoven's Ninth Symphony in a variety of ways. . . . I cannot, however, perceive it as God Save the Queen or as an automobile" (p. 25).[6]

On the other hand, there comes a point at which one cannot perceive a psi experience as indigestion or as an optical illusion. At this point, the exertion of clinging to old beliefs becomes more stressful and more untenable than accepting the validity of new experience. Under these circumstances, after the personal revolution has begun, one looks for confirmation in the annals of experimental science and in the experience of others.

From a historical perspective, we can be certain that many of our truths will become as obsolete as the geocentric model of the solar system. If we consider what reality will appear like a thousand years from now, we must concede, like British biologist J.B.S. Haldane, that not only is the universe stranger than we imagine, but it is stranger than we *can* imagine. We can logically assume that we are not the last conscious animal to evolve. We can predict, logically and psychically, that the next species will exhibit unimaginable physical and mental abilities that we now call, respectively, world class and paranormal.

## CONCLUSIONS

Beliefs are the net effect of our consensus observations and our private experience. When the former is at odds with the latter, the conflicts are mediated with the Jungian character function we each habitually adopt as the arbiter of disparate information. We strive for the subjective feeling of being right and being sane, of embracing a self-consistent reality that is as substantive as the shirts on our backs. When we censor valid data, whatever its source, we sever the thread that connects us to our wisdom. The thread that runs by way of our experience through our faculties of discrimination is strung to the marionette of Belief, which dances for us on the stage of Reality.

Parapsychology seeks to integrate all dimensions of human experience into a cogent whole. To do so, anomalous experiences must initially be accepted at face value and then be subjected to the scrutiny of our intelligence. Parapsychology is not an anti-intellectual science. Rather, it seeks to elevate all abilities to the standard of our intellectual genius. Intelligence is neither synonymous with nor solely a function of the intellect. All modes of experience constitute a unified intelligence. Rejecting one's experience or failing to recognize the hidden dimensions of existence fragments the psyche and alienates the Self from a holistic reality.

In the history of evolution, consciousness afforded survival value initially on the strength of instinct and sensation and then on the basis of intellect. Now it is conceivable that the extrasensory, extrarational functions will accelerate us to the next phase.

For us as physical beings, psi experiences must be made pragmatically useful, while we seek to extract from them clues to the transcendent nature of consciousness. These clues, which are segues to the next stage of evolution, are to be found in the subtle anomalous experiences that our consciousness—at once primitive and overcivilized—is just learning to perceive. Reality testing is a Panel Discussion on Individual Experience, conducted among all modes of information processing.

We conclude with Jung that "at any level of meaning, reconciliation of the opposites is not a matter of logic and reason. Generations of men have struggled to reconcile the search for meaning exemplified in religion, and the search for fact, embodied in science, to no avail. The supposed dichotomy between these two basic urges in men cannot be reconciled through the intellect. Like all opposites, they cannot be resolved by logic; they can only come together at the point of *experience*" (p. 253).[8]

**NOTES**

1. Kant I. *Critique of Pure Reason*. Müller FM, trans. Garden City, NY: Doubleday & Co; 1966.

2. Popper KR. Science: conjectures and refutations. In: Grim P, ed. *Philosophy of Science and the Occult*. Albany: State University of New York Press; 1982.

3. Edge HL, Morris RL, Rush JH, Palmer J. *Foundations of Parapsychology*. Boston: Routledge & Kegan Paul; 1986:87–93.

4. James W. *Pragmatism and Four Essays from* The Meaning of Truth. New York: New American Library; 1955. Original manuscript 1907–1909.

5. James, who was a leading member of the American Society for Psychical Research in the early 1900s, additionally states: "Pragmatism is willing to take anything, to follow either logic or the senses and to count the humblest and most personal experiences. She will count mystical experiences if they have practical consequences" (*Pragmatism*, p. 61). He then asks, "Is 'telepathy' a 'fancy' or a 'fact'? The moment you pass beyond the practical use of these categories (a use usually suggested sufficiently by the circumstances of the special case) to a merely curious or speculative way of thinking, you find it impossible to say within just what limits of fact any one of them shall apply" (Ibid., p. 121).

6. LeShan L. *Alternate Realities*. New York: Ballantine Books; 1976.

7. Jung C. Psychological types. *Collected Works*. Vol 6. Hull REC, trans. Princeton, NJ: Princeton University Press, Bollingen Series; 1971: par. 556. Original work published in 1920.

8. Nichols S. *Jung and Tarot*. New York: Samuel Weiser; 1980.

9. The example of ethylenediaminetetraacetic acid (EDTA) in Western medicine is a case in point. For many years, it was believed that chelation therapy with EDTA reversed coronary artery disease. Studies published in the *American Journal of Cardiology* around 1960 demonstrated apparent electrocardiographic and symptomatic evidence of regression of arterial plaque with EDTA. In corroborative studies over the next several years, most patients showed no improvement, and chelation therapy fell into disfavor, only to be taken up again by some New Age practitioners. When several deaths during therapy occurred in Arizona, some states, including California, outlawed the use of EDTA.

10. One must, at any rate, trust sensations qua sensations. People can indeed feel pain relief from a placebo. Rather than concluding that the sensation proves that one is on the active drug, one must realize that it proves that one can create one's own pain relief.

11. Regrettably, many commercial vendors do make unwarranted claims of scientific proof of the effectiveness of their product. There is an attempt to give lip service to the praxis of Western bioscience, but the methods are not adhered to. This middle ground amounts to a rather curious and unfortunate pseudoscience. It would be more forthright of the companies to simply appeal to the empathy of the consumer. I have personally investigated the claims of a maker of a popular alleged sports performance–enhancing supplement. The spurious and ambiguous nature of the evidence used to support their claims fell just short of fraudulent. Yet many athletes swear by this powder, possibly because of the placebo effect inspired by the scientific-sounding claims.

12. The unreliable nature of intuition also has been ascribed to the artifactual nature of our psychological perception of time, which although perceived linearly, is in fact

simultaneous. Jane Roberts discusses the concept of events beyond the present, both past and future, as a set of probabilities. The one we predict or see or remember may not ultimately be the one that will be or has been chosen or actualized. In this case, we have correctly intuited a probable past or future from which, however, we have diverged somewhere on our experienced timeline.

13. This exercise was developed in the Alternative Therapies Unit of the Department of Out-Patient Medicine, San Francisco General Hospital, to prepare patients to do biofeedback, Psychosynthesis, acupuncture, and other therapies.

14. A controversial issue whose truth value has not been established is advisability of food irradiation. Scientific (intellectual) studies are incomplete, and they may remain inconclusive for decades. Many intuitives believe that food irradiation is a mistake on general principle or direct knowledge. (Some believe, erroneously, that the food becomes radioactive.) Some (empathic) social groups welcome irradiated food as a partial solution to world hunger. The long shelf life of irradiated vegetables appeals to (the physical and economic) needs of farmers and supermarket owners, who favor reduced waste and higher profit. Political opponents question whether food irradiation will justify production of nuclear waste. Although it is impossible to say who is right, we can observe the process of a belief formation in its nascent stage.

15. Maslow A. *Toward a Psychology of Being.* Princeton, NJ: Van Nostrand; 1962.

16. It has been argued that by transcendence, Maslow implies a need-less, ego-less state, similar to nirvana. Ego-centeredness has become a rather pejorative term in New Age psychology. Other psychologists, however, aver that without the ego, there is no Self. I agree with the latter philosophy that even in our most transcendent, nonphysical, form, the individual Self survives with certain creative needs intact.

17. Sexual and political activities fulfill multiple purposes and could be placed in virtually all 15 cells in Table 2.1. Other concepts in the table may equally apply to more than one category.

18. We have had several discussions in the Parapsychology Research Group about the difference between neurotic or psychotic behavior and mystical experience or spiritual emergency. Most of us agree that both types of conditions are distinct entities. Diagnostic labels frequently are misused because of the oversimplification of the current psychopathology model.

19. One problem is semantic: the English language does not have a term such as "grok," from Robert Heinlein's *Stranger in a Strange Land,* to connote the combined sense of knowing, believing, and understanding.

20. Ferguson M. *The Aquarian Conspiracy.* Los Angeles: Tarcher; 1980:190.

21. The analogy admittedly breaks down when we consider that athletic performance is measurable and quantifiable. It is the poorly quantifiable aspect of psi that keeps it in a category apart from the 800-meter hurdle.

22. Schiezer J. Six HIV-infected patients test HIV negative following homeopathic drug therapy. *International Medicine World Report.* April 1991;6:1. (Confirmed by enzyme-linked immunosorbent assay (ELISA); however, polymerase chain reaction (PCR) and p24 antigen tests were not performed.)

23. Assistent NM with Duffy P. *Why I Survive AIDS.* New York: Simon & Schuster; 1991.

24. On the other hand, there is much misguided quackery arising from single anecdotal reports that become overgeneralized without being investigated: a case of faulty empathic information processing.

25.  Abbott R, Wilson PWF, Kannel WB, Castelli WP. High density lipoprotein cholesterol, total cholesterol screening, and myocardial infarction. The Framingham Study.
*Arteriosclerosis.* 1989;8:207–211.

26.  Most people are (statistically) well advised to adhere to the current dogma in
preventive medicine. In opting for lifestyle changes of real or imagined benefit, the
individual is making the choice at a deep level to heal or defeat himself according to
his own plan. A major unanswered question in this chapter and in all of parapsychology
is how to reconcile any single decision with the disparity between statistical reality and
the belief in "miracles."

27.  Abbott EA. *Flatland.* New York: New American Library; 1984. See also the
introduction to the Mathematical Models section in this volume.

# II

# REMOTE VIEWING

Remote viewing, a type of extrasensory perception (ESP), describes a protocol in psychical research in which a person in the laboratory is able to describe, often in great detail, activities, pictures, and locations—"targets"—viewed by another person, even when these targets are thousands of miles distant and blocked from ordinary perception. To describe the origins of remote viewing, we should look at the research that preceded it.

In the 1940s and 1950s, research in ESP was centered (and the term was coined) at the laboratory of J. B. Rhine and Louisa E. Rhine at Duke University. The Rhines were successful pioneers in the development of quantitative psychical research. In his famous card-guessing experiments, J. B. Rhine found that many people were able to correctly identify a statistically significant number of ESP cards (circle, star, square, wavy lines, and cross) that an experimenter had hidden. Although some participants in these experiments frequently obtained extra-chance results, most did not. An unfortunate aspect of this card-guessing procedure was that people did not improve with practice. Rather, even the most successful participants eventually lost their ability. This was called the "decline effect," postulated to be due to the repetitive nature of the task.

In an effort to overcome the decline effect, later researchers abandoned the forced-choice, card-guessing approach to ESP and developed free-response protocols in which there are a wide variety of possible correct subjective responses that can be quantitatively scored by independent judges. One of the most successful series was the dream telepathy experiments carried out in the 1960s and

1970s at Maimonides Hospital by Montigue Ullman and Stanley Krippner. In these experiments, a person in one part of the hospital was asked to mentally send images of art prints into the dreams of a person sleeping in a distant part of the hospital. The dreamers indeed produced dream reports that could be objectively correlated with the pictures viewed by the senders. The researchers credited the success of the dream telepathy experiments to the fact that subjects were encouraged to describe their mental pictures and experiences rather than guess at a limited, predescribed set of targets. We now have good evidence that the memory of a fixed set of possible targets creates mental noise and encourages analytical guessing at targets, both of which strongly interfere with successful psychic functioning.

Remote-viewing experiments are always of the free-response type, in which the viewer does not know anything about the specific target he or she is to describe. Whether the target is to be a picture or a geographical location such as a harbor, a church, or a bridge, the viewer is not shown an inventory of the possibilities. The success of this protocol rests on several psychological factors, such as maintaining the participant's interest.

A possibly important psychical factor in the success of remote viewing is that the viewer has three ESP channels open to him: For one thing, he can see the target clairvoyantly, independently of a sender. In addition, he can get his data telepathically from the sender's mind. Third, he can look into his own future and precognitively sense the location he will be visiting half an hour after the experiment. There is evidence that these three channels operate independently at different times in different experiments. For instance, in some experiments, percipients have noted features of the target that escaped the outbound person's attention, but that were confirmed at a later visit to the target. This occurrence would seem to indicate an element of precognition; however, there is no method to discriminate among the various elements of psi (if indeed they are distinct entities) or to further differentiate the three we have mentioned from psychokinesis. In other words, we may ask, did the receiver *perceive* the target, or did he *create* the "random" generation of the target?

We also are led to ask, in what parts of the brain does remote viewing occur? In certain modules, words are *understood*. In others, words are *expressed*. In still other regions, in the cerebral cortex and several major subcortical structures, vision is understood and expressed. David Van Essen, Charles Anderson, and Daniel Felleman have recently published correlations between visual perception and brain function that suggest biological interpretations of remote-viewing data ("Information processing in the primate visual system: an integrated systems perspective," *Science*. 255;24 January 1992:419).

Because brains and intelligence in animals are more or less alike, we might look for evidence of remote viewing in nonhuman species. Indeed, we are perhaps witnessing such occurrences in the phenomena of homing, migration, and navigation. Nonmigratory birds that are taken thousands of miles from their nests quickly find their way home. After years at sea, salmon return to their mountain-stream birthplaces to spawn. Finch eggs stolen from nests in Minneapolis and hatched in San Jose produce fledglings that winter in Argentina and return to Minneapolis. Pacific Coast monarch butterflies winter in a region from northern California to south of the Mexican border. During the summer months, they range into the Rocky Mountains and up into Canada. The round-trip journey can cover more than 2,500 miles, and requires five or six generations before a great-great-grandchild arrives back at a small grove of trees it has never seen in a country in which it has never been.

Remote-viewing refers to primarily visual perceptions of drawings and geographical locations. Remote *sensing* is a broader term that includes perceptions that are not necessarily visual. For example, dowsing is the remote sensing of water, oil, or some other material or object, often done from a map and not in the physical locale. We can experience remote hearing, remote smelling, or the presence of another person without any known (as yet) physical cues.

In this section, we present four approaches to remote-viewing.

In their study of geomagnetic activity and dream telepathy, Persinger and Krippner continue the seminal work begun at Maimonides as they attempt to further characterize the nature of ESP. Psi phenomena have consistently behaved unlike any known form of energy, certainly not like electromagnetic forces. Yet it is clear from the Persinger and Krippner study that there is an interface between psi and other physical effects, probably through the biophysical medium of the brain. By identifying the brain structures that are most sensitive to the earth's magnetic fields, we ultimately may have clues to the biological correlates of psi functioning.

Russell Targ and his coworkers might be considered the Rhines of this generation for standardizing and perfecting free-response remote-viewing protocols using the most scrupulous scientific methods and rigorous statistical analysis. In Chapter 4, Targ takes a bird's-eye view of his many years of research and reports on the state of the art in remote viewing, a discussion continued in the final chapter on increasing psychic reliability.

Elizabeth Rauscher is unique among psi researchers in having both an extensive repertoire of experimental trials in remote viewing and a detailed theoretical model based on her primary work as a physicist. In Chapter 5, Rauscher shows that the training effect in psi experiments apparently is a stronger variable than time or space.

The history of psi research has been fraught with the dilemma of how to admit and evaluate reports of spontaneous psi occurrences—"field" psi as compared with laboratory psi. Many of the most remarkable psi occurrences—such as "crisis psi"—*by their nature* may be attenuated or impossible under laboratory conditions.

In 1951, Louisa E. Rhine examined 1,600 case reports of spontaneous psi, and over the years, she concluded that they agreed remarkably well with experimental results. Both Rhines called for continued investigation of spontaneous case studies for clues about the nature of psi that could then be tested experimentally.

In Chapter 6, Jean Millay reports both formal and spontaneous remote-viewing occurrences and discusses the neurological and psychological processes underlying the experience. Millay offers an intriguing glimpse of some striking aspects of remote perception and reveals elements, such as emotional coloration, that continue to be elusive to statistical measures.

Over the years, remote viewing has been the recurrent focus of the Parapsychology Research Group. Further experiments in remote perception—and remote activation, such as the psychokinesis experiments at Princeton—will have a major role in the numerous remaining riddles about the nature of psi.

# 3

# Dream ESP Experiments and Geomagnetic Activity

*Michael A. Persinger and Stanley Krippner*

Determination of the mechanism by which telepathy occurs would facilitate its understanding and control. The first step to the isolation of mechanism requires the identification of some measurable variable that is systematically associated with the occurrence of telepathy. Spontaneous telepathic experiences concerning death or crises occur more frequently during days in which the global geomagnetic activity is significantly less than during the days before or after the experiences. A similar pattern has been shown for the Gurney, Myers, and Podmore[1] collection from the nineteenth century,[2] the Sidgwick collection from early in this century,[3,4] and the unverified reports published in *Fate* magazine.[5,6]

The systematic association between specific temporal patterns in daily average geomagnetic activity and the likelihood of a telepathic occurrence does not by itself reveal mechanism. There are at least three classes of explanations. Periods of sudden, relatively quieter geomagnetic activity facilitate telepathy by (a) producing environmental conditions that promote exchange of information between the agent and the percipient, (b) allowing normal telepathic factors already in the environment to be amplified between the agent and the percipient, and (c) evoking transient alterations in brain function such that normal telepathic factors (that do not change with geomagnetic activity) can affect the percipient's sensitized temporal lobes.

The association between geomagnetic activity and spontaneous telepathic experiences suggests the existence of a persistent factor that may serve as an empirical handle by which to study the phenomena. If this utilitarian objective is to be achieved, the geomagnetic activity pattern also should be observable in experimental cases of telepathy. This association also would support the presumption that spontaneous and experimental telepathy are indeed similar phenomena. Several studies have shown statistically significant relations between changes in daily geomagnetic activity and accuracy during remote viewing,[7] the Circular Matching Abacus Test,[8] and, more recently, both Ganzfeld sessions and restricted-choice computer games.[9]

One of the best known examples of experimental telepathy involves the dream telepathy research inaugurated by Montague Ullman, Stanley Krippner, and Charles Honorton during the 1960s.[10–12] These studies were conducted at the Dream Laboratory of the Maimonides Medical Center in Brooklyn. To determine if the geomagnetic effect was evident in these data, the study was designed to examine three hypotheses.

1. Nights on which the strongest experimental telepathy occurred also would be nights that displayed the quietest geomagnetic activity compared with the days before and after (i.e., is the V-shape effect apparent?).
2. Cases that demonstrated weak or questionable telepathy should not demonstrate the V-shape effect.
3. Both the strongest cases of telepathy from the Maimonides studies and the most accurate cases from the spontaneous telepathic experiences from Gurney, Myers, and Podmore should demonstrate the same temporal pattern of daily geomagnetic activity (the V-shape).

## PROCEDURE

### Dream Telepathy Protocol

The typical procedure followed at Maimonides was for the percipient (or subject) to arrive at the laboratory in time to meet the agent—a person who would spend much of the night focusing on the contents of an art print. The percipient's task was to dream about this art print even though it would not be selected until the percipient was isolated from the agent. The percipient also would meet the two experimenters, who would explain the procedures. (On a few occasions in which possible clairvoyance was studied, the art print was selected randomly and was not removed from the sealed envelope, and no agent was used. The percipient was simply instructed to attempt to dream about the art print.)

After electrodes were attached to the percipient's head for the monitoring of brain waves and eye movements, the percipient would have no further contact with the agent until the next morning. An experimenter threw dice that, in combination with a random number table, provided a number that corresponded to a number on a sealed envelope that contained an art print. The envelope was opened once the agent reached his or her private room in a distant part of the building. This art print became the target on which the agent focused during the night.[11,12]

The experimenters took turns monitoring the percipient's sleep. Toward the end of each period of rapid eye movement, the percipient was awakened by an experimenter by way of an intercom and described any dream content that could be recalled. These comments were tape-recorded, as was a morning interview in which the percipient associated to his or her dream recall. The interview was conducted double blind; neither the percipient nor the experimenters knew the identity of the target or the pool of art prints from which the target had been randomly selected.

The target for a given night and the dreams for the night often contained a number of striking similarities, suggesting that an anomaly (so-called telepathy) had occurred. For example, on May 23, 1966, the target was a print of a zebra painted by an unknown Indian artist. The percipient dreamed about a horse show, a horse race, and a striped tie. But it could have been the case that simply by chance any transcript of a night's dreams might have contained passages of striking similarity to any picture to which they might have been compared.[13]

To evaluate the chance hypothesis, the Maimonides team obtained judgments of similarity between the dream content and each of the other potential targets in the pool from which the actual target had been randomly selected. Typically, three judges were used who worked blind and independently from one another with materials that had been mailed to them. They had no information about which picture had been randomly selected as the target. Any extrachance difference between targets and nontargets in their similarity to dream content was considered an apparent anomaly. The target pools typically used by the judges were duplicates that had never been handled by the agents.

Although sometimes percipients evaluated their own dreams against the target pool (before they discovered the identity of the actual target), and although some experiments required the judges to rate target-dream similarities on a 100-point scale, the only form in which data were available for all sessions was a count of judges' hits and misses. If the actual target had been ranked in the upper half of the target pool (e.g., #1, #2, or #3 in a pool of six) for similarity to the dreams and postsleep interview, the outcome was considered a hit. If the actual target had been ranked in the lower half of the pool (e.g., #4, #5, or #6 in a pool of six), the outcome was considered a miss. The median score of the three judges was selected to determine hits and misses.

For the purposes of this study, the ranks were divided into four categories. A "high hit" would be a rank in the top quartile (e.g., #1 or #2 in a pool of eight; #1 in a pool of six); a "low hit" would be a rank in the second quartile (e.g., #3 or #4 in a pool of eight; #2 or #3 in a pool of six). A "high miss" would be a rank in the third quartile (e.g., #5 or #6 in a pool of eight; #4 or #5 in a pool of six); a "low miss" would be a rank in the fourth quartile (#7 or #8 in a pool of eight; #6 in a pool of six). In other words, these four groups represented judges' ranks of successive order from strongest hits to strongest misses.

The data from the first night each subject spent at the Maimonides Laboratory were utilized, and the data from any other nights were discarded. The rationale was quite simple: Some subjects spent only one night at Maimonides; to use the second or third night would have resulted in a smaller pool. If the last night had been utilized, there may well have been a built-in difference between subjects unfamiliar with the procedures (those spending only one night in the laboratory) and those quite familiar with laboratory procedures (those spending several nights). On the basis of this decision, 62 experimental nights were available for analysis—18 "high hits," 29 "low hits," 7 "high misses," and 8 "low misses." The 62 cases represent the total collection of subjects seen between 1964 and 1969 at Maimonides.

## Geomagnetic Data and Analyses

The daily average aa (antipodal) index[14] was selected as the measure of global or planetary geomagnetic activity. The aa index is the oldest continuous geomagnetic index (started in the year 1868) and was used as the measure of global geomagnetic activity for the Gurney, Myers, and Podmore (1886) cases that occurred between 1868 and 1886.[2] By using this index, direct comparisons could be made between the experimental cases from the Maimonides dream telepathy studies and the spontaneous telepathic experiences from *Phantasms of the Living*.

Although the aa values are based on data from only two stations (one in each of the hemispheres), the daily aa index is highly correlated (.95) with other, more well known daily global measures that utilize the magnetic activity from several geomagnetic observatories. The daily values correspond to the mean amplitude (in gammas or nanoTeslas, nT) of the displacement from a standardized baseline. Average daily aa values are derived from the eight 3-hour values (smallest temporal increment). The average daily value (the one used in our analyses) is considered a good indication of planetary activity, as defined by its near-continuous distribution.[15] Although local variations in the amplitude of geomagnetic activity do occur, the average daily temporal pattern of the changes in amplitude are relatively similar everywhere. The only exception to this statement occurs in areas that are subject to transient geomagnetic anomalies during geomagnetic storms in which the effects of stronger static components also can emerge.

Daily average aa values for the northern hemisphere were collected for each of the 7 days before, each of the 7 days after, and on the day each session began. Because most of the dreaming occurred during the early morning of the next day, it was selected as the key day. To be commensurate with previous studies that involved spontaneous experiences,[2,5,6] this twenty-four-hour period was selected as the key day instead of the (evening of the) day before, when the session was started. Mean monthly aa values for months in which the experiences occurred were also listed.

We selected SPSSX MANOVA (multivariate analysis of variance) as the primary statistical procedure because of the statistically significant intercorrelation of geomagnetic activity levels during any 2 to 3 successive days. The basic design was daily geomagnetic activity by group, that is, the log (base of 10) of the daily aa values for 7 days (key day ±3 days) and the two groups (strong cases of telepathy versus the reference cases). Log values were used to reduce the contribution from days that contained extreme outlier values. (This procedure attenuated the problem within acceptable levels as defined by the lack of statistical significance displayed by the multivariate test for homogeneity of the dispersion matrices.) The total of 7 days (key day ±3 days) of geomagnetic activity was selected before the study began to be comparable and compatible with the analyses of spontaneous telepathic experiences.[2,5,6]

To test the first hypothesis, MANOVA was completed for the daily geomagnetic values (that served operationally as repeated measures) and two independent variables: groups (high-hit versus low-hit groups) and gender (male versus female). The latter variable was included because the possible differential sensitivity of females has been inferred from the markedly enhanced incidence of female percipients in spontaneous cases.[16] The numbers of subjects for each group were high hit—male, 12; high hit—female, 6; low hit—male, 20; low hit—female, 9. Because of the small sample size for each of the other two categories (7 for high miss and 8 for low miss) and our reluctance to combine them, these cases were not included in this analysis. (Also, the issue of psi missing was considered to be an additional problem that would be best addressed elsewhere.) To test the second hypothesis, paired (correlated) $t$ tests were completed between the geomagnetic activity for the key day and each of the other 6 days for the strongest telepathic cases (high hits) and weaker cases (low hits) separately.

To test the third hypothesis, the Gurney, Myers, and Podmore database[2] was combined with the Maimonides data. To specifically check the similarity in geomagnetic activity (the V-shape) around the days on which telepathy occurred, a MANOVA was completed as a function of 7 days of geomagnetic activity (key day ±3 days) and the two databases: the strongest Maimonides cases ($n = 18$) versus the primary spontaneous cases ($n = 78$). To minimize the possible weighting from the larger number of cases in the latter group, we decided to compare the experimental cases with a subset of the spontaneous cases that contained a comparable number of subjects. By requesting all of the records that involved the dream modality (which was considered optimal in light of the Maimonides experiments) for one decade (1877 through 1886), a total of 22 cases was obtained. All analyses were completed using SPSSX software on a VAX computer.

**Figure 3.1**
**Mean Daily Average Values in Dream Telepathy Study**

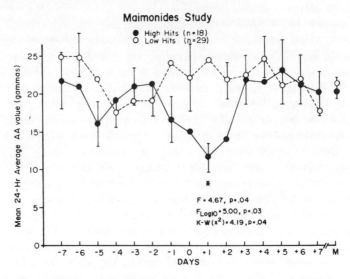

Mean average daily aa values (in gammas) for the days before ( − ), days after ( + ), and days of the beginning of the sessions for the high-hit (closed circles) and low-hit (open circles) dream telepathy groups. Vertical bars indicate standard errors ( ± 1) of the means. M refers to the mean aa values for the months in which the experiences occurred.

## RESULTS

### Verification of Hypotheses

A simple plot of the average daily aa values for the 7 days before, the days of, and the 7 days after the beginning of the sessions for the high hit ($n = 18$) and low hit ($n = 29$) groups is shown in Figure 3.1. The only statistically significant difference between the two groups occurred on the day after the beginning of the session. This day (called the key day for all subsequent analyses) included the late evening and early morning hours during which time the dreaming and telepathic experiences occurred. The statistical significance of the quieter geomagnetic activity during the 24-hour period in which the strongest telepathy occurred was evident for the absolute aa values ($F[1,45] = 4.67$, $p = .04$) (even with the statistically significant difference in group variances [Bartlett-Box $= 21.29$, $p < .001$]) and the log base 10 transformations ($F[1,45] = 5.00$, $p = .03$) that eliminated the statistically significant difference in group variances; a nonparametric test (Kruskal-Wallis) also demonstrated the significant effect ($c^2 = 4.19$, $p = .04$).

The first MANOVA according to the two groups with different accuracy of dream telepathy (high hit versus low hit), gender, and the seven successive days of (log base 10) geomagnetic activity (key day ±3 days) did not reveal statistically significant group (F[1,43]=1.19, $p$=.28), gender (F[1,43]=0.20, $p$=.66), or group by gender (F[1,43]=0.14, $p$=.71) interaction effects. Although there were no statistically significant interactions between gender and the geomagnetic activity on the different days during, before, and after the dreams, and gender (F[6,258]=0.15, $p$=.99) or geomagnetic activity by gender by group (F[6,258]=.012, $p$=.99), there was a significant daily geomagnetic activity by group interaction (F[6,258]=2.97, $p$=.008). The multivariate test for homogeneity of dispersion matrices was not significant ($p$>.05). (The geomagnetic activity by group interaction for the absolute aa values also was statistically significant [F(6,258)=2.21, $p$=.04], even though the dispersion matrices were not homogeneous.)

As can be seen in Figure 3.2A, the source of the interaction was due primarily to the lower geomagnetic activity on the nights of the dreams that contained the greatest accuracy (high hit: strongest telepathy) compared with the nights of the dreams that contained less accuracy (low hit: weaker telepathy). Whereas the geomagnetic activity on the nights of the strong telepathic cases was significantly less (paired $t$[17]=4.55, $p$≤.001) than the monthly average of the months in which the dreams occurred, the geomagnetic activity on the nights of the weaker telepathy dreams was not significantly different from the monthly geomagnetic activity (paired $t$[28=1.49, $p$=.07).

These results supported hypothesis 1, which predicted that the geomagnetic activity should be significantly lower during 24-hour periods in which dream telepathy was strongest, as defined by the greater accuracy of target material. Paired $t$ tests between the log base 10 of the aa values on the key day and for each of the other 6 days demonstrated statistically significant differences between the key day and 3 days before ($t$[17]=3.14, $p$=.003), 2 days before ($t$[17]=2.60, $p$=.009), and 3 days after ($t$[17]=3.58, $p$=.001) for the high-hit group only. There were no significant differences between the geomagnetic activity on the key day and each of the other 6 days for the group of telepathic dreams that were less accurate. These results supported hypothesis 2.

The MANOVA between the two groups of data revealed that the strongest (high hit) telepathic cases ($n$=18) from the Maimonides study and the spontaneous cases ($n$=78) demonstrated that the log base 10 of the average geomagnetic activity (see Figure 3.2B) was significantly lower during the week of the spontaneous cases (that occurred between 1868 and 1886) relative to the experimental cases (F[1,94]=5.18, $p$=.025). Although there were no statistically significant days by group interaction (F[6,564]=0.76, $p$=.06), there was a highly significant difference between the geomagnetic activity across the 7 days, regardless of group factors (F[6,564]=4.29, $p$=.0003). Because paired $t$ tests between the geomagnetic activity on the key days and the 3 days before and after had been already completed for the Maimonides strongest telepathy cases, paired $t$ tests (all 77 $df$) were completed for the Gurney, Myers, and Podmore data. The geomagnetic activity on the key days was significantly lower than all

**Figure 3.2**
**Log of the Mean Daily Values for 24-Hour Periods in Dream Telepathy Study**

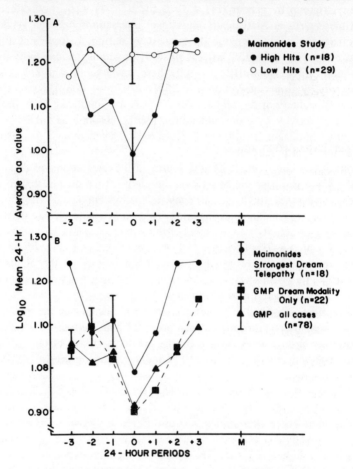

Log (base 10) of the mean daily aa values for the 24-hour periods during, before ( − ), and after ( + ) the key days (0) when (A) strong and weaker experimental telepathic dreams occurred during the Maimonides Series, and (B) spontaneous telepathic experiences (Gurney, Myers, & Podmore, 1886) occurred. M refers to the means of the monthly aa averages. Vertical bars indicate standard error of the mean.

of the other days ( ± 3 days) before or after (*t* values ranged from 2.41 to 4.29). In addition, the geomagnetic activity on the day of the spontaneous experiences was significantly lower than the average values for months in which they occurred ($t[77] = 7.18$, $p < .001$).

MANOVA with the Maimonides data and the 22 cases of *dream modality only* from the spontaneous cases (see Figure 3.2*B*) also showed a significant difference in geomagnetic activity between the days during, before, or after the experiences (F[6,228] = 4.00, $p$ = .0008). Again, there was no significant inter-action between the daily geomagnetic activity and the two groups of data (F[6,228] = 0.61, $p$ = .72). The average geomagnetic activity for the week of the Gurney, Myers, and Podmore cases (dream modality only) also was lower than the week in which the contemporary cases occurred (F[1,38] = 3.80, $p$ = .059). The absence of significant interactions thus supported hypothesis 3 that the two groups should show (statistically) identical temporal patterns for mean daily geomagnetic activity on the days of, before, and after the experi-ences.

### Further Exploration and Analysis

One obvious question that emerged from this research is, What is more im-portant: (a) the *absolute values* of the geomagnetic activity (as defined by aa values), or (b) the *relative change* in geomagnetic activity on the day of the telepathic experience? To answer this question, *T*-score values (by definition a mean of 50 and standard deviation of 10) were computed for the nontrans-formed (i.e., absolute) aa values for each of the 7 days for each case for both sets of data. The *T* score for the aa values for each day for each case was calculated first by subtracting the value for that day from the mean of the scores for all 7 days and then dividing this value by the standard deviation for the 7 days. After multiplying this value (effectively the scores' standard deviation) by 10 and adding it to 50, the *T* score was obtained. Although outliers could still affect the analyses, the amplitude would be minimal because they would be expressed as standard deviations with respect to the mean of the week in which the experience occurred.

The *T* score allowed analysis of the relative change in geomagnetic activity on the key day and for each of the other days with respect to the mean value for the week. If the relative decrease in geomagnetic activity on the day of the telepathic experience was more critical than the absolute value of the geomag-netic activity (in aa units), then the *interaction* (even though the ''repeated'' measure would be invariant [i.e., singular variance-covariance matrix for each cell]) between the high-hit group (strongest telepathy) and the low-hit group (weaker telepathy) should be even more significant than determined in the pre-vious analysis. MANOVA between the *T* scores of the aa values for the key day ±3 days for the two Maimonides groups demonstrated no statistically sig-nificant day by group interactions (F[6,270] = 1.51, $p$ = .17). These results strongly suggested that the *absolute value* of the geomagnetic activity was more critical than the relative change of activity during the weeks of the dreams.

Comparison of the monthly aa values (log base 10) between the Gurney, Myers, and Podmore data and the 18 cases of the strongest experimental dream telepathy results indicated that the geomagnetic activity during the months of the 22 *dream modality cases* (years 1877 to 1886) was less than that during the months of the Maimonides studies (F[1,38] = 14.19, $p$ < .001). There was no statistically significant difference, however, between the geomagnetic activity during the 24-hour intervals of experimental and spontaneous telepathic experiences (F[1,38] = 1.03, $p$ = .32). The lack of a significant difference in geomagnetic activity on the days of the experiences for the two groups (even though monthly values differed) also supports the hypothesis that the *absolute amplitude of geomagnetic activity* rather than the relative change is the critical feature for facilitating telepathic experiences.

## DISCUSSION

The results of this study indicate that the 24-hour periods during which experimental telepathic dreams were most accurate (strongest) were associated with significantly quieter planetary geomagnetic activity compared ±3, 24-hour periods before and after. The V-shaped pattern of geomagnetic activity over days (with the trough occurring on the night of the telepathic dreams) was not observed in cases that were considered to be weaker indications of dream telepathy as defined by an objective ranking procedure. These results support the hypothesis that quieter periods of magnetic activity facilitate the occurrence of experimental telepathic experiences.

The pattern of the geomagnetic activity for the week (key day ±3) of the strongest cases of dream telepathy also was identical (i.e., not statistically distinguishable) from the V-shaped pattern in geomagnetic activity that was observed in the spontaneous telepathic experiences from almost a century ago. This similarity suggests that some geomagnetic factor may influence the occurrence of both experimental and spontaneous telepathic experiences in a similar manner. Comparable V-shaped relations have been observed with other collections of spontaneous telepathic experiences.[5]

Persistence of a geomagnetic factor in telepathic experiences has theoretical and practical implications. First, the similarity of geomagnetic activity patterns around the days of both experimental and spontaneous telepathic experiences suggests that the two classes of phenomena are indeed related. Second, the occurrence of the geomagnetic V-shaped effect, assuming the sample size is appropriate, might be used as an indicator of the occurrence of telepathy within novel experimental designs. Significant differences within any experimental context, despite appropriate controls and valid statistical treatments, may not necessarily involve *traditional* telepathic processes. If the geomagnetic factor continues to be evident with well-established databases of both experimental and spontaneous telepathic cases, then its absence may serve as an indicator of the presence of some other factor that might be generating quasi-psi. Consequently, confusion about telepathy and argumentation between experimenters who use different procedures might be attenuated.

A preliminary answer to the question of whether or not the absolute level of geomagnetic activity rather than a relative decrease in geomagnetic activity is the critical factor was obtained in this study. When *T*-score transformations of the geomagnetic activity for each case were computed for each day with respect to its standard deviation from the week of activity, the differences between the strongest and the weaker experimental cases were not significant. In addition, there was no significant difference between the geomagnetic activity during the 24-hour periods of experiences for either the spontaneous telepathic experiences or the experimental dream reports, despite the elevated mean monthly aa values in the latter cases.

This pattern suggests that aa values of about 10 gammas (95% confidence interval of 8 to 13 gammas) are highly associated with the occurrence of a classic telepathic experience. If the aa values approach 25 gammas or more (95% confidence interval of 18 to 34 gammas), the mean value for the low-hit dream telepathy group, an (accurate) telepathic experience is less likely to occur. The reliability of the approximately 10 aa unit value is supported by the spontaneous cases from Gurney, Myers, and Podmore. The mean of the aa values for the 24-hour periods in which all verified experiences occurred ($n = 78$) was 10 gammas (95% confidence interval of 9 to 12 gammas), whereas the mean aa value for dream-only experiences was 12 gammas (confidence interval of 8 to 16 gammas). It is interesting that the mean aa values for the 24-hour period in which the 133 unverified telepathic experiences from *Fate* occurred was 14 gammas,[5] a value that is expected to be inflated because of poorer controls during case collection. For comparison, the means of the aa values for the days before the occurrence of these experiences ranged between 24 and 26 gammas.

The tendency for both spontaneous and experimental telepathic experiences to occur during the nights of 24-hour periods in which the mean aa amplitudes were about 10 gammas may facilitate the isolation of mechanism. It is not clear whether the optimal condition is the simple occurrence of geomagnetic activity within the range of 10 gammas, regardless of activity during the previous 3 days, or whether the optimal condition occurs when there is a sudden change from some previous higher activity (aa 25 or greater) to within the range of 10 gammas within a 24-hour period. Both the spontaneous cases and the experimental telepathy data indicated that the actual absolute decrease in average daily geomagnetic activity was about 10 to 15 gammas.

The specification of this range of sudden decrease (by 10 to 15 gammas) in geomagnetic activity is important for precise isolation of mechanism. If, for example, some extremely low frequency magnetic field factor[17] is involved with the transmission of information, then its occurrence should be maximally correlated with the 24-hour periods in which the aa values are within the 10-unit range or those days in which the aa values approach 10 after a sudden decrease in activity. Whereas the first option would suggest a steady-state telepathic factor that is linearly related to the presence and duration of geomagnetic activity within the optimal range, the second option argues strongly in favor of a derivative solution that requires the optimal rate of change in magnetic activity within a specific temporal interval.

If, on the other hand, one assumes that the geomagnetic factor is coupled exclusively with its effect on the *sensitivity of the brains* of the people involved in the experience (agent or percipient, depending on the model), then the mechanism would involve some important neuroelectrical or neurohormonal alteration that is sensitive to (a) average daily magnetic activity in the range of 10 gammas or (b) a decrease in average daily geomagnetic activity by about 15 gammas to a value of about 10 gammas. That the human brain may be sensitive to subtle geomagnetic activity within this order of magnitude has been discussed previously.[5,18]

A critique of the geomagnetic effect in traditional telepathic experiences has been developed by Hubbard and May.[19] They have attempted to indict the validity of these studies by implying that (a) there is no strong evidence for the biological effectiveness of either extremely low frequency or ultralow frequency magnetic fields and (b) the aa indices (and indeed magnetic indices in general) are not adequate indicators of geomagnetic activity for parapsychological studies. Although provocative and certainly worthy of consideration, their arguments are neither accurate nor relevant to this study.

First, there are both strong and consistent data that time-varying magnetic fields within the geomagnetic range affect living systems.[20,21] Changes in specific behaviors (e.g., associated with circadian variations) and particular chemical pathways (e.g., indolamines) have been systematically associated with near-natural low-frequency magnetic field exposures. The variability and inconsistency that exist within the scientific literature are in large part associated with inappropriate conceptual aggregation of studies that involve different frequencies, intensities, and systems. To argue that effects of time-varying magnetic fields on living systems are inconsistent (and hence questionable) is equivalent to dismissing pharmacological effects because different drugs produce different responses. In addition, if the controversial nature of an effect was considered a criterion for its rejection, the subject matter of parapsychology would be totally excluded.

Hubbard and May's second major argument involves the alleged decrease in coherence between mean daily geomagnetic activity in different localities. Hubbard and May fail to specify how much discoherence actually occurs and within what latitudinal boundaries. Extreme coherence in geomagnetic activity between stations is important for geophysical modeling. However, intercorrelations of even .80 between the average daily geomagnetic activity near all stations within the continental United States, for example, would be sufficient to demonstrate the geomagnetic field effect, considering the mean decrease of 10 to 15 gammas from a baseline of about 20 to 25 gammas (i.e., about 50% of the amplitude) that is associated with days of strong telepathic experiences. Indeed, even a random selection of two distant stations, such as between Fredericksburg, Virginia, and Anchorage, Alaska, during the last 6 months of 1987 demonstrates a Pearson correlation coefficient of .85 and a Spearman correlation of .92 between the average daily activity (A index) for the two stations.

Even weaker interspatial correlations of geomagnetic activity would not necessarily contest the validity of the phenomenon if the shared variance of geomagnetic activity between loci was the same source with which telepathic experiences were associated.

From an operational perspective, technical discussion concerning the geomagnetic indices with respect to psi phenomena is analogous to an obsession with decimal points when the background fluctuations in the phenomenon involve a large range of integers. Compared with measures of telepathic experiences, the numerical reliability between geomagnetic indices is extremely robust. The arguments concerning precision may be discipline-specific[22] and of questionable relevance to the understanding of psi mechanisms. At most, the discrepancies noted by Bubenik and Fraser-Smith[15] as reported by Hubbard and May[19] would reduce the strength of the geomagnetic effect in telepathic experiences rather than artifactually evoke it.

Despite these interesting questions concerning the degree of variability in the spatial homogeneity of geomagnetic activity, Hubbard and May's argument[19] is not relevant to this study. Because all the Maimonides data were collected in the same place, the problem of different geomagnetic measures at different locations has questionable significance. Similarly, most of the cases for the Gurney, Myers, and Podmore collection occurred within 100 km (the reason our analysis originally was performed) of the sensor that was used for the calculation of the aa values and during a period when human-caused electromagnetic noise would have been much lower than today. The fact that the geomagnetic pattern was similar in both shape and amplitude in two clusters of telepathic experiences that were separated by several thousands of kilometers and by a century challenges the validity of the overconcern with geomagnetic indices.

The issue of cultural electromagnetic signals within the intensity and frequency range of geomagnetic activity, an important component of Hubbard and May's approach,[19] may be useful for the isolation of the mechanism by which the geomagnetic effect occurs. They postulated that a geomagnetic-telepathic effect could be negated because signals generated by a direct-current train system (BART) within the San Francisco Bay Area can exceed background geomagnetic activity by an order of 1 to 3, depending on proximity to the system.[23,24] What Hubbard and May did not state is that (a) the characteristics of these transient signals are markedly different in both form and temporal structure from those associated with geomagnetic storms, and (b) these humanly manufactured signals are effectively absent during the early-morning hours (0100 to 0500 local time) when traditional spontaneous psi experiences tend to occur most frequently. Indeed, the presence of human-made electromagnetic signals and determination of the degree of their similarity to natural patterns may allow innovative approaches to the study of how both classes of stimuli affect the occurrence (suppression or facilitation) of traditional telepathic experiences.

The importance of the absolute value of the geomagnetic activity (or its relative, sudden decrease) as a facilitator of spontaneous or experimental telepathic experiences would argue strongly in favor of on-site measurement as suggested by Hubbard and May. Careful analysis of these records might isolate optimal parameters in the temporal structure of local field variations. Although the daily average geomagnetic measures over months between stations are highly correlated, latitude-specific local hourly variations (especially during solar quiet periods), local human-caused electromagnetic noise, and natural anomalies (e.g., buried ore deposits) are sufficient to affect the local expression of global geomagnetic activity. On-site monitoring and consequent correlation with indices of planetary activity may further reveal the local signatures that modulate the hourly variations in the occurrence and accuracy of telepathic experiences.

## NOTES

1. Gurney E, Myers FWH, Podmore F. *Phantasms of the Living* (2 vols.). London: Tribner; 1886.

2. Persinger MA. Spontaneous telepathic experiences from *Phantasms of the Living* and low global geomagnetic activity. *Journal of the American Society for Psychical Research* 1987;81:23–36.

3. Sidgwick H (Mrs. EM). Phantasms of the living. *Proceedings of the Society for Psychical Research* 1922;33:23–429.

4. Arango MA. *Spontaneous Crisis-Evoked Telepathic Phenomena from the Sidgwick Collection of 1922 and Low Global Geomagnetic Activity*. Ontario, Canada: Laurentian University; 1988. Unpublished fourth-year thesis.

5. Persinger MA, Schaut GB. Geomagnetic factors in subjective telepathic, precognitive, and postmortem experiences. *Journal of the American Society for Psychical Research* 1988;82:217–235.

6. Schaut GB, Persinger MA. Subjective telepathic experiences, geomagnetic activity and the ELF hypothesis. Part 1. Data analyses. *Psi Research* 1985;4(1):4–20.

7. Adams MH. Persistent temporal relationship of ganzfeld results to geomagnetic activity, appropriateness of using standard geomagnetic indices. *Proceedings of Presented Papers: The 29th Annual Convention of the Parapsychological Association* 1986:471–485.

8. Tart CT. Geomagnetic effects on GESP: Two studies. *Journal of the American Society for Psychical Research* 1988;82:193–216.

9. Haraldsson E, Gissurarson LR. Does geomagnetic activity affect extrasensory perception? *Personality and Individual Differences* 1987;8:745–747.

10. Ullman M. Telepathy and dreams. *Experimental Medicine and Surgery* 1969;27:19–38.

11. Ullman M, Krippner S. *Dream Studies and Telepathy: An Experimental Approach* (Parapsychological Monographs No. 12). New York: Parapsychology Foundation; 1970.

12. Ullman M, Krippner S. Experimental dream studies. In: Ebon M, ed. *The Signet Handbook of Parapsychology*. New York: New American Library; 1978:409–422.

13. Child IL. Psychology and anomalous observations: the question of ESP in dreams. *American Psychologist* 1985;40:1219–1230.

14. Mayaud PN. A hundred-year series of geomagnetic data 1868–1967. *IAGA Bulletin* 1973;33.

15. Bubenik DM, Fraser-Smith AC. Evidence for strong artificial components in the equivalent linear amplitude geomagnetic indices. *Journal of Geophysical Research* 1977;82:2875–2878.

16. Persinger MA. *The Paranormal* (2 vols.). New York: MSS Information; 1974.

17. Matsushita S, Campbell WH, eds. *Physics of Geomagnetic Phenomena* (2 vols.). New York: Academic Press; 1967.

18. Becker RO, Selden G. *The Body Electric: Electromagnetism and the Foundation of Life.* New York: William Morrow; 1985.

19. Hubbard GS, May EC. Aspects of measurement and application of geomagnetic indices and extremely low frequency electromagnetic radiation for use in parapsychology. *Proceedings of Presented Papers: The 29th Annual Convention of the Parapsychological Association* 1986:519–535.

20. Ahlbom A, Albert EN, Fraser-Smith AC, Grodzinsky AJ, Marron MT, Martin AO, Persinger MA, Shelanski ML, Wolpow ER. *Biological Effects of Power Line Fields: New York State Power Lines Project Scientific Advisory Panel Final Report.* Albany: New York State Department of Health; 1987.

21. Persinger MA. Increased geomagnetic activity and the occurrence of bereavement hallucinations: evidence for melatonin-mediated microseizuring in the temporal lobe? *Neuroscience Letters* 1988;88:271–274.

22. For examples, see Mayaud PN. *Derivation, Meaning and Use of Geomagnetic Indices* (Geophysical Monograph 22). Washington, DC: American Geophysical Union; 1980.

23. Fraser-Smith AC, Coates DB. Large amplitude ULF electromagnetic fields from BART. *Radio Science* 1978;13:661–668.

24. Ho AMH, Fraser-Smith AC, Villard OG, Jr. Large-amplitude ULF magnetic fields produced by a rapid transit system: close-range measurements. *Radio Science* 1979;14:1011–1015.

# 4

# A Decade of Remote-Viewing Research

*Russell Targ*

Psychic functioning was not invented in the laboratory; rather, it was naturally occurring in the field. When we founded the Parapsychology Research Group twenty-five years ago, we talked about how important it would be, if we were to progress in psychic research, to have some sort of a psychic "battery" to charge us up for a high level of psychic functioning when and where we needed it. We knew that progress in understanding electricity, which had been studied for some twenty-five hundred years, became possible only around the end of the eighteenth century, when an actual electrical battery was made. Then progress was rapid. Demonstrations could go beyond the weak but reliable creation of static electricity by rubbing an amber rod with silk, and beyond merely observing the rare but powerful results of electricity in the field—lightning and thunder.

We needed to set up tests that were reliable and repeatable, that would fit in with ordinary human experience, yet could mold themselves to experimentation in the laboratory. We knew you could demonstrate psychic functioning in a fairly uninteresting and declining way, as with the Zener cards with the five familiar symbols used by J.B. Rhine and L. Rhine in the 1930s. Then there's the spectacular kind of ESP, such as the precognitive dream, that, like the lightning bolt, is not easily repeatable in the laboratory. We wanted to create experiments that a person could do at any time, developing and using intuition rather than the analytical approach that is attempted for card-guessing.

How could we make a battery for a steady source of psychic abilities, for furthering our own psychical research? In 1972, when Hal Putoff and I pioneered experiments in remote viewing—the ability to describe what is going on in some distant place to which you have no ordinary access—we took the first steps toward making an ESP battery. In fact, we were probably among the first people to articulate what the problems in psychic research were in a relatively jargon-free way and to set about correcting these problems, which were really simple ones.

First, we had to overcome people's fear or distrust of psychic phenomena. This began with our choosing the term "remote viewing," picking a neutral descriptive phrase that was free of past prejudices and occult assumptions. We then set up rigorous scientific protocols, including a random protocol for target selection. Next we created an environment in which it was safe to be psychic. Just walking through the entry of SRI International, where the experiments took place, we impressed prospective viewers with the atmosphere of respectability and the multimillion-dollar layout of high-technology equipment. We conveyed the feeling that in a sense, SRI was giving its blessing, and that even though being psychic is a slightly forbidden activity in society, we give you permission to do it now.

In the laboratory itself, the viewers were made to feel at ease—no white lab coats were in evidence. The activities were always happy occasions that we *expected* to be successful. We were not examining people under a microscope to see whether they were part of a weird species of psychics. Rather, we were investigating the remote-viewing phenomenon together; we were partners in research.

In our decade of research at SRI, throughout hundreds of experimental trials, we used no drugs, hypnosis, strobe lights, sensory deprivation, or meditative techniques, nor did we even require belief. In fact, to overcome the problem that Arthur Koestler called the "Ink Fish (Octopus) Effect," in which a skeptic may view a clearly successful ESP demonstration one day and have doubts about its clarity—or even honesty—the next,[1] we encouraged any willing skeptic to take part in a remote-viewing experiment. We found that with patience and encouragement, almost anyone can experience remote viewing.

Everyone seemed to have his own way of "seeing," and we encouraged participants to prepare to "see" in any way they chose. What works for one may not work for another; what works works.

My role evolved as a sort of psychic travel agent, guiding the viewer to learn to distinguish psychic signals from mental noises. I encouraged viewers to stick to descriptive, impressionistic images of the target, and not try to guess at what it might specifically be. In steering viewers clear of analytical judgments— naming the object or describing its function and relating other incidental things about it—I kept them focused on what they were experiencing. We had found that analysis is a source of mental noise and, along with memory and imagination, is the enemy of psychic perception. Because psychic abilities correspond to the intuitive side of life, the more the viewer could be coaxed out of the analytic mode, the more successful the experiment would be.

We also showed that it is much easier to close your eyes and describe a target place that you haven't been to than to guess a star or circle on a card. If you close your eyes and see your own house, for example, you'll know that's not the right answer. But if you see some peculiar, hard-to-describe thing of unknown origin, you're more likely to accept it as the target and not confuse it with some kind of mental noise or imagination or memory. It is the *surprising* character that allows you to get in touch with the psychic image, and the less you know about the target, the more likely you are to see it correctly. So we tried to maximize the surprise element and minimize educated guessing.

We refrained from assigning boring, repetitious tasks so that viewers would remain fresh and interested, thus avoiding a decline effect—the extinguishing of correct responses over time—another disadvantage of the classic card-guessing experiments.

Finally, we gave our viewers feedback and reinforcement so each trial was a learning experience. In our experiments, we found that almost anyone who is assured that it is safe to experience paranormal functioning can learn to do so. Almost anyone could perceive scenes, including buildings, roads, and people, even when the targets were at great distances and blocked from ordinary perception. We concluded that the ability for remote viewing is natural and innate, and anyone who feels comfortable with the idea of having paranormal ability can have it. Our "psychic battery"—the scientific methods and psychological environment we developed in our laboratory—helps to facilitate psychic functioning. We ultimately found that people improved their skills and incorporated them into their lives.

## TESTING THE BATTERY

### Pat Price

Pat Price was a likable, crafty ex-police commissioner and an ex-vice-mayor of Burbank, California. When he first tried an informal remote-viewing experiment with us, he was astoundingly accurate, down to reading (correctly) the labels on file folders in locked file cabinets. With our protocol firmly in place, we invited him to take part in a controlled series of nine remote viewings.

On the first viewing, he not only described the site, he named it (Hoover Tower on the Stanford University campus). As Hal Puthoff said, "It may sound strange, but we still find ourselves burdened to a large degree by the collective conditioning of our society, wondering before every experiment how it could possibly work, and surprised every time it does. We have, however, satisfied

**Figure 4.1**
**Swimming Pool Complex as Remote-Viewing Target**

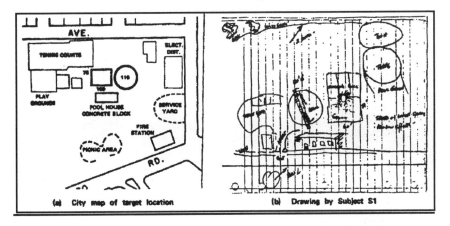

(a) City map of target location     (b) Drawing by Subject S1

Subject Pat Price correctly described a park-like area containing two pools of water. Note an apparent left-right reversal, often observed in psi experiments.

ourselves by exhaustive investigation that the result is genuine, and not an artifact of a flawed protocol.''

The fourth experiment was a classic example of the ''fraud and collusion'' paranoia that can creep into research. This time the director of the division himself took the experimenters to the site to be viewed, rather than offering them a sealed envelope, as was the protocol. Was there some flaw in our protocol? He wanted to find out. While they were away, Price described the site so accurately that Puthoff was to say, ''The excellent quality of the transcript began to raise a paranoid fear in *me* that perhaps Price and the division director were in collusion on this experiment to see if *I* could detect chicanery! Only the concern shown by our director as he tried to figure out how *we* could have fooled *him* brought me back to equilibrium.''

Sometimes Price's stunning accuracies were mixed with inaccuracies, as shown in an experiment in which Price correctly detailed two pools of water in a park, one round and one rectangular (his dimensions were off by only 10 percent); but he was totally incorrect in describing the pools as used for water purification, not swimming, as was the case (Figure 4.1). Puthoff remarked, ''With further experimentation, we began to realize that the occurrence of essentially correct descriptions of basic elements and patterns coupled with incomplete or erroneous analysis of function was to be a continuing thread throughout the remote viewing work. This observation eventually led to a major breakthrough with regard to understanding the connection between remote viewing and brain functioning.''

**Figure 4.2**
**Palo Alto Airport Tower as Remote-Viewing Target**

Palo Alto Airport tower (above) and drawing made by viewer Hella Hammid during local re-mote-viewing experiment. Viewer describes site as a "square tower . . . some technical installa-tion."

## Hella Hammid

Hella Hammid was a professional photographer and an early participant in our experiments who demonstrated to us the importance of feedback. In a 1978 series of six experiments, she gave clear descriptions of three sites that she physically visited after each viewing. For the three sites she did not visit, her descriptions were not accurate. Because she wanted to end on a success, we threw in an extra target, which she described as a "towerlike building . . . square . . . from the top it looks like it has winglike projections on either side of it . . . with something mechanical that needs to be visible from the sky, and that's directional; definitely a kind of marker . . . some technical instal-lation, like a weather station, or an airport tower, or a radar installation or radio. . . . No, it's not radio. It is not that high, and it is not metal" (Figure 4.2).

Hammid correctly identified the target as an airport tower and accurately surmised that it could not have been a radio tower. She could not clearly see what was at the base of the tower, which was both trees and airplanes. Here we have the combination of both the analytical and the nonanalytical.

By 1976, we had carried out highly significant experimental series with Price and Hammid that were published in *Nature* and the *Proceedings of the IEEE*.

**Figure 4.3**
**Louisiana Superdome as Remote-Viewing Target**

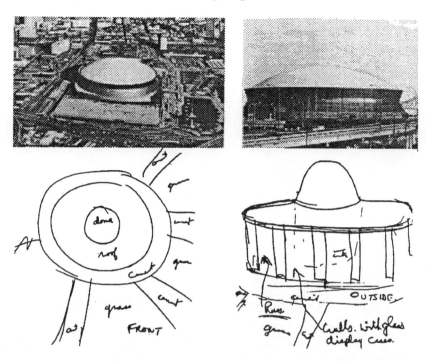

Long-distance remove-viewing experiment—SRI, Menlo Park to Louisiana Superdome. Subject described large circular building with a white dome. October 31, 1976.

## An SRI Physicist

The target was the Louisiana Superdome, to be viewed from the distance of 1,500 miles by a physicist in California. He accurately described the scene as "a large circular building with a white dome" but was hesitant to report his sighting because he felt it looked too much like a "flying saucer" (Figure 4.3).

In another experiment, we were working with a professionally trained artist. This time the outbound team had been sent to the Stanford University Art Museum a few miles from SRI. As I interviewed our participant in his first remote-viewing exercise, he drew fragmentary images around the edge of his page. He then said that the image "sort of coalesced into two geometric solids," which he drew as the building shown in Figure 4.4. You can compare his drawing with the photograph taken by the experimenters at the site.

**Figure 4.4**
**Stanford Art Museum as Remote-Viewing Target**

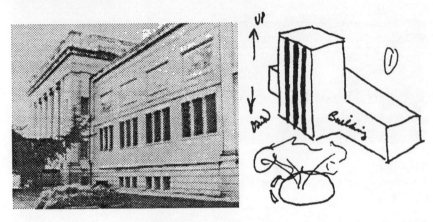

Subject described a building made of two rectangular solids. Note the circular planter in subject's drawing that corresponds to the circular planter in front of the museum.

## WHAT WE'VE LEARNED ABOUT PARAPSYCHOLOGY IN THE PAST TWENTY-FIVE YEARS

In our ESP research, particularly in the remote-viewing experiments at SRI, we had (and still have) no idea of the physical mechanisms behind the experiments we were doing. That's a great disappointment for us as physicists. But we learned a good deal about the psychology of the phenomenon. In our day-to-day activity doing these trials, at one trial per day, it was almost as though we were carrying out a sacrament to the powers controlling the psychic functioning that we were asking to manifest. The sacrament might involve lunch and ice cream, general play and great lightheartedness, with the assumption that when the scheduled experiment time came, we would do the experiment, and we could accept success. As a remarkable outcome of this acceptance, outstanding success is what we often found.

We learned that people with the right degree of acceptance can be taught what they need to know about psychic function in a few days. Hella Hammid, for example, came to us as a control subject. She had never done any psychic work, and yet from the first trial, her work was extraordinary. Typically, four out of six of her trials would be correct. That is like four miracles out of six attempts, or to put it another way, for every six times she tried to walk across the bay on the surface of the water, four times were successful. So to say that it is simply four right and two wrong greatly understates the quality of what she did. But that is just one of the frustrations of the research.

I suggest that the way to increase the reliability of psychic functioning, of increasing the juice in the psychic battery, is to try to carry out each experiment in what I would call a state of grace in which experimenters, judges, subjects, everybody in the environment has reached some kind of harmonious agreement with the universe that what we are doing makes sense and can be accomplished.

## STATE OF THE ART IN REMOTE VIEWING

In the bibliography to *The Mind Race,* researchers George Hansen, Charles Tart, and Marilyn Schlitz report results of their survey of all the published and unpublished remote-viewing experiments at the time (1973–1982). They found that "more than half (fifteen out of twenty-eight) of the published formal experiments have been successful, where only one in twenty would be expected by chance." They also located eighteen unpublished studies, with eight reporting statistical significance. They concluded from this that "the success of remote viewing is not due to reporting bias, in which vast numbers of unsuccessful experiments go unreported."

Given the data from remote viewing in the SRI experiments and others throughout the world over the past twenty years, we have greatly increased our knowledge about this ability. The illustrations in this chapter show the results of some of this work. We have produced three books and more than fifty technical articles describing this work.[2-4] These findings, described by Hal Puthoff and Russell Targ in *Mind at Large,* may be summarized as follows:

1. *Target acquisition.* Remote-viewers can acquire and describe target locations based on the presence of a cooperative experimenter at a distant site or from maps, pictures, or geographical or arbitrary coordinates related to the targets in question. It does not matter whether the person ("beacon") at the distant site is known or unknown by the viewer.

2. *Target attribute perceptions.* Descriptive aspects, such as shape, form, color, or material, are much better described than analytic concepts, such as function or name. At times, analytical data can come through excellently, although written material is only rarely perceived.

3. *Simultaneity and precognition.* Information access appears to be available essentially in real time. Activities at the target site are also often perceived in advance of their occurrence.

4. *Spatial resolution.* Resolution appears to be accurate for targets less than a millimeter in diameter. A pin was correctly described at a quarter-mile distance, and a quarter-inch upholstery button was described at a ten-thousand-mile distance.

5. *Distance effects.* The accuracy and resolution of remote viewing are not sensitive functions of the distance between a viewer and the target over terrestrial distances. In 1984, we had excellent results in experiments carried out between Moscow and San Francisco.

6. *Shielding.* Faraday cage or seawater electrical shielding is not effective in blocking remote-viewing perceptions.

7. *Sensory modalities.* In addition to visually observable details, viewers often correctly describe sounds, smells, and tactile information that can be verified as existing at the target location.

8. *Inhibitory factors.* A viewer's prior knowledge of target possibilities as well as certain psychological and environmental factors may inhibit viewer capabilities by increasing the level of mental noise relative to information signal.

9. *Enhancement factors.* Psychological interest for a viewer together with the necessity and relevance for obtaining the information, seriousness of purpose, training in overcoming and avoiding mental noise, and the presence of a facilitating interviewer to ask questions and help direct the viewer's attention to acquiring relevant information enhance accuracy in remote viewing.

10. *Accuracy.* An analysis of remote-viewing transcripts generated by experienced viewers indicates that roughly two-thirds of viewer-generated material constitutes an accurate description of the target, and about one-third is ambiguous, general, or incorrect. Sometimes near-perfect results are obtained.

11. *Use of redundancy to increase signal-noise ratio.* Redundancy, whereby more than one person attempts to collect data on a given target, has been shown to improve reliability by reducing the effects of individual viewer biases.

12. *Replicability of remote viewing.* Continuing demonstration and replications of remote viewing at laboratories throughout the world indicate that this is a robust human perceptual ability. More than half of all published experimental papers report independent statistical significance.

13. *Distribution of remote viewing in the general population.* The ability appears to be widespread, although latent. Volunteers with no previous history of remote viewing exhibit the ability, indicating that special subjects are not necessary.

14. *Improvement potential.* Viewers trained over a several-year period have shown improved performance in both accuracy and reliability. Viewer reliability tends to improve with practice.

15. *Theoretical considerations.* Because viewers often are able to obtain information that is blocked from traditional means of perceptual access by both space and time, research in remote viewing suggests that modern physics cannot as yet satisfactorily deal with the observed data. These data suggest that the current description of the spacetime metric in which we live is inaccurate or incomplete.

**NOTES**

1. This term refers to how an octopus escapes by secreting a cloud of ink, thus leaving doubt that he was ever there.

2. Targ R, Puthoff HE. *Mind Reach: Scientists Look at Psychic Ability*. New York: Delacorte; 1977.

3. Tart CT, Puthoff HE, Targ R, eds. *Mind at Large*. New York: Praeger; 1979.

4. Targ R, Harary K. *The Mind Race. Understanding and Using Psychic Abilities*. New York: Villard Books; 1984.

# 5

# Longitudinal Comparison of Local and Long-Distance Remote-Perception Phenomena

*Elizabeth A. Rauscher*

I have examined those aspects of human perception that appear to fall outside the range of well-understood perceptual processing capabilities. Of particular interest is a human information accessing "channel" termed *remote perception*. This phenomenon pertains to the ability to access and describe by means of direct mental processes, information sources blocked from ordinary perception, which is secured against sensory access by distance, time, or shielding. I use the term remote perception rather than remote viewing because other sensory experiences, such as those involving smell, feeling, and hearing, have also been shown to arise from distant stimuli.

The research reported here involves the investigation of the remote-perception process. The experiments are designed to eliminate classic sensory modalities and enhance the reliability of the phenomena. On the whole, the experiments conform to the protocol described below. Some of these experiments were focused on the parameters of the physical setups, and some were designed to test specific psychological or paranormal conditions.[1-5] An important finding was that subjects appeared to be capable of learning to develop and improve their remote-perception capabilities. A learning curve seemed to be evident in that later experimenters were more statistically significant. As in other complex scientific experiments, the experimenters may undergo a learning process as well.

## PROJECTS, CORESEARCHERS, AND SUBJECTS

In 1974, I convened the Fundamental Fysiks Group (FFG) at the Lawrence Berkeley Laboratory to study remote-connectedness concepts such as Bell's theorem. The group also discussed the possible existence of psi phenomena and other "non-local" attributes of consciousness. Some of the FFG participants, G. Weissman, S. P. Sirag, and myself among them, developed an interest in performing our own remote-perception experiments.

At the same time, in response to criticism that psi is incompatible with the established theories of physics, I developed a complex hyperdimensional ($N > 4$) geometry to reconcile psi with accepted science, and the work gained acceptance in refereed physics journals. My motivation in developing a multidimensional model was twofold: (1) to reconcile the psi database with the main body of physical theory, and (2) to theoretically describe some of the spacetime-independent features of psi.[2-11]

As a test of this theory, over a period of many years, I conducted local real-time remote-perception experiments in which target location and subject were within half an hour's driving time of each other. To further test the model, we undertook long-distance (thousands of kilometers) and precognitive experiments. I participated in some of these trials when I became a consultant to the SRI International research group of R. Targ, H. Puthoff, and I. Swann. In addition to the long-distance and local remote-perception experiments with the SRI staff, I worked with others from the FFG, such as B. Mayfield, J. Mishlove, H. Mullins, D. Hurt (SRI), and J. Houck, and with B. Rubik.[1,3,5,12]

## PROTOCOL

The phenomenon my coworkers and I investigated is the ability of a person (subject) to "view" or perceive geographical locations (targets) from several kilometers to several thousand kilometers distant from the subject's physical location. (We also used as targets shielded abstract geometrical forms in two and three dimensions, usually less than 30 centimeters on a side.)

The following is a summary of the major elements in our experimental procedure.

1. Person acting as target selector (not otherwise connected with the experiment). This person (a) scouts out a pool of targets within a specified distance of the laboratory, (b) writes detailed traveling directions for the outbound experimenter, (c) places each set of directions in a sealed envelope and the set of envelopes in a locked box. This person has no further involvement in the experiment

2. Laboratory room

3. Remote-viewer (subject)

4. Monitor with recorder and pad of paper in the laboratory room with remote-viewer

5. Target pool (target locations in sealed, numbered envelopes)

6. Random-number generator (RNG) used to select target. The number from the RNG will correspond to a number on the sealed envelope by the target selector

7. Outbound experimental team with recorder and camera

Features of the method include the following.

1. From where the subject sits, he or she knows only the identity of the person or team visiting the location—the outbound experimenters.

2. The outbound team drives several blocks away from the laboratory, opens the sealed envelope containing their destination, and proceeds to the target.

3. The monitor assists the subject in recording and clarifying impressions that are received during the period when the outbound team is at the designated site. The monitor does not know either the specific target location for the particular trial or the pool of locations.

4. The subjects receive feedback when they are taken to the experimental target after the completion of the experiment.

5. Judging is conducted by a person who is independent of the other participants in the experiment. Judging also can be performed by a computer, using feature extraction and analysis. For example, Jahn and Dunne at Princeton developed a matching system using an "alphabet" of 30 similarity descriptors such as indoors versus outdoors, dark versus brightly lighted, and hectic or chaotic versus inactive or homogeneous.[13]

The outbound team typically generated three photographs of different aspects of the remote-target environment and tape-recorded their impressions of the site while they were there. This information, particularly the time-sequencing of events and of transitory motion, was recorded for post hoc analysis. The photographs and tapes were included in the judging package along with the subject's tape-recorded responses and drawings generated in the laboratory room. Our experiments usually consisted of a series of six to twelve individual test sessions. The judging procedure consisted of attempting to match subject transcripts to photographs and taped descriptions of target sites.

In addition to real-time local experiments, precognitive and distant experiments can be conducted. In connection with the time- and distance-independent results from my experimental work, I have developed a detailed mathematical model of remote perception and other forms of psi; this model is presented in Chapter 10.

## EXAMPLES OF REMOTE-PERCEPTION EXPERIMENTS

Typical examples of remote-perception responses are given in Figures 5.1 through 5.6. The subjects generated taped narratives and drawings of their perceptions of remote locations; however, we found that drawings were better descriptors of the targets than the narrative transcripts.

In experiments of this type, there are three significant conclusions: First, we have established that it is possible to obtain a significant amount of descriptive information about remote locations. The descriptions contain accurate and relevant information that is frequently accompanied by incorrect and irrelevant statements (or noise). Second, the physical distance separating the subject from the scene to be perceived, even thousands of kilometers, does not seem to affect the accuracy of perception. Third, the theory of relativity has led to the general acceptance of the concept of a symmetry between spatial and temporal events. In the experiments, we found instances in which a subject was able to describe a remote location before the outbound team had arrived at the site; in a few cases, the subject gave a correct description even before the target location was randomly selected. We deliberately conducted one such experiment in a precognitive mode such that the site was selected after the end of the subject's fifteen-minute narrative. The results are given in Figure 5.6.

## ANALYSIS AND EVALUATION OF EXPERIMENTAL RESULTS

To assist in objectifying the evaluation of remote-perception phenomena, I have developed a 7-point scale, shown below. The scale gives results similar to those of other judging procedures. Although some of our experiments had results at chance expectation, most of our results were statistically significant with a chance probability, or $p$ value, $< .05$. some of our experiments had highly significant results with $p$ values of $< 10^{-6}$, or a million-to-one odds against having such a result by chance.

### 7-Point Evaluation Scale for Target-Transcript Correspondence

7  Excellent correspondence, including good analytical detail (e.g., identifying the site by name) with essentially no incorrect information

6  Good correspondence with good analytical information (e.g., naming the function) and relatively little incorrect information

5  Good correspondence with unambiguous, unique, matchable elements but some incorrect information

4  Good correspondence with several matchable elements intermixed with incorrect information

3  Mixture of correct and incorrect elements but enough of the former to indicate viewer has made contact with the site

2  Some correct elements but not sufficient to suggest results beyond chance expectation

1  Little correspondence

0  No correspondence

**Figure 5.1**
**Local Remote-Perception Target and Response for the Vallambosa Church**

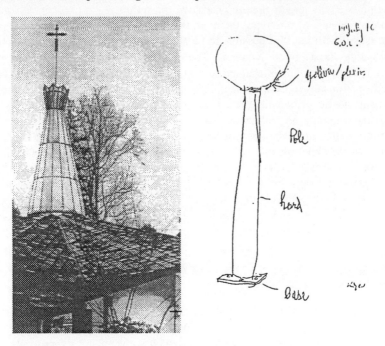

**Figure 5.2**
**Long-Distance Remote-Perception Target and Response for the Underpass at University at El Camino Real, Palo Alto, California**

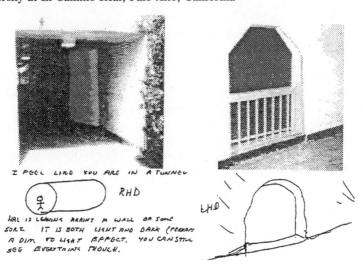

Subject in Huntsville, Alabama. Subject said, "I feel like you are in a tunnel."

**Figure 5.1**

Location of Target: Vallambosa Church, Menlo Park, California.
Subject: Engineer, G. L.
Monitor: H. P.
Outbound Team: E. A. Rauscher and H. M.

Summary of subject's comments: "Looking up to the blue sky. Looks like Elizabeth was looking up at something—a pole or steeple associated with this place, Elizabeth kneelng—Hope is also kneeling; it's something swirling with straight tentacles extending from it—objects whirling around— hazy, swirling—partly man-made and partly natural—they are placed; that's the man-made aspect." The outbound experimenters had first looked up at the yellow plastic church steeple and then knelt and put their hands into the swirling sprinklers.

The outbound experimenter's comments at the site during the last two minutes: "the last two minutes we walked back to the church area . . . I put my arms around one of the cement pillars and hugged it. I noticed that it looked like the kind that had been wrapped with some kind of thing that the concrete was poured into."

Subject's comments on the last two minutes on his tape: "Not your average pole. . . . It looks like that pole was concrete, like an extruded pipe. It has lines that are marked."

**Figure 5.2**

Location of target: Highway underpass at University and El Camino Real Palo Alto, California.
Location of subject: Huntsville, Alabama.
Subject: Engineer, G. O. L.
Monitor: None.
Outbound Team: E. A. Rauscher, H. M. and H. Puthoff.

Summary of subject's comments: "I feel like you are inside a tunnel . . . an outbound experimenter is leaning against a wall of some sort [*true*] . . . it is a dim-to-light effect. You can still see everything though. . . . Hal may be leaning over an edge with an archway opening [*true*] . . . describing the passageway under El Camino on University Avenue."

Outbound experimenters had walked down ramp to enter El Camino and University Avenue underpass, leaned against walls and leaned over railing looking at traffic. (Note: subjects are usually instructed to look for forms and shapes and not to attempt to name the site, as some past experiments appeared to show that this might cause guessing. Hence, the subject said he resisted naming the site.) This experiment was one of a series. As part of this long distance series E. A. Rauscher was the monitor with the same subject for the Superdome target reported elsewhere in this section.

**Figure 5.3**
**Local Remote-Perception Target and Response for the BART Station on Shattuck Avenue, Berkeley, California**

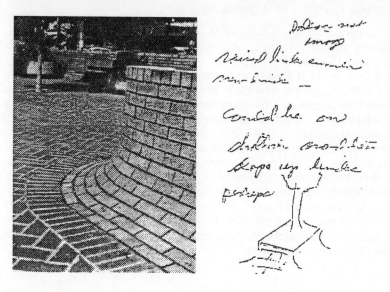

**Figure 5.4**
**Long-Distance Remote-Perception Target and Response for the Bank Plaza and Underground Parking Stairwell in California**

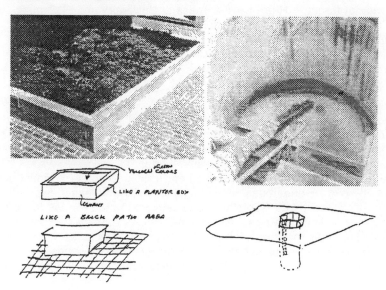

Subject in Huntsville, Alabama.

**Figure 5.3**

| | |
|---|---|
| Location of target: | BART (Bay Area Rapid Transit) station on Shattuck Avenue, Berkeley, California. |
| Subject: | Physicist, E. W. |
| Monitor: | None. A free-response place and time were set within a three-hour time period. |
| Outbound Team: | H. M. and B. M. Experiment designed by E. A. Rauscher. |

The subject, who is a meditator, knew that the outbound team would choose their target and go there for fifteen minutes some time between 2 P.M. and 5 P.M. The subject was to turn on the tape recorder and identify the time and place when the team arrived at the randomly chosen geographical location. Drive time could be anywhere up to two hours and forty-five minutes.

The subject recorded the arrival time at the target as 2:40 P.M. (the actual time of arrival was 2:45). The site was also accurately reported. The subject said later upon receiving feedback (two and one-half months later, after the whole experimental series was analyzed) that he "knew" where the outbound team was and would have named the cross street but could not remember it. The subject mentioned a strong conviction about his choice even though feedback came several months later.

The subject reported during recording, "new brick . . . raised circular brick . . . slopes up . . . could be on Shattuck around trees (planter boxes)."

**Figure 5.4**

| | |
|---|---|
| Location of Target: | United California Bank, Plaza and Underground Parking Stairwell. |
| Location of subject: | Huntsville, Alabama. |
| Subject: | A systems analyst. |
| Monitor: | None. |
| Outbound Team: | E. A. Rauscher, H. Puthoff, and H. Mullins. |

In this long-distance remote-perception experiment, the subject described cement planter boxes, with flowers inside, which were gray on a brick patio area. He also described a cement depression, which is a fountain and an underground space unavailable to the outbound experimental team. This underground space could be reached by a well with a railing around the top that the experimenters were standing near. All these responses by the subject were correct.

The subject wrote the words "grey," "area is greyish," and "grey in color." The underground stairwell is constructed of gray concrete. He wrote "standing in a very confining space, like walls are close." The stairwell is tight confining space. He noted that an outbounder "can look up and see out." From the first flight of stairs, one can see out by looking up.

**Figure 5.5**
**Long-Distance Remote-Perception Target and Response for the House in France**

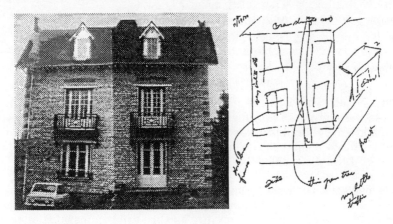

Subject was one thousand miles away.

**Figure 5.6**
**Precognitive Remote-Perception Target and Response for Macy's Shopping Center**

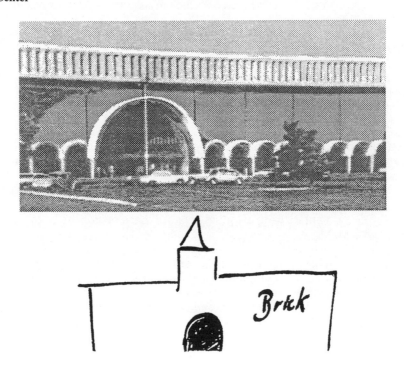

Subject responded with this drawing half hour before target was randomly selected and visited by outbound team.

**Figure 5.5**

| | |
|---|---|
| Location of target: | House in France within 100-mile radius of Paris. |
| Location of subject: | 1,000 miles away. |
| Subject: | Astrophysicist. |
| Monitor: | None. |
| Outbound Team: | O. Costa de Beauregard (nuclear physicist). |

The subject was able to distinguish her intuitive impression from the guessed impression. She reported that if the target location was in Paris, it would be crowded with red tile roofs, but she reported on her "flash" impression that the target (a house) was in an uncrowded area, a quiet location, and had a brown shingle roof. She also reported that it was two stories tall and white stucco (it was actually white stone); that a metal railing around the upper-story windows had been newly painted (true); and that there was a large oriental rug in the living room (true). No apparent major erroneous data were reported.

**Figure 5.6**

| | |
|---|---|
| Location of target: | Macy's shopping center. |
| Subject: | Artist, H. H. |
| Monitor: | Physicist, R. T. |
| Outbound Team: | Elizabeth Rauscher. |

We believe that a subject and monitor can describe a remote target site before it has been randomly selected from the target pool. The following is an example of the accuracy that can be obtained:

4:30 P.M. Subject and monitor went into lab (secluded from outside contact).

4:30 P.M. E. A. R. left lab, went to car and waited.

4:45 P.M. Subject made 15-minute tape recording and sketches.

5:00 P.M. Subject and monitor stopped tape recording.

5:04 P.M. E. A. R. threw die, opened selected envelope, drove to site.

5:15 P.M. E. A. R. arrived at site (Macy's).

5:30 P.M. E. A. R. left site and returned to lab, contacted subject and monitor.

The following is the list of targets that were in the target pool from which the actual target was chosen randomly:

1. Center for Personal Growth—low, modern buildings that are basically dark brown and yellow. Rectangular shapes are prominent and there are extensive garden areas.

2. Busy traffic intersection—concrete and macadam with metal fencing, basically gray colors.

3. Concrete plant—an industrial site consisting of several concrete, wood, and corrugated iron structures. There were giant, semitriangular metal bins holding the various grades of gravel.

4. Large shopping center with courtyard—a red brick building with large white arches. A large parking lot lies in front. (This was the chosen site. The subject's drawing matches the arch and refers to the brick, not part of any of the other possible targets.)

We applied the rating scale for transcript-to-target comparison for both geographical targets and abstract targets consisting of two- and three-dimensional forms.

In 1975, we conducted a series of eight real-time local (RTL) remote-perception experiments that were judged to be nonsignificant by five judges matching transcripts to targets without using the point-evaluation scale. Using the scale, some positive correspondence between transcript and target was found, but the overall results were nonsignificant.

In 1980, we conducted a series of 12 experiments in which subject and target locations were long-distant in the north-south direction. In this series, we used the Princeton 20-point feature-matching protocol and achieved significance with a single-tailed $p$ value of $\approx .01$.[3,4] Using the point-evaluation scale yielded a slightly higher significance, but the difference in the two $p$ values generated by the two judging methods was not significant. All other RTL, real-time distant (RTD), and local precognitive (LP) results were plotted separately, and in the other RTD experiments, the subject and target orientation was in the east-west direction.

Figure 5.7 shows data plotted for the 20 RTL and 20 RTD remote-perception experiments over a 6-year period. In addition, one LP experimental data point is given. The axes represent a plot of $R_S$ versus $t_D$, where $R_S$ is the rating scale for target-to-transcript comparison and $t_D$ is the time or date the experiment was conducted plotted in month intervals. Remote-perception success was evaluated by matching the correspondence of subject transcripts and drawings to the target. All targets were geographical locations, and in most cases, three photographs and an outbound experimenter audiotape were made at the time the experiment was conducted.

From Figure 5.7, we can generate a trend analysis in terms of the relative slope or change in $R_S$ versus time, $t_D$, and we see that the slope for the RTL experiments yields a value of .4 and the slope for the RTD experiments yields a value slightly less, of .3. For the RTD data, both north-south and east-west orientations are grouped together.

The overall average value of the 20 RTL experiments yields $<R_S>=4$, where $<>$ is a symbol for average, and the overall average value of the 20 RTD experiments yields $<R_S>=5$. For all the RTL, we have $p$ approximately equal to .01, and for the RTD, we have a $p$ value equal to approximately .001. Note that the horizontal line $<R_S>=2.5$ represents chance expectation. The results from all our experiments lie on or above this line.

We interpreted the positive slope as a learning curve for both the principal investigators and the subject-participants. Some experimenters were new to remote perception; some were experienced. Nearly all subjects were novices in remote perception before this experiment. I worked with many subjects and other researchers, but all subjects and researchers participated in at least three experiments conducted under my guidance.

It is apparent from my research in psychic phenomena as well as from re-

**Figure 5.7**
**Remote Perception Experiments Conducted Using Geographical Targets**

Comparison of relative slopes of least-squares fits shows accuracy and learning in local
versus distant remote perception.

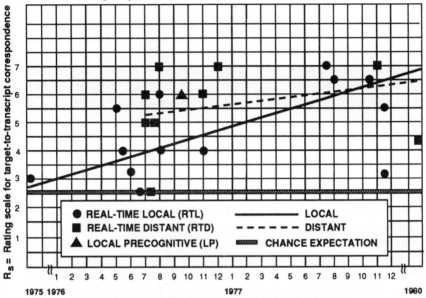

$t_D$ = Date experiment was conducted, in one-month intervals
(Note discontinuities between 1975-76 and 1977-80.)

search that I conducted in accelerator physics that there is an "experimenter
effect." In some standard physics experiments, some researchers are not able
to obtain the results obtained by other experimental groups even when the apparatus and methods used are identical.

There is no attenuation of remote perception over the distance we measured.
In fact, we see that the opposite appears to occur; that is, the long-distance
experiments are more significant than the local experiments. A possible con-
founding factor is that some of the local experiments were conducted first, and
hence the learning effect appears to dominate over any effect of distance.

## GROUP EXPERIMENTS AND EXPERIMENTS USING
## GEOMETRIC TARGETS

In addition to the experiments analyzed in Figure 5.7, which used geographical location targets, we conducted another series of 20 experiments that involved two- and three-dimensional geometric targets, and we used most of the
same subjects in 1976 and in 1977. These experiments had an overall significance with $<R_S> = 6$ and were significant at a $p$ value .000001, or $10^{-6}$.

To gain more data and examine intersubject interaction, we conducted six group experiments in which we had a group of subjects view the same target at the same time. Four group experiments used abstract targets (ATs); two used geographical locations (GLs) as targets.

In 1971, with 56 student volunteers through the University of California Berkeley, we obtained a *p* value of .00001 using ATs. In 1972, through the University of California Stanford Linear Accelerator Collider, 201 students using ATs obtained a *p* value of approximately .01. In 1973, with 16 students at the University of California Berkeley Extension who used ATs, chance results of nonsignificance were obtained. In 1977, through a University of California Extension workshop, 35 students with ATs produced chance nonsignificant results.

In 1978, with 44 subjects, and in 1979, with 32 subjects, using GL we performed experiments with the California Psychical Study Group without significant results. All experiments except the 1973 University of California Berkeley experiment (which was a precognition experiment) were RTL experiments.

Even in the nonsignificant experiments, some interesting subject response correspondences occurred: It appeared that some subjects generated noise in the signal channel of other subjects; that is, specific incorrect subject responses were picked up and repeated by other subjects.

Note that I report the results of *all* the experiments I conducted and in which I participated. The overall significance of the results of these experiments from independent probabilities is many millions-to-one against chance or random expectation. It is important to have obtained significance for both RTL and RTD experiments to test our theoretical hypothesis comparing spatial and temporal properties of the remote-perception phenomenon. At least terrestrially and for precognitive temporal intervals of several hours, there appears to be no attenuation in the significance of the effect, which is consistent with my theory presented in Chapter 10.[6-11]

## MORAL IMPLICATIONS OF SPACETIME-INDEPENDENT PSI MODELS

Our experiments as well as others of their kind show the interconnectedness of people with one another and with all aspects of the environment over great distances. How easily we seem to influence one another and to share thoughts, perceptions, feelings. There are thus potentially an infinite number of ways to tune into and perhaps affect events and people across space and time.

In considering the practical applications of the various abilities we find emerging among people connected with psi research, we must consider the matter of the morality of the uses to which these human capabilities might be put. How can this capacity be used for good? How can we avoid a future in which it could, or would, be used for harm? Knowledge and ethics must go hand in hand.

## NOTES

1. Rauscher EA, Weissmann G, Sirag SP, Sarfatti J. Remote perception of natural scenes shields against ordinary perception. *Advances in Parapsychology*. Metuchen: New Jersey Scarecrow Press, 1975.

2. Rauscher EA, Mullins AJ. The scientific investigation of direct perception across space and time. *Mind Space*. 1977.

3. Rauscher EA, Houck J. Los Angeles area to San Francisco Bay Area remote perception experiment. *Psi Research*. 1985;4:48.

4. Houck J, Nelson RD, Rauscher EA. Addendum to "Los Angeles area to San Francisco Bay Area remote perception experiment": a reevaluation. *Psi Research*. 1986;5:108.

5. Gough WC, Rauscher EA, Houck GB, Gruye V. The status of research on the physics of consciousness: working models and experiments. Staff report of the Committee of Science and Technology, U.S. House of Representatives. 97th Congress, 1st session, Serial G; 1981.

6. Rauscher EA. Some physical models potentially applicable to remote perception. *Bulletin of the American Physical Society*. 1976;21:1305–1306.

7. Rauscher EA. Some physical models potentially applicable to remote perception. *The Iceland Papers: Frontiers of Physics Conference; Select Papers on Experimental and Theoretical Research on the Physics of Consciousness*. Amherst, WI: Essentia Research Assoc; 1979:49–93.

8. Ramon C, Rauscher EA. Superluminal transformation in complex Minkowski spaces. *Foundation in Physics*. 1980;10:661–669.

9. Rauscher EA. The physics of psi in space and time, part I: major principles of physics, psychic phenomena, and some physical models. *Psi Research* 1983;2:65.

10. Rauscher EA. The physics of psi phenomena in space and time, part II: multidimensional geometric models. *Psi Research*. 1983;2:93.

11. Rauscher EA. Complex coordinate geometries in general relativity and electromagnetism. *Bulletin of the American Physical Society*. 1978;23:84–85.

12. Mishlove J. *Interdisciplinary Sciences*. Berkeley: University of California; 1979. Ph.D. Dissertation.

13. Jahn RG, Dunne BJ, Jahn EG. Analytical judging procedure for remote perception experiments. *Journal of Parapsychology*. 1980;3:207–231.

# 6

# Exploring the Visionary Experience

*Jean Millay*

What really happens when we close our eyes to "look" for a vision? Why are telepathic responses "right" when they are right, and why are they "wrong" when they are wrong? Now that much solid research has been done to "prove" that ESP exists,[1-7] mind-to-mind research is moving on to new levels of questioning. It is time to explore the multidimensionality of the total experience of psychic events. It is time to account for the errors as well as the successes. To do so takes us into the symbolism of dreams and the vast complexities of the visionary experience.

Many times over the years during certain times of crisis, my family and I have had to attempt to communicate telepathically because no other means of communicating was possible. Sometimes, even without a crisis, a spontaneous telepathic event would take place. At such a time, a question is always foremost in my mind: Are the thought forms I am experiencing the result of my own projections, or am I receiving a thought from another? For that reason, I would always try to confirm the psychic event with a phone call or letter (when it was possible to do so). Such confirmation has demonstrated that mind-to-mind communication has worked for us—children, parents, and grandparents alike. Later, I was both amused and irritated to discover that some of my professors at the university held the opinion that "telepathy *cannot* exist, therefore it *does* not." Because my own experiences had been woven into the fabric of my life from childhood, and because I could teach my children to enhance such experiences as my grandmother had taught me, I decided to devote my research and my art to the study of telepathic and visionary processes.

This path has included the study of things that normally sighted people share fundamentally: (a) the early development of hand-eye coordination in children through art;[8-10] (b) the structure of the visual system;[11,12] (c) the possible projection of images back through that structure onto the experience of the external;[13] (d) the vibration of the EEG (electroencephalogram, or brain waves) of the occipital areas of the cerebral cortex;[14-16] and (e) the need for the eyes to track an image to actually "see" it.[17,18] Also, as an art teacher for many years and as a mother and grandmother, I've had the opportunity to study the development of children's art and thought processes through three generations.

If you are facing the sun with eyes closed, do patterns begin to develop in the reddish glow of sun-brightened eyelids? If, in a darkened room, a soft, flickering light is projected onto your closed eyelids, do you see different patterns when the flicker rate is changed? More than 100 students were willing to participate in such a flickering-light experience and draw pictures of their images immediately afterward. Among the students in my study, a light that flickered six to nine times per second often produced a mandala pattern made up of small dots of red and green or red and blue. When the flicker rate was speeded up to eleven to fourteen times per second, the patterns began to resemble instead red (or black) and white interference waveform patterns. At faster flicker rates, the images fused together. (Old movie projectors began at eighteen frames per second and were later speeded up when sound was added.)

The contrasting dot patterns drawn by most of the students participating in the flickering-light study is particularly interesting when we consider that the resting EEG pattern (alpha rhythms) of the occiput of the cerebral cortex is 8 to 10 Hz (cycles per second), about the same range as our flickering light. The theta brain wave rhythms are between 4 and 7 Hz. This suggests to me that the patterns seen in the experiment represent a projection of the structure of the rods and cones of the eye. For example, try closing down a projector image to a tiny point at the lens. The image you see projected on the wall is the filament of the projector bulb. Similarly, a pinhole in cardboard will allow the shape of a partial eclipse of the sun to shine through onto another surface. When a flickering light on the eyes matches the resting pattern of the EEG at the occiput, I believe that we are looking *at* what we are seeing *with*. The dots are the rods and cones of the eye, projected outward.

H. Crane and D. Brown studied the way the eyes track an image as the mind determines the content of a picture or columns of numbers.[17] When something was easily understood, the eyes tracked it instantly and moved on. When the picture contained an unusual element, the eyes traced and retraced the image over and over again. The eye apparently needs to trace the edges of contrast for the mind to record the event of "seeing." When "seeing" has occurred, the search strategy resumes until the picture is fully cognized. If at the end a different conception of the picture flashes into the mind, the seek-and-search strategy resumes, with renewed emphasis on the dissonant elements in the picture.

When columns of numbers are added, the eyes scan smoothly and quickly until an error in addition occurs, in which case the scanning flow is disrupted and the eyes stumble back to the offending column. How is it that the mind knows when a correct summing event has occurred (to stop the fast scanning motion)?

Conversely, R. Pritchard studied what the eye sees when it cannot track an image. To accomplish this, Pritchard experimented with a projector mounted on a contact lens, which stabilized the image on the retina.[18] As the images in Figures 6.1A show, part of the stabilized image disappears when the eye cannot track it. Figure 6.2A shows an example of a partial telepathic response. Only the knee is seen at first. Many such partials occurred in the studies we have done over the past twenty years along with a typical comment that begins, "Flashed on an image of . . ."

I believe that the "telepathic eye" does not track because telepathy is the aspect of vision through which an image is created on the visual cortex directly from thought forms and visual association. Often the "flash" of an image follows a part of the *shape* of the target, but not the *concept,* and is, therefore, judged to be a "miss."

R. L. Gregory has stated that "the retina is actually a specialized part of the surface of the brain which has budded out and is sensitive to light. . . . What the eyes do is to feed the brain with information coded in neural activity."[11] The brain selects and organizes the incoming signals according to the experience and expectations of the individual. R. Gottlieb (an innovative eye-care specialist) wrote: "Vision is more a product of the mind than of the eyeballs."[12] It is just this quality of vision that I find the most interesting. I call it the "fuzzy edge of reality"—the edge between what can be seen, what we make of it, and what we visualize about that which the eye does not actually see.

If I ask you to close your eyes and visualize a rose or something else you already know, you don't have to peek at a rose to create the image. The same is true when attempting to receive an image telepathically. So, what do you see when you close your eyes? The incoming neural activity may not be from light that is sensitizing the retina but can be dominated by a thought form. This thought form can create an image that a person might then draw.

When you close your eyes to look for an image that I am sending to you, you may very well "see" an image. That image is related to your own dynamic, to other energies in the environment, to the thought forms that I am actually sending to you, or to your response to me as though we were in conversation. Of course, the dynamic of your memories and of mine are going to be unique. This includes the way we remember our experiences; the personal

**Figure 6.1**
**Methods of Analyzing Telepathic Attempts to Improve Performance**

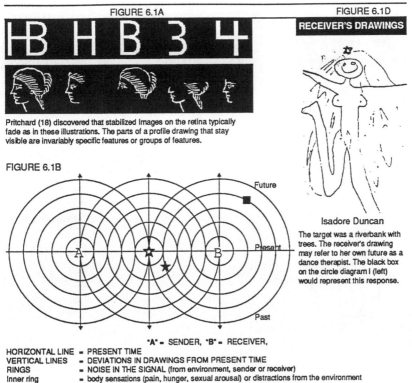

FIGURE 6.1A

Pritchard (18) discovered that stabilized images on the retina typically fade as in these illustrations. The parts of a profile drawing that stay visible are invariably specific features or groups of features.

FIGURE 6.1B

Future

Present

Past

"A" = SENDER, "B" = RECEIVER,

FIGURE 6.1D

**RECEIVER'S DRAWINGS**

Isadore Duncan

The target was a riverbank with trees. The receiver's drawing may refer to her own future as a dance therapist. The black box on the circle diagram I (left) would represent this response.

| HORIZONTAL LINE | = PRESENT TIME |
| VERTICAL LINES | = DEVIATIONS IN DRAWINGS FROM PRESENT TIME |
| RINGS | = NOISE IN THE SIGNAL (from environment, sender or receiver) |
| Inner ring | = body sensations (pain, hunger, sexual arousal) or distractions from the environment |
| Second ring | = emotional overlay which could affect any attempt at communication. |
| Third ring | = memory associations with the color and shape being received |
| Fourth ring | = clarity of a mind that can reach out beyond its daily thoughts to the thoughts of another or to an external object |

FIGURE 6.1C

| 20 POSSIBLE SHAPES | 10 SAME COLORS | THE SAME WORD | 20 POSSIBLE CONCEPTS | 20 POSSIBLE MOODS | THE SAME DRAWING |
|---|---|---|---|---|---|
| 38% | 23% | 23% | 21% | 19% | 12% |

Each trial used three 3" X 5" cards: one target, one sender's response and one receiver's response. These were given to five independent outside judges who compared the receiver's response to the target and the sender's drawing for similarities. Figure 1C indicates the percentage of receivers' responses that the judges felt met the criterion from a suggested list of similarities. In this part of the study, 11 teams participated producing 290 telepathy trials. In a later study with 5 teams, 90 trials produced similar results.

**Figure 6.2**
**Remote-Viewing Target and Response: Examples of Partial Image Reception**

| FIG. 6.2A | FIG. 6.2B | FIG. 6.2C |
| --- | --- | --- |

**TARGET**

**SENDERS' DRAWINGS**

**SENDERS' COMMENTS**

Indian Gods

View of the **world** from the moon -
Space, curves,
cloud formations

**RECEIVERS' DRAWINGS**

1st just caught this than seem xch to be legs of person who's body curves underneath (dotted pad)

a wave

**RECEIVERS' COMMENTS**

Right side of face feels like light but steady pushing.
No clear images - no strong ones.
Also flashed on a pineapple and woman with short dark hair and a lei.

Penguin, Whale
Black & White
green hills

Going down road on some sort of coach toward castle.

**World** spinning around -
rolling hills.

symbolism of our visions, dreams, and memories; the dominant cognitive style we each use most often (verbal, visual, kinesthetic, emotional, etc.).

Our innate ability to receive telepathic messages successfully can be enhanced by creating an environment that allows us to focus intently on the subtle visions and sensations through which psychic information comes into consciousness. A comfortable room at home may be the best, but in a formal laboratory setting, an electromagnetically shielded room may be the best way to cut down on the external distractions.

One study by M. King explored the similarities and differences of personal memory systems.[19] Each of her high school students demonstrated a memory train all the way back to the time when the first memory was established. When the students were asked to report the first thing that came to mind about certain letters in the alphabet, they reported either the first song or the first pictures. These differences will prove to be valuable to people who want to improve their communication with one another. If I associate a cup of hot tea with comfort and healing and you associate it with the painful experience of being scalded when you were a child, our communication may seem to break down, although we are sharing the same subject matter.

Figure 6.1B shows the variety of attentional distractions that can influence telepathic communication positively or negatively. The center of each circle (A and B) represents each person attempting to communicate telepathically. When the sender's focus is clearly on the target (center star), the message is received. When the focus of the sender or receiver is distracted by other thoughts (body sensations, emotions, past or future events, etc.), then the final drawing done by the receiver will be influenced by such distractions. Time distortions are also common (e.g., the receiver might make an accurate drawing of a previous target in the set of five or of a target not yet chosen). The response called "Isadora Duncan" (Figure 6.1D) has been plotted on the circle diagram as a square. This response did not match the target of a river bank, but it did provide the receiver with an important insight about her future career.

The circle map (Figure 6.1B) can be useful for couples (or their counselors) who choose to use telepathy as a means of exploring the preconscious dynamics of their interpersonal communication. For people who use different cognitive processes, even face-to-face communication often is difficult. Frustrated family members may experience less difficulty in their day-to-day interactions if they would explore together the question of how each one thinks differently.

When information about cognitive style is applied to attempts at telepathic communication, more success often is possible. In one of our studies, the receiver, Greg Schelkun, was trying to pick up on the images he thought his wife, Priscilla, was sending to him. After the first five trials, all unsuccessful, Greg and Priscilla discussed the issue. When she told him she didn't like to visualize but was trying to send a feeling about the target, he was then able to receive the feeling as well as at least part of the image. Three out of the next five trials were successful.

Warcollier reported on the mixing of types of perception between feeling, imagery, and verbal responses.[20] One of the psychics in his experiments could much more easily draw an image than talk about it. Warcollier concluded that "there is little doubt that the use of language can cause difficulty in receiving a telepathic impression, because the medium of exchange in telepathy is not language." Many of those participating in our studies would agree with this. Only two of our sixteen teams seemed to be more successful with verbal telepathic responses. Yet Holland emphasizes the idea that all the types of perception may be used.[21] (Holland is an osteopath who teaches his medical students an intuitive skill he calls "perceptual transference," the ability to perceive what is going on inside another person's body by using one's own body as a diagnostic instrument to read the other's sensorium.)

Evidence that visual intelligence can operate quite independently from verbal intelligence is given in Figure 6.2B and C from our telepathy studies.[13,15] The pictures drawn by the receivers are very different from their verbal responses. In Figure 6.2C, there is a word match ("world"), but the images are different. In Figure 6.2B, it is the image that matches the sender's drawing (a similar type of drawing of a face), but the words ("whale, green hills") do not relate to the image.

The illustrations used in this chapter have been collected from several types of experiments that students, colleagues, and I have conducted over 20 years. Reports of this work have been published in more complete detail in other journals.[15,22,23] All participants were interested in exploring ways to improve their own interpersonal communication. We were just as interested in the ways that misses occurred as we were in the types of hits that happened. There were no rewards for getting it right.

In remote viewing, the entire environment becomes the message being sent. We conducted nearly 100 trials of this type. The other type of telepathy was based on target pictures pasted on $3'' \times 5''$ cards. We conducted 380 trials of this type between 1974 and 1980. The target pool for these trials always contained at least 100 cards. None was used more than once in the first set of 290 trials. The cards were shuffled each time before the sender was asked to choose one randomly. We found that it is easier to sort the potential telepathic images from our own internal thought processes if the actual target is unknown to everyone before it is chosen.

Each team was asked to do five trials in a row before any feedback for accuracy was given. Five independent outside judges first attempted to match the responses with the drawings and targets using the blind-match method. The matching was done within the same set of five trials that each team did at one time. The judges were expected to match one in five by chance (20%), even if no drawings were similar. The results of that judging were used in the correlations with the EEG synchronization studies.[13,16,23] J. Johnston wrote a summary of this work, and it is included in Chapter 18.

A group of independent outside judges then compared the results of the first set of 290 trials on a scale of six types of similarity: shape, color, drawing, mood, word, and concept. The diagram in Figure 6.1C shows the distribution of those similarities. Because these trials were not judged in sets of five (as in the blind matching) but were referred to a list of twenty types of shapes, moods, and concepts and ten colors, the 20% score for chance no longer applies. By far the most dominant similarity was shape (37%) followed by color (24%). Examples of such similarities are seen in Figure 6.3A through D.

Hardy, Harvie, and Koestler considered how much matching could be done of pictures drawn by two persons at different times and places, unrelated to attempts to communicate with each other.[24] They found some remarkable similarities indeed. This information might challenge claims of true telepathic responses. When we consider the types of drawings we share in learning to read, it is no wonder why free-response drawings done spontaneously by different people from similar education systems might match. If two persons who were not artists were both asked to draw ten pictures quickly from imagination, what might they choose to draw? Probably simple things from memory, such as a house, a mountain, a flower, a cat, a dog, a tree, or a boat. As King discovered, the memories that come quickly are based on our first ones—often the ones formed by the outline drawings of the verbal picture-symbols that are used in our early readers or coloring books.[19] Naturally, we could expect some of these drawings to show the type of similarity Hardy, Harvie, and Koestler reported.[24] Today, if we were to ask children to draw animals from memory, we would find many Donald-type ducks, Ninja-type turtles, and a Mickey Mouse.

For this reason and to avoid the automatic recall of the line drawings we share in memory, a wide variety of images was used for our target pool. These were taken from drawings and photos of landscapes, buildings, animals, people, and statues. After the sender selected a target, he or she was asked to redraw the image, using any of ten colored pens. The receiver also had a box of pens with the same ten colors, and five numbered blank cards. If the two drawings, done simultaneously under testing conditions, demonstrated enough similarities, our judges would consider the response to be nonrandom. Clear examples of nonrandom similarities can be seen in Figure 6.4A through C. Notice that there are four dots on the headband of both the bull (in the target) and the Norseman (in the response). The horns match, and in both, the yellow and red lines coming from the background also match. The symbol of the Egyptian ankh is a clear example of visual transfer of information. Notice that the tarot card star over the head of the person has been reversed in the response.

Examples of telepathy using one sender and two independent receivers, James Dowlin and Tom Byrne, both professional artists, are shown in Figure 6.5A and B. Dowlin and Byrne were on opposite sides of the video studios at Santa Rosa Junior College. In another part of the studio, I had selected a $3'' \times 5''$ target card (from a pool chosen by others). Television cameras on each of us separately showed how the shapes of some images were being drawn simulta-

**Figure 6.3**
**Remote-Viewing Target and Response: Examples of Overall Image Similarities**

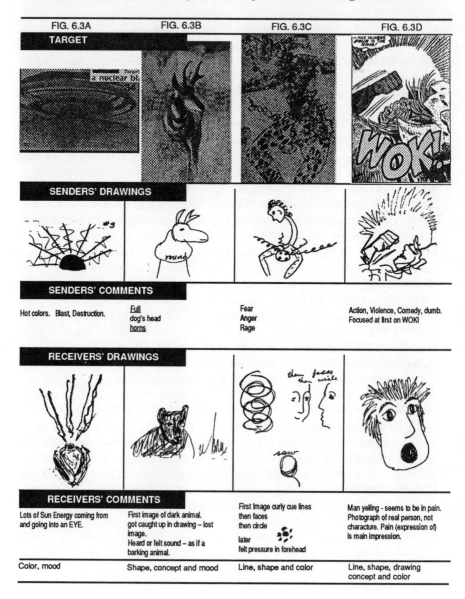

neously. Bob Budereaux, in the silent TV mixing room, recorded one such event as a live-time superimposition of telepathic drawings with similar shapes.

This type of research needs to be repeated in the future. I predict exciting results that will add needed information to our accumulating database about the entire process of mind-to-mind communication.

The same artists also responded to a remote-viewing experiment while in the television studio. I went to a randomly chosen site (one of the buildings on campus) and drew sketches of it from the outside (Figure 6.5B). As I entered one of the biology classrooms, I drew pictures of fish, a stuffed owl, and an eagle. Byrne's drawing of the same building is much better than the one I drew (Figure 6.5C). Figure 6.5D shows Dowlin's responses during that period. At first, Dowlin interpreted the curved shapes to suggest that I had gone to an appliance store. He embellished this with a cart. Later, the curves became arches of a building, and then the wings and the head of a bird emerged in his drawings at the same time I was sketching the stuffed owl across campus. Dowlin is such a superb artist that the images he is channeling do not have to make sense. He said that he just begins to draw and he doesn't know what images will emerge. This suggests that he does automatic drawing the way some people do automatic writing while in trance. Because Dowlin can draw anything he can visualize, his work provides us with a rare look at the stream of visions that can pour through one's mind.

This process of receiving unknown telepathic imagery and blending it with internal visual association is one of the most interesting aspects of human consciousness yet to be studied in the field of human science. Uri Geller has exhibited another aspect of this ability. During their experiments at SRI International, Targ and Puthoff did a series of warm-up trials using different electromagnetically shielded rooms around the complex.[1] I noticed that if Geller didn't know what the image he had received was supposed to be, he might draw it upside down or sideways. Once, when the target was a Christmas tree with a star on the top, Geller drew an image of a two-story set of stairs. Although I was sitting outside the shielded room, I could feel that he was confused, perhaps because he had only part of the image. I changed my sending strategy. After that, Geller received the image of the star and automatically placed it on the top of the page (in the sky). At that point, he rotated his drawing 90 degrees and came bursting out of the room in high spirits: he knew that the target was a tree with a star on top rather than the two-story set of stairs. I asked him where he had been standing in the room. He had been facing east, whereas I and the rest of the team in the outer room, had been facing the target image in the south—a 90-degree difference. Perhaps the type of detailed research on the primate visual system being done by D. Van Essen, C. Anderson, and D. Felleman can eventually tell us more about the mysterious visionary process observed that day.[25]

Among the most fascinating material that was judged among the misses in the blind-matching statistics of the study published in 1978 are bits and pieces

**Figure 6.4**
**Remote-Viewing Target and Response: Examples of Nonrandom Similarities**

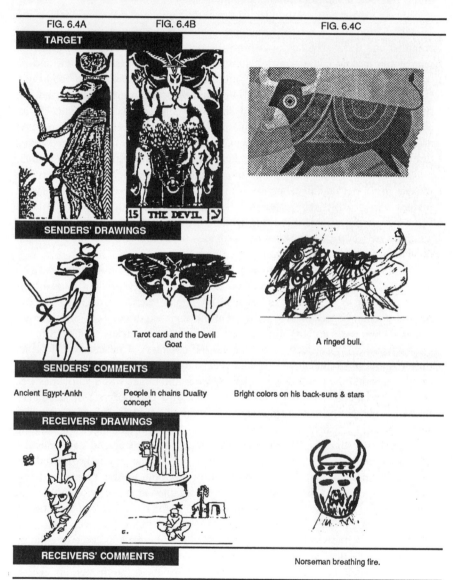

**Figure 6.5**
**Remote-Viewing Target and Response: Two Responses to Same Target**

of subconscious material that relate to the inner process of the receiver. Because information from the receiver's own higher intelligence may be coming through on subtle levels, the subconscious images have a chance to communicate to the conscious mind during the quiet time devoted to the telepathic exercise.

Most of the telepathic teams who participated in the study were men-women couples. Two men, however, who were musicians and had been friends through grammar school, made up one of the teams. Two women formed another team; they were college roommates who had been friends since high school.

The receiver of the women's team had hoped to get married and start having children, but her boyfriend had moved away. To console herself, she got a new puppy. She was still feeling sad during our experiments, and the dynamics of this emotion colored all her attempted telepathic responses. Few of the first set were judged as hits, although afterward, she could see her own process in what she thought was the psychic "conversation" between her and her friend. When the target was a dog, she drew a pregnant lady. When the target was a nude male, she drew a buffalo and wrote that her former boyfriend's nickname was "Buffalo." She mentioned a ballet tutu on one card as though it were an afterthought not related to her main image. The ring diagram (Figure 6.1B) shows that her focus of attention was continuously being distracted to the emotional inner ring, and all her major responses revolved around those emotions.

The dance theme was coming from another place. For example, three months after the experiment just described, a second set of trials was conducted. At this time, words about dancers again appeared as afterthoughts on the margins of her cards. Once she wrote, "Belly dancer, huh?" as if she was surprised by the comment and didn't expect it to be part of the experiment. In this set, her primary responses were judged to be more successful than before, even though the occasional dance comments that continued did not relate to the targets or to her main responses. On her final response, the dancer triumphed. Although the target was a river and the sender wrote about swimming there, the response was a drawing of a radiant nude with a star over her head. The title of this one is "Isadora Duncan" (Figure 6.1D). Years later, this woman became a successful dance therapist, a profession she did not expect of herself back in the student days of our experiments. Yet a part of her knew her real talent, and during those still moments of reaching for a telepathic response, she made contact with that higher Self. Her earlier confusion eventually was conquered by her innate creativity and compassion.

One of the most famous and interesting demonstrations of the influence of the subconscious during a formal experiment occurred at SRI.[1] I had been asked to draw a farmer with a pitchfork as a message to send to Uri Geller who was in an electromagnetically shielded room. Puthoff was guarding the room Geller was in, and I was with Targ in his office several buildings away across the SRI complex. Geller had a standard-size pen and drawing pad on his lap. I was asked to draw on a large poster-size paper with a large marking pen. After Targ chose the subject matter, I went into a light trance state and drew quickly, filling the page. After seeing the pitchfork, at the last moment (still in trance—without thinking), I added horns and a tail and wrote "Devil" on the page. Geller drew the tablets of Moses with the word "God" on them. Then he drew an apple with a snake or a worm. The last drawing by Geller transformed the large, round head of the crude drawing of the farmer into the earth with the tablets of Moses behind it instead of horns. A pitchfork was being driven away toward the edge of the page (Figure 6.6A). Later, when Geller saw the target drawing, he became thoughtful. He said it was against his religion to mention the name of the devil in the temple. Perhaps his subconscious mind was receiving but rejecting the image at the same time.

In one of my later experiments with the teams in Sonoma, a picture of George Washington on a coin came up as a target. The words on the coin are "In God We Trust" (Figure 6.6C). Part of the telepathic response was "A devil with pitchforks." Another example of the reversal of the God-Devil theme is seen in Figure 6.6B. Here, the receiver wrote, "Flashed on an angel." Flying saucers and little green men were included, along with a galaxy of stars.

When only a series of 10 to 20 trials are conducted and only the binary set of hits versus misses are reported, certain aspects of the process can be overlooked. Because we accumulated a variety of data on the similarities of nearly 400 trials, much additional surprising information came to the surface. For example, similar types of misses by different teams show dream-like symbolism. Of the first 290 responses, only 4 (1 in 72) suggested a church or a temple. Three of these were paired with a target picture of a nude or seminude woman. The fourth response (a pagoda with a red curving roof) was paired with a cheerleader in a red sweater with her arms curving upward. The woman of each team was sending the image to her lover, who gave this type of response. Each temple was drawn with some similar lines or shapes seen in the sender's drawing. These can be seen in Figure 6.7A through D. Not all the targets, which were pictures of women (twenty-nine in all), received such responses. Some were partials (as in Figure 6.2A); some were accurately matched; and some were missed for reasons unknown to me.

After finding this repeated relation between the temples and the women, we took a second look at the response to the target, Shirley Temple as a child star in a dress with many ruffled petticoats. The visual response was a drawing of a radiant sunset. The verbal response was "Rays of sunlight bursting out of a billowing cloud formation. Feelings of great power there, in Cecil B. DeMille's picture of God, Heaven, etc."

The reverse of the dream-like pairing of imagery can be seen in Figure 6.7E. A picture of the Greek Parthenon is paired with a picture of a woman and a moon. In Christian times, some spiritual healers, although branded as witches, still honored the Greek goddess Diana. Her symbol is the moon.

The moon as a feminine symbol and the sun as a masculine symbol are old ideas that can be observed in the art of many cultures. When considering sym-

**Figure 6.6**
**Remote-Viewing Target and Response: The God/Devil Theme**

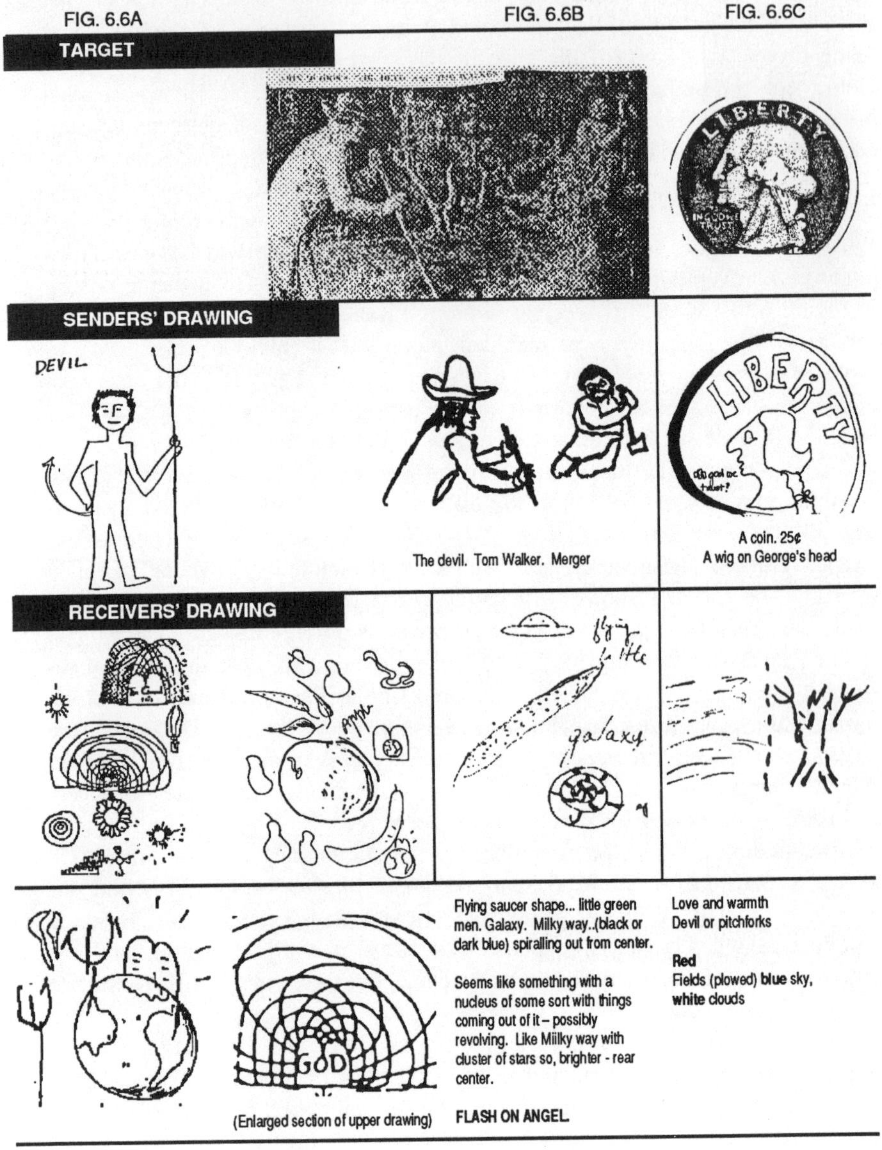
FIG. 6.6A
FIG. 6.6B
FIG. 6.6C
TARGET
LIBERTY
SENDERS' DRAWING
DEVIL
LIBERTY
The devil. Tom Walker. Merger
A coin. 25¢
A wig on George's head
RECEIVERS' DRAWING
galaxy
GOD
(Enlarged section of upper drawing)
Flying saucer shape... little green men. Galaxy. Milky way..(black or dark blue) spiralling out from center.
Seems like something with a nucleus of some sort with things coming out of it – possibly revolving. Like Miilky way with cluster of stars so, brighter - rear center.
FLASH ON ANGEL.
Love and warmth
Devil or pitchforks
Red
Fields (plowed) blue sky, white clouds

**Figure 6.7**
**Remote-Viewing Target and Response: Transpositions from 290 Telepathy Tests**

| FIG. 6.7A–Team 3 | FIG.6.7B Team 11 | FIG. 6.7C Team 8 | FIG. 6.7D Team 8 | FIG.6.7E Team 2 |
|---|---|---|---|---|

**TARGET**

**SENDERS' DRAWINGS**

**SENDERS' COMMENTS**

| Cool air on wet skin; surge of water, swirling, Naked skin, soft stirring hair. | Voluptuous, big. | Soft, sensual; a pure power from within: abandon, loving openness." | Exuberance, Energy, Light Hearted. All-American | Tried to visualize building; its antiquity.. (Team mate) as a Greek woman there; the constancy of this structure. |

**RECEIVERS' DRAWINGS**

PAGODA

**RECEIVERS' COMMENTS**

| Mystical, serene, pensive, enshrouded. | Temple, galaxy | European cathedral, Felling of massiveness. Weather is cold there-- cold stone. | Japanese or Chinese Garden with Pagoda-lots of greenery around-small pond. | Dark night. Halo around moon. |

About one target in ten was a picture of a single woman similar to those above. One response in seventy-two (four responses) was a church, temple, or a pagoda, with some shape or color similarity to the woman on the target.

bolism, the response to the target in Figure 6.8A becomes funny. A lunar eclipse of the sun indeed! In Figure 6.8B and C, a variety of classic dream symbolism about sexuality becomes apparent. In Figure 6.8D, the embracing couple from the Tantric tradition of art is translated into an embracing couple from Western art, from a statue by Rodin.

When we began to do remote-viewing experiments, we started to follow the model used by Targ and Puthoff.[3] James Dowlin, however, would sometimes start drawing before the scheduled time of the experiment because he was in the mood. He seemed to draw a running account of our activities, moment by moment, before we actually arrived at our remote destination. We decided to explore this further without telling him by deliberately moving from place to place during the testing hour. We asked friends in California (Sola Smith, Cheryl Wells, Mark Harris, and Greg Schelkun) to draw images and tape-record comments at any time during predetermined days and hours while we were traveling in Hawaii. We told them we would be on Maui for the first two events and on the big island of Hawaii for the next two. While there, we asked friends to make up a list of very different environments and to choose one for us randomly. Each of the islands has many unique environments. On Maui, for example, we could have been in, on, or under the water. We could have been walking in the desert-like area of Mount Haleakala, or shopping in the tourist centers at Lahaina, or eating at one of the big hotel buffets, or riding a bicycle down the side of the volcano.

The first target turned out to be the Seven Sacred Pools. We kept up a running account of our visions and experiences on a tape recorder during the entire hour, half of which we spent at the pools (Figure 6.9A). Before the hour was up, we drove back to Hana Bay along a road that is only one lane part of the way, although it is used by two-way traffic. The tall trees closed over the road, and on the tape, I mention, ''It feels as though we are driving through a tunnel.'' Schelkun correctly identified all our first activities, including finding us at Hana Bay (Figure 6.9B).

Near the end of the hour, we stopped at a store to get some suntan lotion and food for ourselves and for the stray cat who usually nursed her kittens on the doorstep. On our arrival, the cat raced into the room and sat expectantly in front of the small refrigerator. The rather dark, late-afternoon photos I took of the store and the cat may be difficult to see in Figures 6.10A and 6.11A, but Dowlin's drawing of the store and of ''a dog expecting food'' is clear and definitely an example of nonrandom remote viewing (Figure 6.11B). In addition to providing us with drawings, our California participants also tape-recorded their impressions of our adventures. The tapes and drawings were mailed the same day to an independent monitor (Saul-Paul Sirag), who kept them until we reported our activities on our return.

The participants also did well in their taped reports. After three relatively successful sessions, we called the series to a halt. On the big island, both active volcanoes were erupting at the same time. The energy of such an event was

**Figure 6.8**
**Remote-Viewing Target and Response: Examples of Symbolism**

FIG. 6.8A          FIG. 6.8B          FIG. 6.8C          FIG. 6.8D

TARGET

SENDERS' DRAWING

SENDERS' COMMENTS

Warm, loving, exciting
natural flesh sweet skin

the kiss  women / man
holding heads - eyes closed

touch - feel - soft - hairy body

RECEIVERS' DRAWING

RECEIVERS' COMMENTS

Lunar eclipse of Sun. Sun is really
bright - very clear picture.
Fire feeling - full of energy.

1. Black Piano / Keyboard
2. On stage

1. Like Kirlian Leaf
2. Pistol
3. Football

"The lovers" by Rodin

dominant for me and my family, who live within sight of them. It was on the minds of the receivers too, but the pictures of volcanic eruptions that they all drew were contaminated by the world news of the event on television.

Figure 6.12 is difficult to explain, but it had a profound impact on my life. The illustrations in Figure 6.12B through D were drawn by James Dowlin of Santa Rosa after a series of remote-viewing trials held in the nearby town of Petaluma had been finished. Although the experiment was officially over, Dowlin, one of the participants, was strongly moved to continue drawing. At that point, he had never been to my apartment.

Shortly thereafter, I invited the remote-viewing experimental team to my place in Petaluma for a celebration dinner. When he came to the party, Dowlin brought me the images he had drawn of my apartment. Figure 6.12A is a small, framed sketch by William Mayo that was hanging on my wall. Dowlin drew two versions of the sketch with the nude lying on sofa cushions (Figure 6.12B and C). My place was small, without a sofa. The only image of a sofa was that in the Mayo sketch.

Because of the accuracy of the other images, I then looked for the "letter of importance & opened . . . on the floor" (Figure 6.12D). There was such a letter, which had been sent to my old address and saved for me; the letter announced a conference in Brazil. I could not afford to go, and it was too late to submit a paper. I had ignored the letter when I first received it, forgot it, and it had fallen on the floor under the desk. Because Dowlin's drawing had called my attention to it and because he had said it was important, I answered the letter, mainly to send in my new address. The next year a telegram came inviting me (and offering to pay my way) to demonstrate my stereo biofeedback light sculpture at the next conference on parapsychology in Brazil. The letter on the floor had been important indeed! But where does such a message come from? If it is from my own unconscious mind, how does the artist know to draw an image of it from a distance of ten miles away? (Perhaps my spirit guide had a chance to talk to his spirit guide while my conscious mind slept.) If it is precognition, then does precognition *create* the conditions for the future event to take place? For such a strange event, perhaps the answers are equally strange to most of us.

More research into this fascinating world of mind-to-mind communication is clearly needed. For those who still think that "telepathy does not exist," I say, open your mind and explore your inner visions. Each of us can begin our own exploration into the profound mechanisms of consciousness and into our own multidimensional potential to communicate with one another. When we do, lovers can learn to be more loving; families can learn to listen to one another, honoring their individual differences as well as their genetic similarities; communities can grow in compassion; and the world can learn to understand itself. I hope that in the future of education, perceptual development will be regarded as a valid method of expanding intelligence. It will be necessary training for those who would become scientific observers of nature, healers of the earth,

**Figure 6.9**
**Remote-Viewing Target and Response: Maui Waterfall and Hana Highway**

FIGURE 6.9A

REMOTE VIEWING EXPERIMENT

Waterfall at the Seven Sacred Pools in Maui

Photo of the Hana Highway from the air (from postcards)

RECEIVER'S DRAWINGS

FIGURE 6.9B

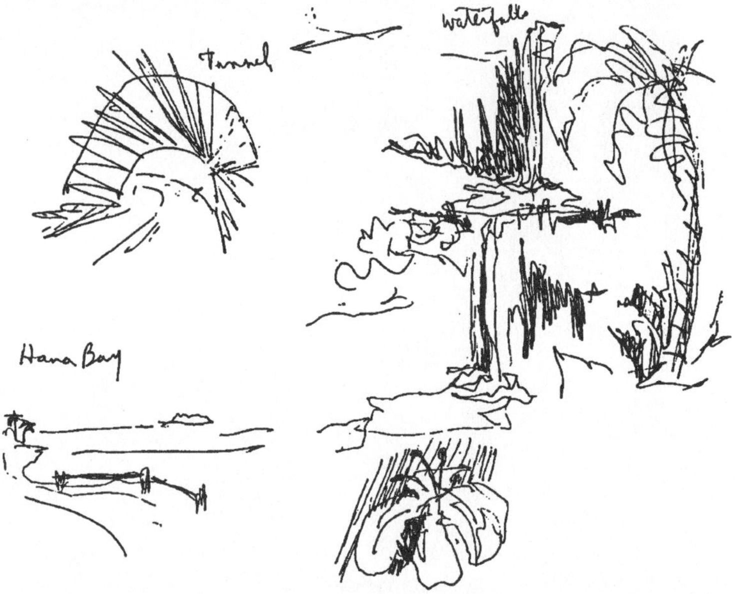

Example of Greg Schelkun's drawings of the accurate location of the remote team.

**Figure 6.10**
**Remote-Viewing Target and Response: Photo of Small Grocery Store in Maui**

| FIGURE 6.10A | FIGURE 6.10B |
|---|---|

**REMOTE VIEWING EXPERIMENT**

Photo of store in Hana taken by remote team

C. B. of the remote team parked the car by this store and went inside to buy food. J. M. of the remote team took this photo and went into the store briefly for suntan lotion. She said, "I won't stay, because the hour scheduled for remote viewing is not up yet," and went back to the car.

Notice the small high windows of both the building and the drawing.

**RECEIVER'S DRAWINGS**

Example of Jim Dowlin's accurate drawings of the location of the remote team.

**Figure 6.11**
**Remote-Viewing Target and Response: Stray Cat Waiting for Food**

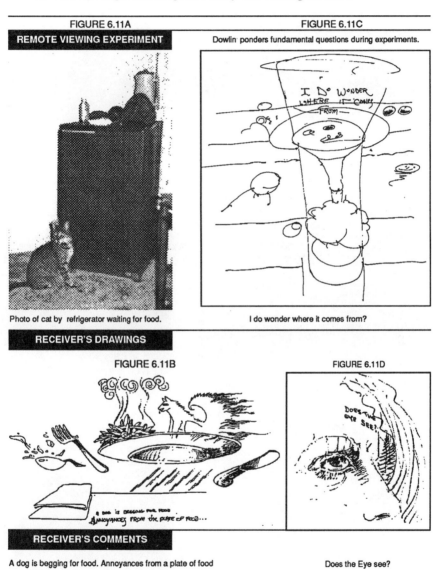

FIGURE 6.11A

**REMOTE VIEWING EXPERIMENT**

Photo of cat by refrigerator waiting for food.

**RECEIVER'S DRAWINGS**

FIGURE 6.11B

FIGURE 6.11C

Dowlin ponders fundamental questions during experiments.

I do wonder where it comes from?

FIGURE 6.11D

**RECEIVER'S COMMENTS**

A dog is begging for food. Annoyances from a plate of food

Does the Eye see?

Example of Jim Dowlin's responses to the remote-viewing experiments.

**Figure 6.12**
**Remote-Viewing Target and Response: Important Letter on the Floor**

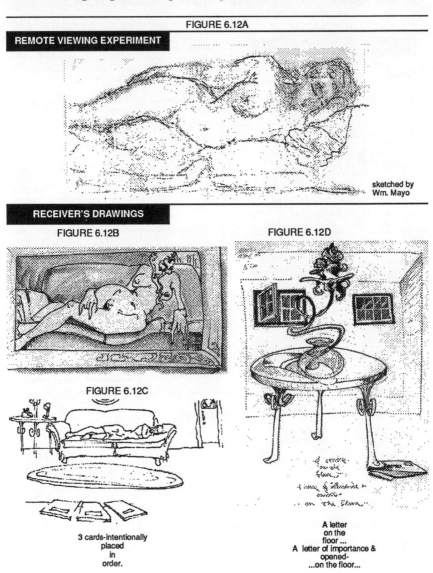

FIGURE 6.12A

REMOTE VIEWING EXPERIMENT

sketched by
Wm. Mayo

RECEIVER'S DRAWINGS

FIGURE 6.12B

FIGURE 6.12D

FIGURE 6.12C

3 cards-intentionally
placed
in
order.

A letter
on the
floor ...
A letter of importance &
opened-
...on the floor...

Example of Jim Dowlin's responses to the remote-viewing experiments.

and leaders of societies. We have found, through many forms of feedback, that we can learn to increase our ability to focus attention. Focus of attention is the key to intelligence. That means we can learn to become more intelligent as well as more creative. Creativity will not be seen as some special talent of the few, but as a process of each human expressing the uniqueness of his or her own perceptual organization.

## NOTES

1. Targ R, Puthoff H. Information transmission under conditions of sensory shielding. *Nature*. 1974;252:602–607.

2. Krippner S. *Song of the Siren*. New York: Harper and Row, 1975.

3. Targ R, Puthoff H. *Mind-Reach*. New York: Delacorte Press, 1977.

4. Targ R, Harary K. *The Mind Race*. New York: Villard Books, 1984.

5. Harary K, Targ E, Targ R. Report presented to the Parapsychology Research Group, San Francisco, 1985.

6. Krippner S. Dream telepathy revisited. Report presented to the Parapsychology Research Group, San Francisco, 1984.

7. Rauscher E. Theoretical and experimental exploration of the remote perception phenomena. Proceedings of the Eleventh International Conference on the Unity of the Sciences. University of Pennsylvania, Philadelphia: 1982;2:1443.

8. Millay J. An approach to the discovery and education of the visually oriented student. Report presented at University of California Berkeley: 1962.

9. Kellogg R. *Analyzing Children's Art*. Palo Alto, CA: Mayfield Publishing Co; 1969.

10. Pasto T. *The Space Frame Experience in Art*. New York: AS Barnes & Co; 1964:66.

11. Gregory RL. *Eye and Brain: The Psychology of Seeing*. New York: McGraw-Hill; 1966:7.

12. Gottlieb RL. *The Psychophysiology of Nearsightedness*. Saybrook Institute, San Francisco; 1977. Dissertation.

13. Millay J. Exploration into the nature of the visionary experience. Heinze RI, ed. Proceedings of the International Conference on the Study of Shamanism, Independent Scholars of Asia. Berkeley, CA: 1984.

14. Kamiya J. Conscious control of brain waves. *Psychology Today*. 1968;1:56–60.

15. Millay J. The relationship between phase synchronization of brain waves and success in attempts to communicate telepathically: a pilot study. San Francisco: Saybrook Institute; 1978.

16. Johnston J, Millay J. A pilot study in brain wave synchrony. *Psi Research Review*. 1983;2:71–91.

17. Crane H, Brown D. Unpublished studies done between 1968 and 1972. Report presented to the Parapsychology Research Group, San Francisco, 1987.

18. Pritchard R. Stabilized images on the retina. *Perception: Mechanisms and Models, Readings from Scientific American*. San Francisco: Freeman; 1972.

19. King MB. View from a classroom using biofeedback and other tools. *Association for Humanistic Psychology Newsletter*. 1979:5:26–27.

20. Warcollier R. *Mind to Mind*. New York: Farrar, Strauss & Strauss & Co.; 1948, 1963.

21. Holland C, Holland J. Perceptual transference: a scientific basis for intuition and other paranormal experiences. Report presented to Parapsychology Research Group, San Francisco, 1991.

22. Millay J. Brain-wave synchronization: a study of subtle forms of communication. *The Humanistic Psychology Review*. 1981;3:9–40.

23. Millay J. Brain-mind and the dimensions beyond space-time. Proceedings of the International Conference on the Study of Shamanism, Independent Scholars of Asia. Berkeley, CA: 1985.

24. Hardy A, Harvie R, Koestler A. *The Challenge of Chance: A Mass Experiment in Telepathy and Its Unexpected Outcome*. New York: Vintage Books, 1975.

25. Van Essen DC, Anderson CH, Felleman DJ. Information processing in the primate visual system: an integrated systems perspective. *Science*. 1992;255:419–422.

# III _____

# PHYSICS

The four physicists represented in this section have in common a deep interest in the nature of consciousness and the possibility of bringing it into the orbit of physics by way of quantum theory.

Herbert and Sirag have known each other since 1973, when they met at the Institute for the Study of Consciousness in Berkeley, and have been discussing ideas about physics and consciousness ever since, especially at Esalen[1] Physics conferences and the Consciousness Theory Group. Herbert and Sirag got to know Rauscher in 1975 during their participation in her weekly seminar called "The Fundamental Fysicks Group" at the Lawrence Berkeley Laboratory. The main topic of discussion was Bell's theorem and its implications. Burns became acquainted with Sirag, Herbert, and Rauscher in the early 1980s in various meetings of the Parapsychology Research Group and other groups, such as the Consciousness Research Group, which she cofounded in 1987.

It is perhaps striking that Sirag does not mention psi, and Herbert mentions psi only to say that his quantum approach to consciousness will not explain telepathy. It has long been the strategy of Herbert and Sirag to try to explain consciousness in a physical theory in such a way that psi phenomena might find a natural home.

There have been many suggestions (e.g., Walker) that quantum connectedness (Bell non-locality) might account for telepathy.[2] Herbert, who is an expert in this aspect of quantum theory, comes down decisively against it. His argument should be carefully considered. If he is right, telepathy will require a broader theory than quantum mechanics.

Within physics itself, we know that a broader theory than quantum mechanics is necessary. Such a theory is the goal of what used to be called *unified field theory* and is now called the *theory of everything*. Such a theory would contain both quantum theory and general relativity (Einstein's theory of gravity) as subtheories.

Sirag's approach is to propose that such a supreme theory is necessary to account for consciousness. He assumes that in such a theory a place for psi is more natural, but he does not develop this idea here. The most startling consequence of current approaches to theories of everything is that they require spacetimes of at least 10 dimensions. It is hardly novel to suggest that hyperspace (a space of more than three dimensions) might provide scope for consciousness theory. Such an idea only becomes interesting when the details are provided. Sirag's strategy is to fit mathematical structures in the hyperspace physics to aspects of consciousness such as cognition and volition. This is only a raw beginning. One might think that affect is still untouched by this approach.

Herbert suggests that "subjective experiences consist of the feelings that accompany quantum changes." In other words, the quantum change is an outer manifestation, whereas the subjective experience is an inner manifestation of the same event.

The words inner and outer may be more than metaphor. They suggest the possibility of a geometric approach.

In the geometry of the supreme theory, the quantum jumps correspond to jumps from one discrete point to another in a set of discrete points, making a symmetrical structure in a certain hyperspace that Sirag calls *reflection space* because the jumps are a kind of mathematical reflection. The points are not states but correspond to states. Rather, the points are, in a sense, the inner manifestation of the states. Here we have an "inner" and "outer" that may match up with the inner and outer aspects of quantum jumping to which Herbert refers.

As has been emphasized by prominent quantum theorists such as Weyl and Wigner,[3] symmetry plays a deep role in physics. By symmetry we mean a change in a system that leaves some aspect of the system unchanged. In effect, the quest for a theory of everything is a quest for the deepest symmetry. We want to know what remains invariant under the widest possible set of transformations. With reference to consciousness, this is perhaps what we mean by the self, something that remains the same through all the changes of a lifetime and perhaps even remains invariant beyond the change called death.

One important aspect of supreme theories today is the concept of broken symmetry: A system that is highly symmetrical at one level may be much less symmetrical at a lower level. The difference in levels may correspond to differences in dimensionality.

With this idea, we can make contact with the main theme of Burns' paper, "the arrow of time." Ordinarily, in basic theories of physics, time is symmetrical. The theory remains the same even if we switch the direction of the time arrow in the description of some phenomenon. If we make a movie of the phenomenon, we can run the movie backward and the theory will still provide a perfectly good description.

Some of the supreme theories have a way of introducing a time asymmetry by symmetry breaking, and this time asymmetry corresponds to the expansion of the universe.

This is not discussed in my chapter, and I mention it here because it may be relevant to Burns' chapter. She considers a combination of quantum theory and thermodynamics as a larger theory and finds it necessary to go beyond this larger theory to explain certain psi data (psychokinesis [PK] dice experiments). She points out that the problem of the arrow of time—the basis for time asymmetry—is an unsolved problem with many proposed solutions. She discusses these proposals and favors the idea that the collapse of the quantum wave function may be the fundamental basis for time asymmetry. Although the evolution of the wave function is time symmetric, the collapse that occurs during any measurement is a change from a host of possibilities to one actuality. Because this one actuality is selected randomly, the collapse process is not time reversible. However, citing Walker's discussion of PK as the ability of a subject to select the actuality in a quantum collapse process, she points out that this would violate the second law of thermodynamics. This implies that a larger theory than quantum theory plus thermodynamics is necessary to embed a theory of consciousness sufficient to include psi.

Burns, in her discussion of thermodynamics, is concerned mainly with the second law, which she describes in some detail. It is useful to mention the first law, the fact that energy is conserved. This relates to the discussion of energy by Sirag that he presented in a panel discussion at the Parapsychology Research Group. The relevance of energy conservation here is that energy conservation can be derived from the time *translation* symmetry: the fact that a basic physics experiment does not depend on when it is done. This connection between energy and time derives from the definition of action as the product of energy and time and the law of least action, which plays a basic role in classic mechanics and becomes even more important in quantum mechanics.[3,4]

Note that the time symmetry discussed in Burns' chapter is time *reversal* symmetry, which is a different matter. Broken time reversal symmetry corresponds to entropy increase. Unbroken time translation symmetry corresponds to energy conservation. This suggests that there must be some connection between energy and entropy, and there is: The second law states that entropy always increases. Another way to state this law (in addition to the statements in Burns' chapter) is that the availability of energy always decreases.[4] Moreover, quantum uncertainty also ties energy and time together: The uncertainty in energy times the uncertainty in time must be greater than or equal to Planck's constant, which is in units of action. It is because Planck's constant is in units of action that the law of least action plays such a fundamental role in quantum theory.

Rauscher's paper explores the possibility of explaining paranormal phenomena by invoking faster-than-light connections. These tachyonic connections are not based on quantum non-locality and are consistent with Einstein's theory of special relativity. Although special relativity forbids superlight speeds for particles of ordinary matter, it would require that a particle with imaginary rest mass always move faster than light speed. Such hypothetical particles of imaginary rest mass are called *tachyons*. The word imaginary here means that the rest mass is multiplied by the factor $i$, equal to the square root of minus one. This factor occurs naturally in the context of complex numbers $z$, which are ordered pairs of real numbers $(a,b)$; that is, $z = a + ib$. Thus the natural framework for such a theory is not spacetime but complexified spacetime. This is an eight-dimensional real vector space formally equivalent to the four-dimensional complex vector space $C^4$.

Physicists have investigated the properties of complex spacetime in the context of the *twistor theory*, which is a major approach to quantum gravity.[5] In fact, a twistor can be regarded as a complex two-plane in complex spacetime. The set of all these two-planes constitutes the set of points that make up a space called *projective twistor space*. It is these points, rather than spacetime points, that are regarded as fundamental.

To provide a possible link between Rauscher's complex spacetime and Sirag's formalism, I might mention that complex spacetime is implicit in the group algebra C[OD]. Embedded in this algebra is the unitary group $U(2) \times U(2)$, which could be given the name *complexified conformally compactified spacetime*. This is exactly the form of spacetime needed for twistor theory.[5] Moreover, there are profound connections between twistor theory and superstring theory, which is the other major approach to quantum gravity.[6]

I should mention that superstring theories are beset with tachyons, and great ingenuity is required to get rid of these pesky beasts because they wreak havoc with causality. Rauscher's approach to tachyons implies that perhaps some of them may be tame enough to account for strange, acausal psi phenomena.

These remarks should suggest the interconnectedness and unity of ideas in physics and may perhaps help to explain the feeling that even consciousness must somehow be entailed in the basic structure of physics, especially as this structure underlies a supposed "theory of everything." It usually is thought that this program of physics is reductionistic. Perhaps it is, but notice that it is a reduction accompanied by a countervailing expansion of mathematical ideas. Moreover, the manner in which the mathematical ideas interlock would seem to be a holism of vast proportions.

Saul-Paul Sirag

## NOTES

1. Esalen Institute, Big Sur, California.

2. Walker EH. The quantum theory of psi phenomena. *Psychoenergetic Systems.* 1979.

3. Wigner EP. *Symmetries and Reflections,* Woodbridge, CT: Ox Bow Press; 1979.

4. Feynman R. *The Character of Physical Law.* Cambridge, MA: MIT Press; 1965.

5. Penrose R, Rindler W. *Spinors and Space-Time Vol 2.* New York: Cambridge University Press; 1986.

6. Peat FD. *Superstrings and the Search for the Theory of Everything.* Chicago: Contemporary Books; 1988.

# 7

# Energy

*Saul-Paul Sirag*

**Saul-Paul Sirag:** I want to talk about something perhaps more mundane,[1] which is *energy*. The reason for this is that Russell [Targ] has been complaining about people's use of the word energy. At least he complained once to Jean [Millay] about somebody using the term psychic energy, and so I thought that it might be a good idea to give a brief presentation on what physicists mean by energy and how energy came into the physicist's lexicon and how that might relate to explanations of psi or nonexplanations of psi, as the case may be.

So I studied up a little bit on the history of energy in physics, and actually I was quite surprised. I brought with me an old physics book—I collect old physics books; whenever I see one, I buy one. This is quite old, published in 1837, and one of the most interesting things about it is that the word energy doesn't occur anywhere in this book *[audience laughter]*. Now that corresponds to the fact that there wasn't a physics of energy in 1837. You might think that this is just a book that was at a high school level, and so it wasn't really up with the current physics of even 1837. But actually how energy came into physics is an amazing story.

Newtonian mechanics is, in a sense, the beginning of real physics. Of course, the Greeks talked about physics—they invented the word, they invented the concept, and so on—but there wasn't really a mathematical body of theory. There

From the Panel Discussion on the Nature of Reality, Parapsychology Research Group General Meeting, May 1988 were some mathematical formulas that the Greeks knew, but they didn't amount to much. We really think of physics as starting with Newton's equations.

One of the interesting things about Newton's work for us here—and it's frequently overlooked because ever since Fritjof Capra's book came out, Newton has been made sort of the bad guy *[audience laughter]* who made the world mechanistic and deterministic, and in the twentieth century quantum mechanics comes along and rescues us from all that *[audience laughter]*—that's the short version of the Capra book *[loud audience laughter]*. Capra wasn't the only one saying that; lots of people have said that, but he said it very eloquently, and so a lot of people have that view of the history of physics.

But as a matter of fact, Newton's equations were, in a sense, a very magical set of equations because there was really no model, there was no *mechanism* whatsoever in Newton's equations. Newton's equations imply instantaneous action at a distance. He was severely criticized for this in his day, and it was in that context that he very angrily said, "I don't make hypotheses." Of course he made hypotheses, but he meant that he didn't have an underlying model. There are no strings attached between the moon and the earth; how in the world can the moon affect the tides?—that's what people said. In fact, the French described Newton's theory as an *occult* theory for that reason because he had an occult force that acted at a distance instantaneously.

Actually, Newton realized that that was a lack in his theory, that there wasn't any underlying mechanism whatsoever. What he really believed and what he said was that space is God's sensorium. So in other words, his explanation for why the equations worked was that God made them work, so it was totally magic. However, people became familiar with those equations, and what happens when you become familiar is that the very familiarity makes it seem ordinary, makes it seem unmagical.

So it became sort of the paradigm of a mechanistic theory, and as I say, it's not mechanistic at all. However, the aspect of it, which is important, which is what really impressed people, is that it was completely *deterministic*. That is to say, if you knew the positions of the planets at one point in time, then you knew the positions of the planets at any point in time. You just had to crank through the equations and you would get the position. Of course, you couldn't do it very far into the future in those days because they didn't have computers yet, but with computers and with improved mathematical techniques, we can do that quite handily.

But those are just details. The important thing is the matter of principle. The theory was, in principle, deterministic. So at first, there was a kind of worship, an awe of Newton, once people got over the shock of how magical the equations were. There was a kind of awe at the determinism, the perfect determinism of the equations, and of course, they were very successful. There were even books published that were the analog of Capra's book in the sense that they said that Newton's equations were a way of seeing the mind of God. In other words, physics at that time was being used as a way of supporting certain religious ideas. Newton himself thought of his equations that way, and other people did very much.

After about a hundred years of that, a reaction started setting in due largely to poets and philosophers like Blake who were objecting to the stifling feeling that came from the philosophy of determinism, the idea that everything was set from the word go, so to speak. Blake wrote many lines of poetry about Newton—I think he has a long poem called "Newton," in which he asks to be saved from Newton's *sleep*. I think it was, "God save us from single vision and Newton's sleep." What Blake meant by that was an opposition to the supposed determinism of the universe. Determinism portrays the universe as merely a clockwork—that was the catchword for Newton's theory. Newton himself didn't say that, of course, because Newton was all too aware that there wasn't any clock-like mechanism. A clock is a beautiful mechanism, whereas the planets are not. The only analogy that is valid there is the fact that a clock is deterministic and Newton's laws regarding the planets are deterministic, but otherwise, the analogy totally breaks down. The clockwork is kind of like a dead thing because once it's wound up, it just goes on until it winds down, and that's the end of the world, presumably.

A reaction set in, among the romantic poets especially, and an interesting thing is that out of this romantic reaction to Newton's determinism, the word energy started being bandied about, particularly among these philosophers and romantic poets.

**Question [2]:** Did Newton use the word energy?

**Saul-Paul Sirag:** No, Newton never used the word energy.

**Physicist A:** When was kinetic energy invented?[3]

**Saul-Paul Sirag:** I'm gonna tell about that! *[audience laughter]*. No, there's no kinetic energy in Newton's work. It's all a matter of force, F = MA, and the force of gravity obeying the inverse square law—that's essentially Newton's theory of gravity, and it's not a field theory. It's an action-at-a-distance theory.

Actually, "energy" wasn't at first used in the physics context, that's the point I'm making. It was used in a personal context, that is to say, a personal freedom context, the romantic context, literally.

**Physicist B:** What did the word mean?

**Saul-Paul Sirag:** *Ergon* means *work,* and energy is the ability to do work. It's the feeling of being able to move freely. It's the opposite of the feeling of determinism, I suppose. And it's a feeling of vitality.

**Physicist C:** Like it says, "Energy is pure delight."

**Saul-Paul Sirag:** Yes, that's from Blake. The term really arose in that context, and the only scientists who were thinking along the lines of an energy paradigm, you might say, were really fringe scientists in that period.

There was a German doctor named Mayer who is supposedly the discoverer of the conservation of energy. But the way he discovered it was, as you might guess, by paying attention to food, feeding rats, and weighing things. Of course, it was a rough kind of measurement that he could do in that way at that time, and he did crude little experiments that improved a little bit over the years. But he had a hard time getting that work published. Then when it was published— by the way, his paper was published in 1842, so that explains why there's no "energy" in here *[tapping old physics book]* whatsoever—hardly anybody knew that the thing was published. It wasn't published in the major journals at that time; several major journals turned down his paper.

Then in England, Prescott Joule, a self-taught amateur experimenter, was also independently trying to understand energy. One of things that was the impetus for his work was the development at the time of machinery that used energy in our terms today, like the steam engine, which was an important machine. But you see, the steam engine was invented by James Watt, who knew no physics whatsoever. I mean, these were just inventors, they were really fringe people, they didn't know Newton's equations. Newton's equations wouldn't have helped them one iota anyway. Knowing Newton's equations, you couldn't build a steam engine. There's nothing in there that helps you. Nothing about heat.

In other words, the concept of energy arises in the context of thinking about heat. And the problem with heat is that it's subjective before you have any equipment, before a thermometer is invented, let's say. Heat is a feeling, after all—you feel hot, you feel warm. You can have two people in the same room— one guy says its hot, and the other guy says it's cold *[audience laughter]*. You know that problem—one guy wants the window open, the other guy wants it closed. So how can you make a science out of something so subjective as temperature—the feeling of heat?

So energy was gradually brought into the realm of physics by people like Mayer and, especially, Joule. By the way, our unit of energy in the metric system is the joule, which is one watt-second, if that means anything to you. It's not a large amount of energy, if you think about how many kilowatts of electricity you use in a day.

What Joule was able to do was to make energy respectable by doing a simple, ingenious experiment that showed an exact correspondence between the amount of heat energy and the amount of mechanical energy. In other words, he was able to define a notion of mechanical energy. He did several kinds of experiments, but I suppose his most important experiment along that line was just having a paddle moving very slowly in water or oil and measuring the change in temperature of the water as the paddle rotated a certain number of times. These were long, laborious experiments that he did, and you can imagine that the statistics on them were poor. He had to do many, many runs. It was very much like an ESP experiment *[audience laughter]* in the sense that he did many runs and he got wildly different numbers and he just averaged them to come out with these equivalences.

Hardly anybody was interested in that work. It just seemed too far off the beaten path. Joule read his paper at a scientific meeting, and no one was interested in his first experiment. So he got permission to read another paper a couple of years later when he'd improved his experiments a lot. And since there hadn't been any interest in his first paper, they were only going to give him ten minutes to read this paper in the midst of a lot of other papers being given. Fortunately, in the audience of that second paper of his was an up-and-coming 23-year-old physicist, a guy who became Lord Kelvin later on, and he saw the significance of this paper. He gave Joule a lot of feedback from the audience and then went off and did his own experiments and really developed the whole field of heat. So we have the Kelvin temperature scale, and the unit of heat in absolute units is the Kelvin.

Now the point of all this is to show how physics is a kind of a living being in a sense—it feeds on ideas and it grows. There are lots of prejudices in it, of course, but new ideas come into it, many times from the fringes of physics. A new idea comes in and gets calibrated in some way that makes sense to the rest of physics when it makes contact with some existing part of physics—not necessarily with all of physics because physics, especially at that time, was compartmentalized.

For instance, there were at the same time in the early 1800s, important developments going on in electricity and magnetism. It was in 1820 that Oersted first discovered that electricity and magnetism had something to do with each other. In fact, this book, published in 1837, this is after 1820, ends with a short section on electricity and a short section on magnetism, and there's not the slightest hint that the two have anything to do with each other. So this book is quite behind the times *[audience laughter]* so far as electricity and magnetism are concerned but . . .

**Psychologist:** Saul-Paul, I found a school textbook while I was looking for science textbooks that didn't seem to think that they had anything to do with [each other] either. They had different sections on each one, and there was nothing that would pull the whole electromagnetic spectrum together even in this textbook recently published for junior high school students.

**Saul-Paul Sirag:** Well, this book came long before Maxwell's electromagnetic spectrum was invented in the late 1800s. Oersted's work was quite startling, and it took a long time for it to get into the textbooks, obviously, but the point I'm making here is that energy didn't immediately have to hook up with electromagnetism—it wouldn't have helped it much to hook up immediately with electricity and magnetism because that was a pretty far out field anyway. It had to hook up with something that was absolutely staid and established, which was mechanics, Newtonian mechanics. It was then, in thinking about heat, that the idea of kinetic energy comes in. You see, there was a theory developed about that time called the *kinetic theory of heat*. This was the idea that heat is due to the random motion of atoms or small particles of some kind, that is, due to the random kinetic energy of those particles. So really kinetic energy comes into the picture first by way of heat and then it gets generalized by way of the work of Joule. That is to say, the notion of energy gets generalized, so that it includes not just kinetic energy but potential energy. That's how energy comes into the discussion of gravity, by way of potential energy.

**Physicist A:** When did that happen?

**Saul-Paul Sirag:** In the early 1800s. Joule and Kelvin had a lot to do with that. For instance, I can give this book a charge—people talk about charging—giving something an energy charge, maybe by staring at it—a flaky use of the word energy—but I can give this thing a charge simply by lifting it *[lifts book off table]*. Now it has more potential energy than it had down here on the table because I lifted it in the gravitational field. Now, Newton didn't have the notion of a gravitational field. Remember Newton's idea was that gravity worked totally by action at a distance. There's no field involved, so the field idea comes in by way of the energy idea. It actually comes in by way of potential energy, and what we say is that the potential energy is actually stored in the gravitational field. So when I lift it up, this thing here has potential energy because of where it is in the gravitational field. Now, if I drop it *[clunk]*, that potential energy is, we say in physics, transformed into kinetic energy.

So the field idea became useful in physics with the idea of potential energy being transformed into kinetic energy and doing work with that kinetic energy, and gradually, the field idea took over physics, especially in the hands of Maxwell. In the late nineteenth century, he used the field idea—the electric field idea and the magnetic field idea—to understand light itself.

Now, the first person to apply the field idea to electromagnetism wasn't Maxwell. It was Faraday, who drew lines of force explaining electrostatic fields and magnetic fields, but he was being influenced by the field thinking of the energy paradigm, you might say, that was going in that period. Now in the twentieth century, one could say that the field idea in physics is the predominant one and the particle idea is secondary.

For a while, one could say that the field idea was in a kind of abeyance or eclipse because in making the field idea consistent with quantum mechanics, tremendous difficulties were encountered because of the infinities due to the self-action of particles like an electron in a field. That was partly solved by Feynman in the late forties for electromagnetism. But the field idea didn't seem to work for other forces, such as the weak force and the strong force—the nuclear forces in other words—until the late sixties and early seventies when Weinberg and Salaam and Glashow worked out the field theory for the weak force and other people worked out a field theory for the strong force. And, of course, Einstein conceived a beautiful field theory for gravity, the definitive field theory for gravity around 1915. Now all the forces are understood in terms of fields—you might say "energy" fields.

So the point of this history is simply that an idea that seemed flaky at first became the key idea in all realms of physics. One can't predict exactly what the future of physics will be. It could even happen that some better idea will come along and eclipse the field idea, but right now, it looks like that idea is very solid and will be here to stay.

So—let me just stop there. There are lots of different things that can be said, but I'll answer some questions.

**Physician:** Saul-Paul, what about the curvature of spacetime explaining gravity rather than its being a force? Is that something you would recognize as already eclipsing the field idea?

**Saul-Paul Sirag:** Well, no, that *is* a field idea. It's a strange kind of field, a curvature field, let's say. Let me define what a field is. That's one thing that people find mysterious, this use of the word field in physics. A field is sort of what it sounds like—it's a spread-out, smooth structure. In other words, it's a smooth assignment of a quantity to every point of some space.

For instance, the simplest possible example, I suppose, is a temperature field, where every point in this room has a temperature associated with it and the temperature changes smoothly from one part of the room to any other part of the room. If I measure the temperature as I move along any line in the room, the temperature will change gradually. It will change at different rates, going on different paths throughout the room, but it will change gradually. Now that's an example of what we call a *scalar field* because we're simply assigning a different number, namely the temperature, and a single number is a scalar.

If we assign sets of numbers, then we might have a *vector field*. An electric field is an example of a vector field. We assign three numbers to each point in spacetime for the electric field and three numbers for the magnetic field. So, to answer your question about gravity, the way gravity is thought of in Einstein's theory is that every point of spacetime has associated with it a set of numbers that correspond to the curvature of space at that point, and that curvature in effect is the gravitational field. That's an example of a *tensor field*. The electromagnetic field is also a tensor field.

**Physicist A:** Saul-Paul, let me give you an example of a problem with what we mean by an *explanation*. You've given us several physically correct descriptions of gravity. You've had a number of things to say, all of which are understandable in terms of contemporary physics about gravity, but that nonetheless somebody might find unsatisfactory at a deeper level. I'm obviously not criticizing what you said because what you said is correct.

But if some child comes home from school and says, "We were taught today about how God runs the universe," all the parents would throw up their hands and say, "That's terrible! How could your teacher say that?"

"Well, I asked the teacher why the moon controls the tides and the teacher said, 'Well, the moon exerts a force on the water.' " And the child wanted to know, how does that work?—and the teacher said, "All particles of matter attract one another—it's called the law of universal gravitation. Each atom in the universe has a property that exerts a force on every other atom. That's the nature of matter, that all material objects attract one another." And the child says, "Well, why is that?" and the teacher says, "Well, God made them that way, that's how we know what matter is, the fundamental property of matter is that all matter attracts all other particles of matter."

There are many things that we would like to have described in the most infinitesimal description, the point where you run out of answers that you can give meaningfully to questions beginning with "why." That's why children get beaten up by their parents, *[audience laughter]* because every question that can be answered can be followed by another question at a smaller level: "Yes, but why is that so?" That may be one of the problems we're having describing psychic functioning.

Steve Braude, who's a philosopher, is challenging the so-called small-is-beautiful theory of description when he says that you may not find ultimate elementary psi particles that explain how psi functioning works. Psi just may not have that level of description, the same way we haven't found elementary particles of time that explain how time works. I think that this is the problem with describing gravity—we all feel we understand how gravity works, we can write descriptions of gravity and we don't ask why it is that these particles attract each other . . .

**Saul-Paul Sirag:** But we do! You see, the thing is that physicists are never satisfied with the answers that we have. I mean, we have to defer answers to the future all the time. Certainly Einstein, for instance, wasn't satisfied with Newton's answers about gravity, and one of the main reasons that he wasn't satisfied is simply that Newton's theory . . .

**Physicist A:** . . . didn't give the right answer!

**Saul-Paul Sirag:** That's not the main reason. That's just a clue that there's something wrong with the theory. There was only one discrepancy that was known when Einstein was first working on gravity, and that was that the revolution of the perihelion of Mercury wasn't correctly predicted by Newton's theory. But there was also something philosophically unsatisfying about it for Einstein, which is this action-at-a-distance business. So Einstein was trying to come up with a theory of gravity that wouldn't have that terribly unattractive feature about it.

However, we're not completely satisfied with Einstein's theory, or any theory. We do keep asking these questions, "Why?" If a theory says that there are just all these forces—and that's what our theories do say, they say that there are four forces—we attempt to unify the forces.[4] The reason we're trying to unify the forces is because we're not satisfied with just an answer that says there happen to be these four forces, and they happen to have these particular properties.

You see, we want to go to the next level, which is exactly what the kid wants to do. Theoretical physicists actually play six-year-old kid—that's really what we're doing, we're playing that particular game. So we ask, why do these forces work the way they seem to want to work, why do they have the characteristics they do? As Einstein put it, he wanted to know whether God had any choice in the matter, which is his way of saying that he wouldn't really be satisfied with an ultimate theory of physics unless the theory could be shown to be so unique that that was the only way to do it. He never got close to that, but that was the goal, that was his vision. We're still attempting that, and yet we may never reach there.

**Psychologist:** I'm really interested in all this, but one of the reasons I particularly wanted you to discuss energy is because of our original argument about energy: When spiritual healers say that they are going to "put energy through" somebody, the physicists say no, no, that's not what energy is. I really wanted to talk about the semantics problem between physics and the psi realm. People who do spiritual healing or people who are exploring these realms seem to be quite at ease with using the word energy. What word should they use instead?

**Saul-Paul Sirag:** Well, maybe you're misunderstanding me. I'm not saying that they shouldn't use the word energy at all. I'm just saying . . .

**Psychologist:**. . . a lot of people tell me I shouldn't use that word . . .

**Saul-Paul Sirag:**. . . what I'm saying is that you shouldn't use the word energy in that context and think that you necessarily mean the same thing the physicist means by it.

**Psychologist:** How would we discriminate between those two concepts, the physics concept and the New Age concept?

**Saul-Paul Sirag:** Well, you have to make the point I just stated. But there's another point I want to make that I think is equally important. Remember, Newton didn't discover energy, smart as he was. All the people who were contemporary with him were smart too, and they didn't discover the notion of energy. One of the peculiar things about the notion of energy and one of the reasons that the idea of energy was discovered so late in physics is that it's invisible, it's a behind-the-scenes kind of thing, and . . .

**Comment:**[2] They just called it work. Work is force times distance. They had energy back then, it was just a different name.

**Saul-Paul Sirag:** Well, energy is related to work but it's different.[5]

**Psychologist:** When [Physicist C] was quoting Blake's equating energy with pure joy, we saw that Blake was using "energy" in the psychological sense before physicists came along and grabbed the word away from us.

**Saul-Paul Sirag:** Well, we used the word heat in a psychological sense before physicists gave precise notions of heat by inventing thermometers. But the point I want to make here is that the principle of the conservation of energy is interesting from the point of view that you're raising. Healers talk about putting energy into things. One thing that you have to realize is that we in physics use principles like conservation of energy to discover new forms of energy because we can use it as a bookkeeping criterion. If we do an experiment in a confined region, which means that we're able to keep track of all the energy flows, so to speak, and we find that our numbers just don't add up, that there's something missing, then we suspect that there's something going on in there that we haven't identified.

The best example of this that comes to mind is in radioactive decay. This is kind of like an alchemical change in which one type of atom changes, or decays, into another type of atom. What happens typically is that a fast electron, called a *beta particle,* that's measurable comes out. However, there's always a tiny mass discrepancy, and there's also a discrepancy in spin. That was our first clue that there might be some overlooked type of particle, which was proposed by Pauli—he and Fermi called it the neutrino—around 1930.

Now at that time, Bohr wasn't willing to countenance such a strange particle that would have no charge, no mass, but just a half unit of spin—that's it—and that would account for the energy going off. Instead, Bohr was willing to give up the principle of conservation of energy. He said that maybe on a subatomic level the principle of conservation of energy is just approximately obeyed. But most other physicists clung to the notion of conservation of energy. And by hanging on to that principle, they were able to deduce—not prove, mind you, just deduce—that there must be some other type of particle.

Now, it was more than 20 years after that—it wasn't until 1956—that the neutrino was actually shown to exist. So for 20 years there was a great deal of doubt as to whether the principle of conservation of energy even held at the quantum level or whether it was just a classic notion.

Now, the reason I'm bringing this up is that it may be that what New Age people are calling "energy" may in fact be some unusual kind of energy that we don't know about yet in ordinary physics. If that's the case then, there must be some kind of experiment we can do in which we do all of the bookkeeping on the energy flows involved, and lo and behold, there's a little bit missing. Now, chances are that would be a difficult kind of experiment. But I'm just thinking that in principle, if these people are using the word energy in some way that relates to the physics of energy, then that's the sort of thing one would expect in the long run, however long the long run is.

**Question:** [2] What can you say about the historical concept of the luminiferous ether with respect to energy fields—and healing—inasmuch as it may have some mass effect?

**Saul-Paul Sirag:** The luminiferous ether was invented by nineteenth-century physicists who established the wave theory of light. It got its more or less definitive form in Maxwell's equations. The ether was simply invented to answer the question of what is waving in a light wave, and in Maxwell's case, what is waving in the electromagnetic wave. The problem with Maxwell's luminiferous ether was that it had properties that were, to say the least, contradictory. But people lived with that because in physics, there are always conundrums going on. That was the great conundrum of the late nineteenth century, the luminiferous ether.

Then a crucial experiment was done by Michelson and Morley, who attempted to find out the velocity of the earth with respect to the luminiferous ether. Maxwell's equations implied that that was possible. In fact, Maxwell himself proposed the experiment—he was aware that that's what his equations implied. As you know, they came up with a negative result; that is to say, they came up with the result zero. Einstein explained that result by saying that there isn't any luminiferous ether. And Einstein explained the relation between electromagnetism and ordinary mechanics by the special theory of relativity.

Now, one might say that in quantum mechanics, a kind of ether has been reinvented, called the *quantum vacuum,* that has many properties of the old luminiferous ether and many new properties, properties that are magical in the quantum mechanical sense. For one thing, the quantum mechanical vacuum is exceedingly active. It's just seething with stuff going on, and we picture particles and fields coming in and out of the vacuum all the time. That's the big mystery of the late twentieth century, you might say, the quantum mechanical vacuum. It's playing the role, in a sense, that the luminiferous ether played in the nineteenth century, and nobody knows what the result is going to be. But some Einstein might come along and get rid of that too in some magical way, and that would undoubtedly create a profound change in physics. What that may have to do with psi and healing who knows?—but it's a fundamental thing.

**NOTES**

1. More mundane than the highly metaphysical discussion of reality in the first part of the panel discussion.

2. Unknown meeting attendee. Voice not recognized from audiotape.

3. In 1807, Thomas Young proposed the name energy for the older term *vis viva*— mass times velocity squared. However, "energy" was considered too disreputable a term by most physicists until the 1840s.

4. The four known types of forces are the electromagnetic, gravitational, weak atomic nuclear, and strong atomic nuclear.

5. The idea of *force times distance* as an independent concept called *work* (and other names) was introduced in the 1820s after "energy" was proposed for *mass times velocity squared* (1807). Cf. Thomas Kuhn, *The Essential Tension*. Chicago; 1977:84.

# 8

# Quantum Reality and Consciousness

*Nick Herbert*

Speculations concerning the origin of inner experience in humans and other beings have been few, vague, and superficial. They include the notion that mind is an "emergent property" of active neural nets,[1] or that mind is the "software" that manages the brain's unconscious "hardware." To these soft speculations I would like to add my own: the conjecture that mind is not a rare phenomenon associated with certain complex biological systems, but is everywhere, universal in nature, a fundamental quantum effect more akin to the mass and charge of the electron than to complicated computer operations.

The notion that consciousness might be a quantum effect is not new. In 1924, Alfred Lotka, one of the founders of modern theoretical biology, guessed that the then-new physics of the quantum might someday account for the phenomenon of human awareness.[2] Neurobiologist Sir John Eccles recently proposed that a nonmaterial mind gains control over the matter of the human brain by way of quantum mechanical acts performed on certain intrinsically inefficient neural synapses.[3] World-class mathematician John von Neumann[4] and Nobel laureate Eugene Wigner[5] claim that quantum theory is actually formally incomplete and that the least drastic way to make quantum theory mathematically consistent is to introduce consciousness as the necessary accomplice of every quantum jump. Despite its support by certain prominent physicists and biologists, no serious experimental program has yet been conceived, let alone carried out, to test the quantum consciousness hypothesis.

What is quantum theory, in a nutshell?[6] The oddest thing about quantum theory is that it describes the world differently, depending on whether you look at it or not. When you don't look, the theory treats objects not as real things, but as "vibratory possibilities," oscillating opportunities for something real to happen.

On the other hand, when an object is observed, it always looks ordinary, taking on just one of its previously numerous possibilities. During the act of observation, the quantum description shifts from a spread-out range of possible attributes (unlooked-at object) to single-valued actual attributes (looked-at object). This sudden observer-induced switch of descriptions is called the "collapse of the wave function" or simply the "quantum jump." The nature of the quantum jump is the biggest mystery in quantum physics: Does this abrupt shift in quantum description correspond to an actual change in the real world, or is it a mathematical fiction like the International Date Line, a purely conventional discontinuity? The quantum model of consciousness holds that quantum jumps are real and that all conscious beings live at some location where quantum possibility turns into actuality. Our subjective experiences consist of the feelings that accompany that quantum change in some part of our brains. In a sense, the business of consciousness is to actualize possibility. Our inner experience during each quantum jump is our reward for this job.

Half-baked attempts to explain consciousness, such as mind as software or mind as emergent property, do not take themselves seriously enough to confront the bare experimental facts, our most intimate database—how mind itself feels from the inside. One piece of suggestive evidence for a quantum model of mind is that our experience of ordinary sentience is somewhat congruent with what quantum theory says is happening during an observation. Looking inside, I do not feel like "software," whatever that might mean, but indeed like a shimmering center of ambiguous possibility around which more solid perceptions and ideas are continually precipitating. This rough match of internal feeling with external description could be utterly deceptive, but it at least shows that a quantum model of mind can begin to successfully confront the introspective evidence in a way no other mind models even attempt.

What other aspects of quantum theory besides the sensation of the quantum jump might we look for in human consciousness? Three features of quantum theory seemed so strange to Albert Einstein that he refused to accept them: they are randomness, thinglessness, and interconnectedness.

Quantum randomness means that the quantum jumps occur at random, with no discernible physical cause. The quantum consciousness assumption proposes that the causes of quantum jumps do indeed lie outside of physics. They are psychological in origin, the results of the inner intent of some immaterial mind. A key part of quantum consciousness research will be learning to distinguish conscious matter from unconscious matter by looking for deviations from ordinary quantum statistics. Conventional quantum theory represents the default statistics for unconscious matter. Minds are able to violate these statistics, usually unintentionally, in the same way that thoughtfully we can violate the English language statistics that loosely govern our speech. For instance, there is a novel, "Gadsby" by Ernest Vincent Wright, that does not contain a single instance of the letter "e."[7]

Quantum thinglessness refers to the state of a quantum system when it is not being observed. I described the unobserved state as a bundle of possibilities. But the real situation is much more ambiguous. Quantum possibilities are not well defined like dice possibilities, but depend on the measurement context. The quantum state is like a set of blank dice whose faces are assigned only after the gambler has decided which game he wants to play. Depending on the game chosen, the blank dice will take on numbered faces, playing-card faces, or colored faces, just as a quantum system takes on momentum or position possibilities, depending on the measuring instrument used to investigate it. Because of their sensitivities to the measurement context, quantum systems possess a deeper kind of uncertainty than that of classical systems. Quantum systems are not only random like dice but, unlike dice, they do not even know what game they are playing until the observer makes that choice for them.

If consciousness is a quantum effect, we might expect it to possess this double level of uncertainty also, a deeper form of doubt than simple ignorance concerning which preexistent possibility might manifest. Soviet physicist Yuri Orlov mathematically described one possible model of a type of "deep doubt" that might arise in a quantum kind of mind.[8] Given a quantum situation with only two possible outcomes, such as the polarization attribute of light, the observer's freedom to choose a different measurement context expands the number of conceivable measurement outcomes to a twofold infinity of polarization pairs. Instead of a simple yes-or-no situation, the range of doubt concerning a photon's polarization spreads out onto the surface of a sphere. Orlov proposes that ordinary two-valued human uncertainties—"Did I see a 'wolf' or a bundle of 'wool' in the twilight?"—may, under some circumstances, be similarly expanded into a spherical form of ignorance. So far, Orlov's model of mind (smuggled out of a Soviet prison camp) has made no connection with the way humans actually experience the ambiguous background out of which clear choices emerge and present themselves to the will.

Quantum connectedness is also a more complex type of interaction than its classical counterpart. A classical connection must be "local," that is, mediated by fields that fall off with distance and transmit forces at light speed or slower. Quantum connections, on the other hand, are unmediated, unmitigated (no degradation with distance), and immediate (faster than light). The quantum connection, alas, is also invisible: it never shows up as a statistical change in the pattern of many quantum jumps but acts only on the level of individual jumps. Any superluminal message sent via the quantum connection from one person to another cannot be deciphered by its human recipient because it is scrambled by quantum randomness, masked by an unbreakable code to which only Nature and her subquantal sentient representatives hold the key. Although this superluminal linkage can never be directly observed, the real presence of the quantum connection has been verified in an indirect but undeniable way by way of Bell's theorem and the associated Clauser-Aspect experiments.[9] Because of its statistical invisibility, this peculiar connection would not be of much use in explaining telepathy—direct mind-to-mind transmission of statistically stable patterns. But it might account for certain far-flung harmonies between like-minded people, such as the remarkable concordance in the behaviors of identical twins raised apart[10] or, manifesting as lucky, one-of-a-kind events, create "fortunate coincidences" that put us in touch with people, ideas, and things helpful to our development.

The quantum theory of mind is one tentative approach to the solution of the mind–body problem. It suggests that the essence of subjectivity is the intentional transformation of deeply ambiguous possibilities into concrete actualities. Furthermore, this activity, although conditioned by physical laws, does not arise from physical causes: Our choices are truly free, from physical determinism at least. In addition, our minds may be connected by inner nontelepathic links that coordinate human action into a larger harmony than that produced by external forces.

## NOTES

1. Minsky M. *Society of Mind*. New York: Simon & Schuster; 1985.

2. Lotka A. *Elements of Mathematical Biology*. New York: Dover reprint; 1956.

3. Eccles JC. Do mental events cause neural events analogously to the probability fields of quantum mechanics? *Proceedings of the Royal Society*. 1986;227B:411.

4. von Neumann J. *Mathematical Foundations of Quantum Mechanics*. Princeton, NJ: Princeton University Press; 1955.

5. Wigner E. *Symmetries and Reflections*. Bloomington: University of Indiana; 1967.

6. Herbert N. *Quantum Reality: Beyond the New Physics*. New York: Doubleday; 1985.

7. Wright EV. *Gadsby: A Story of Over 50,000 Words Without Using the Letter "E"*. Wetzel Publishing Co; 1939.

8. Orlov YF. The wave logic of consciousness: A hypothesis. *International Journal of Theoretical Physics*. 1982;21:37.

9. Herbert N. *Faster Than Light: Superluminal Loopholes in Physics*. New York: New American Library; 1988.

10. Tellegen A, Lykken DT, Bouchard TJ, Jr. Personality similarity in twins reared apart and together. *Journal Personality and Social Psychology*. 1988;54:1031.

# 9

## Time, Consciousness, and Psi

*Jean E. Burns*

One might suppose that the conscious experience of time can be described solely in terms of properties of the physical world. Indeed, a great deal of empirical data in neurophysiology demonstrates a dependence of the content of conscious experience on encoding in the brain.[1] And a great deal of empirical data in psychophysics demonstrates that the content of visual, auditory, and other sensory experience has a correspondence with the physical quantities it represents.[2] Furthermore, psychophysical experiments show that our experience of time intervals is dependent on encoding in the brain. For instance, for very short time intervals, a subject may know that two events have occurred but be unable to specify which came first; thus we are limited in temporal discrimination by encoding in the brain.[3]

Time in the physical world has two aspects, clock time and the arrow of time, which are not described in the same way by physical laws. Therefore, if we are to ask what the relation is between the conscious experience of time and physical time, we should ask this question with respect to each aspect of physical time.

To explore this relation, a comparison must be made between the description of conscious experience and the description of the physical world (i.e., physical laws). We should note that not all qualities characteristic of conscious experience correspond to known physical properties. For instance, the quality of awareness is fundamental to conscious experience, yet this quality does not appear in any known physical law. Therefore, the conscious experience of time and time in the physical world do not necessarily correspond in all respects.

In making a distinction between the description of consciousness and the description of the physical world, no ontological relation, such as physicalism or dualism, is implied herein. Physicalism holds that consciousness arises out of the physical world, and a quality of consciousness that is different from known qualities of the physical world can be described as *emergent*.[4] Dualism holds that consciousness is an independent realm, and a quality of consciousness that is different from known qualities of the physical world is described as *independent*. There is no known empirical way, however, to distinguish between an emergent quality and an independent quality.[5]

To make a comparison between the conscious experience of time and its physical aspects, we first describe physical time, in both its aspects. We will see that the fundamental nature of the arrow of time is not well understood and discuss some competing hypotheses about its nature. We will then discuss the relation between the conscious experience of time and physical time. We will see that our experience of the relative duration of time and of the temporal ordering of events probably derives from encoding in the brain and corresponds to clock time in the physical world. The hypothesis that consciousness can do processing independently of the brain, made in a number of recent models of consciousness, suggests that our understanding of the arrow of time should be broadened.[6] Finally, we will discuss the relation of psi to the arrow of time; we will see that data in parapsychology may have profound implications for our understanding of the arrow of time.

## NATURE OF TIME IN THE PHYSICAL WORLD

In the physical world, time intervals can be described by readings on a clock, and in this respect, the description of time is fairly simple. The conception of time in the physical world is made more complicated by the time reversibility of the dynamical laws that describe physical processes, the block universe of relativity, and the nature of irreversible processes.

### Time Reversibility of the Dynamical Laws of Physics

The state of a system in the physical world can be described by dynamical laws (classical or quantum mechanical), with time occurring as a parameter in these laws. All the dynamical equations of physics are time reversible; this means that for a given trajectory that is a solution to a dynamical equation, the equation is satisfied, regardless of the direction in which the particle travels the trajectory. For instance, a planet can travel around the sun in either direction.

The fact that the dynamical equations are time reversible also could be interpreted to mean that a particle can traverse a dynamical trajectory either forward or backward in time. We suppose that particles travel only forward in time because backward travel is contrary to common experience, not because this idea is incompatible with the dynamical laws.

If we suppose, in accord with common experience, that there is an arrow of time, that is, all physical processes move forward in time, the dynamic laws provide a simple concept of clock time: It specifies the number of times a periodic cycle, such as the swinging of a pendulum or the orbiting of a planet, has been completed, and thereby measures the duration of time between different events. The concept of clock time is made more complicated by considerations from relativity.

### Block Universe of Relativity

In relativity, the dimension of time occurs as a geometric parameter, similar to spatial dimensions, and sometimes the physical world described by relativity is called the *block universe*. Two sorts of separations between events in space-time can occur: those that are time-like and those that are space-like. Two events that have a time-like separation can always be viewed from a suitable reference frame as taking place at the same spatial location. Alternatively, this idea can be expressed by saying that events that occur in the history of any individual object will always have a unique ordering in time, such that the sequence of events occurring to that object will be the same in any reference frame. For that reason, the history of an object can be viewed as being on a "worldline" in four-dimensional spacetime.

On the other hand, if space-time events are so far separated spatially that light, which travels at a finite velocity, cannot travel from one event to another in the time between the events, the events have a space-like separation, and there is no unique temporal ordering between them. Therefore, according to the laws of relativity, it is not possible to classify all events as happening either before or after any given reference event.

Thus the time-reversible dynamical equations and relativity together describe a universe that is in a state of being; that is, the states of its constituent particles are specified at each point of time, and no deviations from these specified states are allowed. Even a random process can be represented as a series of predetermined events on a worldline in such a universe. This view is not consistent with the idea that the universe as a whole exists at a particular time, Now, and is evolving from present moment to present moment. For that reason, Einstein, in letters to friends, wrote: "For us who are convinced physicists, the distinction between past, present, and future is only an illusion, however persistent," and "You have to accept the idea that subjective time with its emphasis on the now has no objective meaning."[7]

In an alternative view, Stapp has proposed that the physical world is characterized by two kinds of time: Einstein time and process time. Einstein time is the time part of the space-time continuum, and process time describes events in a uniquely ordered sequence.[8] To be compatible with the relativistic restriction that events with space-like separations cannot have a unique temporal ordering, the theory provides that an ordered sequence of events can only occur in a bounded region of spacetime. Thus, as Stapp described it, "the actual is represented not by an advancing, infinitely thin slice through the spacetime continuum, but rather by a sequence of actual becomings, each of which refers to a bounded space-time region."

In another alternative view, Moon, Spencer, and Moon have proposed a modification of special relativity in which universal time can occur (i.e., events on different worldlines can evolve simultaneously).[9] Relativity theory as developed by Einstein holds that the velocity of light is the same in each reference frame. Moon, Spencer, and Moon, in analyzing the possible conditions in which universal time could occur, have shown that only one postulate about the velocity of light can predict the possibility of universal time for all reference frames in arbitrary translational motion; in this postulate, the velocity of light depends on the velocity of the source. They pointed out that binary star data, which was considered to have established the validity of Einstein's postulate, is equally well explained by their formulation.

### Arrow of Time

Because the dynamical laws of physics are time reversible, a molecular system cannot move toward any preferred microscopic state. Everyday experience, however, shows that many physical processes do show a preferred direction: For instance, heat transfers from hot to cold, but not the reverse; at a given temperature and pressure, chemical reactions proceed in a given direction; if an egg is dropped, it breaks, but a broken egg does not spontaneously recombine. Processes such as the above can serve to define an arrow of time. Because such processes are inconsistent with the dynamical equations, there has been a continuing discussion in physics during the past century over their fundamental nature. We will discuss time asymmetric processes with respect to molecular interactions, the collapse of the quantum mechanical wave function, the expansion of the universe, the decay of the neutral K meson, and quantum randomness. We will see that, despite numerous attempts to understand the arrow of time, there is no consensus as to its fundamental nature.

### Molecular Interactions

Processes that involve molecular interactions can be readily observed, on the macroscopic level, to move toward an equilibrium state. Thus one would expect that, using kinetic theory, it would be possible to model molecular action on the microscopic level, and average over this action to describe irreversible processes (those that take place in only one direction) on a macroscopic level. Indeed, an equation derived by Ludwig Boltzmann more than 100 years ago often is used for this purpose; however, the Boltzmann equation includes an ad hoc term, the "collision term," and the modeling of irreversible processes comes from this term. Many attempts have been made over the years to resolve the question of what the collision term represents. As Davies has reviewed, the hypothesis that under repeated collisions, the velocities of molecules are reshuffled at random, together with some other simple assumptions, can be used to derive a detailed expression for the microscopic collision term.[10] An averaging shows that on the macroscopic level, a function (the H function) derived from the latter expression is irreversible. The time symmetry of this function is not compatible with time reversibility, and one of the assumptions made in deriving it presupposes that molecular states after collision are different than before collision, and hence presupposes irreversibility.[10]

As Zeh has reviewed, attempts have been made not only in kinetic theory, but also in statistical mechanics to find the relation between microscopic processes and irreversible macroscopic processes.[11] In statistical mechanics, a quantity is averaged over all possible microscopic configurations, given macroscopic constraints on the system (such as the total energy). Even in statistical mechanics, the H function will not show irreversibility unless a "coarse-grained" average, which takes into account only macroscopically available information instead of complete information about microscopic states, is used.[11] Sometimes irreversibility is described as a phenomenon that is statistical and solely macroscopic in nature: Under repeated collisions, particles change energy and momentum and thus occupy many microscopic states, and an equilibrium state can be described as the most probable macroscopic state (the macroscopic state that corresponds to the most microscopic states). Thus, using the results of the "coarse-grained" average, sometimes irreversibility is characterized as a phenomenon in which processes are reversible on a microscopic level, but tend to their most probable state. The view that irreversibility is solely a macroscopic phenomenon is unsatisfactory in that it provides no explanation as to how a macroscopic process that lacks time symmetry can derive from microscopic processes that are symmetric in time (this point is called Loschmidt's objection). Also, we have no explanation as to why irreversibility cannot be derived from ordinary averaging, but only from averaging in which information about the system is left out.

## Quantum Mechanics and the Collapse of the Wave Function

Zeh, in examining the possibility that irreversibility has a quantum mechanical origin, has noted that quantum statistical mechanics has an inherent difference from classical statistical mechanics because a quantum system contains correlations between its parts, and is, therefore, nonlocal, whereas a classical system is inherently local.[11] Nevertheless, as Zeh has discussed, in quantum statistical mechanics, as in classical statistical mechanics, an irreversible process cannot be described by averaging over a system that follows time-reversible dynamical laws, but it can be predicted for macroscopic variables if one does not take into account the full microscopic description.

An alternative possibility is that the arrow of time might be associated with collapse of the quantum mechanical wave function. This "collapse" can be described in the following way: There is a difference in description of events between that given in quantum mechanics and that of ordinary reality. In quantum mechanics, events are described in terms of a wave function that describes mutually exclusive possibilities. Ordinary reality is characterized by definite events. Although there is no formal resolution of this discrepancy in descriptions, it usually is supposed that a quantum system makes a transition to a definite state by "collapse" of the wave function.[12]

Zeh has proposed that collapse of a wave function that describes macroscopic variables is an irreversible process.[11] He showed that collisions of very low energy photons with a system would destroy the quantum correlations of the system (because of the lack of correlation of the photons) and thus could be viewed as causing continuous collapse of the wave function; he also showed that such interactions would be associated with a net increase in entropy. (Irreversible processes are characterized by an increase in entropy; we will discuss entropy in more detail in another section.)

Zeh has noted that opinions differ as to whether collapse of the wave function is an irreversible process, associated with an increase of entropy, or is characterized by a gain of information, associated with a decrease in entropy.[11] Walker[13] and Goswami[14] have proposed that collapse of the wave function is not a physical process, but is produced by the action of consciousness, and they also disagree on the latter point: Goswami has proposed that collapse produces irreversibility, whereas Walker has held that it is associated with a gain of information to the physical system involved.

### Expansion of the Universe

If the universe is assumed to be homogeneous on a large scale and to be in uniform expansion from an initial point event (the big bang), an observer in a comoving reference frame (a frame that moves with the expansion) can associate events with the sequence of states that the universe passes through.[10] The time scale defined by the expansion, called *cosmic time,* can be viewed as no more than a parameter in the block universe. If for all events with a space-like separation an absolute temporal ordering is specified to be the ordering determined by the comoving frames, then cosmic time could be associated with irreversibility. Thus it has been proposed that cosmic time provides the master arrow that determines the direction of all other time asymmetrical processes.[11] Because no molecular processes are completely isolated from cosmological-related processes such as the production of energy at the center of stars, the arrow of time for all such processes could be linked to the cosmic arrow.[11]

The equations of general relativity that describe the expansion of the universe are time symmetric, although the universe could expand indefinitely or recontract, depending on the curvature of space.[10] Thus if the universe were completely homogeneous, expansion could not lead to thermodynamic nonequilibrium. If a master arrow is associated with expansion, a seed of inhomogeneity must have been present from the beginning, or else a spontaneous breaking of the symmetries of homogeneity and time isotropy must occur at later times.[11]

With regard to the latter point, Hawking has proposed that the universe can be described by two kinds of times: ordinary time and *imaginary time*.[15] By doing a quantum mechanical analysis (a sum over histories) with imaginary time, he showed that if the early universe had no more inhomogeneity than the minimum allowed by the uncertainty principle, amplification of this initial fluctuation could account for all the inhomogeneity of the present time. Hawking's imaginary time was constructed as a mathematical artifice to solve a computational problem;[15] it is akin to Einstein time and is not proposed to be related to irreversibility. Because a master arrow must be associated with inhomogeneity in the universe, the latter result suggests that the arrow of time might be intrinsically associated with quantum uncertainty.

### Decay of the Neutral K Meson

Only a single exception is known to the rule that the dynamic laws are time symmetric, and this is one of the decay modes of the neutral K meson, also called the K-zero meson. This particle is only produced at high energies, and it is unstable, with a short lifetime. Thus there are probably few of these particles in the universe, and consequently they probably interact very little with the rest of the matter in the universe. It is not known how or whether this decay mode might be related to the arrow of time associated with ordinary physical processes.

### Being Versus Becoming

A system in which irreversible processes take place can be described by an entropy function, that is, a function that increases monotonically in time and specifies an equilibrium (attractor) state.[16] It is known that the evolution of any dynamical system along a well-defined trajectory, such as the orbiting of a planet around the sun, has zero entropy change. Thus Prigogine has proposed that dynamical systems may not always have well-defined trajectories.[16] He has further proposed that trajectory and entropy are complementary quantum mechanical qualities, with a detailed formulation that defines entropy as a quantum mechanical operator.

Prigogine has characterized the states associated with these complementary qualities as *being,* the state in which the trajectory of a system is known, and *becoming,* the state in which the evolution of the system is not predetermined.[16] Prigogine's formulation produces the conclusion that a system can be described by two sorts of time: the clock time of the dynamical equations and *internal time,* a quantum mechanical operator whose eigenfunctions describe the system at a sequence of times, from the far past to the distant future, and whose eigenvalues specify the age of the system.[16] (Eigenfunctions and eigenvalues are mathematical functions and quantities, respectively, that describe quantum mechanical states.) The reversible aspect of a system is described by all eigenfunctions of the internal time, but the contribution of these eigenfunctions to the irreversible aspect is modified by a function that decreases monotonically from 1 in the far past to 0 in the distant future.[17] Thus the irreversible aspect of a system contains contributions from the past and the nearby future, but no contributions from the distant future.[17]

As we noted earlier, one view of molecular irreversibility holds that it is a macroscopic phenomenon only, which occurs as a consequence of a "coarse-grained average" used in making observations of a system, although objections can be made to this view. Prigogine differs from this view by holding that randomness occurs at a microscopic level.[16,17] He has pointed out that many dynamical systems, including any three-body system, are characterized by weak stability, a condition in which the trajectories of neighboring points diverge by arbitrarily large distances after sufficient time, and he has proposed that irreversibility is produced by such diverging trajectories. Even in such a system, any given trajectory is deterministic, so irreversibility is still not accounted for.

### Quantum Randomness

To understand the possible relation between quantum randomness and the arrow of time, we should first discuss the uncertainty principle. In quantum mechanics, a particle does not have definite attributes, but rather has a collection of possible, mutually inconsistent attributes; for instance, it might have a fairly definite position, but a spectrum of possible momentum values. The particle only attains definite attributes on "measurement" (also described as "collapse of the wave function"), but the nature of this measurement process is not understood.[12] And the uncertainty principle places a limitation on how well certain attributes, such as position and momentum, can be simultaneously known.

It is known that a probabilistic process (i.e., a process in which information about past history is not preserved) produces an increase in entropy.[17] Therefore, it is possible that irreversibility derives from probabilistic processes at the microscopic level. The dynamical laws do not describe such processes. If quantum uncertainty not only limits our knowledge about a system, but also introduces randomness into it, then irreversible processes could be produced by the cumulative effect of quantum uncertainty in molecular collisions.

The latter idea represents an extension of the usual view of the uncertainty principle. This hypothesis answers a number of questions that have come up in the various attempts to derive irreversibility from the dynamical laws. For instance, as we have seen, irreversibility can be explained in kinetic theory by making the assumption that molecular velocities are reshuffled at random under collision. This assumption is not consistent with the dynamical laws, but it is consistent with the hypothesis that quantum uncertainty produces random change during collisions. Similarly, in both quantum and classical statistical mechanics, irreversibility can be explained by using an average in which information about microscopic trajectories is dropped; in a random process, information about past history is in fact lost. This idea also is consistent with the idea that the arrow of time is associated with expansion of the universe through inhomogeneities produced by quantum uncertainty. We will return to the hypothesis that irreversibility is associated with quantum randomness in our discussion of parapsychological data.

## TIME AND CONSCIOUSNESS

The conscious experience of time measured in psychophysical experiments has to do with duration of time as measured by a clock rather than with irreversible processes. Thus it seems reasonable to suppose that our experience of time duration derives from clock time in the physical world by way of encoding in the brain.

It is true that the subjective experience of time duration can be expanded, such that time appears to slow down. An expansion effect also can be seen in other sensory experiences. For instance, in comparing colors, one ordinarily compares one category of color with another: this color is red and the other is blue. But in comparing different shades of blue, say, one can become aware of many shades of blue, all slightly different from one another. In this respect, an expansion in scale is not unique to time. So even with respect to the slowing down of time, it is reasonable to suppose that our experience of time duration is associated with encoding in the brain and derives from clock time in the physical world.

### Consciousness and the Second Law of Thermodynamics

The second law of thermodynamics has several equivalent formulations. Basically, it states that irreversible processes can be described by an entropy function. As we noted earlier, an entropy function increases monotonically in time and specifies an attractor (equilibrium) state. Alternatively, entropy can be described in terms of the degree of disorder of the components of a system, with the equilibrium state corresponding to maximum disorder.[16] At the molecular level, entropy describes the degree of randomness in the distribution of positions and velocities of the molecules in the system, and the equilibrium state corresponds to the maximum disorder possible for given external constraints such as temperature and pressure. The second law was originally formulated for systems near equilibrium. It can be readily observed that any physical system, even if far from equilibrium, will tend toward an attractor state. For instance, at a given temperature and pressure, a chemical system, even if far from equilibrium, will proceed in a definite direction toward an attractor state. Thus the second law is now used in descriptions of systems far from equilibrium.[16]

The reason for discussing the second law at this point is that a number of researchers have proposed that consciousness can do processing independently of the brain.[6] The types of processing proposed are free will and holistic information processing; free will would make a selection from alternative programs in the brain, and holistic information processing would correlate, modify, or activate encoding in the brain.[6] Such independent processing could occur even if all the content of conscious experience is encoded in the brain.[6] It has been shown by several researchers that independent processing by consciousness violates the second law of thermodynamics.[6]

Reasoning for the above conclusion can be given as follows: Although the brain is an open system, far from equilibrium, physical processes will nevertheless tend toward their attractor states. If an independent process is to affect encoding in the brain, through activation or modification, then some physical process in the brain must move in a different direction from that in which it would otherwise have gone. Thus the second law must be violated.[18] Following a somewhat different line of reasoning, Jahn and Dunne have pointed out that holistic information processing must contradict the second law because such processing can organize information.[19]

Thus if independent processing exists, the state of becoming described by Prigogine must be associated both with increasing disorder through processes in the physical world and with increasing order through processing by consciousness. Although the decrease in entropy associated with the latter action is, in principle, measurable, it would probably be small and not in reach of current measurement. If it were not for data in parapsychology, we would have to consider the possibility of independent processing by consciousness as pure speculation. Such data, however, can provide an important means for exploration of the nature of becoming and the arrow of time.

## PSI AND TIME

The various phenomena of extrasensory perception (remote viewing, telepathy, precognition, and so on) violate the second law of thermodynamics because they consist of the introduction of order (information) where it did not previously exist. With regard to precognition, Prigogine's theory predicts that the description of an object in its aspect of becoming depends on its entire past and the near future, but not the distant future. Some studies suggest that precognition falls off with increasing time lapse between the prediction and the event; not all researchers agree that such attenuation occurs.[20] Thus not enough is known about precognition to provide any evidence relevant to the theory above.

As has been discussed by several researchers, psychokinesis (PK) also violates the second law.[18,19,21,22] (The arguments are similar to those given above for consciousness.) The results of a study by Rauscher of material (metals and crystals) that was bent or broken by PK is consistent with this view.[23] The material showed more movement along crystal boundary dislocations, compared with that bent or broken in a comparable way by normal means, and the microstructure of the material subject to PK appeared to be annealed. PK appeared to release stress in the material and to increase the ordered crystal pattern array.

An analysis by Walker[24] of some PK experiments is highly relevant to hypotheses about the nature of irreversibility. Psi is independent of physical conditions with respect to the type of physical substance, type of physical process, and physical complexity involved.[25,26] Yet experiments in which cubes tumbled down an incline showed that PK-induced deviation is dependent on the material and design (solid or hollow) of the cubes.[27] Walker assumed that the initial quantum uncertainties in position and angular orientation of a cube were amplified on each successive bounce of the cube, in the same way that any ordinary (macroscopic) deviations would be amplified in a collision. The initial uncertainties are exceedingly small but depend in a known way on the total mass and the density distribution of the cube. Walker showed that the initial uncertainties will increase exponentially with the number of bounces and reach a macroscopic size fairly quickly, and he assumed that PK can act to order this uncertainty in a certain direction. Walker's predictions of deviations for cubes of different materials and design closely match the experimental results.

The experiments on which Walker's analysis was based were performed more than thirty years ago and should be carried out with more modern techniques to confirm the experimental results. Walker's results suggest that PK can order the randomness associated with quantum uncertainty. Because such an ordering process would be a counterpart of irreversibility (which produces disorder), these results also suggest that irreversibility and the arrow of time are connected with quantum randomness.

## SUMMARY AND CONCLUSIONS

To describe time in the physical world, one must describe not only clock time, which is associated with the time-reversible dynamic laws and the block universe of relativity, but also the arrow of time, which is associated with irreversible processes and the second law of thermodynamics. The physical nature of the arrow of time is not understood, and it is not known whether irreversible processes are macroscopic or microscopic.

It is likely that clock time is common to consciousness and the physical world. Independent processing by consciousness inherently produces order in the physical world, whereas irreversible processes produce disorder; thus these contribute to becoming in different ways.

Psi, like independent processing by consciousness, violates the second law of thermodynamics, and in this respect, it follows properties of consciousness rather than those of the physical world. Thus data about psi can be an important tool in exploring the nature of consciousness and the arrow of time. In particular, the dependence of PK-induced deviations on the material and design of tumbling cubes can be explained in terms of an ordering of quantum randomness. This result implies that PK and irreversible processes are counterparts, one producing order and the other disorder, and thereby suggests that irreversible processes occur at a microscopic level and that the arrow of time is connected with quantum randomness.

## NOTES

1. Blakemore C. *Mechanics of the Mind*. New York: Cambridge University Press; 1977.

2. Gescheider GA. *Psychophysics: Method, Theory and Application*. Hillsdale, NJ: Lawrence Erlbaum; 1985.

3. Uttal WR. *The Psychobiology of Mind*. Hillsdale, NJ: Erlbaum Associates; 1978:420.

4. Gregory RL. *Mind in Science: A History of Explanations in Psychology and Physics*. New York: Cambridge University Press; 1981.

5. Burns J. Contemporary models of consciousness: Part I. *Journal of Mind and Behavior*. 1990;11:153–172.

6. Burns J. Contemporary models of consciousness: Part II. *Journal of Mind and Behavior*. 1991;12:407–420.

7. Prigogine I. *From Being to Becoming*. New York: WH Freeman; 1980:203.

8. Stapp HP. Einstein time and process time. In: Griffin DR, ed. *Physics and the Ultimate Significance of Time*. Albany: State University of New York Press; 1986:264–270.

9. Moon P, Spencer DE, Moon EE. Universal time and the velocity of light. *Physics Essays*. 1989;2:368–374.

10. Davies PCW. *The Physics of Time Asymmetry*. Berkeley: University of California Press; 1974.

11. Zeh H-D. *The Physical Basis of the Direction of Time*. New York: Springer-Verlag; 1989.

12. Herbert N. *Quantum Reality*. New York: Doubleday; 1985.

13. Walker EH. The quantum theory of psi phenomena. *Psychoenergetic Systems*. 1979;3:259–299.

14. Goswami A. The idealistic interpretation of quantum mechanics. *Physics Essays*. 1989;2:385–400.

15. Hawking SW. *A Brief History of Time*. New York: Bantam Books; 1988.

16. Prigogine I. *From Being to Becoming*. New York: WH Freeman; 1980.

17. Prigogine I. Irreversibility and space-time structure. In: Griffin DR, ed. *Physics*

*and the Ultimate Significance of Time*. Albany: State University of New York Press; 1986:232–250.

18. Burns J. Consciousness and psi. *Psi Research*. 1986;5(1/2):166–205.

19. Jahn RG, Dunne BJ. *Margins of Reality*. New York: Harcourt Brace Jovanovich; 1987.

20. Stokes DM. Theoretical parapsychology. In: Krippner S, ed. *Advances in Parapsychological Research, Volume 5*. Jefferson, NC: McFarland; 1987:77–189.

21. Mattuck RD, Walker EH. The action of consciousness on matter. In: Puharich A, ed. *The Iceland Papers*. Amherst, WI: Essentia Research Associates; 1979:112–159.

22. Rush JH. Physical aspects of psi phenomena. In: Schmeidler GR, ed. *Parapsychology: Its Relation to Physics, Biology, Psychology, and Psychiatry*. Metuchen, NJ: Scarecrow Press; 1976.

23. Rauscher EA. The physics of psi phenomena in space and time: Part I: Major principles of physics, psychic phenomena and some physical models. *Psi Research*. 1983;2(2):64–88.

24. Walker EH. Foundations of paraphysical and parapsychological phenomena. In: Oteri L, ed. *Quantum Physics and Parapsychology*. New York: Parapsychology Foundation; 1975:1–53.

25. Burns J. Current hypotheses about the nature of the mind-brain relationship and their relationship to findings in parapsychology. *Proceedings of the LE Rhine Centenary Conference*. New York: Praeger; 1992 (in press).

26. Kennedy JE. The role of task complexity in PK: A review. *Journal of Parapsychology*. 1978;42:89–122.

27. Forwald H. An experimental study suggesting a relationship between psychokinesis and nuclear conditions of matter. *Journal of Parapsychology*. 1959;23:97.

# IV _____

# MATHEMATICAL MODELS

In the two chapters that follow, Saul-Paul Sirag and Elizabeth Rauscher summarize several features of their complex cosmological theories and relate their models to the properties of consciousness. The models require the existence, at least mathematically, of a hyperspace of many more dimensions than the three we experience in the ordinary physical world. The advanced technical level of the chapters should not obscure their profound implications for how psi phenomena may be interpreted in the current language of physics.

The psychological ramifications of the two theories may be viewed as analogous to the allegory in Edwin Abbott's Victorian classic *Flatland*. In this evocative novelette, Abbott satirizes the narrow-minded perspectives of his time and draws associations between the ignorance of Flatlanders and the scientific dogmatism, religious parochialism, and prejudices of unexamined experience in his own society.

Flatland is a two-dimensional world whose inhabitants are plane figures: lines, polygons, and circles. Flatlanders have experience only of the two-dimensional plane of their known universe, and therefore cannot conceive of up or down.

The protagonist and narrator of the story, A. Square, is the first in his society to peek into worlds of other than two dimensions. First, he has a dream about a world with one dimension in which he tries to convince its king of the existence of the real world, Square's world, of two dimensions.

The next day, as Square relaxes at home, a supernatural event takes place: a circle of growing diameter spreads across the floor. Shortly he is to understand that this miraculous occurrence is caused by Lord Sphere, descending from the third dimension, who manifests in Flatland in the only way possible: as a cross-sectional representation of his larger self. Sphere appeals to Square to envision the extrapolation of the circle that the latter can see to the invisible part in the higher dimension.

Square vehemently rejects the possibility of a third dimension, and Sphere becomes increasingly frustrated. Effectively forced to perform a more tangible miracle, Sphere invades Square's cupboard from the up dimension that Square cannot see and removes an object. Square sees that the doors to his two-dimensional cupboard have remained locked the entire time, yet Sphere reappears in another part of the room clutching the displaced object. With the experience of this demonstration, Square is compelled to accept the existence of the higher dimension, which he can yet barely comprehend or imagine. Square eventually is ridiculed and imprisoned for trying to convince the authorities of Flatland of the existence of the higher dimensional space he has experienced.

The parallels between "miracles" in Flatland and so-called psychic phenomena in our universe are quite apparent. For many years, field theories of psi predominated, particularly in the former Soviet Union, where parapsychologists favored bioplasmic energy models. However, psi experiments in Faraday cages, which shield most of the electromagnetic spectrum, and those using time and distance as variables suggest that psi does not behave like the known energy fields of electromagnetism, strong and weak nuclear forces, and gravity. There seems to be no degradation of the signal with distance (certainly nothing like an inverse square relation) or with elapses of long periods of time.

In Flatland, the inhabitants must use time to view objects across space. To view superimposed objects in a row, or even to read a word, a Flatlander must crawl the perimeter from one object or letter to the next. The idea of viewing sequential objects simultaneously or of seeing all the letters in a word or of viewing a farther object before a nearer object is out of the question. Yet for a creature with a bird's-eye view in 3-space, whole words and long arrays of objects are visible "all at once." It seems that in higher-dimensional space, time has a different meaning than in lower-dimensional spaces. In *Flatland*, Lord Sphere pokes a finger down from 3-space onto Square's intestines, another miracle, as Flatlanders cannot see or touch the inside of their own bodies. Square feels the effect on his gut but cannot see from whence it came. Would Lord Sphere be considered a psychic surgeon in Flatland?

Thus geometrical or hyperspace theories of consciousness, by analogy to Flatland, offer attractive models for psi events. A key assumption under this reasoning is that linear, unidirectional time as we experience it—going from Monday to Tuesday or from one letter to the next in Flatland—is an illusion. In fact, the entire universe exists all at once in all its actualized and probable manifestations. Event A may be experienced ten years before event B in 3-space. But in the curled-up dimensions of a hyperspace filled with all possible events, Event A may be short-circuited to Event B such that B may be experienced before A.[1]

In his introduction to Flatland, A. K. Dewdney, says: "Abbott made of the Flatlanders' ignorance a metaphor suggesting that we solid folk are no better off when it comes to higher realities. . . . We, like the Flatlanders, cringe before the possibility of ascent. . . . The physical dimension embraces Flatland and all of its inhabitants. The metaphysical dimension embraces the world 'above' Flatland both in its implied relationship to the Flatlanders and in the symbolic content of that relationship for us."[2]

Of Lord Sphere's appearance in Square's plane, Dewdney says, "We recall how sages and divines from all spiritual traditions—including Christianity—have reported encounters with angelic or 'higher' beings which appeared out of nowhere."

And according to Dewdney,

Abbott took a divinity degree at Cambridge, was a devout clergyman and staunch supporter of the established church, taking as his special role the defense of the church against all forms of irrationality and superstition. A great admirer of Sir Francis Bacon and the enquiring rational mind which he exemplified, Abbott sought a complete reconciliation and harmony between his scientific convictions and his religious faith. There are hints among his many religious writings that he saw himself in an almost prophetic role as an exemplar of a new faith which had no dependence on "credulity." In [many] books Abbott tells us what must be taken on faith and what must be explained in Christianity. Again and again he attacks miracles as illusions or false reports and attempts to replace a belief in miracles by a faith in the supernatural, a second category which to most readers appears hardly distinct from the first. Yet for Abbott, the Supernatural means that which is both "obvious" and "obviously above" nature. . . . Flatland may well be Abbott's attempt to make the Supernatural credible (if not exactly explainable in any strict sense) as a kind of higher-dimensional influence.

Rauscher was, to her knowledge, the first to propose a hyperdimensional mathematical model of consciousness, in particular the psi function. The model proceeded from her earlier work in 1964 on multidimensional cosmological models and was further developed in 1974. In 1978, she met Ceon Ramon at the Institute for Applied Physiology, Astronomy, and Medicine, She credits Ramon with invaluable contributions to the current form of this theory.

It is interesting to note that Sirag, like Abbott, comes from a religious background, having been born the son of Christian missionaries in Borneo. Although his parents had hoped he, whom they named Paul, would follow them into the ministry, the self-rechristened Saul-Paul pursued his calling in physics. In this mission, Sirag, like Abbott, has always attempted to syncretize the universal human need to satisfy a rational curiosity about the nature of things with the need to experience the transcendence of that reality. Both science and religion promise to achieve this syncretism, but neither succeeds.

Ultimately, Sirag and Rauscher, like Dewdney, citing Roger Penrose, ask, "What is the relationship between the laws of our universe and the fact that it exists? . . . Given its laws, does it exist because in some mathematical sense it must, or does it exist as the creation of some 'outside' agency?" If, further, we replace Abbott's name in this passage from Dewdney, we would say that "Sirag and Rauscher are promoting a view of reality in which the natural and supernatural worlds exist together in the harmony of a multidimensional framework. All would seem logical, they are telling us, if only we could see."

Beverley Kane

## NOTES

1. For further reading, see Freedman DZ, Nieuwenhuizen P. The hidden dimensions of spacetime. *Scientific American*. May 1985.

2. All quotations are from Abbott EA. *Flatland*. Introduction by AK Dewdney. New York: New American Library; 1984.

# 10

# A Theoretical Model of the Remote-Perception Phenomenon

*Elizabeth A. Rauscher*

As indicated by the title, this chapter deals with two diverse fields of knowledge: the field of space-time physics and the nature of the human mind.[1] The purpose of this chapter is to explore whether the concepts of complex space-time physics can be applied to understanding a few of the natural processes that take place in the human mind. We will focus our attention on information transfer between two events in complex space-time and its similarity to the information transfer of precognitive or "simultaneous" time events between two persons without ordinary means of communication (or one person and the universal consciousness) in real time.

This chapter is written in a general format with a minimum of mathematical equations so as to be comprehensible to a wider audience, rather than to be limited to physicists. In the third section of this chapter, the mathematical concepts of the complex spacetime are reviewed. Differences between real and complex spacetime also are discussed in detail.

The remote and local connections of the events in complex spacetime are analyzed in the fourth section. Mathematical procedures show that two events separated in real time and space have local connections in the imaginary time frame. This means that the two events are connected with each other in complex spacetime, and there is a possibility of information transfer between two events before an event happens in the real space time frame. The concepts of scalar and vector potentials, which are the source terms for information, are described in the fifth section. Application of the physical theory of complex spacetime to the nature of the human mind is explored in the sixth section. In this section, we will focus our attention on precognition, "simultaneous" time events, information transfer in the human mind, and the causal connections between two persons for such events. Application to information storage and retrieval in the human mind as viewed in complex spacetime is discussed in the seventh section. A summary of the chapter, its relation to human consciousness, remote perception, and the nature of consciousness is given in the last section.

## MAJOR PRINCIPLES OF PHYSICS AND PSYCHIC PHENOMENA: POINCARÉ INVARIANCE, ANALYTICITY, AND UNITARITY

A major consideration in this work is using the remote-perception experimental database to deduce the relevant physical principles and laws that govern paranormal functioning. A common objection to the existence of psychic functioning is that it appears to be in conflict with the laws of physics. I attempt to demonstrate the possible compatibility of psychic phenomena with the laws and content of physics and to develop a model with predictability.[2] I also examine the limits of specific physical theories in modeling psychic phenomena.[2]

I suggest that we can use physical principles to assist us in understanding psi phenomena. Further, the psychic database may shed light on some of the current problem areas in physics, such as the foundations of quantum mechanics, geometrical models of spacetime, and relativity theory.

I discuss the following general areas: first, the major principles of physics and their relation to and reconciliation with psychic phenomena; second, an examination of higher-dimensional geometries, including complex coordinate geometries with regard to the possible resolution of precognition and causality (this model not only demonstrates the constancy of precognition and causality, but also suggests a fundamental relation between Maxwell's equations and the structure of relativity theory)[2,3]; third, consideration of the constraints of remote-perception data on the structure of the spacetime metric.

Three major universal principles are used to determine the structure and nature of physical laws. These are Poincaré invariance and its corollary Lorentz invariance (which expresses the spacetime independence of scientific laws), analyticity (which is a general statement of causality), and unitarity (which can be related to the conservation of physical quantities). These principles can apply to macroscopic as well as microscopic phenomena. Poincaré invariance has implications for both macroscopic and microscopic phenomena, and unitarity is a condition on the wave function description in quantum physics. The quantum description of elementary particle physics has led to detailed formation of the analyticity principle in the complex momentum plane.[4] Table 10.1 lists three principles of physics with a brief explanation, such as causality, and ap-

**Table 10.1**
**Principles of Physics and Their Suggested Relation to Psychic Phenomena**

| Principle | Poincaré Invariance | Analyticity | Unitarity |
|---|---|---|---|
| **Brief Statement of Principle** | Homogeneity of spacetime | Causality | Conservation of Probability |
| **Physical theory related to principle of physics and psychic phenomena** | Complex geometry and remote connectedness | Complex geometry | Entropy models and vacuum state polarization |
| **Psychic phenomena** | Remote perception | Precognition | Psychokinesis |

plication to a complex coordinates model or, for psychokinesis (PK), the physics of vacuum state polarization.[5]

I have studied the relation of these models to psychic phenomena. In particular, I am considering a multidimensional geometrical model that appears to reconcile precognition and causality in a self-consistent theoretical framework. I have examined complex physical variables that can be tested for their consistency with the main body of physics and also may demonstrate a fundamental relation between relativity and electromagnetic phenomena.[2] With this model, a precognitive advantage can be calculated.[2] The limits of a simple Lorentz invariant model of precognition also are being examined. I believe that it is possible to demonstrate that psychic phenomena is not denied by the structure of physical law but is compatible with Poincaré invariance and causality.

In applying physical models or theories to the psychic phenomena database, it should be possible to make predictions and design experiments for further research, that is, apply the methodology that defines a science. This is one of the major goals of my research.

There are many fruitful areas in physics to explore in relation to paranormal phenomena. One possible area is the description of causality in relativity and the application of this condition to higher-dimensional spaces. These models can be considered as possible information-accessing channels. It is most vital in constructing any model of psychic phenomena to use a correspondence principle such that one does not hypothesize a physical theory that is inconsistent with the prediction of and compatibility to normal physical data.

Any model of psychic phenomena should be pragmatic, in that it is consistent with the phenomena and predicts the outcome of experiments and also is consistent with the main body of physics. There are few restrictions on the ability of human consciousness to access remote information that involves a physical process rather than psychological states. I will start with the development of a model of remote perception constructed to be consistent with the PK phenomena.

Let us start from some concepts developed in physics that describe the way in which events occur in space and time. Einstein's relativity theory is designed to deal with relations between causes and effects in spacetime in a careful and precise manner. Remote perception involves correlation of events in spacetime between the activities of an outbound experimenter and a subject's description made and recorded in the laboratory.

## CONCEPTS OF REAL AND COMPLEX SPACETIME

Many readers are familiar with the concept in Einstein's special theory of relativity based on the use of four-dimensional spacetime. The main tenet of the theory consists of describing physical processes in three dimensions of space and one dimension of time. The law of causality holds true in such a spacetime whether we are traveling faster or slower than the velocity of the light. This means that cause always precedes the effect. Concepts of simultaneity and precognition do not exist in real spacetime. Concepts of space and time assume a new dimension when we encounter velocities greater than that of light. Research on the nature of faster-than-light particles (tachyons) shows that space and time coordinates are exchanged with each other along the direction of motion.[2,6] Normal to the direction of motion, the quantities become imaginary. These transformations, in the language of physics, are known as superluminal Lorentz transformations (SLT). (The term superluminal refers to a signal or information traveling faster than light.) Mathematically, they can be represented as

$$t' = x,$$
$$x' = t,$$
$$y' = -iy,$$
$$z' = -iz, \tag{1}$$

where the primed quantities ($x'$, $y'$, $z'$, and $t'$) refer to the moving frame and the unprimed quantities refer to the stationary or rest frame.

The coordinates $x$, $y$, $z$, and $t$ are real quantities that form a four-dimensional real space. Similarly, $x'$, $y'$, $z'$, and $t'$ also are real quantities in the moving frame. A person who is moving in a rocket at infinite velocity will view the time component as changed into the space coordinate ($x'$ component), and the remaining two dimensions of space, $y'$ and $z'$, become imaginary with respect to a person on the ground (rest frame). In other words, one could say that along the direction of motion, an event appears to be a "time point" that is extended in space. If, for example, this event is a tachyon traveling at infinite velocity, it would appear to be extended over all space in the laboratory frame or rest frame. The principle of causality is still not violated. Information about the tachyon is available to all observers in the rest frame. Local communication between the observers will be either subluminal or maximum at the velocity of light, but there will always be a finite amount of time involved in communicating between two local observers in the same frame of reference. Thus the laws of physics do not change or show any unusual properties when examined in four-dimensional real space either at subluminal ($v < c$) or at superluminal ($v > c$) velocities of motion. Here $v$ is the velocity of motion and $c$ is the velocity of light.[7] By examining the motion of a tachyon in complex spacetime, a new picture emerges. A unique mixing of space and time vectors is observed under SLT in complex spacetime, which exhibits both remote and local spacetime event connections. This unique mixing of space and time vectors is not present in four-dimensional real spacetime. The concepts and properties of complex spacetime are described below.

The concept of complex spacetime is not new. It has been used in the theory of general relativity by Hansen and Newman,[8] and recently it has been applied to the study of the properties of tachyons.[9] The space and time vectors are complex quantities in complex spacetime, defined as follows:

$$x = x_{Re} + ix_{Im},$$
$$y = y_{Re} + iy_{Im},$$
$$z = z_{Re} + iz_{Im},$$
$$t = t_{Re} + it_{Im}, \tag{2}$$

where $x$, $y$, $z$, and $t$ are now complex quantities, with subscripts Re and Im referring to the real and imaginary components of the complex quantities. The real and imaginary components themselves also are real quantities. It is the combination, such as $x = x_{Re} + ix_{Im}$, that makes them complex quantities. If the imaginary components are zero in the equation above, then we get back the four-space in which Equation (1) is defined.

Here I have introduced a complex eight-dimensional space consisting of six dimensions of space and two dimensions of time. A slice through this space gives four real dimensions consisting of three dimensions of space and one dimension of time.

It also has been suggested that to understand the appearance of imaginary quantities in superluminal transformations, time should be represented by a three-dimensional vector, $t_x$, $t_y$, and $t_z$, and that only its modulus, $|t| = (t_x^2 + t_y^2 + t_z^2)^{1/2}$ has a direct physical meaning.[2,9] This means that a clock will only measure the modulus $|t|$ of time and not the components of time. This concept of three-dimensional time is based on the symmetrical role of space and time intervals in relativistic physics.[9] For the purposes of this formalism, the following is defined:

$$t = \hat{x}t_x + \hat{y}t_y + \hat{z}t_z,$$  (3)

where

$$t_x = t_{x,\text{Re}} + it_{x,\text{Im}},$$
$$t_y = t_{y,\text{Re}} + it_{y,\text{Im}},$$
$$t_z = t_{z,\text{Re}} + it_{z,\text{Im}}.$$  (4)

As before, Re and Im refer to the real and imaginary parts of the complex quantities. For example, both $t_{\text{Re}}$ and $t_{\text{Im}}$ are real quantities.

Equations (2) through (5) represent the basic structure equations for complex spacetime. The properties of the superluminal Lorentz transformation will be examined next in this section.

The transformation laws for infinite velocity in the positive $x$ direction ($v_x = \infty$), as given by Equation (1), are slightly modified because of the inclusion of three temporal dimensions. The modified transformation laws from the moving frame to the rest frame are as follows:

$$t_x' = x,$$
$$x' = t_x,$$
$$y' = iy,$$
$$z' = iz,$$
$$t'_y = -it_y,$$
$$t'_z = -it_z.$$  (5)

All quantities are complex in Equation (5), as defined by Equations (2), (3), and (4).

Consider an event $P$ in the rest frame and the corresponding event, $P'$, in the moving frame. A graphic representation of a complex plane in one space and one time dimension and location of an event $P$ is shown in Figure 10.1.

Event $P$ in complex coordinates can be written as

$$P = (x + it_x, \ y + it_y, \ z + it_z).$$  (6)

By use of Equations (2) and (4), we can rewrite Equation (6),

$$P = ((x_{Re} - t_{x,Im}) + (x_{Im} + t_{x,Re}),$$
$$(y_{Re} - t_{y,Im}) + i(y_{Im} + t_{y,Re}),$$
$$(z_{Re} - t_{z,Im}) + i(z_{Im} + t_{z,Re})). \tag{7}$$

The superluminal transformation in complex spacetime will transform the even $P$ to $P'$, which will be given as:

$$P' = (x' + it'_x, y' + it'_y, z' + it'_z). \tag{8}$$

Using the transformation laws given by Equation (5), we can rewrite the coordinates of the event $P'$. We get,

$$P = (t_x + ix, t_y - iy, t_z - iz)$$
$$= ((t_{x,Re} - x_{Im}) + i(t_{x,Im} + x_{Re}),$$
$$(t_{y,Re} + y_{Im}) + i(t_{y,Im} - y_{Re}),$$
$$(t_{z,Re} + z_{Im}) + i(t_{z,Im} - z_{Re})). \tag{9}$$

Comparing Equations (7) and (9), we see that a superluminal transformation in complex spacetime not only changes real quantities to imaginary ones, but also changes the mixing of real and imaginary parts of the spatial and temporal vectors. This unique mixing is not present in real spacetime. For comparison, see Equation (1), where coordinates of the events $P$ and $P'$ in real spacetime do not show any mixing. The next section examines the remote and local event connections in complex spacetime and their application to precognitive and synchronous events.

## PRECOGNITIVE AND "SIMULTANEOUS" EVENT CONNECTIONS

For graphical representation, let us consider only $x$ components of space and time. We have $x = x_{Re} + ix_{Im}$ and $t_x = t_{x,Re} + it_{x,Im}$. A further simplification can be achieved by assuming that there is only real space separation present between two causal events. In such a case, we can let the imaginary component of the space go to zero (i.e., $x_{Im} = 0$). Thus the only dimensions present in a simplified complex spacetime are the $x_{Re}$, $t_{x,Re}$, and $t_{x,Im}$ components. This gives us one dimension of space and two dimensions of time.

The relation of events in the spacetime should be examined as shown in Figure 10.1a. Two events, $P_1(x = 0, t = 0)$ and $P(x \neq 0, t \neq 0)$, are shown in Figure 10.1a. Projection of the event $P$ on the real space axis is marked as event $P_2(x=0,t_{x,Re}=0)$, and the corresponding projection on the real time axis is marked as event $P_3(x=0,t_{x,Re}\neq0)$. An event $P_4(x=0,t_{x,Im}\neq0)$ is located on the imaginary time axis. Events $P_1$ and $P_2$ are separated in space but simultaneous in time. Similarly, $P_1$ and $P_3$ are separated in time but located at the same point in space.

In Figure 10.1b we see that the two events $P_1$ and $P_2$ are disconnected in the real dimensioned space ($x_{Re}$) that appear to be connected through another event, $P_4$, in higher-dimensional complex spacetime. This gives rise to possible implications for remote connectedness of the events in complex spacetime.

The proper distance between two events, commonly known as length of the line element, d$s$ is defined as:

$$
\begin{aligned}
\mathrm{d}s^2 &= x^2 - ct^2 \\
&= (x_{Re}^2 + x_{Im}^2) - c^2(t_{x,Re}^2 + t_{x,Im}^2) \\
&= (x_{Re}^2 - c^2 t_{x,Re}^2) + (x_{Im}^2 - c^2 t_{x,Im}^2)
\end{aligned} \tag{10}
$$

$$\underbrace{\qquad\qquad}\qquad\underbrace{\qquad\qquad}$$

Normal condition        Remote connection

This will be the line element between the two events $P_1$ and $P_2$. Here we need to regress for a moment to define a few terminologies used in physics. The spatial distance between two events, $P_1$ and $P_2$, is $x$, which is from $x=0$ to $x=x$, but the proper distance is d$s = (x^2 - c^2t^2)^{1/2}$. The separation between two points in four dimensions is measured as a combination of spatial separation and the length of time needed to go from one point to the other. The spatial separation is a fixed quantity, but the proper distance is a variable quantity, depending on the velocity of motion (or time of travel), and could become zero or negative under certain conditions. It is known as *proper time* when it becomes negative. Details of this can be found in any textbook on relativity of the electromagnetic field.[10]

To satisfy the causality condition, the shortest possible line element between the two events must be zero (i.e., d$s=0$). To achieve this condition, we see from Equation (10) that time and space components need to be mixed together. That is, we use the imaginary time component to effect a zero space separation.[2] Figure 10.1b represents the case in which there is no precognitive time element, or $t_{x,Re}=0$, between events $P_1$ and $P_2$. In the simplest case, where $x_{Im}=0$, we get

$$
\mathrm{d}s^2 = 0 = x_{Re}^2 - c^2 t_{x,Im}^2 \tag{11}
$$

**Figure 10.1**
**Location of Four Events in a Complex Plane**

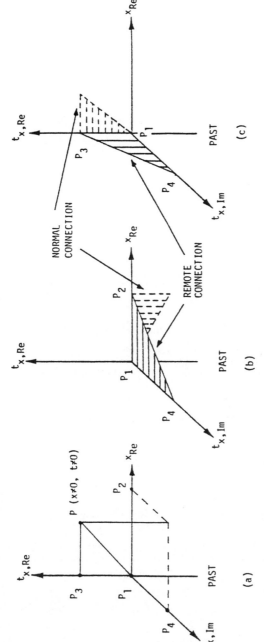

(a)

(b)

(c)

(a) $P_1$ is at the origin. Event $P$ is marked by non zero spatial and temporal separation from the origin. $P_1$ and $P_2$ are separated in space but synchronous in time. $P_1$ and $P_3$ are separated in time, but there is no spatial separation. Event $P_4$ is located on the imginary time axis.

(b) Remote and normal connections of events $P_1$ and $P_2$ as viewed by an observer at $P_4$ such that space-like separation, $x(P_2) - x(P_1)$, between the events $P_1$ and $P_2$ is zero.

(c) Remote and normal connections for zero time-like separation between the events $P_3$ and $P_1$ as viewed by an observer at $P_4$, such that, $t(P_3) - t(P_1) = 0$.

or

$$x_{Re} = ct_{x,Im} \tag{12}$$

Equation (11) shows that we need an imaginary time axis to satisfy the causality condition between the two synchronous events $P_1$ and $P_2$. In other words, events $P_1$ and $P_2$ are connected by another event, $P_4$, on the local event connections that exist at velocities faster than the velocity of light $(c<v<\infty)$.

In this section, we have explored the description of precognitive and synchronous or simultaneous time events within the structure of complex spacetime.[9] Findings of this section can be summarized as follows:

1. Remote and local event connections exist in complex space time geometries.
2. There is a unique mixing of space and time vectors under the influence of superluminal boost.
3. The velocity of information transfer for precognitive and synchronous time events could be faster than the velocity of light $(v>c)$ or instantaneous $(v\rightarrow\infty)$.

In the next section, we examine the possible physical sources of information transfer at velocities greater than light. These sources could be considered electric or magnetic potentials related to electric or magnetic charges.

## SCALAR AND VECTOR POTENTIALS IN COMPLEX SPACETIME

Information transfer and storage may take place by means of electric or magnetic fields or electrical charges. In complex spaces, the electric and magnetic fields exhibit unique properties that are different from the properties exhibited in real spacetime. Here we focus our attention on velocities greater than light (superluminal cases). The transformation laws for subluminal cases are well worked out and can be found in any standard book on electromagnetic fields.[10]

Electric and magnetic fields can be represented by a combination of scalar and vector potentials. The transformation of these potentials under the influence of superluminal boost in complex spaces is a current topic of research and controversy in special relativity.[11–13] In this work, a brief summary of the results is now presented and applied to signal transfer for precognitive and synchronous time events.

Consider two events in moving and rest frames: an electromagnetic signal given out by event $P'_1$ will travel toward $P'_2$ with the velocity of light, $c$, and will still look like an electromagnetic signal when it arrives at $P'_2$. For example, a flash of light will look like a flash of light at the point of origin or at the point of reception in the moving frame. If the same flash of light emitted at $P'_1$ in the moving frame is observed in the rest frame, then the situation is quite different. We can analyze it as follows: A flash of light is composed of electric and magnetic field vectors that can be related to scalar and vector potentials by the following equations in the moving frame:[9,13]

$$E' = -\nabla'_r \phi' - \delta A'/\delta t',$$
$$B' = -\delta \phi'/\delta t', \tag{13}$$

where $E$ is the electric field, $B$ is the magnetic field, and $A$ and $\phi$ are scalar and vector potentials. Here primed quantities refer to the moving frame and $\nabla_r$ is the gradient operator in three spatial coordinates.

Under the influence of the superluminal boost, $E'$ and $B'$ will transform as follows:[9,12,13]

$$E' = -\nabla_r \phi - \delta A/\delta t = E,$$
$$B' = -\nabla_r x \phi, \tag{14}$$

where $\nabla_t$ is the gradient operator in three temporal coordinates or rate of change in time. We see from Equation (14) that the electric field remains the same under the influence of SLT, but the magnetic field transforms into an unrecognizable form that would require a vector form of $\phi$ and is not related to electric or magnetic charges. This means that a faster-than-light particle (tachyon) will behave as a purely electrical charge in the rest frame. If the information transfer between two persons is by means of tachyonic signals, then the associated electric fields within the information storage and retrieval system (the human brain, for example) will change during the precognitive and synchronous time events. This could be one of the possible source terms for information exchange in PK effects. This property of electric fields associated with tachyons and the unique mixing of space and time vectors in complex spacetime, as described in previous sections, can be applied to examine the complete behavior of precognitive and synchronous time events. This formalism is one example of a complex coordinate model of psi.[2,9,13]

In the next section, we apply the theoretical concepts developed so far to the experimental results of paranormal phenomena (PK effects).

## APPLICATION OF COMPLEX SPACETIME GEOMETRIES TO THE EXPERIMENTAL RESULTS OF PK EFFECTS

This chapter gives a detailed account of the experimental research work in remote perception carried out at several laboratories in the United States and in European countries.[14–16] Remote perception, or remote viewing, has been well studied from the scientific point of view by several research groups over the past two decades. In these experiments, a subject is asked to describe by written, graphic, or oral means an unknown remote target location at which another person is stationed. During the course of the experiment, there is no normal sensory mode of communication between the two persons. The following inferences can be drawn from a vast amount of experimental data.[14,15,16]

1. Information can be transmitted over large distances without loss of clarity of reception (nonlocal and remote connectedness). I have conducted local, long-distance, and precognitive experiments to test this model.

2. The information transfer channel has noise in it (probabilistic nature of remote spacetime connections).

3. Information can be transmitted during, before, or after the remote-perception experiments (no time dependence; future event can be perceived in the local spacetime frame, represented as remote connectedness in the complex time coordinate).

The three inferences drawn from these experiments can be explained by use of the superluminal transformations in complex spacetime. Nonlocal and remote connectedness of the events can be used to show that information is available instantaneously at every point in the space. Thus information about a target can be transmitted over long distances by remote connectedness of local events in the present time. Information about a future event also is available in the local time frame, and it would be feasible to extract this information by means of a perception channel in complex spacetime. The foregoing discussion can be applied here to explain the remote-viewing experiments as well as PK effects.

## APPLICATION TO INFORMATION STORAGE AND RETRIEVAL IN THE HUMAN BRAIN-MIND

Remote and local event connections in complex spacetime also can be applied to examine information storage and retrieval in the human brain-mind. In this presentation, I will not try to differentiate between the brain (physiologic part) and the mind (thinking part), but rather attempt to examine the manner in which information flow and storage is possible within the framework of complex spacetime.

Information in the human brain (or in the consciousness related to mind) is stored as a function of frequency and amplitude, commonly known as a holographic model.[17] Information is retrieved or accessed through the *Fourier transform* technique, which converts frequency and amplitude information into the more familiar form of space and time coordinates as commonly visualized. If information transfer between two persons or between one person and the universe is taking place faster than the speed of light (or instantaneously), then complex spacetime models can be applied. SLTs in complex spacetime exchange space and time vectors along the direction of motion and convert real quantities to the imaginary ones normal to the direction of motion. It will be interesting to examine the behavior of Fourier transforms under the influence of the superluminal boost. It is out of the context of this chapter to go into mathematical details here, but we can see that exchange of space and time vectors also will convert a Fourier transform from the time domain to the frequency domain and vice versa. Therefore, it is feasible to have a continuous exchange going on between frequency and time under the influence of superluminal boost.[13] Thus, if two persons (or one person and the universe) can tune in to each other, there will be a continuous exchange of information for past, present, and future events as described by Fourier transforms in the frequency plane. Therefore, the human mind can access precognitive, or past event information, in the local time frame by use of some kind of a perception channel.

Because almost all psi phenomena appear to be statistical in nature, there is always some inherent noise present in a perception channel. (We will not go into quantum mechanical or quantum geometrical processes to examine the amplitude and noise levels present in the physical or conscious channels of perception.) This noise also will occur in Fourier transforms between the frequency and time domains. Thus the perceptual channel for precognitive or any other type of event also will become noisy.

In addition, there will be several event connections available on the imaginary time axis that can satisfy the causality conditions for precognitive and synchronous time events on the real space and time axes. A combination of inherent noise and the multiple event connections will give rise to the probabilistic nature of information transfer in a perception channel. The speculative hypothesis suggested above might explain the noise associated with PK-type random number–generator experiments.

## SUMMARY AND DISCUSSION

This chapter examines the properties of SLTs in complex space-time and their application to precognitive and synchronous time events. There is a unique mixing of space and time vectors and remote and local connectedness under the influence of the superluminal boost in complex spacetime. Real and imaginary parts of complex quantities are interchanged in going through SLTs. Similarly, space and time components are interchanged along the direction of the motion. In addition, we need to satisfy the causality condition in the complex space that requires that the proper length of the line element, $ds$, should be zero. The imaginary time component is required to satisfy this causality condition. An event located on this imaginary time axis will be simultaneously connected to events separated in real space and real time (see Figure 10.1). Therefore, by going into one higher-dimensional space, it is feasible to extract information in the local time frame for an event separated in real space and time. Here the term "separated in real time" means that an event is located in the future or in the past with respect to the local time frame.

From the discussion above, we see that an observer (or, more correctly, a participator) located on the imaginary time axis can perceive precognitive and past events in present local time and space. Similarly, information about a synchronous event also will be available to an observer even though the event and the observer are far away from each other. This is feasible if and only if the observer is located on the imaginary time axis.

The concepts of complex and imaginary time are needed in physics and mathematics to describe some physical phenomena that are not describable in real spacetime. Imaginary time does not exist by itself in the nature of physical reality as we are familiar with it. However, at superluminal velocities, an observer in the rest frame will see the quantities normal to the direction of motion become imaginary [Equation (1)]. If time is represented as a three-dimensional quantity, $t = (t_x, t_y, $ and $t_z)$, and if we are moving along the $x$ direction, then $t_y$ and $t_z$ components of time will become imaginary in the rest frame of the observer [Equation (5)].

Creation of imaginary time in such a manner at superluminal velocities $(v > c)$ and the exchange of space and time vectors along the direction of motion allows one to satisfy the law of causality and yet have remote and local event connectedness in complex spacetime. These concepts have been used here to show that precognition, synchronous time events, and related paranormal phenomena (PK effects) are possible within the conceptual framework of science.[18,19]

How does the work presented here relate to the nature of human consciousness? This is a difficult question, but perhaps science does provide some means to examine the conscious nature of people. We have applied the concepts of physics in complex spacetime to study precognitive and synchronous time events, which commonly are known as paranormal phenomena. It is useless to discuss the validity of these phenomena. A skeptic will always doubt these effects, and a believer will always have a blind faith in them. A skeptic needs to experience these phenomena to believe in them, and a believer needs to question further to learn more about them. It is reasonable to assume, based on the current scientific evidence, that these phenomena do exist and that they do have some influence on the subconscious part of our minds, which in turn influences our spiritual nature.

**NOTES**

1. I was the first to propose a hyperdimensional mathematical model of consciousness, in particular the psi function. This work proceeded from my earlier work in 1964 on multidimensional cosmological models and was further developed in 1974. In 1978, I met Ceon Ramon, who made invaluable contributions to the current form of this work. Ceon Ramon was at the Institute for Applied Physiology, Astronomy, and Medicine, Seattle, WA.

2. Rauscher EA. Some physical models applicable to remote perception. In: Puharich A, Josephson B, eds. *The Iceland Papers*. Amherst, WI: Essentia Research Assoc.; 1979:49–93.

3. Rauscher EA. Electromagnetic phenomena in complex geometries and nonlinear phenomena. PSRL-3107A and *Bull Am Phys Soc*. 1983;28:351.

4. Chew G. The analytical S-matrix. In: *Frontiers of Physics*. New York: WA Benjamin Inc.; 1964. Also, private communications; 1976.

5. Rauscher EA. Quantum electron interactions in plasmas. *J Plasma Phys*. 1968;2:517.

6. Fineberg G. Tachyons. *Phys Rev*. 1967;159:1089. Also, private communication; 1971.

7. Tachyons or superluminal signals alone will not explain precognition in ordinary four-dimensional spacetime. G. Fineberg states that signals at the velocity of light will gain only a few nanoseconds per foot into the future.

8. Hansen RO, Newman ET. *General Relativity and Gravitation*. 1975;6:216.

9. Ramon C, Rauscher EA. Superluminal transformations in complex Minkowski spaces. *Foundations of Physics*. 1980;10:661.

10. Lorrain P, Corson D. *Electromagnetic Fields and Waves*. San Francisco: WH Freeman & Co; 1970.

11. Nagi OPS, Rajput BS. *Lettere Al Nuovo Cimento*. 1981;32:117.

12. Corbon HC. *Il Nuovo Cimento*. 1975;29:415.

13. Ramon C, Rauscher EA. Superluminal transformation of scalar and vector fields in complex spaces. Manuscript in preparation.

14. Puthoff HI, Targ R. A perceptual for information transfer over kilometer distances. *Proceedings IEEE*. 1976;64:329.

15. Rauscher EA, Siraq SP, Weissmann A. *Advances in Parapsychology*. Methuen, NJ: Scarecrow Press; 1975.

16. Jahn RG. The persistent paradox of psychic phenomena: An engineering perspective. *Proceedings IEEE*. 1982;70:136.

17. Pribram K. Problems concerning the structure of consciousness. In: Globus G, ed. *Consciousness and the Brain*. New York: Plenum; 1976:161–184.

18. The eight-dimensional complex space $M_4$ is related to five-dimensional Kaluza-Klein geometry. The spinor calculus of the Kaluza-Klein geometry is mappable 1-to-1 to the twistor algebra of complex eight-space, and the spinor calculus is an excellent framework for accounting for the coupling of the electromagnetic field to the gravitational field.

19. Charon JE. *The Complex Relativity*. Paris: Albin Michel Press; 1987.

# 11

# Hyperspace Reflections

*Saul-Paul Sirag*

The idea that space is more than three-dimensional is at least as old as Plato, who, in his Parable of the Cave, suggested that we usually identify ourselves with our three-dimensional shadows rather than with the higher-dimensional beings we really are.[1] This idea was rejected by Aristotle and subsequent generations of physicists. Recently, however, theoretical physicists working on unified field theory have found it necessary to postulate the physical reality of hyperspace, defined as a space of more than three dimensions (3-d). These proposed physical hyperspaces are 10-d or 26-d or even higher-dimensional spaces.[2]

Mathematicians began describing abstract (nonphysical) hyperspaces in the nineteenth century. They could do this because the ideas of classical geometry of 2-d and 3-d could be extended in various ways. For instance, a coordinate system can be set up in a 2-d space so that any point can be located by two numbers (e.g., latitude and longitude on the 2-d surface of the earth, or the *x-y* axes of a 2-plane). Thus, by extension of this idea, three numbers would locate any point in a 3-d space, and n numbers would locate any point in an n-d space.

All 2-d spaces are either flat or curved, and this distinction can be generalized to any number of dimensions. Roughly speaking, a curved space of any dimension is a space that cannot be flattened without tearing. The unsuccessful attempt of mapmakers to construct an untorn, undistorted flat map of the earth's surface led to this fundamental distinction between flat and curved.

Thus ordinary 3-d space and 4-d spacetime seem to be flat and were believed to be flat by physicists until Einstein's theory of general relativity (1915) proposed that gravity corresponds to curvature of 4-d spacetime. This implied that 3-d space could be curved and might form the 3-d sphere $S^3$ when viewed as a whole, that is, at the cosmic scale.

An ordinary globe or sphere is called a 2-sphere or $S^2$. The area of a 2-sphere is $4\pi r^2$ and thus finite if the radius r is finite, whereas the area of the flat 2-plane of high school algebra extends to infinity and is thus infinite in area. A finite-size space such as the 2-sphere is called a compact space.

It is an open question whether the 3-d space in which dwell the planets, stars, and galaxies is a (flat) 3-plane of infinite volume, a sphere $S^3$ of finite volume $2\pi^2 r^3$, or some other curved space (of finite or infinite volume). This is a question to be answered by observational cosmology—the telescopic study of distant galaxies—in conjunction with theoretical cosmology, which is the mathematical description of the large-scale structure of space and time in accordance with Einstein's (1915) theory of gravity, called the general theory of relativity.

Einstein's theory says that gravity is not a force acting at a distance (as in Newton's theory), but rather is the movement of particles along the geodesics (straightest possible paths) in a curved 4-d spacetime. The curvature of spacetime, which is allowed to vary over every point of spacetime, is an expression of particle masses.

The fact that spacetime carries properties of 4-d distance (called interval) and curvature makes it clear that spacetime is a space, in fact a hyperspace, from the point of view of geometry.

The precedent set by general relativity suggested to physicists that it might be possible to bring other forces into the geometrical picture by increasing the dimensionality of the physical hyperspace.

In the 1920s, Kaluza and Klein proposed a unification of general relativity and electromagnetism by introducing a 5-d hyperspace generated as a product of spacetime (4-d) and a circle (1-d)—just as spacetime is a product of 3-d space and 1-d time. They showed that particles moving on geodesics in the 5-d hyperspace project down to paths of particles moving in 3-d space under the combined action of gravity and electromagnetism. This projection is the 5-d analog of the ordinary projection of a 3-d body onto a 2-d shadow. Shades of Plato! The reason we don't see the fifth dimension is that, as Klein calculated from quantum-theoretic considerations, the circle is very tiny—around $10^{-30}$ cm. In other words, we would have to be smaller than this size to be able to move around in the extra dimension. Not even a proton, which is around $10^{-13}$ cm, could explore this region.

This unification of gravity and classical electromagnetism was an astounding achievement. It was praised by Einstein, who could see its beauty and the possibility of applying it to the problems of quantum mechanics. It was, however, forgotten for many years because it did not account for the nuclear forces, which occupied the attention of most theoretical physicists in the 1930s and 1940s.

The Kaluza-Klein scheme has recently been revived by physicists seeking to unify all the forces.[3] In these new hyperspace schemes, the hyperspace is a mathematical structure called a *principal fiber bundle:* a space of B + F dimensions, where B is the dimensionality of a base space (e.g., spacetime) and F is the dimensionality of a fiber, a copy of which is attached to each point of B. There is a projection of the fiber space down to the base space such that all the points of a single fiber project onto a single point of the base space. Moreover, the fiber is not only a space, but also a set of symmetry transformations called a Lie group (after the nineteenth-century mathematician Sophus Lie). The symmetry transformations act on the fiber. In other words, the Lie group acts on itself. It does this by moving its points along geodesics in the fiber. In unified field theory, spacetime is considered the base space.

A geodesic path is a "free-fall" path, which means that an object traversing a geodesic feels no force. A skydiver (before opening his parachute) and an astronaut floating in orbit are in free-fall and do not feel any force, except the electrical and nuclear forces holding the atoms and molecules of their bodies together. General relativity teaches that gravity is not a force, but consists of the movement of particles in free-fall paths (geodesics) in curved spacetime. The Kaluza-Klein scheme generalizes this idea to include all the so-called forces. To do this, the correct fiber bundle must be chosen from the myriads of fiber bundles available in mathematics.

The path of a particle moving along geodesics in the hyperspace of the fiber bundle can be projected to a path in the base space (i.e., spacetime). The spacetime path will not be a geodesic, but a path seemingly acted on by a force (or set of forces) characterized by the structure of the fiber. Given the fact that the geodesics occur in the hyperspace (i.e., the fiber bundle), it is only natural to assume that this hyperspace is the true reality of the theory and that the occurrences in the base space are only appearances.

It is necessary not only to choose just the right fiber (i.e., symmetry group) to make this scheme describe the real physical world, but also to choose the right spacetime.

It has been discovered that spacetime must be at least 10-d to make the theory consistent with both the rules of general relativity and the rules of quantum mechanics.[3] Moreover, the most popular scheme, called *superstring theory,* replaces the point particles of quantum field theory with vibrational modes on tiny lines, called strings, which can be closed (like circles) or open (like threads). This scheme requires a 10-d spacetime: The 1-d strings move in a 9-d space, and as they move, they sweep out a surface in a 10-d spacetime. From the Kaluza-Klein point of view, the fiber (i.e., symmetry group) in the most popular version of superstring theory is the $E_8 \times E_8$ Lie group, which is 496-d. This group is generated by a 16-d structure that I call a "reflection space," which possesses symmetry properties that facilitate the cancellation of "anomalies" that would otherwise make the theory inconsistent. These symmetry properties correspond to the packing of hyperspheres in 8-d space. The closest possible sphere-packing in 8-d space is 240 7-d spheres around a central 7-d sphere. This 8-d space is the reflection space of a group called $E_8$, whose dimensionality is $240 + 8 = 248$. The full symmetry group of the standard superstring theory is a product of two of these groups, $E_8 \times E_8$, whose dimensionality is double that of $E_8$, that is, 496-d, with a 16-d reflection space. Note that when we form product spaces the dimensions add: The product of a 1-d space and a 1-d space is a 2-d space. The word product is justified by the fact that metrical content multiplies; for example, 2 cm along $x$ and 3 cm along $y$ defines an area of 6 cm.[2]

(Incidentally, I use the term reflection space because, as will be explained below, a kind of mathematical reflection takes place in such a space, which technically is called the "dual space of a Cartan subalgebra of a semisimple Lie algebra.")

Most of the current work in superstring theory is devoted to explaining how four of the spacetime dimensions expand in accordance with the currently favored big-bang theory of cosmology, whereas the other six dimensions remain small (about $10^{-30}$ cm in radius) and thus become internal dimensions. Other work is devoted to reducing or extending the standard 496-d fiber in various ways. But it would seem that physical hyperspace is here to stay.

Evidence for the physical reality of hyperspace could come from predictions made from superstring theory, especially as it relates to the earliest stage of the universe—at the Planck time $10^{-43}$ seconds after the start of the big bang. For example, various exotic particles may have been constructed at this time, some of which may still exist.

The strategy of this chapter is to assume the reality of the hyperspace (in particular, the reflection space) and to use this assumption to speculate about the nature of consciousness in the context of the mind–body problem. Verifiable consequences of this strategy will provide indirect evidence for the reality of the physical hyperspace.

The mind–body question can be posed as follows: Are the mind and body fundamentally different entities? If so, how do they interact? (This is the problem of dualism.) If not, why do they seem so different? (This is the problem of monism.) In 1637, Descartes defined a kind of dualism of mind and matter by defining matter as *res extensa* and mind as *res cogitans*.[4] This has made the problem of interaction acute, for, it is argued, how can matter, which is extended in space, interact with mind, which is not extended in space? To answer this criticism of Cartesian dualism, psychiatrist J. Smythies,[5,6] following the lead of philosopher C. D. Broad,[7] has proposed a non-Cartesian dualism: Mind *is* extended in a spacetime that is connected to but different from ordinary physical spacetime. If we reduce 4-d spacetime to a 2-d spacetime, we can picture this as two sheets of paper (each representing a 2-d spacetime, one mental and one physical) that intersect each other in a line. In general, when two spaces intersect, we call the space that the two spaces have in common the intersection space. The dimensionality of the intersection space depends on the dimensionalities of the two intersecting spaces as well as on the manner of intersection.

The Broad–Smythies scheme is not a model of mind–body interaction, but provides a general framework for such a model. My approach is to look for a unified field theory hyperspace structure that entails the intersection of two spaces. It is clear that this intersection structure must be a special kind of space. In fact, I propose that it is the reflection space of the unified field theory itself.

A reflection space is a mathematical concept inspired in part by Lewis Carroll and in part by the kaleidoscope. Alice in Carroll's *Through the Looking Glass* assumed that she could go from the world in front of the mirror to a similar world behind the mirror. We smile at this childish naivete and know that no such thing is possible in the physical world of ordinary mirrors. Mathematicians, however, have discovered abstract reflection spaces that function much as Alice imagined her world to function.[8,9]

To understand the mathematician's reflection spaces, we shall first describe an ordinary kaleidoscope and then describe the mathematical reflection spaces abstracted (and generalized) from it. If you set two ordinary physical mirrors in 3-d space at 60 degrees to each other and stand between them, you will see four extra mirrors as reflections of these mirrors, so that you will see five copies of yourself, that is, six images including yourself. This is similar to the way a kaleidoscope works. To see this, set up two mirrors at 60 degrees to each other, with their edges resting on the floor. (A pair of hinged mirrors works best.) The part of the floor between the mirrors is called the *fundamental region*. Place some pattern in this fundamental region. When looking down at the fundamental region from above, we see the pattern reflected five times, making six images of the pattern, thus deriving a hexagonal (snowflake) design. A toy kaleidoscope is nothing but a miniature version of our hinged mirrors mounted in a tube with bits of colored glass in the fundamental region of the viewing screen.

To abstract a mathematical reflection space from the physical kaleidoscope, we regard the 2-d viewing screen of the kaleidoscope as a 2-d mathematical reflection space. In general, an n-dimensional reflection space with n basic mirrors can be defined.

We can describe the mathematical definition of a reflection as follows: A reflection is a transformation of all the points in the reflection space from one side of a mirror plane to the other side and vice versa. This transformation must reverse the direction of all the vectors attached at 90 degrees to either side of the mirror. This transformation also must leave the mirror fixed and leave the measure of distance in the space unchanged. This definition of reflection requires a mirror to cut the space in half. Moreover, repeating a reflection restores the original space just as if it had not been transformed. We write

$r^2 = 1$, where r is a reflection and 1 is the identity transformation, which is to say "do nothing." The reflections that correspond to the mirrors bordering the fundamental region are the basic reflections. Any possible reflection in a particular reflection space is merely a combination of some or all the basic reflections in some particular order. In fact, the set of all possible combinations of basic reflections in a given reflection space form an algebraic structure called a *reflection group*.

Each reflection group acts in its own reflection space, which is defined by the placement of mirrors, each of which bisects the reflection space. A line in a plane has two sides, but a line in 3-d space has an infinity of "sides." Therefore, a line cuts a 2-d space into two parts, whereas it takes a 2-d plane to cut a 3-d space into two parts. Similarly, a 3-d hyperplane cuts a 4-d hyperspace into two parts. This means that the mirrors of various n-dimensional reflection spaces will have to be hyperplanes of dimension $n - 1$. To describe the mutual orientations of the mirrors with respect to each other, we make use of a mirror vector (of unit length) attached to each mirror at a right angle. We attach these mirror vectors at the point where all the mirrors intersect.

For the kaleidoscope viewing screen, setting the mirrors at 60 degrees to each other makes the mirror vectors point 120 degrees away from each other. In generalizing the kaleidoscope viewing screen to n-space, we shall consider only the case of the n basic mirror vectors set at 120 degrees to each other.

We define these reflection spaces as spaces generated by basic mirror vectors separated by 120 degrees. There are other reflection spaces known to mathematics, but these kaleidoscopic reflection spaces with basic mirror vectors set at 120 degrees to each other are the simplest and the most useful.[10]

It is known that there are three types of these simple reflection spaces, called A, D, and E. A and D constitute two infinite series of reflection spaces. For each dimension n, there is an $A_n$ type—$A_2$ being the ordinary kaleidoscope view screen. For each dimension n beyond 3, there is a $D_n$ type. The type E is called exceptional because within this category, only reflection spaces $E_6$, $E_7$, and $E_8$ exist. Moreover, all these reflection spaces are hierarchical in the sense that the $A_n$ reflection space contains the $A_{n-1}$ reflection space; $D_n$ contains $D_{n-1}$, and $E_8$ contains $E_7$, which contains $E_6$. Also, $D_n$ contains $A_{n-1}$, whereas $E_n$ contains both $A_{n-1}$ and $D_{n-1}$.

Now there is a deep sense in which one of these reflection spaces (with all its lower-dimensional embedded spaces) must be the kaleidoscopic "viewing screen" for the physical world.

According to quantum mechanics, the only observable quantities in the world are certain numbers called *eigenvalues* of observation "operators." A unified field theory supposedly describes all the basic eigenvalues and observation operators of the world. Reflection spaces are central to this task because the observation operators form a basis for a reflection space, whereas the eigenvalues are sets of numbers in the reflection space that define the mirror vectors and their "duals." In this by now standard scheme, the force particles correspond to the mirror vectors. The matter particles correspond to dual vectors that can be derived from these mirror vectors by a certain nonreflection transformation of the reflection space itself. (Technically, the mirror vectors are called "roots" and the dual vectors are called "weights."[11])

Note that observation is an aspect of consciousness. In this context, it is significant that mathematician John Von Neumann and physicist Eugene Wigner have proposed that consciousness be the ultimate repository of quantum observations.[12] One consequence of the non-locality of quantum mechanics, as proved by Bell's theorem, is that this consciousness of Von Neumann and Wigner must be a universal consciousness.[13,14] Thus it becomes plausible to regard some appropriate reflection space as the space of universal consciousness.

In 1974, the $A_4$ reflection space was used by Georgi and Glashow to unify three forces.[15] The four dimensions of the $A_4$ reflection space were allocated as follows: electromagnetism (1-d), the weak force (1-d), and the strong color force (2-d). [Their theory usually is called the SU(5) grand unified theory because SU(5) is the continuous symmetry group—or the fiber as described above—associated with $A_4$.]

To bring gravity into the unification scheme, much larger reflection spaces seem to be necessary. This is related to the fact that a 10-d spacetime is required. Hundreds of physicists are working on superstring theory in which the reflection space of $E_8 \times E_8$ (described above) is the repository of observable charges.[16–18] This scheme is plausible only because of the hierarchical structure embedding the $A_4$ reflection space in that of $E_8$.

I have been working on an alternative route to unified field theory in which I introduce a finite group called the octahedral double group OD, whose 48 elements provide an explanation for the three families of matter particles.[19–21] Accounting for these families is considered the deepest problem of unified field theory. So my strategy has been to start with the deepest problem, rather than to deal with this problem after an enormous mathematical machinery is in place.

In quantum field theory, a set of n particles generates an n-dimensional space. Because the 48 elements of the OD group can be given particle labels, they will generate such a space. Moreover, this space will be an algebra, because the 48 elements are group elements. This is the OD group algebra, written as C[OD]. This is a linear algebra that has a "regular" representation consisting of $48 \times 48$ matrices. This group algebra has a 10-d subalgebra that could play the role of a 10-d spacetime for a version of superstring theory. Seven of these 10 dimensions form another subalgebra that can be identified with the $E_7$ reflection space because of an amazing theorem that makes a one-to-one correspondence between the A-D-E reflection spaces and the symmetries of certain Platonic structures:[22]

$A_n$ corresponds to the symmetries of an $(n+1)$-sided polygon.

$D_n$ (n greater than 3) corresponds to the symmetries of an $(n-2)$-sided polygon, assuming we can turn the polygon over.

$E_6$, $E_7$, and $E_8$ correspond to the symmetries of the tetrahedron, octahedron, and the icosahedron, respectively.

This theorem implies that the entire 133-d Lie algebra $E_7$ (generated from the $E_7$ reflection space) intersects with the 48-d group algebra C[OD] in such a way that the $E_7$ reflection space is the overlap region (called $C^7$). In analogy with the Broad–Smythies hypothesis that mental spacetime and physical space-time are partially separate spaces that interact by way of the *intersection* between them, I propose that:

$E_7$ is universal mind (both consciousness and "the unconscious");

C[OD], since it includes spacetime, is universal body;

$C^7$, the $E_7$ reflection space, which is the intersection between $E_7$ and C[OD], is universal consciousness.

In this theory, the physically observable charges reside in the $E_7$ reflection space $C^7$. In the standard superstring theory, these charges would reside in the 16-d reflection space of $E_8 \times E_8$. In the standard theory, however, one projects immediately down to the reflection space of $E_6$, skipping over $E_7$ for certain technical reasons. The $E_6$ reflection space is contained in that of $E_7$, whereas the $E_7$ reflection space is contained in that of $E_8$. The main problem of the standard theory is making appropriate contact with the "low energy" particle structure—the charges residing in the $A_4$ reflection space—which describes the three (nongravity) forces well known to physics. This means that one has to provide a role for the other charges in the $E_6$ reflection space. This role could be a mental one if a different strategy for a unified field theory were used.

My strategy is to use the $E_7$ reflection space $C^7$ as a bridge to the "low-energy" particle structure described by the group algebra C[OD]. All the charge structure in the reflection space is a structure of observable quantities, hence the connection with consciousness.

Because $C^7$ is universal consciousness, it is necessary to describe how individual conscious entities emerge from this theory. To describe this, we must first describe how ordinary spacetime couples to $C^7$. The ordinary spacetime of this theory is a substructure of the universal body C[OD]. The 3-d part of spacetime is the sphere $S^3$, whereas time is in $C^7$, or rather in a space written as $C^7/W$, where W is the $E_7$ reflection group acting in $C^7$. In other words, all the reflections acting in $C^7$ generate $C^7/W$ as a new 7-d space that has special features. Most important, $C^7/W$ is time plus the 6-d control space of a "catastrophe structure."[23–25]

A *catastrophe* is a structure with a system and a set of control parameters on which the system depends in such a way that a small change in one or more of the control parameters corresponds to a large change (perturbation) in the system.

We can consider a path in $C^7/W$ to be the path of an individual consciousness. Because of the structure of the intersection between $E_7$ and C[OD], every point of $S^3$ can be considered a copy of $C^7/W$. Movement in $S^3$ is correlated with movement along a path in $C^7/W$. Moreover, a small change along such a path can correspond to a large change in $S^3$. Hence a small change in consciousness can correspond to a large change in a body that is a set of points in $S^3$.

The six control parameters correspond to the six internal dimensions of the 10-d superstring space of this theory. This implies that every point of ordinary spacetime has access to six control parameters. A body is a large number of points in ordinary space, and a brain is a means of accessing, in a richly interconnected way, a large number of paths in $C^7/W$.

Many more aspects of $C^7$ seem suggestive of aspects of consciousness. For example, the $E^7$ mirror vectors generate an error-correcting code—the Hamming-7 code—which is well known to communication engineers. The dual vectors generate the $E_7$ quantizing scheme (i.e., analog-to-digital conversion).[26] There also is the $E_7$ "contact" structure and the $E_7$ "quiver." The list goes on and on.

The richness of these reflection-space structures can be surmised from a proposition of Russian mathematician V. I. Arnold: "To easily checked properties of one set of associated objects correspond properties of the others which need not be evident at all. Thus the relations between all the A, D, E,-classifications can be used for the simultaneous study of *all simple objects,* in spite of the fact that the origin of many of these relations (for example, of the connections between functions and quivers) remains an unexplained manifestation of the mysterious unity of all things" [emphasis added].[25]

Because the A-D-E classification structure is hierarchical, higher-dimensional objects contain the lower-dimensional objects. This suggests that if the $E_7$ reflection space corresponds to consciousness, there are higher and lower realms of consciousness. In this regard, $E_6$ and $E_8$ are especially interesting, since these three are the only exceptional structures in the A-D-E scheme. And these exceptional structures are the link to non-simple structures.

In 1864, Maxwell unified electricity and magnetism in such a way that he produced an electromagnetic theory of light. This unification made the startling proposal that visible light is merely a tiny part of the electromagnetic spectrum.

Similarly, because we today are unifying all the forces, something new, analogous to light, should come out of our endeavors. I propose that a theory of consciousness should emerge and that such a theory should imply that "ordinary" consciousness is but a small part of a spectrum of realms of consciousness. Because, through Arnold's work, the A-D-E classification is itself a small part of a vast scheme that deals with non-simple mathematical objects—for example, chaos—there are many realms for us to explore.[24]

**NOTES**

1. Plato. The republic. In: Hamilton E. and Cairns H., eds. *The Collected Dialogues of Plato.* Princeton, NJ: Princeton University Press; 1961:747–749.

2. Duff MJ. Recent results in extra dimensions. In: Piran I. and Weinberg S., eds. *Physics in Higher Dimensions*. Singapore: World Scientific; 1986:40–91.

3. Appelquist T, Chodos A, Freund PGO. *Modern Kaluza-Klein Theories*. Menlo Park, CA: Addison-Wesley; 1987.

4. Descartes R, cited in Gregory RL, ed. *The Oxford Companion to the Mind*. Oxford; 1987.

5. Smythies JR, ed. Is ESP possible? *Science and ESP*. London: Routledge & Kegan Paul; 1967:1–14.

6. Smythies JR. In: Koestler A, Smythies JR, eds. As peets of consciousness. *Beyond Reductionism*. Boston: Beacon Press; 1971:233–257.

7. Broad CD. *The Mind and Its Place in Nature*. London: Routledge & Kegan Paul; 1927.

8. Coxeter HSM. *Regular Polytopes*, 3rd ed. New York: Dover; 1973.

9. Coxeter HSM. *Complex Regular Polytopes*, 2nd ed. New York: Cambridge University Press; 1991.

10. Gilmore R. *Lie Groups, Lie Algebras, and Some of Their Applications*. New York: Wiley-Interscience; 1974.

11. Georgi H. *Lie Algebras in Particle Physics*. Reading, MA: Benjamin/Cummings; 1982.

12. Wigner EP. *Symmetries and Reflections*. Woodbridge, CT: Ox Bow Press; 1979.

13. d'Espagnat B. *In Search of Reality*. New York: Springer-Verlag; 1983.

14. Herbert N. *Quantum Reality*. Garden City, NY: Doubleday, Anchor Press; 1985.

15. Georgi HA. Unified theory of elementary particles and forces. *Scientific American*. April 1981:48–63.

16. Green MB. Superstrings. *Scientific American*. September 1986:48–60.

17. Green MB, Gross DJ. *Unified String Theories*. Singapore: World Scientific; 1986.

18. Peat FD. *Superstrings and the Search for the Theory of Everything*. Chicago: Contemporary Books; 1988.

19. Sirag SP. Why there are three fermion families. *Bulletin of the American Physical Society*. 1982;27:31.

20. Sirag SP. An $E_7$ unification scheme via the octahedral double group. Contributed paper at 23rd International Conference on High Energy Physics; 1986; Berkeley, California.

21. Sirag SP. Consciousness: a hyperspace view. In: Mishlove J., ed. *Roots of Consciousness*. Tulsa, OK: Council Oak Press. (In press.)

22. McKay J. Graphs, singularities, and finite groups. *Proc. Symp. Pure Math.* 1980;37:183–186.

23. Gilmore R. *Catastrophe Theory for Scientists and Engineers*. New York: Wiley-Interscience; 1981.

24. Arnold VI. *Singularity Theory*. New York: Cambridge University Press; 1981.

25. Arnold VI. *Catastrophe Theory*. Berlin: Springer-Verlag; 1986.

26. Conway JH, Sloane NJA. *Sphere Packings, Lattices and Groups*. New York: Springer-Verlag; 1988.

# V

# BIOSCIENCE

In this section, we descend from the abstract, ethereal realms of physics to become grounded in the most tangible domain of earthly existence—our own biological identities. We may at this point pause for a moment and wonder at the entire scheme of biochemical reality. All that we know and do is through the instrument of the body and its intermediary, the physical brain. Yet we can imagine other universes in which consciousness did not choose to manifest as biological matter.

Our universe, as a special case of all possible and indeed all extant universes, is contextualized by the philosophy of Jane Roberts, speaking as (some would say "channeling") her oversoul personality, Seth. In this view, consciousness permeates timeless universes as a formless, sense-less, undivided whole that at times desires to know itself in an infinitude of manifestations, including the physical. Consciousness, or spirit, is born into flesh to experience energy made into substance. Seth extends the equivalence of mass and energy ($e = mc^2$) to include ideas and thoughts. The energy of awareness, the soul's idea of itself, condenses into the mass of the organism. Similarly, the Kabbalah of mystical Judaism teaches that the Ain Soph, The Great Nothingness, comes into differentiated awareness, eventually manifesting in physical form in successive nodes on the Tree of Life. Although both Eastern and Western religions disparage the sins, pains, and pleasures of the flesh, Seth/Roberts tells us that "the body is not *just* a vehicle for the spirit. It *is* the spirit in flesh," born of the Universal Consciousness into Original Grace.[1]

As a physician, I note that people are likely to have their first transcendent or supernormal experience through the medium of their bodies, during illness or strenuous exercise. Virtually everyone accepts the mind–body connection implied by the effect of psychological stress on the body. There is nothing mystical in the concept that under stress, one is likely to develop indigestion, headaches, high blood pressure, and rashes. Stress as a cause of illness is a euphemistic concept that both hints at and obscures the specific information encoded by the body for the conscious mind. Understood as a decryption exercise, stress management is the process of deciphering the body's messages through techniques such as Psychosynthesis, with its subpersonality stratification, dreamwork, and dialoguing with symptoms.

The emerging field of psychoneuroimmunology (PNI) makes the mind–body communication protocols even more explicit. Barrett's chapter on PNI as the bridge between science and spirit surveys the state of the art in psychosomatic medicine. The most stunning implication of Barrett's thesis is that there is no fundamental difference between the mind's conscious ability to flex the muscles, mobilize self-healing powers, or send and receive telepathic information.

Brown and Quincy further blur the distinction between mind and body by addressing the chemistry of consciousness. It is no accident, Brown suggests, that plants evolved with substances that are psychoactive in the human brain. In Sethian reality, sequential evolution is an artifact of our linear time sense, from present back to past and ahead to future. In the true simultaneous time, all species exist at once. Plants and animals represent the complementary selves of All-That-Is, a single consciousness exalting in its myriad forms like a tree with many leaves.

Neurophysiologist Sir John Eccles postulates that there will be no species beyond *homo sapiens*. The buck stops here, in his view, because of cessation of selection pressure on the gene pool, presumably as a consequence of humankind's technological conquest of the environment. Quincy, however, suggests that paranormal functioning may confer a survival advantage. If this is true, we will evolve into a new species with highly developed psi abilities. In that next phase, no doubt polarized by advances in microprocessor-based prostheses, genetic engineering, and nano-robotic biovectors, we must ask what will become of the body. Will the body become vestigial at Childhood's End as evolution closes the loop into undifferentiated consciousness?

Rubik and Rauscher offer evidence that some unnamed influence with quantifiable effects on bacterial cultures may elucidate the scientific basis for psychic healing. How finely tuned our cells are to subtle influences is further revealed by the fact that norms for serum electrolyte values, as determined by clinical laboratory quality-control surveillance, fluctuate with sunspot cycles.

The bioscience chapters point to the exquisite sensitivity and yet the resilient sturdiness of biological systems. This combination of properties suggests that with, for instance, the cellular effects of ELF (extremely low frequency) radiation, the body–mind, in its infinite strength and wisdom, can *choose* to utilize the new energies or neutralize any potential for damage or both.

As the millennium draws near, we seem destined for many more centuries of highly technological research in molecular biology. At some distant time, we will have to leap the impasse at which our most reductionistic advances in biochemistry will not yet explain the emergent properties of the brain and their relation to the body.

Beverley Kane

**NOTES**

1. Roberts J. *The Nature of Personal Reality*. Englewood Cliffs, NJ: Prentice-Hall; 1974.

# 12

# Psychoneuroimmunology—The Bridge Between Science and Spirit

*Sondra Barrett*

A new field of science and medicine, psychoneuroimmunology (PNI), has evolved out of the interaction of psychology, neurobiology, immunology, theology, yoga, shamanism, and the space program. The union has not been an easy one, nor is it condoned by all its peers—yet. PNI started off on the shaky ground of psychosomatic medicine, which claimed that emotions and stress influence illnesses such as asthma, allergies, and rheumatoid arthritis. That the psyche could influence the soma was not a popular idea in academic medicine forty years ago. Now, some "accidents" of science, corroborated by the unprejudiced observations of astute investigators, add impetus to PNI's theories of mind–body connectivity.

## ANATOMICAL CONNECTIONS

Underlying the beginnings of this infant discipline was the quest to identify biological links between the nervous system and the immune system.[1-3] It must be kept in mind that until recently, it was believed that the immune system operated independently of any other system in the body. Because immune cells could function normally in the test tube, it was assumed that they were outside regulation by any internal or external factors.

Initial studies showed that there were nerves connected to the thymus, the primary organ of the immune system. Damage to the brain, specifically the hypothalamus and left cerebral hemisphere, was shown to damage the immune system.[4] Similarly, vaccination, which stimulates an immune response, was seen to accelerate the electrical firing of specific (noradrenergic) neurons in the hypothalamus.[5] In other words, there was now anatomical evidence that the nervous and immune systems can communicate with each other. Further evidence came when it was demonstrated that cells of the immune system, the lymphocytes, have receptors for many of the chemicals synthesized in the nervous system, such as growth hormone, adrenalin and noradrenalin, prolactin, acetylcholine, substance P, endorphins, and enkephalins.[6-9] Lymphocytes also can synthesize some of the same substances made by the nervous system, such as corticotropin and endorphins.[10] Conversely, astrocytes, cells in the brain, can produce interleukin-1, an effector of immune reactivity once thought to be made only by the immune cells.[11] Not only are there anatomical links between these two systems of the body, but they also share many of the same biochemical functions.

## CONDITIONING THE IMMUNE SYSTEM

The coup de grâce that launched PNI into legitimate interdisciplinary dimensions was the controversial discovery by Robert Ader, a psychologist, and Nicholas Cohen, an immunologist, that the immune system could be trained just like a reflex. In other words, it could be conditioned to do new things.[12] A new assumption came to modern science: If the immune system could learn behaviorally, then it must be part of or at least influenced by the mind. Conditioning, one form of learning, often occurs without conscious perception of the process.

Pavlov's classical conditioning of the dog with a dinner bell set the stage for a scientific protocol to study learning and the immune system.[13] Ader set out to discover how animals are conditioned to adverse stimuli. In his experiment, he fed rats saccharin-sweetened water paired with a one-time injection of a drug that would cause gastrointestinal upset. The association of the ill feeling with the sweet taste resulted in subsequent aversion to the saccharin-sweetened water. When thirst overpowered the aversion, the rats were obliged to drink the saccharin water. Unexpectedly, some of the animals died of infections during the extinction trials, and the mortality rate tended to vary directly with the amount of saccharin originally consumed. What was happening? Ader, in discussing the pharmacology of the drug he used, cyclophosphamide (Cytoxan), with immunologist Cohen, learned that this chemotherapeutic agent used in cancer treatment also suppresses the immune system. Even when the rats were no longer exposed to Cytoxan, they continued to suppress their immune systems in response to the sweetened water alone. Together, Ader and Cohen went on to confirm that the immune system can be suppressed through a classical conditioning paradigm. Subsequently many investigators have substantiated and expanded their work.

Other findings have shown that the senses are powerful triggers for conditioning the immune system. In the 1920s and 1930s, Metal'nikov, at the Pasteur Institute, injected bacteria into animals while simultaneously scratching their skin. Later, scratching alone evoked a large increase in white blood cell count and antibodies to the bacteria previously injected.[14] Besides taste and touch, the smell of camphor as well as visual cues have been used in association with agents that suppress or enhance immune capabilities.[13,15] In a series of experiments, Spector and associates conditioned interferon and natural killer cell activity by using a synthetic immunostimulant, Poly I:C, paired with the odor of camphor. Conditioning occurred after nine sessions. Poly I:C mimics the action of a virus, which acutely raises levels of interferon and natural killer cell activity. The odor of camphor alone, before conditioning, had no effect on immune functions.[14] In human studies, conditioning stimuli have been the odor of incense, rhythmic drum patterns, and unusual patterns of stroking the skin.

Jeanne Achterberg, author of *Imagery and Healing*[16] and *Bridges of the Bodymind,*[17] once suggested that perhaps someday people with cancer could take a mint paired with an antitumor drug. Eventually they could stop taking the drug and get the same beneficial effects with the mint, eliminating toxic side effects such as vomiting and hair loss.

## PLACEBO EFFECT

Any effect produced in the absence of an identifiable causal agent raises the question of whether a placebo (from the Latin for "I shall please") response is being triggered. The placebo effect has long been a nuisance to drug companies doing placebo-controlled studies to test new pharmaceutical agents. After all, how can a new sleeping pill be proved effective and commercially viable if experimental subjects who are strong placebo-responders sleep even better with an inert pill?

Although the mechanisms of the placebo response are not well understood, factors that influence placebo effects include the physician–patient relationship, the person's belief system, and environmental and cultural components. The existence of the placebo response implies that beliefs about one's own curative abilities can stimulate the necessary physiological systems that mediate healing. The psychological factors most commonly implicated are suggestion, expectation, anxiety reduction, and the hope and will to live. It has been suggested by Ader, Wickramasckera, and others that conditioning also may account for the placebo effect.[18,19] Wickramaskera says: "All effective interventions have the potential for Pavlovian conditioning and triggering a placebo response. The response to any active ingredient includes two components: a placebo and an active component."

Virtually every physiological response in the body, including blood flow, pain control, and cancer cytotoxicity has been subject to a placebo effect, and in most studies, the placebo accounts for at least 30% of all observed effects.[20]

Its changes can be positive or negative, producing the same effect as the active drug and the same unpleasant side effects.

In the one area of placebo studies, the biological mechanism is understood. Jon Levine and his colleagues at University of California San Francisco reported that placebos appear to modulate pain relief through release of endorphins, the brain's opiate-like pain-killing substances.[21]

## ATTITUDES AND SURVIVAL

The existence of the placebo effect opened the door for seeking to understand if and how belief, attitude, and states of mind affect the physical body. Much of the initial work in this area looked epidemiologically at the psychological differences between those people who stayed well and those who get sick. An excellent overview of the historical work is found in Blair Justice's book, *Who Gets Sick.*[22] Suzanne Kobasa, a pioneer in attitudes and health, studied executives from the Illinois Bell Telephone Company during the stressful time of federal deregulation and showed that certain mind states contributed to health and hardiness.[23] In Kobasa's subjects, the factors most predictive of healthy coping were the three Cs: *challenge*—the perception of a threat or change as a challenge, a problem looking for a solution; *control*—the ability to do something about the situation versus a feeling of victimization; and *commitment*—the sense of purpose in life, that there is something important to accomplish. The three Cs, which Kobasa deems the *hardiness factor,* have been shown to be the basis for resilience and survival in brutal circumstances, such as during the Holocaust and in prisoner-of-war camps.

Many attitudes, such as trust and nurturing, that contribute to health and well-being are formed, for the most part, during childhood. It is widely known that loving touch is essential in human infant survival and growth. One study found that if baby rats were gently handled every day from birth to weaning (22 days), they showed much smaller stress hormone responses than unhandled rats, an effect that lasted until "old age"—24 months.[24]

The importance of childhood upbringing is implicated in the relation between learned hostility and coronary heart disease. Cultural differences in children shed some light on how attitudes learned as children influence later health and behavior. For example, a central feature of the typical Japanese personality is *amae,* the expectation of being treated well and with kindness by others. Child-rearing practices in Japan include close physical contact, little separation from the mother, and preference for maternal–child closeness over strict discipline. The child abuse common in the United States is virtually nonexistent in Japan.[25] Traditional Japanese mothers avoid expressing negative emotions toward or about the child and take care to spare the child embarrassment. The parental attitude toward the child is that he or she is good, wonderful, and clever.[26] This early benevolent environment coupled with preliminary research findings of lower hostility scores among urban Japanese men led Williams and coworkers to postulate that the attitude of the Japanese toward their children is a contributing factor to lower rates of coronary heart disease in Japan compared with these in the United States, where child-rearing is very different. As discussed below, hostility has been identified as a key psychological factor in coronary artery disease.

The challenge for researchers and practitioners of PNI is to find ways to teach healthful attitudes to those who haven't learned them as children. A specific goal is to help people shift from a helpless mode to one in which they experience control and mastery. Subjected to uncontrollable stress from which they could not escape, animals were more likely to experience infections, increased tumor growth, and other experimentally induced diseases.[27,28] This led to the understanding that in people, too, helplessness and lack of control have long-range effects on mental and physical health. Furthermore, helplessness and optimism can be learned. As suggested by Martin Seligman, helplessness in one stressful situation often is carried over to others.[29]

The importance of a sense of control to overall health increases as we age. Research in the area of aging and autonomy has suggested that the ability to choose one's environmental surroundings is important in healthy aging. Adverse effects on health after admission to a nursing home were in part a function of the amount of individual control over the move. Prospective residents given a choice about when and where they moved as well as about some specifics of the living arrangements showed little decline in level of health and psychological well-being.[30] Lack of control has adverse effects on emotional states, performance, and subjective well-being.[31] As we age, the locus of control often changes from internal, or directed from within, to external, or imposed from without.

PNI provides a scientific structure for understanding the biology and psychology of how attitudes or emotional states, like optimism, or internal locus of control impact the immune system, the quality of life, and longevity.[32] PNI research also provides us with the rational incentives to search for empirical ways to alter consciousness to improve health. Negative emotional states, such as depression,[33] loneliness,[34] hopelessness,[35] and bereavement[36] suppress immune function, making a person more prone to illness. Anger, another so-called negative emotion, appears to have its first effects on the cardiovascular system rather than the immune system. In the 1950s, Meyer Friedman and Ray Rosenman introduced the concept of coronary-prone or Type A behavior—the fast-paced, impatient "hyper" person—to help explain the increased incidence in coronary artery disease in twentieth-century Western societies.[37] More recently, Redford Williams and others showed that not all Type A behaviors were life-threatening.[38,39] Hostility, lack of trust, and cynicism seem to be the damaging components of Type A behavior.[40]

Are there ways a person can counterbalance or change self-defeating attitudes and emotions and continue in a state of health despite great upheavals? It is the mandate of PNI to search for and develop these behaviors. With the benefit of Soviet science, we find clues to altering emotional behavior and physical responses—the mind–body dialogue.

## THE SPACE PROGRAM, ATHLETICS, AND YOGA

Pioneering work on stress by Nobel laureate Hans Selye established that our emotions and mental states dramatically influence activities of the autonomic nervous system, such as hormonal activity and blood flow.[41,42] Excitement or anxiety can increase blood pressure and heart rate and cause blood vessel constriction, producing cold hands and feet. Worry, depression, or performance anxiety can slow other body and brain functions.

During our day-to-day existence, we all experience emotional ups and downs, but there was one arena in which emotional instability was unacceptable—the Soviet and American space programs. In the early 1950s, initial efforts of the Soviet space program were aimed at exploring the possibility of using the techniques of yoga to teach cosmonauts to control psychological and physiological processes while in space. Yoga is an ancient Eastern mental and spiritual system in which the practitioner can learn to regulate functions such as temperature, heart rate, and mental concentration. Using the traditional teachings, the Soviets developed methods of control that depend on feedback signals between the body and the mind. The training emphasized voluntarily control of heart rate and muscle tension as well as of emotional reactions to stressful situations like zero gravity. Before this work, most scientists, unfamiliar with or skeptical of yoga, believed that these autonomic, automatic functions were outside conscious control.

Similarly, in the early phases of the American space program, National Aeronautics and Space Administration (NASA) scientists predicted that during prolonged lunar spaceflights, astronauts would experience irregular blood pressure and heart rate along with emotional lability. To combat these effects, rather than risk drugs that had never been tested at zero gravity, NASA began to explore self-regulation through meditation and biofeedback. In a spaceflight simulator, the astronauts were taught how to preprogram their minds and bodies for optimal space performance. Yet even with their self-regulation abilities perfected, when the astronauts returned from orbit, they showed some damage to immune function and decreased bone density. The latter was in part attributed to hypersecretion of adrenal stress hormones, the corticosteroids.[43]

What was learned in space projects like Apollo—the disciplined use of imagination, the importance of mental rehearsal, and biofeedback—contributed to PNI's investigations into which specific self-regulatory methods are most effective in reversing the negative effects of stress, emotions, and thoughts.

From their success with controlling automatic responses in the cosmonauts, Soviet scientists set out to discover how emotional reactions, detrimental to peak athletic performance, could be regulated consciously before competition. They discovered that certain mental training techniques helped to combat stress and heighten physical abilities. The power of visualization and imagery to alter physical performance was first evident in recent times in weight lifting, golf, skiing, and tennis. Many *Inner Game of* — books were written in the 1970s, using imagery, mental rehearsal, and relaxation to improve performance in these sports.

Superior athletic performance brought to public awareness the effects of stress, attitude, and mental training on physical training and prowess. In his book *Peak Performance,* Charles Garfield describes how athletes identify the signs of stress and negative emotions as shortness of breath, lost coordination, cramped muscles, and the inability to perform optimally.[44] In other words, when an athlete is worried about his or her performance, the body responds in ways that makes performance less successful.

The body–mind methods that have been perfected for optimal performance in astronauts and athletes are finally entering the health arena. From the traditions of yoga, a new body–mind technology is achieving scientific respectability and proving to be useful "medicine" in many health-promoting settings.

## RELAXATION RESPONSE, MEDITATION, AND PRAYER

Harvard physician Herbert Benson studied yogis and other people engaged in meditation practices for biological clues to possible health benefits. His work has contributed substantially to integrating yoga with a modern understanding of stress. Central to Benson's definition of the relaxation response is his idea that the body operates in a yin-yang, on-off manner. For every *on* reaction, or stress response, he believes that there must be a corresponding *off* response.[45,46]

Benson showed that the relaxation response, exemplified in transcendental meditation, improves hypertension and irregular heart rhythms. Since his initial studies, it has been learned that meditation is effective in alleviating presurgery anxiety and the adverse effects of cancer chemotherapy and can decrease a diabetic's need for insulin. By putting the body in a state of altered consciousness and lowered biochemical arousal, a more balanced homeostasis is achieved.

Benson expanded his study of the biological effects of meditation to discover its heart- and consciousness-opening abilities. He began to see a relation between meditation and prayer. The study of prayer seems to have no place in science, yet a much-quoted study done by cardiologist Randy Byrd at San Francisco General Hospital looked at the effect of prayer in 393 persons who had suffered a myocardial infarction (heart attack).[47] Compared with a control group of 201 patients, the 192 patients named in prayer had fewer complications while in the cardiac care unit. The prayed-for group had between five and seven Protestants, Catholics, and Jews across the United States praying for them each day. Those praying were given the patient's name, diagnosis, and condition and were asked to pray for the beneficial healing and quick recovery for each person. In this experiment, the patients were not told of the prayers, nor did the people praying personally know those whom they were praying for. Although such a unique study is highly suggestive, it is difficult to design and execute studies in the accepted methodologies of science to test these subtleties.

## SOCIAL TIES THAT BIND

Similarly, characterization of the potential of personal relationships to benefit health and longevity has seemed implausible as a biological experiment. Work by dedicated investigators, however, is beginning to show what we intuitively might expect: that the kinds of relationships we have affect our risk of disease. The residents of Roseto, Pennsylvania, have most of the risk factors for heart disease—a high-fat diet, obesity, smoking—yet they have significantly lower rates of heart disease than the rest of the United States.[48] Why? The conclusion was that this is a close-knit community in which the social ties are strong.

Other ground-breaking work on the importance of the quality of relationships, intimacy, and health came first from epidemiological studies and then from research by James Pennebaker and his associates. Prospective epidemiological studies showed greater morbidity and mortality in people with fewer close relationships.[49] Both the quality of relationships and their disruption influence immune function.[50] Furthermore, Pennebaker, Janice Kiecolt-Glaser, and Richard Glaser showed that being able to express emotions from past traumatic events improves not only immune function in the test tube, but also health.[51] In Pennebaker's original experiments, college students who had been sexually or physically abused as children spent fifteen minutes a day writing about their early traumas.[52] In their journals, they emphasized their feelings rather than the narrative of the events. After a trial of only four consecutive days of writing, long-range effects were apparent. The students had stronger lymphocyte reactivity, used the student health service significantly less frequently for illness, and had less subjective distress than a control group of students who wrote about random, nonemotional things. Failure to confront a buried trauma forces the person to live with it in an unresolved manner; actively confronting it allows for understanding and assimilation.

The salutary effects of intimate relationships and the ability to disclose emotional traumas were further demonstrated in support groups for breast cancer patients in research by Stanford psychiatrist David Spiegel.[53] After one year, patients reported only subjective changes such as mood improvement and pain reduction. Then, unexpectedly, in a ten-year follow-up, a difference in survival time was discovered in those patients who had been in the support group. Such compelling evidence of prolonged survival resulting from group psychotherapy suggests that one major change in the practice of medicine should be the inclusion of psychosocial support as an integral part of any cancer therapy program.

## FUTURE HEALTH AND MEDICINE

PNI is in a position to create a solid theoretical framework for preventive medicine. By continuing to provide experimental data, as much as possible, on the mind–body connection, PNI will clarify how mental states confer susceptibility to and protection from illness. Concomitantly, PNI clinicians will define practical means of strengthening the internal environment.

The clinical applications of this information may be of profound value for people with AIDS (acquired immune deficiency syndrome), cancer, and autoimmune diseases such as rheumatoid arthritis. Even in the absence of unequivocal laboratory data on the beneficial effects of imagery and relaxation on immune function and longevity, these modalities are being effectively used for improving the subjective quality of life in people with illness or stress.

This chapter has focused on the objective aspects of PNI. It provides the reader with a context in which to interpret future work on the effects of consciousness-altering modalities on health. Medical science tends to emphasize quantitative, reproducible outcomes from quantifiable, reproducible interventions. In our efforts to seek out the hard facts, we also must acknowledge the role of spirit in healing. The effects of subtle energies may be more elusive, less universal than those of, say, penicillin. But the results for the individual are no less dramatic.

Medically, PNI will offer insight into how, beyond the chemical changes, consciousness affects the body. Philosophically, PNI promises to leap from its formal proofs to an elucidation of the spiritual component of healing and the quest for purpose so essential to health and quality of life.

## NOTES

1. Bulloch K, Pomeranz W. ANS innervation of thymic-related lymphoid tissue in wild-type and nude mice. *J. Comp. Neurol.* 1984;228:57–68.

2. Cabanac J. Les nerfs du thymus. *Bull. Assoc. Anat.* 1931;25:92–100.

3. Bulloch K. Neuroanatomy of lymphoid tissues: a review. In: Guillemin R et al, eds. *Neural Modulation of Immunity*. New York: Raven Press; 1985:49–85.

4. Cross RJ, Markesbery WR, Brooks WH, Rozman TL. Hypothalamic-immune interactions. I. The acute effect of anterior hypothalamic lesions on the immune response. *Brain Res.* 1980;196:79–87.

5. Besedovsky HO, Sorkin E, Felix D, Haas H. Hypothalamic changes during immune response. *Eur. J. Immunol.* 1977;7:323–325.

6. Pert CB, Ruff MR, Weber RJ, Herkenham M. Neuropeptides and their receptors: a psychosomatic network. *J. Immunol.* 1985;135:118–122.

7. Malinski W, Grabezewska E, Ryzewski J. Acetylcholine receptors of rat lymphocytes. *Biochem. Biophys. Acta.* 1980;663:269–273.

8. Payan DG, Goetzl EJ. Modulation of lymphocyte function by sensory neuropeptides. *J. Immunol.* 1985;135:783–785.

9. Hazum E, Chang KJ, Cuatrecasas P. Specific non-opiate receptors for $\beta$-endorphins on human lymphocytes. *Science.* 1970;205:1033–1035.

10. Smith EM, Blalock JE. Human leukocyte production of corticotropin and endorphin-like substances. *Proc. Nat. Acad. Sci.* 1981;789:7530–7534.

11. Fontana A, McAdams KP, Kristensen F, et al. Biological and biochemical characterization of interleukin-1 from glioma cells. *Eur. J. Immunol.* 1983;13:685–688.

12. Ader R, Cohen N. Behaviorally conditioned immunosuppression. *Psychosom. Med.* 1975;37:333–340.

13. In Pavlov's experiment, a dog was given food at the same time a bell rang. The dog would salivate in response to the food while hearing the bell. Eventually the dog would salivate at the sound of the bell alone, when no food was presented.

14. Metal'nikov S, Chorine V. Role des reflexes conditionnels dans l'immunite. *Ann. Inst. Pasteur.* 1926;40:893–900.

15. Ghanta V, Miramoto R, Solvason B, and Spector HN. Neural and environmental influences on neoplasia and conditioning NK activity. *J. Immunol.* 1926;135:848–852.

16. Achterberg J. *Imagery and Healing.* Boston: Shambhala; 1985.

17. Achterberg J, Lawlis F. *Bridges of the Bodymind.* Champaign, IL: Institute for Personality and Ability Testing; 1980.

18. Ader R. Conditioned immunopharocological effects in animals: Implications for a conditioning model of pharmacotherapy. In: White L, Tursky B, Schwartz G, eds. *Placebo: Theory, Research and Mechanisms.* New York: Guillford Press; 1985:306–323.

19. Wickramasekera I. A conditioned response model of the placebo effect: Prediction from the model. In: White L, Tursky B, Schwartz G, eds. *Placebo: Theory, Research and Mechanisms.* New York: Guilfford Press; 1985:255–287.

20. O'Regan B. Placebo effects: a review. *Investigations,* Institute of Noetic Sciences. 1988;2:1–31.

21. Levine J, Gordon NC, Fields HL. The mechanism of placebo analgesia. *Lancet.* 1978;2:654–657.

22. Justice B. *Who Gets Sick.* Los Angeles: Jeremy Tarcher; 1988.

23. Kobasa SC. The hardy personality: toward a social psychology of stress and health. In: Sanders GS, ed. *Social Psychology of Health and Illness.* Hillsdale, NJ: Lawrence Erlbaum; 1982.

24. Schaneberg SM, Field TM. Sensory deprivation stress and supplemented stimulation in the rat pup and preterm human neonate. *Child Development.* 1987;58:766–768.

25. Doba N, Hinohara S, Williams RB. Studies on Type A behavior pattern and hostility in Japanese male subjects with special reference to CHD. *Jpn. J. Psychosom. Med.* 1983;23:321–328.

26. Stevenson H, Azuma H, Hakuta K. *Child Development and Education in Japan.* New York: WH Freeman; 1986.

27. Riley V. Psychoneuroendocrine influences on immunocompetence and neoplasia. *Science.* 1981;212:1100–1109.

28. Laundenslager ML, Ryan SM, Drugan RC, et al. Coping with immunesuppression: inescapable but not escapable shock suppresses lymphocyte proliferation. *Science.* 1983;221:565–570.

29. Seligman MEP. *Helplessness: on Depression, Development and Death.* San Francisco: WH Freeman; 1975.

30. Rowe J, Kohn R. Human aging: usual and successful. *Science.* 1987;237:143–149.

31. Krantz D, Schulz R. Application of personal control. *Adv. Environ. Psychol.* 1980;2:23–57.

32. Pelletier KR, Herzig D. PNI: towards a mind-body model. A critical review. *Advances.* 1988;5:27–56.

33. Schleifer S, Keller SE, Meyerson AT, et al. Lymphocyte function in major depressive disorders. *Arch. Gen. Psychiatry.* 1984;41:484–486.

34. Kiecolt-Glaser J, Garner W, Speicher C, et al. Psychosocial modifiers of immunocompetence in medical students. *Psychosom. Med.* 1984;46:7–14.

35. Goodkin K, Antoni MH, Laney B. Stress and hopelessness in the promotion of cervical neoplasia. *J. Psychosom. Res.* 1986;30:67–76.

36. Bartrop RW, Lazarus L, Luckhurst E, Kiloh LG. Depressed lymphocyte function after bereavement. *Lancet.* 1977;1:834–836.

37. Friedman M, Rosenman R. Association of specific overt behavior patterns with blood and cardiovascular findings. *JAMA.* 1959;169:1286–1290.

38. Blumenthal P, Williams RB, Kong Y, et al. Type A behavior patterns and coronary atherosclerosis. *Circulation.* 1978;58:634–639.

39. Matthews KA, Haynes SG. Type A behavior patterns and coronary risk: update and critical evaluation. *Am. J. Epidemiol.* 1986;123:23–96.

40. Williams RB, Barefoot JC, Haney TL, et al. Type A behavior and angiographically documented coronary atherosclerosis in a sample of 2287 patients. *Psychosom. Med.* 1988;50:139–152.

41. Selye H. *The Stress of Life.* New York: McGraw-Hill; 1956.

42. Selye H. The physiology and pathology of exposure to stress. *Acta;*1975.

43. Wronsky TJ, Morey ER. Alterations in calcium homeostasis and bone during actual and simulated space flight. *Med. Sci. Sports Exerc.* 1983;15:5410–5414.

44. Garfield CA, with Bennet HZ. *Peak Performance. Mental Training Techniques of the World's Greatest Athletes.* New York: Warner Books; 1984.

45. Benson H, with Klipper MZ. *The Relaxation Response.* New York: William Morrow; 1975.

46. Benson H, Beary J, Carol M. The relaxation response. *Psychiatry.* 1974;37:37–46.

47. *Brain Mind Bulletin.* 1986;11:7.

48. Bruhn JG. An epidemiological study of myocardial infarctions in an Italian-American community. *J. Chronic Dis.* 1965;18:353–365.

49. Cohen S, Syme SL. *Social Support in Health.* New York: Academic Press; 1985.

50. Kiecolt-Glaser J, Fisher L, Ogrocki P, et al. Marital quality, marital disruption and immune function. *Psychosom. Med.* 1987;49:13–34.

51. Pennebaker J, Manger SD, Tiebout J. Confronting traumatic experiences and health among Holocaust survivors. *Advances.* 1989;6:14–17.

52. Pennebaker J, Kiecolt-Glaser J, Glaser R. Disclosure of traumas and immune function: health implications for psychotherapy. *J. Consult. Clin. Psychol.* 1988;56:239–245.

53. Spiegel D, Kraemar HC, Bloom JR, Gottheil E. Psychological support for cancer patients. *Lancet.* 1989;2:1447–1449.

# 13

# Human Volitional Effects on a Model Bacterial System

*Beverly Rubik and Elizabeth A. Rauscher*

What are the dynamics of healing and health? What is the purpose of illness and death? Are all living systems interconnected in some fundamental manner? Does such a fundamental connectedness involve a fundamental non-local aspect of human consciousness? Is this interconnectedness mediated by an energy or an informational process?

In this study, we address these and other vital issues that relate to a better comprehension of the nature and properties of living systems and life in general. We examine healing as a restoring phenomenon that involves fundamental and natural processes of living systems.

Health is everything; it is a positive, glowing state of mental, physical, and spiritual well-being. It is wholeness in function and not simply the absence of disease. The term "dys-ease" only provides a contrast to the state of wholeness or health. It is readily apparent that there is a natural healing property or restoring force, an innate intelligence, that all living things appear to possess. Small afflictions of the human body, ignored, soon heal without action of the conscious mind. Only when the wound or disease is severe or permanently disabling does the impetus to understand the process of healing and how it can be implemented come to the fore.

Historically, the practitioners of healing in our Western tradition have shifted from the practice of an art to the practice of science. Most modern physicians would agree that they are only assisting in the natural healing process of the body, rather than effecting any cure. As one practicing physician said, "note the word *practice* connected with the word *medicine.''* The healing process today remains largely a mystery. Yet modern scientific methodology and knowledge give us tools to scientifically explore healing and apply this knowledge to alleviate suffering and amplify health. To date, most medical research has been based on the study of the invasion of the physical body, the alleviation of disease, and symptomatic relief, sometimes by means of drastic chemical and surgical intervention. An alternative and complementary approach would be to focus on health itself—how to obtain it and how to maintain it naturally. Health is manifest at the physical, emotional, and mental levels as a wholism such that understanding this vital resource may involve exploring spiritual and psychic health as well.[1]

Can one only heal one's self, according to the saying, "Physician, heal thyself"? Or can others aid in the process? The methodology of Western medicine assumes that others can assist the patient in regaining his or her health. It appears that one can determine one's own movement toward or away from health by one's attitude, as is evidenced by psychosomatic illnesses. Some accidents, or the state of being accident prone, may be attributed to one's own state of mind. How much does one's attitude and self-awareness govern one's health, and how much can be induced and amplified by another person?

The laying on of hands is an age-old tradition and is portrayed, for example, in art of ancient Egypt and Babylon. It has since been part of all cultures and has its place in our science-dominated culture as well, as evidenced by the work of Olga and Ambrose Worrall and others.[2] It is largely considered to be paranormal, however, and outside orthodox science and medicine. Section 3 of the American Medical Association Principles of Medical Ethics states that "a physician should practice a method of healing founded on *scientific* basis and should not voluntarily associate professionally with anyone who violates this principle."

The scientific methodology exists in which to test the effects of laying on of hands under controlled laboratory conditions. Our extensive research of healers' laying on of hands on a model bacterial system was conducted with Dr. Beverly A. Rubik, then of John F. Kennedy University (Orinda, California), and Dr. William Van Bise, Tecnic Research Laboratories (San Leandro, California). (Van Bise and Rauscher also have extensively examined the interaction of electromagnetic fields with biological systems in healing.)

## OBJECTIVES

Regarding the possibility of an energy exchange between living organisms, we conducted three comprehensive studies in which we examined the intentional effects of a well-known healer, Dr. Olga Worrall, on the growth and motility of a model bacterial system, *Salmonella typhimurium,* which Rubik has studied for six years.[1] These three studies were conducted in February 1979, April 1980, and December 1981. A fourth study was done in November

1982, and two additional studies are planned, using the volitional effects of Dennis Adams of California.

The purpose of this work is to (a) investigate the fundamental process of the laying on of hands; (b) elucidate the mechanism of a healing process on a well-characterized organism; and (c) demonstrate that our methodology yields a strong and persistent phenomenon that we and others can replicate. Thus we envision our work as an important contribution to the increased credibility and scientific acceptance of the effects of healers on the healing process.

Our experimental design involves the following criteria: (a) that the organism used to study healer effects be previously well characterized and experimentally familiar to us; (b) that real-time control (healer-untreated) samples, identical to test samples (healer-treated), be used; (c) that it be possible for the healer to obtain immediate feedback as to her effects on the system; (d) that the parameters used to measure the viability of the target organism vary relatively rapidly, are quantifiable, and hence are subject to statistical analysis; (e) that permanent records of both test and control samples are made; and (f) that after the healer treatment, data is gathered under double-blind conditions, such that any conscious bias on behalf of the experimenters may be eliminated.

Bacterial motility (swimming behavior), measured by means of a stroboscopic microscope with attached camera, and bacterial culture growth, measured by means of light absorption in a spectrophotometer, are the two parameters we used that satisfy all these criteria.[3,4]

## METHODS

*S. typhimurium* was grown at 30° C. on a gyratory shaker in flasks that contained a liquid medium designed for the species, Vogal-Bonner citrate, with 1% glycerol added as a carbon source (food supply). The bacteria were actively growing and used directly for experimentation.

In the growth experiments, identical samples were prepared by means of sterile technique transferring 15-milliliter portions of the culture to sterile capped test tubes.[5] For the motility studies, glass microscope slides containing 3 microliters of bacterial suspension under a coverslip were prepared in the presence of the healer. Chemical agents used to damage either motility or growth of the bacteria were diluted with bacterial media and added to the samples before any healer treatment.

Healer treatment consisted of Dr. Worrall holding her hands near, but not touching, the bacteria for about two minutes. As a control, we had a laboratory technician who was uninformed about the purpose of our experiments hold sample test tubes for two minutes. During healer treatment, control samples were removed from the room to eliminate possible healer effects at moderate distances. After treatment, samples were labeled and data gathered. In the motility experiments, the bacteria were observed and photographed immediately after healer treatment and at intervals up to 20 minutes post healing. In the growth experiments, light absorption of the cultures at a wavelength of 620 nanometers was monitored in a spectrophotometer up to 48 hours post healing.

Quantification of healer effect was based on measuring differences in the viability curves (numbers of bacterial survivors over time) between treated and control samples.

## RESULTS

We found similar trends in the data of each of the bacterial growth experiments for each antibiotic (growth inhibitor) used, as well as a dose–response effect. That is, for smaller concentrations of the antibiotic, the healer treatment produces a greater positive effect on bacterial growth than that resulting from healer treatment of bacteria in larger concentrations of the antibiotic. A dose–response effect is one criterion for a real and definite effect in medical research. It appears that the bacteria respond more positively to healer treatment when they are less damaged by an antibiotic.

We also found that in each of the three major studies, the time course of the effects of healer treatment on bacterial growth rate is relatively constant and depends on the specific antibiotic. For each healer-treated bacterial sample, the viability curve features are similar for each antibiotic used. These characteristic curves are one indicator of consistency in and reproducibility of our experimental data, rendering them more valid.

A summary of the conditions and results of all our experiments is presented in Table 13.1. The data is expressed as the percentage of difference of healer-treated samples over control and is calculated from the numbers of bacterial survivors (bacteria per milliliter $\times 10^9$) at equivalent numbers of bacterial generation times (time for a bacterium to divide in two). Each experiment consists of about 30 data points that measure the number of bacteria at time intervals in control and treated cultures. The bacterial generation time was determined by examining the light absorbance of cultures incubated at a constant temperature and measuring the time at which the culture had doubled in opacity. At 37° C., a bacterial generation time is about one hour. Spectrophotometric absorbance is a standard methodology for determining the number of viable cells, and at 620 nanometers, an absorbance of 0.03 corresponds to a concentration of 3.0 $\times 10^8$ *S. typhimurium* per milliliter.

In the control sample exposed to the laboratory technician control, the non-healer with nonhealing intentions had no effect on treated samples versus controls.

On two occasions during the experiments, Olga Worrall spontaneously volunteered unsolicited information that subsequently or contemporaneously proved to be correct. In one instance, on placing her hands near the growth-inhibited bacterial samples, she exclaimed that these were "like starving children." These samples in fact contained the methionine-minus mutagens. Because all the samples appeared identical, there were no clues to lead her to this information. On

**Table 13.1**

**Summary of Results from Healer-Influenced Bacterial Growth Experiments 1979, 1980, and 1981**

| Bacterial Culture Conditions | Generation Time (Hours) | % Average Difference of Healer-Treated Over Controls* |
|---|---|---|
| Normal, 1981  24 | + 23% | |
| Normal, 1979  16 | 0% | |
| **Growth Inhibition Using Antibiotics:** | | |
| 1 mg/ml Tetracycline, 1981 | 23 | +121% |
| 10 mg/ml Tetracycline, 1980 | 21 | + 28% |
| 10 mg/ml Chloramphenicol, 1981 | 22 | + 70% |
| 100 mg/ml Chloramphenicol, 1979 | 16 | + 22% |
| 100 mg/ml Chloramphenicol, 1980 | 21 | + 34% |
| 100 mg/ml Chloramphenicol with naive participant acting as healer | 23 | 0% |
| **Mutagens Present, 1981:** | | |
| 0.05 M Sodium nitrite | 31 | - 57% |
| 0.05 M sodium nitrite plus 10 mg/ml Tetracycline | 23 | + 50% |
| 0.05 M sodium nitrite plus 100 mg/ml Chloramphenicol | 23.5 | + 76% |
| Nutrient starved by removal of methionine to methionine auxotroph, 1980 | 23 | 0% |
| Motility inhibitor 50 mg/ml phenol present, 1979 | | + 7% |

* Percent difference is defined as (T-C)/C x 100%, where T = average number of bacteria in healer-treated samples, and C = average number of bacteria in control samples.

other occasions, Worrall placed her hands around a test tube labeled #20 and stated that it was anomalous and that she felt much "energy" associated with it. Data gathered subsequently on the growth of sample #20 indeed proved that it was an anomaly showing growth several times faster than all other samples. Such unplanned occurrences seem to hold no place in the scientific literature, but we believe them to be highly significant.

## DISCUSSION

There is an apparent exchange of energy and information between living organisms. This process appears to involve a form of mind–matter interaction that may be related to both psychic healing or so-called laying on of hands on living systems and psychokinetic interaction with inanimate systems.

Our results indicate that healer treatment produces significant growth and motility increases over control cultures in the presence of various chemical inhibitors. This leads us to hypothesize a general effect of healer intervention on cells, consistent, for example, with the possibility of field effects. One possibility is the existence of specific electromagnetic frequencies associated with laying on of hands that enhances vitality. In subsequent studies, we plan to replicate some of our previous experiments and examine field characteristics associated with Worrall during her treatment. Theoretical studies and planned additional experiments are now in progress.[6–8]

We would like to conduct future work to determine the level of cellular activity at which healing occurs, that is, whether it is at, for example, the level of extranuclear organelles, transfer ribonucleic acid, or deoxyribonucleic acid. We also plan to monitor certain physiological parameters of the healer, such as electroencephalography, electrocardiography, and Galvanomic skin response. Ambient electromagnetic, magnetic, and electrostatic fields before, during, and after an experimental session will also be examined. In addition, we plan to examine pulsed, low intensity–specific frequency and waveform effects on the bacteria cultures in the absence of a healer. Different healers will participate in our experiments. The mechanism of healing, blastimal cell formation, and regeneration of tissue will be examined in theory and by experimental examination.[9]

## NOTES

1. Rubik BA. *A Systems Approach to Bacterial Chemotaxis.* Berkeley: University of California; 1979. Dissertation.

2. Worrall A, Worrall O. *The Healing-Touch.* New York: Harper & Row; 1970.

3. Rauscher EA, Rubik BA. Effects of motility behavior and growth rate of *Salmonella typhimurium* in the presence of Olga Worrall. In: *Research in Parapsychology.* Metuchen, NJ: Scarecrow Press; 1980:140–142.

4. Rauscher EA, Rubik BA. Human volitional effects on a model bacterial system. *Psi Research.* 1983;2(1):38.

5. Spudich JL, Koshland DE, Jr. Quantitative assay for bacterial chemotaxis. *Proceedings of the National Acadamy of Science USA.* 1975;72:710–713.

6. Rauscher EA. Healing and psychokinesis as negentropic processes. Preprint *PSRL-241.* June 1982.

7. Rauscher EA. The physics of psi phenomena in space and time. *Psi Research.* 1983;2(2):87.

8. Rauscher EA. Application of human volition mind-matter interactions. *Applied Psi.* 1984;9, and *Archaeus* 1984;2(7):71.

9. Rauscher EA, Van Bise W. The dynamics of electromagnetic healing effects on in vitro and in vivo biological systems. Preprint *PSRL-10796;*1984.

# 14

# The Evolution of Consciousness Intertwined with the Evolution of the Science of Plants

*Dean Brown*

*. . . in media res . . .*

The evolutionist Lucretius, in his monograph *De Rerum Naturum,* reminds us that we are always in the middle of things. When we consider the progression of consciousness, we look backward in time to the beginning and forward in time to the end. Today, at the precise center of this very moment, we stand in the middle of that progression.

From the beginning of time up to this moment, all life has evolved symbiotically—each living entity has emerged in harmony with one another. In particular, it is impossible to contemplate humankind, both socially and as individuals, without accepting our interdependence with all living creatures, especially the plants. We and our food plants have genetically modified each other from the beginning. The same holds for our fabrics, poisons, medicines, and mental states. Even oxygen, the primal source of our mental and bodily energy, derives from the plants. We have all come along together.

Our scientific understanding of the interplay between plants and civilization has developed in a tendential sequence, as a vector of increasing sophistication, pointing from plant origins to domestication to foods to beverages to commerce to medicines to psychoactives to ethnobotany. I here expand that magnificent vision.

Perhaps there are a million species of plants altogether. Lynn Margulis, in her book *Five Kingdoms,* estimates that about 500,000 have been classified. About 3,000 are known to be edible, palatable, and nutritious. Eating habits worldwide are generally restricted to only six: corn, wheat, rice, beans, cabbage, and potatoes. Among the million plants that might be set upon our table, we live on only six!

What a long way we have to go. Many new foods (even many old foods) await us in our future. Surely in their own future time some of them will be preferred to what we eat today.

Reasoning statistically, there may be perhaps 5,000 plants with consciousness-affecting properties. Humankind knows and uses about 300. In common use, there are less than 10, particularly tobacco, opium, coca, cannabis, *Psilocybe,* and peyote. Add several socially acceptable plant products—sugar, alcohol, and caffeine. Many new consciousness plants lie in our future. Surely some of them will be preferred.

Before I proceed with ingested plants, consider the importance of other plants and plant materials in the everyday elevation and diversification of consciousness.

* Fabrics. I (and many others) require cotton as the sole fabric allowed to be in contact with my skin. My clothing, in soft, breathing, humankind-evolved cotton, is essential to my ability to feel, think, and act in comfort. It enhances my senses, my being, and my functioning. I insist on it.

* Flavors. Food seasonings are not important in nutrition, but they elevate the intensity and the qualities of my sensitivities—my moods and the efficacy of the incarnation of my lunch.

* Aesthetics. Our peace of mind depends on being with plants in landscaping, plants at home, in the office, in the hospital, at the airport, ubiquitous in our works of art. Their presence is essential to the quality of consciousness.

In one of those mysteries of nature, most of the psychoactive chemicals from the plant world fall into two vast and complex categories, alkaloids and glycosides. Alkaloids and glycosides contain rings and radicals that are isomorphs to those that carry on the processing in our central nervous systems.

Is it only an accident that plants produce chemicals so intimately aligned to animals' complex makeups? Continuing study of these strange molecules fails to reveal any value that they could possibly have for the plants that produce them. But their value for humans and their impact on consciousness has been interwoven with us throughout the entire track of our evolution.

William Blake, in "The Marriage of Heaven and Hell," says: "If the doors of perception were cleansed every thing would appear to man as it is, infinite." The alkaloids and glycosides present us with a vast spectrum in many dimensions for experiencing and exploring the "many mansions in our Father's house."

It is difficult to grasp the profound and subtle influences that plants have already made on consciousness, modifications of perception that have accreted through countless generations. The greatest effects are buried deeply in our behavior and ways of thought—genetically, socially, and aesthetically. They are embedded organically in the invisible substrate of our reality.

In the future, how much more so! Consciousness up to this point has largely evolved spontaneously, without much overt intervention on our part with organic chemistry, genetic engineering, or applied psychology.

But now, suddenly, the situation has become qualitatively different. Now we are manipulating the symbiosis of humans and plants with awareness, intentionality, purpose, and skill. Now, in this late twentieth century, we have passed a critical turning point.

In the flow of time from past to future, things occur at an exponentially increasing rate. In a historical context, we enjoy living on the cusp of intelligence. With modern science, information, attitudes, and perspectives, progress in the adaptation and synthesis of plant chemicals in the next twenty years will equal that of all history up to this point. Extrapolate that to 100 years, to 10,000!

Every food and medicine that we ingest has side effects, most of them undesirable, sometimes discovered much later. Take, for example, Bayer heroin (made around the turn of this century for heroes!) and aspirin. Plant chemists with sharper tools, greater command of their science, and better focus of their efforts will progressively manage the adverse effects and intensify the desired ones. Most significantly, they will lead us to refine our paradigms on precisely what it is that is desired. Here is the point at which genetics, biology, psychology, aesthetics, philosophy, and religion converge.

Here is the place to confront and examine our underlying subliminal beliefs, values, and goals. Here is the place to express and fulfill our humanness. Here is the precise center of the discipline of ethnobotany. Here is the vortex where the moral and ethical dimensions of science come into focus. Here culminates our ultimate existential question: When these materials will have been identified and produced, distilled to their ideal quintessences, how shall we choose to use them?

The answers will reveal the profiles and contours of the human mind and its thrust into the future, into its ultimate fulfillment. We will have produced a snapshot of the elements of consciousness. We do not have the option to do otherwise.

Coda: And so we come full circle from the future back to that most ancient wisdom, the tantras and the vedas—with their quest for that revered plant, soma—today unknown.

# 15

# Consciously Creating Conscious States

*Cheri Quincy*

How can we bring consciousness to the search for unusual or usually unconscious perceptions, moods, and behaviors? How can we use the tools we already have? How can we learn of what we are capable? Conscious responsibility for our responses to and personal control of our chemistry would seem to be basic to our individual liberty and the pursuit of happiness.

When is change called education, and when is it brain damage? Changes can be stimulating or inhibitory; they can be amplifying or extinguishing, novelty-generating or routine. Changes can result in increased information and choices, or they can decrease the amount of information in the system and lead to stereotypic behaviors and boredom. Habits are a repetitive, stable internal form, but they are rather notoriously ineffective for dealing with rapidly changing environments or variable or fluctuating stressors or for generating creative solutions to complex problems.

Conscious intention seems to be effective in generating powerfully desired states. That deliberate augmentation or stimulation of various neurotransmitters has been used for the enhancement of sexual behavior, for example, is strong evidence for the ability of people to use any particular neurotransmitter state for whatever behavior they are trying to evoke and a powerful example of our general ability to assign meaning to our chemistry on a conscious or nearly conscious basis.

Whatever we experience happens on a background of molecular chemistry. If there are associations, how can we begin to understand and use them to

expand human experience and range of perception? Many states of consciousness can be characterized by their associated chemical events. In what ways
can this neurochemistry help us understand our experiences of altered or paranormal states?

The chemistry of our moods and behaviors is extremely complex and can be
thought of as both reflecting and creating the electrical activity within our nerve
networks. But some generalizations can be made, based on both objective and
subjective observation.

## NEUROTRANSMITTERS

Chemical exchanges between the cells of our nervous system are part of the
language of mental events. The major neurotransmitters (dopamine, serotonin,
adrenalin, acetylcholine, endorphins, and many others) as well as hormones
drive our daily lives, influencing movement, thinking, mood, reactions, pain,
sleep, hunger, and thirst.

### Adrenalin States

The adrenalin state commonly is recognized as a state of fight or flight. At
the chemical level, we clearly have a cause-and-effect molecular process, but
the mental interpretation of that message varies with individual experience and
a person's ability to develop useful alternative behaviors. If we exercise no
creativity, we repeat the behavior that succeeded first. In most personal histories, our first adrenalin state was birth, and our first adrenalin-associated behaviors may have been fear, anger, and rejection, or they may have been excitement and love.

Adrenalin itself does not *determine* any behavior. Our *interpretation* of the
meaning of our detection, consciously or unconsciously, of the molecule adrenalin leads to our choosing a behavioral response. David Bohm has said that
*meaning* is the link between mind and matter.[1]

Is it possible to *decide* that an adrenalin rush means excitement rather than
threat? We can observe our responses and evaluate them by paying attention.
By exposing ourselves to novel stimuli and creating new ways of responding,
we can expand our chemical language.

Creativity-evoking behavior training requires the ability to extinguish a habit
by decoupling a stimulus–response loop. Many people actively seek the adrenalin state by riding roller coasters, skydiving, or watching scary movies. When
the adrenalin rush is interpreted as excitement and exhilaration, the body may
generate interleukins, extremely potent immunoprotective molecules, some with
antiviral and anticancer properties. Medically, a hyperadrenergic state is associated with Type A behavior, anxiety, panic attacks, and overachieving.

An adrenalin level interpreted as fear results in the production of corticosteroids, which suppress the immune system. Adrenalin can be blocked by the

prescription drug propranolol (Inderal). Inderal can decrease stagefright, test-taking anxiety, panic attacks, palpitations, migraine headaches, angina, and hypertension, but prolonged use may lead to slow heart rates, depression, anhedonia, and low-energy complaints.

The relative activity of our adrenergic system regulates the amount and kind of information we select to notice. (This is clearly demonstrated by the selective perception of a person in a state of paranoia: Everything he or she notices is threatening.) What is the optimal level of adrenalin for the perception of paranormal events? Sometimes hyperactive or highly emotional states seem to empower telepathic communication—many spontaneous reports involve an emergency—but controlled telepathy experiments have not required intense hyperadrenergic states.

## Dopamine States

Dopamine is another potent neurotransmitter. Its activity is increased by cocaine. The resulting state is similar to that induced by the related chemical family—amphetamine (crystal, ice) and some diet pills. Amphetamine stimulation usually is associated with high-energy feelings, a very directed and narrow focus of attention, self-centeredness, and egotistic, compulsive, hyperactive, hypersexual, and anorexic behavior states. Some evidence has led to the hypothesis that schizophrenia results from an excess of dopaminergic transmission.[2] Again, the chemistry *allows* a range of behavior but does not coerce.

In treating the selective dopamine deficiency condition Parkinson's disease, for example, there is a narrow range of balance in dopamine stimulation below which there is immobility and above which lies mania, insomnia, and hallucination.

## Serotonin States

Operating in a delicate balance with the dopamine-language neurons are those that use serotonin for communication. Serotonin augmentation leads to effects suggesting that the serotonin receptor family is involved in the chemistry of feelings of well-being, anxiety, depression, and appetite. Medicines like fluoxetine (Prozac) that enhance serotonin levels are used in the treatment of depression and anxiety. In the setting of empathic interpersonal counseling situations, phenethylamines (MDA, MDMA, etc.) were widely used until they became illegal.[3] L-Tryptophan, a serotonin precursor, was used as a relaxation- and sleep-inducing dietary supplement (until tainted synthetic preparations caused a Food and Drug Administration ban). D-Lysergic acid (LSD) also interacts with serotonergic synapses, among its other neurotransmitter effects. Serotonin states of consciousness are associated with deeply empathic feelings in religious contemplation and meditative states. The serotonin state seems to promote truthfulness and intimacy with decreased fear of emotional upset.

### Endorphin States

Endorphin and enkephalin chemistry usually is introduced as the body's own internal morphine system, the opioid peptides. Endurance athletes, near-death accident survivors, conscious natural childbirthers, and warriors are some who understand this state experientially. It can be characterized as a state of (mental) ecstasy resulting from the dissociation of the mind from the body. This naturally occurs under the onslaught of overwhelming information overload associated with pain and a threat to physical survival (often manifested as out-of-body experiences). Endorphins abolish pain and other bodily sensations. Is a lack of pain awareness a prerequisite for paranormal states? If so, how much? In morphine-, heroin-, or other opiate-associated states of consciousness, there is a decrease in blood flow to the brain, metabolism, and electrical activity across the entire sensory-motor cortex that correlates with progressive loss of attention, focus, and memory. With larger amounts, unconsciousness, coma, and death may occur, as complete mind-brain-body dissociation occurs.

### Natural Psychotropic Agents

Many kinds of neurotransmitters or their chemical precursors exist in our ecosystem naturally. They include the chemicals in plants such as marihuana, caffeine, nicotine, psilocybin, mescaline, coca, belladonna, and ergot or derivatives such as alcohol. In addition, many common foodstuffs (the psychoactive or mood foods), milk, peppers (and other nightshades), cheeses (and other tyramine-containing foods), chocolate, sugar, and others have behavioral effects through their action on endogenous (internal) neurotransmitters. Others are cognitively active because of habituation or associations (placebo effects and cultural expectations).

### HORMONES

Other kinds of molecules—hormones—mediate the various repeating cycles of our physiology. Cortisones, sex hormones (e.g., estrogen, prolactin, testosterone), thyroid, and the releasing factors have major effects on the local or general *eigenstate,* or local baseline, of the nervous system. It is rather remarkable that they have only recently been popularly recognized as major psychoactive molecules as well. Admittedly, we have long recognized that a pregnant woman behaves differently. Even folk wisdom presumes that this is due to major hormonal shifts. Similarly, the use of male hormones—anabolic steroids—by athletes is associated with a dramatic increase in overtly aggressive behaviors and violence. An epidemic in the number of women complaining of premenstrual syndrome (PMS) has again brought endocrinology to the public eye. Studies suggest that PMS may be a disease of imbalanced interpersonal communication on a pheromonal level. (The interpersonal effects of secreted molecules used to be considered magic or paranormal.) Decreased endorphin sensitivity also may be involved in PMS.

We are on the verge of recognizing that we are truly animals who live in the world of seasons and reproduction, growth, and involution cycles. It is presumed that the major life cycle changes of conception, birth, puberty, menopause, and life span are probably under hormonal control or influence. How do these molecules interact with our states of consciousness, and further, do we have any conscious way of interacting with them?

Perhaps it might be better to consider that we are already altering and interfering with our endocrinology on a global scale. We have added synthetic hormones to increase food production, and we prescribe synthetic hormones for a multiplicity of conditions, such as the often overdiagnosed hypothyroidism. In the West, it is not unusual for a woman to start taking hormones at puberty, add progesterone for PMS, change to estrogen plus progesterone at menopause, and continue until she dies. Does this affect the range of states of consciousness available to women in this culture?

One of the effects of taking exogenous hormones is to alter the composition of the molecules secreted by our adult sweat glands. That is, hormones change our pheromones. That and other denials of our chemical identities have possibly limited our ability to respond to smells and odors, our molecular communication with others. The olfactory richness of communal or tribal life has nearly been eliminated from urban *homo sapiens* (although other odors have filled the airspace). Cumulative transgenerational and intergenerational skills and information are being lost with every migration and refugee camp. Any experience with extrasensory communication as a function of the "what's in the air" is being lost. In truth, such communication is sensory; we're just not sensing it anymore.

## "EXTRA"-SENSORY PERCEPTION

Conscious perception occurs through special senses: the skin and associated specialized nerve receptors, the retina of the eye, taste, smell, and hearing. But not all perception is noted consciously. Most is *not* conscious. Immune perception, the ability to distinguish one molecule from another, is incredibly precise. The process takes place throughout the entire body, seldom enters the realm of consciousness, and simultaneously handles hundreds of microorganisms from viruses to parasites, often without causing symptoms or awareness. In addition, humans also are affected by vibratory, electromagnetic, gravitational, meteorological, and, possibly, paranormal stimuli.

## EMOTIONAL STATES: ACCESSIBLE AND CONTROLLABLE

As anyone who has ever been overcome by the baser urges knows, drives emanating from the hypothalamic-pituitary axis are extremely difficult to ignore. Thirst, hunger, sleep, warmth, mothering, and lust are only a few of the behaviors seemingly hard-wired into our physiology. But adrenalin will override many of these in the short term, as will other powerful endogenous or exogenous psychoactive agents. Some (stressful) states of consciousness are known to have effects on our endocrinology—for instance, the miscarriage or irregular menstruation that results from an emotional shock or loss.

Clearly, then, if the chemistry works both ways, which comes first? The extreme emotions associated with near-death states seem to catalyze major changes in both the behaviors and the mood of those who have experienced them. Alternatively, a convincing (near) death experience seems to be just as effective in catalyzing long-term behavioral and emotional-spiritual changes.[4] In either case, these changes in states of consciousness take place within a few seconds or minutes and sometimes involve remote viewing, telepathy, and spiritual contacts.

If these states are truly accessible to us, then only education in alternative states of consciousness and recognition of their power will save us from the helplessness implicit in a "Twinkie defense" or other violent acts committed while in a state of "temporary insanity."[5] Powerful, yes, but uncontrollable, no. We must always be willing to consider our chemistry as only one of the factors involved in our decisions and actions.

In addition, almost all sensory data is filtered through a judgmental cortex that frequently refuses to recognize what it doesn't expect. The patterning resulting in optical illusion can be generalized to belief systems and is one of the drawbacks of socialization to a consensus state of consciousness. This unconscious or automatic filtering of information by the cerebral cortex also is an efficient way to reduce information overload, habituate behaviors, and resist new ideas.

## CHOOSING STATES OF CONSCIOUSNESS

We seem to be in a state of destabilization of our molecular, hormonal, and temporal rhythms. Irregular work and sleep schedules, increased use of synthetic foods and medicines, and ubiquitous, accidental toxic exposures yield new chemical experiences both beneficial and detrimental. Increased interpersonal density results in increased stimulus density. The number of messages we must respond to may overwhelm anomalous or more unusual messages of the paranormal variety. Finding our personal *eigenstate* or center has become more difficult. We have destabilized and overloaded our input systems, and the result is *stress* (evolutionary pressure). People who can select new, useful information by conscious tuning of their neurochemical state may have a survival advantage.

With increased input to all our sensory systems and with stress, we have two of the preconditions for a jump in our level of understanding or the intelligent creation of new states of consciousness. Note that intelligence is not a particular state of consciousness, but the ability to access or create states of consciousness when it is useful to do so to most effectively interact with the universe. Changing circumstances require innovative solutions; we are limited only by the tools (chemicals, foods, sounds, lights, emotions, sensations, movements, thoughts) we use and how we intentionally use them together—use them for a purpose. At this point, we are limited only by our models of the possible and the preconceptions that limit our perceptions. To be able to consciously recognize what we now call paranormal or to use altered states or voluntary control of internal states, we must integrate them into our models of reality. "There is no monolithic, external, objective set of facts to which we can appeal in determining what is medically real. . . . Meanings and metaphors are powerful determinants not only of what we observe, but of what we *can* observe." [6] I suggest that the process will involve metaphors of sensitivity, recognition, relationship, and responsibility and the redefinition of acceptable social relationships and states of consciousness.

How do we consciously interact or assist in the process of growth? We tend to remain in the first state that "works" or in a previously learned compromise, rather than selecting a state of consciousness that is optimum after a careful exploration of multiple options using chemical tools (hormones, food, and other psychoactive molecules), rhythmic mechanical tools (sound, biofeedback, ecstatic dance, yoga, massage, hypnosis, and television), intellectual tools (verbal, written, virtual), and spiritual practices.

Human beings have a remarkable capacity for creating states of consciousness that facilitate complex behaviors and relationship interactions. The experiences that we have come to call parapsychological may represent the edges of our electro-mechanical-chemical receptor interpretation system. Many of these paranormal events could represent the results of novel states of consciousness that allow perceptual expansion. Rather than discard input that doesn't fit, we may have discovered new information access skills to cope with the challenges of our society. Many of these experiences depend on interpersonal connection and trust. Our challenge is to develop models that validate this information and to teach this skill for our continued survival—as a species and as individuals— and continued creative growth.

## NOTES

1. David Bohm, quoted in *Brain/Mind Bulletin*. 1985;10:1–2.

2. Kandel ER, Schwartz JH. *Principles of Neural Science*. 2nd ed. New York: Elsevier; 1985:22.

3. Shulgin A, Shulgin A. *Pihkal: A Chemical Love Story*. Berkeley, CA: Transform Press; 1991.

4. Grof S. *Beyond the Brain*. Albany: State University of New York Press; 1985.

5. In the famous "Twinkie defense," Dan White, convicted killer of San Francisco Mayor George Moscone and Supervisor Harvey Milk, argued that he was a victim of temporary insanity brought about by eating junk food.

6. Dossey L. *Meaning and Medicine*. New York: Bantam Books; 1991:132.

# VI

# PSYCHOLOGY

Psychology, the science of mind, as an intellectual and pragmatic discipline, appears fully developed in our most ancient literature: Gilgamesh, the book of Job, the Vedas, Beowulf. The masterpieces of Cervantes and Shakespeare can be studied as learned treatises on applied psychology. The idioms change with the times; the substance remains valid. The chapters in this section bring a modern expression of the age-old discipline—the idiom of contemporary science with its emphasis on experimental design, verifiability of results, and induction of patterns of data into rational hypotheses and theories. Psychology as a science is now expanding to meet other sciences, notably physics, biology, and medicine. The stimulus of fresh thinking resulting from these fertile boundary discontinuities is exhilarating.

Traditionally, psychology is chiefly concerned with perceptions, moods, motivations, and a person's management of experience and events. Where lies the boundary between psychology and parapsychology? Perhaps parapsychology is a smaller domain of phenomena and experience embraced fully within the universe of psychology. More likely, parapsychology is that part of psychology that is not yet understood. The contributions in this section illustrate how modern research is thrusting out into areas once reserved for physics, sociology, the healing arts, aesthetics, creativity, and broader realizations of the true nature of intelligence.

Many of the aspects of perception and intelligence studied in this section involve seemingly disparate processes that simultaneously go on in a person's awareness. New emphasis on biological modularity (Cubelli, ''A Selective Deficit for Writing Vowels in Acquired Dysgraphia,'' in *Nature,* September 19, 1991, 258) suggests how cognitive abilities correlate with brain and central nervous system functions. For example, the peculiar ways in which subjects verbalize perceptions of remote-sensing targets suggest that we investigate the physiologic aspects of our experiments. Other modularity phenomena can be found in the literature on idiot savants and prodigies, conditions that suggest a provocative area for more research on the neurobiological correlates with parapsychology.

Another area for more emphasis is state dependency: We have strong indications of state-dependent learning, state-dependent memory, state-dependent reproducible behavior patterns, and state-dependent perception. In fact, reality itself is state-dependent! Do the results of an experiment depend on the mood of the experimenter or the subject, on the setting and the ambience of the experiment? Most researchers believe that they do, but these factors seldom are controlled for in most formal research as generally reported.

An important part of state dependence is the effect of other people on subjects in an experiment. A subject cannot avoid being influenced by people present (or even by people not present), their belief systems, their expectations, and the subject's perceived relationship to them. In a limited sense, these parameters affect experimental design. In a broader and even more interesting sense, they show that reality itself is strongly colored by group mind and individual mind. Individual mind—if a person were in perfect isolation for a long time, what would his stream of consciousness be like? Could he avoid the effect of external influences on his perceptions?

Biologically and psychologically, we are, each of us, compelled to explain, digest, and rationalize our experience. This compulsive trait also must be taken into account in parapsychological research, with regard to both subjects and those conducting the research. The compulsion is so strong that there is a tendency to draw untenable conclusions. The presentations in this section have gone to great lengths to protect against these subtle biases.

Dean Brown

# 16

# Alternate States of Consciousness: Access to Other Realities

*Ruth-Inge Heinze*

Whether we admit it or not, we all experience different states of consciousness. While we are sleeping, for example, our consciousness appears to be at rest, but dreams arise and we cross thresholds and enter different realities not easily accessible during so-called ordinary, *consensus* reality. There are other occasions when access to different realities opens up spontaneously, even while we are awake. Such openings may occur when conditions and prerequisites coincide naturally. When we begin to look for the causes and conditions of these sudden shifts in consciousness, we may discover that shamans have been able to access other realities at will for thousands of years and that everybody else can develop these faculties as well.

Do we have a general consensus of what consciousness is? Most of us know whether we *are* conscious of one thing or not and, most of all, do register when we *become* conscious of something. The latter usually happens when a need and the intention to expand our consciousness arise. The need and the intention then create the basis for the expansion of consciousness.

In this chapter, I want to prove that we have the capability of accessing different states of consciousness and do so for various purposes. Knowing how also will enable us to speak more professionally of the different states of consciousness experienced by most of us, especially by shamans.

Research in the fields of comparative religion, anthropology, and psychology informs us that when we enter a specific state of consciousness, the characteristics and especially the quality of our perceptions and, consequently, our way of thinking and feeling change. For example, comparing waking consciousness with the state our consciousness is in when we are dreaming, we have to admit that the quality of what we are experiencing in dreams differs considerably from the quality of what we are aware of in ordinary, consensus reality.

In the following, I want to concentrate on available techniques to open doorways to other realities. All of them have been used by shamans for more than 15,000 years. Meditation manuals, documentation on shamanic trances, and scientific reports (e.g., of hypnotists) tell us that nonordinary realities can be accessed and influenced through thoughts, words, and actions on the material level. Mystics speak of a reversed process, that is, that nonordinary realities can influence the material world.

Looking at the available data, it is important to recognize the state-specific set of rules operating on each level. One major difference between realities is that, as has been said above, when our consciousness transcends the ordinary level of consciousness, the commonly agreed on rules of time and space no longer apply. On the experiential level, we then begin to see the possibilities that quantum physics, mysticism, science, and religion may find ways to bridge what at one time split apart.

Before discussing the different techniques to access other realities, I want to clarify that I use the term *alternate* states of consciousness instead of *altered* states of consciousness[1] to avoid the implication that a state has been artificially altered. I maintain that each of the different states, accessed by the techniques described below, does not coexist, but alternates with other states of consciousness.

Looking closer, we may recognize a movement toward either hyperactivity or hypoactivity, mind expansion or dissociation, increased control or increasing loss of control. Even when we occasionally observe areas of overlap and sometimes even flooding, a certain state of consciousness becomes distinguishable when it has reached its peak and demonstrates all its state-specific properties.

Tart speaks of

a unique configuration or system of psychological structures or sub-systems. The parts or aspects of the mind that we can distinguish for analytical purposes (such as memory, evaluation processes, and the sense of identity function) are arranged in a certain kind of pattern or system. . . . The nature of the pattern and the elements that make up the pattern determine what you can and cannot do in that state. In dreaming, flying by an act of will is possible. I wouldn't want to say that is totally impossible in consensus consciousness, but it certainly is not easy. (p. 4).[2]

And Ludwig speaks of "alterations in thinking, change in sense of time and body image, loss of control, change in emotional expression, perceptual distortion, change in meaning and significance, a sense of ineffability, feelings of rejuvenation and hypersuggestibility."[3] Both findings confirm my hypothesis.

**Figure 16.1**
**Fluctuations of Consciousness between Ordinary and Alternate States**

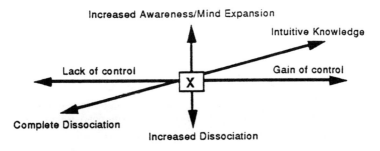

X represents the ordinary state of consensus reality.

The range of possible alternate states appears to be almost infinite. We are just starting to map out states that we have learned to access for certain purposes.[1,4–6] Our "hidden observer"[7] watches the fluctuations of our consciousness between ordinary and nonordinary realities but may not always be present when we enter certain states of consciousness. For example, in cases of deep dissociation, which I call *flooding,* people may lose control temporarily or for longer periods, depending on the depth of the dissociation. The diagram in Figure 16.1, where x represents the state of consensus reality, illustrates this point.

When we begin to cultivate awareness and control, we progress on the diagonal toward *intuitive knowledge,* which is the highest point in the upper right quadrant. This state indicates full control and complete awareness (i.e., being and knowing without objectification and discursive thinking). The lowest point on the diagonal, in the lower left quadrant, is *complete dissociation,* multiple personality, or possession. With respect to this lowest point, Jung spoke of "unconscious, autonomic complexes," which appear in such a state "as projections because they are not associated with the ego" (p. 99).[8] Possession either has to be exorcised or is professionally utilized by shaman and mediums.

To give an example for how cautious we have to be when we want to define a certain state let us consider shamans who call a spirit into their bodies and surrender their consciousness to the spirit who begins to act through them. They must be plotted in the lower right quadrant because although they enter possession, which is a dissociative state and a state of temporary flooding, they have at least partial control over consciously accessing and leaving this state after its purpose has been fulfilled. Schizophrenics belong to the lowest point in the lower left quadrant because they have neither recall nor control over this state of consciousness. When going on a "magical flight," meditators and shamans have to be plotted in the upper right quadrant because they experience and control the expansion of their consciousness at all times to the point where they enter intuitive knowledge and just "be."

The following techniques and conditions facilitate access to states of consciousness other than the present state of my readers.

1. *Extreme Temperature Conditions*. The heat of a sweat lodge, for example, increases pulse rate and induces nausea, dizziness, and syncope (fainting). As with fevers, high body temperatures seem to activate the immune system, detoxify the body, and release emotional and cognitive blockages, facilitating spiritual experiences. Spiritual exercises (e.g., meditation, prayer, evocation of saints in Christianity or Wakan-Tankan in Native American tradition), on the other hand, do not only calm down the mind, but also result in a calming of bodily functions, which allows a different kind of heat to arise.

We have, therefore, to distinguish between physical heat that penetrates our bodies from the outside, leading to increased physical functions (also influencing our emotional, mental, and spiritual levels of experience), and spiritual heat generated during meditation and prayer by stilling physical functions, which allows quiet transcendence and entry into a different reality. I predict that future research will yield more conclusive results toward the quality of states that can be entered through consciously induced changes in temperature from either the outside or the inside.

2. *Physical or Sensory Deprivation*. In the flotation tank, for example, the boundaries between self and nonself dissolve. The body is not restricted by clothing. Neither sensory nor motor systems are in play. At this point, unusual shifts into slower alpha activity have been reported by Heron and Zubek, Welch, and Saunders (pp. 33–35).[9]

Aside from restricted mobility and visual-sensory deprivation, sleep deprivation and seclusion also lead to alterations in consciousness. Food and water deprivation have an effect on the pituitary and adrenal glands that directly affects the hypothalamus and hippocampal-septal systems.[10]

On a vision quest, individuals fast, do not drink, and forgo sleep for three or more days and nights. Through abstinence, the life energy is "redirected toward healing, or to produce states of bliss."[9,11]

3. *Pilgrimages*. Many oral traditions around sacred places—the sacred mountains of the Taoists, sacred trees, tombs of saints, sites of revelations (e.g., Lourdes, France; Fatima, Portugal; Medjugorge, Yugoslavia)—speak of religious trances occurring at these sites. Such trances cause a shift of attention and activate the pilgrims' self-healing powers. The question of whether these miraculous shifts are the result of the placebo effect, the pilgrim's expectations, geographical and meteorological conditions, or outside intervention cannot be answered conclusively because we don't have the tools to prove whether a single one of these agents or all the above caused the shift. We can, however, establish medical records that document the physical condition of individuals before and after their pilgrimage. We also should continue with our research of

sacred sites that have been and are still used by shamans (e.g., Sedona in Arizona and Mount Shasta in California).

4. *Sonic Driving.* We have archaeological documentation (e.g., petroglyphs) that the effect of drumming and rattling on the central nervous system was known already in prehistoric times. Whether in religious or nonreligious context, chanting also seems to produce shifts in consciousness.

Research on rhythmic sensory stimulation was first conducted in the 1930s. The Walters then found in the 1940s that "stimulation of other receptors gives even more convincing results, particularly when a very large group of sensory units can be excited simultaneously and rhythmically, for then the central electrical response is correspondingly larger" (p. 85)." [12]

Jilek elicited responses to auditory driving at the fundamental of each stimulus frequency (usually three to four beats per second) (p. 86).[12] When Neher exposed clinically normal people to low-frequency, high-amplitude acoustic stimulations produced by instruments similar to the deerskin drums used by North American Indians, he observed on the electroencephalograph that different sound frequencies were transmitted along different nerve pathways in the brain (p. 86).[12] (He had, however, reinforced the acoustic effects by flashing lights; that means he did not control for all variables.) With the rise of neoshamanic groups, we now have the opportunity to conduct more accurate fieldwork on the use of *sonic driving* without becoming intrusive to shamans who practice in traditional societies.

5. *Kinetic Stimulation and Hyperventilation.* Extensive running and dancing result in overbreathing and oxygen depletion, which, coupled with hypoglycemia, causes the appearance of slow wave activity (2 to 3 cycles per second) and hallucinatory experiences, as do other forms of exertion.[10] I witnessed, for example, in India and Southeast Asia ritual dancing that produced dissociative states before firewalking and other physical feats.

I observed, especially with spirit mediums, who not always use kinetic stimulation, that a change in breathing patterns occurs. Noteworthy also is the *energy darshan* practiced in Asia (e.g., during the ritual initiation of disciples).

To compare these practices with those in the United States, rebirthing comes to mind in which the desired state is activated with the help of quick breathing. Energy stimulations also can be observed in the use of Reiki. Apprentices report that they experience a strong surge of energy during initiation.

Dance, rhythmic music, lights, and several breathing techniques, used by many psychotherapists today, are indeed techniques that combine elements from various shamanic traditions. Stanislav Grof, for example, uses holotropic breathing, certain body postures, lights, and music, and Felicitas Goodman found that certain postures, assumed during rattling, produce specific imagery, even in ethnically not related individuals whether they lived in prehistoric times or live in contemporary societies.[13,14]

6. *Use of Chemical and Hallucinogenic Substances.* Weston La Barre wrote

about the peyote cult, and Harner discussed extensively the use of hallucino-
genics in shamanic and other religious ceremonies.[15,16]

Shifts in states of consciousness that produce chemical changes in the brain
need not be activated by hallucinogenic substances; the intention and concentration of an individual may suffice without any outside help. Research to investigate the latter possibility has begun, and we anxiously await the first results.

Jilek talks about the endogenous opioid agents enkephalin and beta-endorphin and possibly other neuroendocrine peptides, such as neurotensin and
bradykinin which, for example, may play an important role in the integration
of pain information (p. 85).[12] Beta-endorphin injections have antidysphoric,
antidepressant, anxiolytic, analgesic, and disinhibiting effects within five to ten
minutes after injection that last from one to six hours. Kline speculates that
beta-endorphin, produced by the anterior pituitary, may be the body's own way
of producing and controlling affective states.[12]

The endorphins can be found in the limbic system, the thalamus the peri-
aqueductal gray matter, and the substantia gelatinosa of the spinal cord. They
also are in areas of the brain that regulate respiration, motor activity, endocrine
control, and mood.

Achterberg points to the role of the enkephalins as "endogenous immunom-
odulators" that assist the immune system in fighting disease (p. 137–141).[9]
The entire natural pharmacopoeia can indeed be reinforced. Achterberg added
consciously used imagery, which also plays a role in the placebo effect (p. 84–
87).[9]

7. *Hypnosis and Deep Sleep.* These are well-documented means to access
different states of consciousness. Historically, sleep therapy has been used already (e.g., in classical Greece at Epidauros).

Tart recorded brainwaves (EEG), galvanic skin resistance responses, and heart
rate in a woman who frequently had out-of-body experiences during sleep (pp.
27–28).[9] During these experiences, alpha activity was 1½ cycles per second
slower than the subject's normal alpha, and there were no rapid eye movements, which normally accompany dreaming. There also was no physiological
arousal despite her heightened mental activity.

Hypnotherapy and other techniques of focused attention are effectively used
today by trained professionals. Hypnotism has proved to be a technique to
bypass an individual's "erroneously limited belief system" and to circumvent
"the all too narrow limits of ordinary everyday consciousness."[17] This statement alerts us to the wide area of unexplored territory. Extreme deprivation
during a vision quest often is reinforced by hypnotic suggestions with which
individuals prepare themselves for the visionary states.[18] The visions then signal, illuminate, and provide guidance for the transformative process of a sha-
man-to-be. I did not find any study that explored in depth the use of hypnosis
by shamans, either self-hypnosis to bring about and enhance their trance states
or their use of hypnosis to shift the attention of their clients to put them into a

healing frame of mind, which includes posthypnotic suggestions. I observed at numerous occasions the conditioning of shamans that showed similarities to the preparations of actors who condition themselves before each performance for the role they are going to play.

8. *Meditation.* In my book *Trance and Healing in Southeast Asia Today,* I discuss research on wakeful relaxed states in which reduction in oxygen consumption occurs together with changes in carbon dioxide elimination (p. 84).[12] The rate and volume of respiration, when reduced, causes a slight increase in the acidity of arterial blood, marked by a decrease in blood lactate level. The heartbeat slows down, and there is a considerable increase in skin resistance and alpha brainwave patterns with occasional theta waves.

We have numerous manuals on different kinds of meditation, from Patanjali's yoga sutras[19] in Hinduism to the "insight meditation" *(satipatthana sutta)*[20] in early Buddhism as well as the tantric meditation systems of Hinduism and Mahayana Buddhism; the meditations of Taoist, Sufi, and Hasidic masters; and the *Exercises of St. Ignatius*[21] in Christianity. They all use breathing techniques and suggest focusing the mind; some use specific forms of visualization. The *Visuddhimagga,* for example, suggests forty subjects of meditation *(kammatthana).* All these meditation techniques additionally prescribe certain body postures.[14]

When mental and spiritual health is the purpose of all these meditation techniques, do we find similar ultimate goals? The Abhidhamma speaks of 121 mental states that can be cultivated through meditation until practitioners reach *nirvana* (complete extinction of material attachments), whereas Hindu, Sufi, and Hasidic masters talk about the union with the Divine. There seems to be a difference between nirvana, the Void, and the union with the Divine. Shamans usually maintain that they communicate with the world of spirits, closer to our human world. Only a few speak of a High God (e.g., Wankan Tankan of the Sioux). Chinese shamans expressedly communicate with mediators between the High Gods and the human world (e.g., Kuan Yin, generals of the Three Kingdoms, etc.).

9. *Ritualization.* Access to alternate states of consciousness is facilitated by ritualization, which (after all participants agreed on the purpose of the ritual) requires the following seven steps:

1. Preparation of the environment. Since time memorial, it has been the task of shamans and priests to create a safe place where the unusual can happen. Visible boundaries are established—for example, by placing *sima* stones around the *bot* (ordination hall in Thai monasteries) or by forming a circle in shamanic practices. Such preparations create a state of readiness and raise the expectations; they also prepare practitioners for the experience of the unusual, the meeting with the supernatural world.

2. Purification of the site and all participants (with incense, sage, or water).

3. Separation. The ordinary reality has to be left behind and nonordinary reality is entered ritually.

4. Entrance into the alternate state. In this *liminal* state, ordinary rules are suspended and spiritual forces can be invoked.[22]

5. Communion. Participants come indeed into the presence of the Divine and experience the mystical union of being connected with everybody and everything else.

6. Celebration. The presence of the Divine is celebrated with food and often dance.

7. Closure. After having expressed gratitude for its manifestation, the Divine is sent off and a ritual closure protects, on the one hand, the spiritual world from pollution and, on the other hand, participants from emotional overload.

8. Integration. After participants have returned to ordinary reality, ritualists facilitate the integration of the experience into daily life.[23,24]

## CONCLUSIONS

Michael Winkelman has provided us with a survey of psychophysiological research on the effects of trance-inducing procedures that lead "to a state of parasympathetic dominance in which the frontal cortex is dominated by slow wave patterns originating in the limbic system and related projections into the frontal parts of the brain."[10] Such investigations are helpful for distinguishing pathological from nonpathological cases. The main criterion appears to be the faculty to consciously access and exit alternate states of consciousness and to be able to recall the experience.

Science has to establish new categories for individuals who are capable of monitoring their shifts of attention and who can access other realities at will, a faculty that not only is of benefit to practitioners, but also serves the community. The conscious evocation of alternate states of consciousness has already proved to be beneficial in setting the self-healing process in motion and increasing our state of well-being.[9]

It is important to note that despite their excursions into other realities, masters of different states of consciousness function well in their communities in contrast to individuals who have no control over the different states of consciousness they are experiencing, and therefore fit the pathology suggested in the DSM-III *(Diagnostic and Statistical Manual of Mental Disorders, Third Edition.)*[23,25] More detailed results about alternate states of consciousness can be expected from ongoing and future research.

## NOTES

1. Tart CT. *Altered States of Consciousness*. New York: John Wiley & Sons; 1969.

2. Tart CT. *Waking Up: Overcoming the Obstacles of Human Potential*. Boston: Shambhala, New Science Library; 1986.

3. Ludwig A. Altered states of consciousness. *Archives of General Psychiatry*. 1960;15:225–234.

4. Fischer RW. A cartography of the ecstatic and meditative states. *Science*. 1974:897–904.

5. Fischer RW. A cartography of the ecstatic and meditative states. In: Woode R, ed. *Understanding Mysticism, Its Methodology, Interpretation in World Religions, Psychological Evaluations, Philosophical and Theological Appraisal.* Garden City, NY: Image Books; 1980:286–305.

6. Krippner S. Altered states of consciousness In: White J, ed. *The Highest State of Consciousness.* New York: Doubleday; 1972:1–5.

7. Hilgard ER. *Divided Consciousness: Multiple Controls in Human Thoughts and Action.* New York: John Wiley & Sons; 1977.

8. Jung CG. Hull RFC, trans. *The Structure and Dynamics of the Psyche.* Bollingen Series VI. New York: Pantheon Books, 1960.

9. Achterberg J. *Imagery in Healing, Shamanism and Modern Medicine.* Boston: Shambhala, New Science Library; 1985.

10. Winkelman M. Trance states: a theoretical model and cross-cultural analysis. *Ethos.* 1986;14(2):174–203.

11. Foster S. Crying for a vision, the purpose circle, and emergence. In: Heinze R-I, ed. *Proceedings of the Third International Conference on the Study of Shamanism and Alternate Modes of Healing.* Madison, WI: A-R Editions, Inc.; 1987:264–271.

12. Heinze R-I. *Trance and Healing in Southeast Asia Today.* Berkeley/Bangkok: Independent Scholars of Asia, Inc. White Lotus; 1988.

13. Grof S. *Beyond the Brain—Birth, Death and Transcendence in Psychotherapy.* New York: State University of New York Press; 1985.

14. Goodman FD. Body posture and the religious altered state of consciousness: an experimental investigation. *Journal of Humanistic Psychology.* 1986;26(3):81–118.

15. La Barre W. *The Peyote Cult.* New York: Schocken Books; 1971.

16. Harner MJ. *Hallucinogens and Shamanism.* New York: Oxford University Press; 1973.

17. Erickson M, Rossi E, Rossi S. *Hypnotic Realities: The Induction of Clinical Hypnosis and Forms of Indirect Suggestion.* New York: Irvington; 1976.

18. Rogers SL. *The Shaman: His Symbols and His Healing Power.* Springfield, IL: Charles Thomas; 1982.

19. Prabhavananda S, Isherwood C, trans. *How to Know God, The Yoga Aphorisms of Patanjali.* New York: New American Library; 1969.

20. Ven. U Silananda, Heinze R-I, eds. *The Four Foundations of Mindfulness.* Boston: Wisdom Publications; 1990.

21. Mottola A, trans. *The Spiritual Exercises of St. Ignatius.* New York: Doubleday; 1964.

22. Van Gennep A. *The Rites of Passage.* Vizedom MB, Cafees GL, trans. Chicago: University of Chicago Press; 1960.

23. Heinze R-I. *Shamans of the Twentieth Century.* New York: Irvington; 1991.

24. Heinze R-I. The ritual process: translating the ineffable into ritual language. In: Heinze R-I, ed. *Proceedings of the Seventh International Conference on the Study of Shamanism and Alternate Modes of Healing.* Berkeley, CA: Independent Scholars of Asia, Inc.; 1991:1–17.

25. *Diagnostic and Statistical Manual of Mental Disorders, 3rd ed.* Washington, DC: American Psychiatric Association; 1980.

# 17

# Firewalking—A New Look at an Old Enigma

*Larissa Vilenskaya*

In 1983, I met Tolly Burkan, a Californian who had learned the art of firewalking from a student of a Tibetan yogi. Tolly claimed that within three to four hours, he could teach any person to walk on red-hot coals unharmed. At one of Tolly's workshops, I was inspired to firewalk and found it to be an elating, exhilarating, and profound experience. I went on to teach firewalking and gave several dozen workshops in the United States and Europe. As I taught, I discovered firewalking to be not only a deep personal experience, but also an excellent tool for healing, spiritual growth, and psychological development.

As I continued teaching and performing firewalks, my interest changed to a deep curiosity about the whole phenomenon. I have written elsewhere about the implications of the nature of firewalking.[1-6] Whereas the ancients and many contemporary firewalkers have attributed their abilities to spiritual powers, scientists look to commonly understood properties of human physiology and the physical universe to explain the mystery.

In this chapter, I will discuss various hypotheses that have been made to explain this phenomenon: physical hypotheses, psychophysiologic hypotheses, belief systems, altered states of consciousness, and mind over matter. These hypotheses are not mutually exclusive, and more than one may be a significant factor in understanding this ancient enigma.

## PHYSICAL HYPOTHESIS

The firewalking phenomenon can be formulated as follows: Certain people apparently possess immunity to the influence of temperatures sufficiently high enough to be detrimental for the human organism. The tissues of mammals cannot stand temperatures higher than 60° C. (140° F.), since protein begins breaking down, and skin exposed to a temperature of 75° C. (167° F.) will blister within one second of contact. At a temperature of 250° C., the effect on the protein, muscles, fatty tissue, and nerves of the foot would be devastating in only a fraction of a second.

Although most research to date has examined the physical aspects of firewalking [7-10] and has offered *physiological* hypotheses, [11] other ideas have been advanced to explain the phenomenon. Alternative hypotheses concerning firewalking and fire immunity include psychological, psychophysiological, and religious theories and must be thoughtfully considered.

Within the framework of classical physics, three primary propositions attempt to explain firewalking. The first and most simplistic belief is that the firewalkers have callouses on their feet. The second is that the surface across which individuals pass during firewalking ceremonies (hot stones or the hot coals of a wood fire) provide low heat conductivity, and therefore any person making quick, even steps can perform a short firewalk without injury. [12-17] A third position is that the natural moisture of the foot protects a person while passing across the coals. [7,9]

Because there were a number of Europeans with noncalloused feet who participated in firewalking ceremonies without harm to themselves, the first explanation can be easily rejected. [18-20] Furthermore, although some participants may walk quickly and take only a few steps, this appears to be insufficient to explain the lack of burns, given the extremely high temperatures involved [21,22] and the fact that 60-foot-long firewalks have been performed without injuries to the participants. [23,24]

The low thermal conductivity hypothesis has been widely publicized in terms understandable by nonphysicists. [25,26] The main proponents, Leikind and McCarthy, stress the distinction between thermal conductivity and heat. They explain that even though the coals seem hot, the firewalkers will be burned only over an extended period, not instantaneously, because of the low thermal conductivity of the coals. Leikind and McCarthy have not submitted quantitative data to suggest a maximum tolerance time.

Furthermore, chemist Mayn Reid Coe walked on hot iron, a surface that is a much better conductor of heat than basaltic stones or wood coals, without injury. [7] Friedbert Karger, a West German nuclear physicist who studied firewalking in Fiji using temperature-sensitive paints, reported that a firewalker stood for seven seconds on a rock with a temperature over 600° F. (p. 58). [8] During his study of fire-handlers, anthropologist Steven Kane observed instances when a person held each hand stationary at the midpoint of a torch flame for ten to fifteen seconds without injury.[27] Such reports provide evidence that refutes the hypothesis of low thermal conductivity as the major explanation of fire immunity.

The auxiliary hypothesis of classical physics, that the feet of firewalkers are protected because of natural moisture on them, often is referred to as the Leidenfrost effect.[7,9] The name derives from the eighteenth-century physician Johann Leidenfrost, who noted that at temperatures lower than 200° C., water droplets on a smooth, heated surface will evaporate quickly. At higher temperatures, a vapor barrier builds up around each droplet, and it vaporizes much more slowly. At temperatures about 500° C., the droplets again vanish rapidly.

Enlisting this information to explain firewalking, proponents of the Leidenfrost view state that the natural moisture on the walker's foot partially vaporizes at high temperatures and provides a primary protection. This depends on the ability of water to achieve a spheroid state.[7,28] The phenomenon is encountered by the breakfast chef who sprinkles water on the pancake griddle and sees that when the temperature is high, the droplets do not vaporize immediately, but turn to spheres and remain a moment dancing on the griddle. (One can easily surmise that a coal bed is a far cry from the smooth, nonporous griddle surface required for such effects.[29]) According to this theory, the sweat on the feet of the firewalker enters the spheroid state of water. In doing so, the sweat does not vaporize instantaneously, but serves to protect the firewalker from burn.

Yet, since the Leidenfrost effect is stated to occur only within a fixed temperature range, how can we explain successful firewalks outside that range? The temperature of the coal bed (ranging from 100° to 800° C.) has been both above and below the Leidenfrost limits, without the occurrence of burns (p. 27).[20] Temperatures at the lower end of the Leidenfrost range for water or sweat (about 200° C.) are still more than sufficient to produce a painful burn in a short time. Furthermore, burns have occurred within the Leidenfrost range.[16] McClenon pointed out that the Leidenfrost effect does not occur at temperatures lower than 200° C. (390° F.). Because this temperature is still high enough to cause burns, it does not explain firewalks performed over "cool" firebeds, including one firewalk performed by James McClenon during cold and rainy weather in Japan.[20]

As far as the higher end of the Leidenfrost range is concerned, the *Guinness Book of World Records* indicates that during the firewalk of "Komar" (Vernon E. Craig) of Wooster, Ohio, performed at the International Festival of Yoga and Esoteric Sciences, Maidenhead, England, on August 14, 1976, the temperature of the coals recorded by a pyrometer was 1494° F. (812° C.).[30] A group of eleven persons led by Steven Neil Bisyak of Redmond, Washington, participated in a firewalk with an average temperature of 1546° F. (841° C.) on December 19, 1987, at Redmond.[31]

In discussing the Leidenfrost hypothesis, Ingalls pointed out that moisture on the feet would present a disadvantage: It would cause hot embers to adhere to the soles and increase the time of contact with the hot surface and the danger of injury.[28] Ironically, James Randi, who is known for his debunking of extraordinary phenomena, notes that Sri Lankan firewalkers believe that foot moisture causes embers to stick and carefully dry their feet before walking (p. 31).[14]

Jearl Walker, from the Department of Physics of Cleveland State University, has been a proponent of the Leidenfrost hypothesis of firewalking. Walker himself attempted firewalking several times until he suffered third-degree burns on both feet. Walker warned that his explanation is sufficient for a short firewalk "unless the walker has an unusual tolerance for pain" (p. 131).[9] He did not specify how short the "short" is. Therefore, one has no way to tell whether standing on a hot surface for 7 seconds, observed by Karger,[8] or holding a hand stationary in a torch flame for 10 to 15 seconds[27] falls into the "short" category.

In addition, the Leidenfrost hypothesis requires that the steps not be too fast, so that sufficient sweat can build up on the foot while in the air, midstride. In actual practice, the time range of steps varies considerably between, for example, the fire dancers of Greece and the firewalkers of America.[1,10,31] An account of Greek firedancing emphasized that the firedancer's time of contact with the burning coals was "extremely variable."[32] Another account stated that "Thracian firewalkers somehow dance over . . . white-hot beds, and sometimes kneel down in the center for several minutes."[33]

Finally, the laws of physics do not, by themselves, satisfactorily explain the numerous cases in which some firewalkers have been burned, while others remained unharmed.[19,22,27,34-36] Feinberg describes a mass firewalk in Sri Lanka (Kataragama) in which about 100 devotees crossed a 20-by-6-foot fire pit: "On the night we watched the firewalking at Kataragama, twelve people were burned badly enough to go to the hospital, and one of them died. . . . A young English clergyman who visited Ceylon a few years ago . . . volunteered to walk the fire with others. He . . . spent the next six months in a hospital, where doctors barely managed to save his life.[37]

The hypothesis that explains firewalking strictly according to known physical properties, then, cannot give a satisfactory answer as to why some people are burned during the same firewalk when others are not.

## PSYCHOLOGICAL HYPOTHESES

Recent attempts to understand the interrelation of mind and body have begun to shed light on the phenomenon of altered states of consciousness and fire immunity. Andrew Weil summarized a psychophysiologic perspective as follows:

Several different mechanisms may take part. Changes in blood circulation might help conduct heat away from body surfaces or reduce the flow of heat to vulnerable tissues. Changes in the functions of local nerves might suppress the activity of neurochemicals that mediate pain and inflammatory reaction to strong stimulation. . . . A more hypothetical possibility is some as-yet-undiscovered capacity of the nervous system to absorb potentially harmful forms of energy, transform them, and conduct them away from the body surface. . . .

I think the abilities are quite natural, the results of using the mind in certain ways (or not using it in ordinary ways) and so allowing the brain and nerves to alter the body's responsiveness to heat (p. 249).[11]

In Weil's opinion, psychoneurological mechanisms that may contribute to successful firewalking include the following: (a) absence of fear or any effort at defense that produces neuromuscular tension; (b) deep relaxation; (c) the presence of someone experienced and unafraid; (d) concentration, produced by techniques such as chanting or hypnosis (pp. 253[38] and 254).[11] In current research, within these categories, only (c), the presence of an experienced firewalker, and (d), concentration, were apparent in a significant measure.

The emergence of the relatively new field of psychoneuroimmunology may augment knowledge of the mind–body interaction as it relates to fire immunity. Recent research has documented correlations among psychological events, endocrine secretion, and modulation of immunity.[39–46] The studies indicate a connection between the hypothalamus, the limbic system, and the most evolved part of the cortex, the frontal lobes, which may affect certain aspects of immunity.[47,48] Such findings may lead to further information about an interface between the mind–body interaction and extraordinary practices such as firewalking.

## BELIEF SYSTEMS

The *power of belief* refers to the individual's relinquishing some degree of personal power to forces greater than himself, be they the natural forces of the universe, the power of a placebo, or the power of God. Although contemporary firewalk instructors strengthen the power to believe in the possibility of safety, Stillings has stated: "No firewalk instructor that I know of claims that any one belief system is necessary for success" (p. 58).[29] Thus the specific belief system held by the firewalker is not as important as the fact that there is *a* belief system in place.

One example of the power of belief is from Leikind, who gave a physics lecture about the low thermal conductivity of the coals and then led a group of people through the firewalk unharmed. In his own way, Leikind used a well-ensconced belief system with appropriate imagery, "a system with some 300 years of paradigm support behind it" (p. 58).[29] In other words, Leikind acted as a firewalk instructor by using the basic belief principle of firewalk preparation—in this case, belief in the laws of physics.

The most common conviction expressed by firewalkers is the attribution of their firewalking abilities to a belief in the power of God or "friendly spirits" that protect the participant. Similar to the magical thinking described in the literature of anthropology and mythology, the firewalking literature contains numerous references to firewalking adepts who believe in mysterious forces and supernatural powers that protect them from ordinary harmful external influences.

In India, the *devtias* who perform firewalking claim to be protected by their personal deity, or *Isht,* who is invited to come into and act through them during the firewalk.[49] In Greece, the firedancing Anastenarides are believed to possess *dinami*—spiritual or supernatural power to perform miracles—which enables them both to firewalk and to "gain access to supernatural knowledge" and perform diagnosis and healing (p. 124).[50]

Within our own culture, devotees of the Free Pentecostal Holiness Church, who participate in numerous feats of firehandling,[27,51] evoke a biblical passage to explain their ritual use of fire without harm: "When thou walkest through the fire, thou shalt not be burned; neither shall the flame kindle upon thee" (Isaiah 43:2).

The essential concept is the belief that the Holy Ghost moves into the worshipers and takes possession of their faculties, rendering them capable of carrying out works of God, that is, fire-handling, snake-handling, healing the sick, prophecy, and so forth.

Physician Andrew Weil says that extraordinary abilities are natural to all human beings, and that the question of how mind and body interact is the next frontier of medical research. Yet both Weil and Pearce conclude that belief is the key—that the power of belief accounts for all the anomalies of innate healing, the placebo effect, and such extraordinary phenomena as firewalking.[11,52,53] Weil specifies that "belief that counts is gut-level belief that stirs emotions and connects to the body through the centers of the deep brain. It is based on experience as well as thought and must be psychosomatic to begin with, bridging the barrier between modern cortex and primitive brainstem" (p. 253).[11]

In addition, Weil addresses the universal human tendency to externalize belief in saints and deities, rather than recognize one's own spiritual power. He postulates that we may need to project belief onto external objects, such as placebos or gods, to reap the benefits of our innate power, since there is an apparent barrier between the cortex and the deep brain centers that control psychosomatic events (p. 250).[11]

Regardless of the universality of the power of belief or the belief system utilized to protect one from injury, Evaggelou suggests that this hypothesis may not pertain to noninjurious firewalks by nonbelievers.[54] But Evaggelou does not consider that belief in natural forces may be as effective as belief in deities. One might conjecture that every firewalker believes in something, regardless how disparate the belief systems may be.

## ALTERED STATES OF CONSCIOUSNESS

Spiritual or other beliefs could result in an altered state of consciousness, and the contention that firewalkers and fire handlers are in a trance or an altered state of consciousness has frequently been expressed in the literature.[21,23,27,55,56] There have been few attempts to assess experimentally the states of consciousness involved. After interviewing participants of firewalking workshops, Blake found that of 52 respondents, 38% reported perceptions inconsistent with consensual reality (i.e., the coals felt cool or wet), 67% described their experience as euphoric, 54% expressed a feeling of timelessness, and 81% described a shift in their energy while firewalking (p. 57).[55]

A Greek Anastenarides firedancer has described the experience in the following way: "If the Saint [Constantine] calls you to go into the fire, then you don't feel the fire as if it were your enemy, but you feel it as if it were your husband or your wife. You feel love for the fire. . . . You go into the fire freely. . . . When the Saint gives you courage, you feel love for the fire. You feel hope. You have a longing to enter the fire" (p. 281).[50]

Devotees of the Free Pentecostal Holiness Church claim to achieve the state of "anointing," which they describe as follows: "It makes a different person out of you"; "I about lose sight of the world for a while"; "It's like a good cold shower"; "You feel just like your hands are in a block of ice. I've had it all over me"; "You feel queer all over, like you stick your finger in electricity"; "It's like a bolt of lightnin' goes through you"; "It's so wonderful. You can feel it in your flesh. You're conscious, but everything looks just beautiful to you" (pp. 376–377).[27]

Stillings suggests that simply looking at the hot coals glowing bright orange and knowing that one will step on them in a few seconds can lead to an altered state of consciousness because this action is outside our ordinary behavior.[29] The underlying issue in this case concerns those factors that cause a person to enter an altered state, and how radical a shift in attention must be before one's state is considered to have been "altered."

Because there have been insufficient studies of the relation between firewalking and altered states of consciousness, the role of hypnosis, trance, and other kinds of altered states remains a topic for further study.

## MIND OVER MATTER

The final assumption, the hypothesis of mind over matter, however loosely defined, is proffered by both advocates of psychokinesis (PK) and those writers who postulate that physical reality is mutable and that people, through their minds, are capable of changing physical laws.[52,53,57] Psychics have been touting this approach for ages. In contemporary terms, PK is defined by parapsychologists as "the direct influence of mind on a physical system without the mediation of any known physical energy or instrumentation—that is, the extra-motor aspect of psi'' (p. 191).[58] Firewalking might involve a mind-over-matter effect that is a heretofore undiscovered electrostatic cooling mechanism. Stillings suggests that cooling effects produced by strong electrostatic fields can be quite dramatic, as in the cool winds that reputedly may blow across the seance table. He believes that "the mind and body, in certain altered states, are capable of mentally producing strong electrostatic fields surrounding the legs and feet of firewalkers and can then protect the subject by cooling the coals" (p. 17).[29]

Interestingly enough, many firewalkers report tingling sensations, like slight electric shocks, on the bottoms of their feet during and after firewalking.[18,22,59,60] There has been no research reported to date and no known attempts to measure electrostatic fields during firewalking or fire handling.

Leshan suggests that firewalking may not be possible in our ordinary reality, but it can probably be done in an alternate reality.[61] Similarly, Pearce proposes that we can create our own reality, even one that entails a change in physical laws.[53]

## SUMMARY

The hypotheses that have been advanced through the ages to account for the phenomenon of firewalking range from the esoteric to the mundane and come full circle with the overlap between ancient spiritual beliefs and contemporary parapsychological hypotheses.

Hypothesis-builders tend to fall into two general categories: (1) those who explain firewalking within a framework defined by the currently understood properties of the known physical universe and (2) those whose hypotheses fall outside the commonly accepted scientific laws. In the latter category are those who ascribe the mysterious phenomenon to external agencies, and those who believe that the human mind is capable of powers that are not yet fully understood. Controversy abounds and further research is necessary.

Several writers invoke natural processes to explain what might allow for some people to cross burning coals unharmed: the low conductivity of the embers, which will radiate heat without burning skin, and the protection offered by sweat on the feet. Some psychologists postulate a fear of failure that inhibits firewalkers from reporting blisters they sustained while firewalking.

Psychophysiologists meanwhile study the mind–body relationship, and sometimes profess that the power of an altered state of consciousness provides protection—whether that state is induced by the hypnotic skills of a firewalk leader or the social reinforcement of the group. Physiologists also may study the role of endorphins, the hypothalamus, and the limbic system in fire immunity.

Psychologists, anthropologists, and contemporary firewalking instructors all agree on the importance of a strong belief system in enacting the firewalk. Trust in the power belief, as evidenced in the ability of the belief in spirits and deities to protect the "faithful," thus characterizes the most widespread consensus about firewalking.

There also is a strong possibility that several factors may operate simultaneously. A Fijian firewalker, who believes that his spiritual deity protects him from the fire, adeptly summarizes the overlapping of several hypotheses: "It's really mind over matter. . . . There are . . . endless incantations until each man is prepared to do just about anything. It's like hypnosis" (p. 68).[62]

Spiritual and physical hypotheses for firewalking may blend, each gracefully allowing for and including the precepts of the other. If so, the basis for a multilevel explanation of this phenomenon emerges: Belief can build on some natural phenomenon and can evoke other natural processes. Further research is needed, but from what is already known about fire immunity, we must support Steven Kane's conclusion that "there appears to be more than a little objective truth in the communicants' assertion that 'it takes faith' to handle fire" (p. 382).[27]

## NOTES

1. Vilenskaya L. Firewalking: a new fad, a scientific riddle, or an excellent tool for healing, spiritual growth and psychological development? *Psi Research*. 1984;3(2):102–118.

2. Vilenskaya L. Firewalking: renewing an old tradition to raise consciousness. In: Heinze R-I, ed. *Proceedings of the Second International Conference on Shamanism*. Berkeley, CA: Independent Scholars of Asia; 1985:58–65.

3. Vilenskaya L. Firewalking and beyond. *Psi Research*. 1985;4(2):91–109.

4. Vilenskaya L. Psi in mental healing, with observations from firewalking. Presented at the Panel Discussion States of Mind in Psychic Healing, 28th Convention of the Parapsychological Association, August 1985; Medford, Massachusetts. (Abstract in Weiner DH, Radin DI, eds. *Research in Parapsychology*. 1985:158.

5. Vilenskaya L. Symbolism of fire, firewalking and individual belief systems: do we create our own reality? In: Heinze R-I, ed. *Proceedings of the Sixth International Conference on Shamanism*. Berkeley, CA: Independent Scholars of Asia; 1989:107–132.

6. Vilenskaya L, Steffy J. *Firewalking: A New Look at an Old Enigma*. Falls Village, CT: Bramble Company; 1991.

7. Coe MR. Fire-walking and related behaviors. *Psychological Record*. 1957;7(2):101–110.

8. Doherty J. Hot feat: firewalkers of the world. *Science Digest*. August 1982;67–71.

9. Walker J. The amateur scientist: drops of water dance on a hot skillet and the experimenter walks on hot coals. *Scientific American*. 1977;237:126–131.

10. Xenakis C, Larbig W, Tsarouchas E. Zur psychophysiologie des Feuerlaufers [To psychophysiology of firewalkers]. *Archiv für Psychiatrie und Nervenkrankheiten*. 1977;223:309–322.

11. Weil A. *Health and Healing: Understanding Conventional and Alternative Medicine*. Boston: Houghton Mifflin; 1983.

12. Langley SP. The fire walk ceremony in Tahiti. *Nature.* 1901;64:397–399.

13. Fulton R. An account of the Fiji fire-walking ceremony, or vilavilairevo with a probable explanation of the mystery. *Transactions and Proceedings of the New Zealand Institute.* 1902;35:187–201.

14. Leikind BJ, McCarthy WJ. An investigation of firewalking. *Skeptical Inquirer.* 1985;10(1):23–34.

15. Price H. A report on two experimental fire-walks. Bulletin II. London: University of London, Council for Psychical Investigation; 1936.

16. Price H. *Fifty Years of Psychical Research.* London: Longmans, Green; 1939.

17. Roth K. The fire-walk in Fiji. *Man.* 1933;33:44–49.

18. Gudgeon WE. Te umu-ti, or fire-walking ceremony. *Journal of the Polynesian Society.* 1899;8(29):58–60.

19. Freeman JM. Trial by fire. *Natural History.* 1974;83(1):54–62.

20. McClenon J. Firewalking at Mount Takao. *Archaeus.* 1983;1(1):25–28.

21. Ianuzzo G. Fire-immunity: psi ability or psychophysiological phenomenon. *Psi Research.* 1983;2(4):68–74.

22. Kenn CW. *Arii-Peu Tama-Iti: Fire-walking from the Inside.* Los Angeles: Franklin Thomas; 1949.

23. Coe MR. Safely across the fiery pit. *Fate.* June 1978;84–86.

24. Hopkins EW. Fire-walking. In: Hastings J, ed. *Encyclopedia of Religion and Ethics, Vol.* New York: Charles Scribner & Sons; 1951 (first printing 1913):30–31.

25. Baker B. A skeptical view: doubting academics wage a flamboyant battle to debunk society's fascination with popular theories. *Los Angeles Times;* April 21, 1985.

26. Garrison P. Kindling courage. *Omni.* April 1985;44–48, 84–85.

27. Kane SM. Holiness ritual fire handling: ethnographic and psychophysiological considerations. *Ethos.* 1982;10:369–384.

28. Ingalls AG. Fire-walking. *Scientific American.* 1939;160:135–138, 173–178.

29. Stillings D. Observations on firewalking. *Psi Research.* 1985;4(2):51–60.

30. *Guinness Book of World Records 1988.* New York: Sterling Publishing; 1987:83.

31. *Guinness Book of World Records 1989.* New York: Sterling Publishing; 1988:31.

32. Ballis T, Beaumanoir A, Xenakis C. Anastenaria. *Hellenic Armed Force Medical Review.* 1979;13:2.

33. The mystery of firewalking. *Human Behavior.* 1978;7(3):51.

34. Darling CR. Fire-walking. *Nature.* 1935;136:251.

35. Feigen GM. Bucky Fuller and the firewalk. *Saturday Review.* July 12, 1969:22–23.

36. McClenon J. Firewalking in Sri Lanka. *Psi Research.* 1983;2(4):99–100.

37. Feinberg L. Fire walking in Ceylon. *Atlantic Monthly.* May 1959;73–76.

38. Weil A. *The Marriage of the Sun and Moon.* Boston: Houghton Mifflin; 1980.

39. Ader R, ed. *Psychoneuroimmunology.* New York: Academic Press; 1981.

40. Borysenko J. Psychoneuroimmunology: behavioral factors and the immune response. *ReVision.* 1984;7(1):56–65.

41. Locke SE, Colligan D. Mind cures. *Omni.* March 1986:51–54, 112–114.

42. Locke SE, Horning-Rohan M. *Mind and Immunity: Behavioral Immunology, an Annotated Bibliography 1976–1982.* New York: Institute for the Advancement of Health; 1983.

43. Oubre A. Shamanic trance and the placebo effect: the case for a study in psychophysiological anthropology. *Psi Research.* 1986;5(1/2):116–144.

44. Prince R. The endorphins: a review for psychological anthropologists. *Ethos.* 1982;10(4):303–316.

45. Prince R. Shamans and endorphins: hypotheses for a synthesis. *Ethos.* 1982;10(4):409–423.

46. Rogers MP, Dubey D, Reich P. The influence of the psyche and the brain on immunity and disease susceptibility: a critical review. *Psychosomatic Medicine.* 1979;41:147–165.

47. Achterberg J. Imagery in Healing: *Shamanism and Modern Medicine.* Boston: Shambhala, New Science Library; 1985.

48. Geschwind N, Behan P. Left-handedness: association with immune disease, migraine, and developmental learning disorder. *Proceedings of the National Academy of Sciences.* 1982;79:5097–5100.

49. Pathak R. The India devtia: fire-walking deity. *Fate.* June 1970:90–99.

50. Danforth LM. *The Anastenaria: A Study in Greek Ritual Therapy.* Princeton, NJ: Princeton University; 1978. Dissertation.

51. Schwarz BE. Ordeal by serpents, fire and strychnine. *Psychiatric Quarterly.* 1960;34:405–429.

52. Pearce JC. *The Crack in the Cosmic Egg.* New York: Pocket Books; 1973.

53. Pearce JC. *Magical Child Matures.* New York: E. P. Dutton; 1985.

54. Evaggelou I. *I Goiteta Tou Mistiriou [The Fascination of Mystery].* Athens: Dodoni; 1971.

55. Blake J. Attribution of power and the transformation of fear: an empirical study of firewalking. *Psi Research.* 1985;4(2):64–90.

56. Gaddis VH. *Mysterious Fires and Lights.* New York: David McKay; 1967.

57. LeShan L. *The Medium, the Mystic and the Physicist.* New York: Ballantine Books; 1975.

58. Mir M, Vilenskaya L. *The Golden Chalice.* San Francisco: HS Dakin; 1986.

59. Menard W. Firewalkers of the South Seas. *Natural History.* 1949;58:8–15, 48.

60. Ross I. I joined the firewalkers. *Fate.* April 1966:46–50.

61. LeShan L. *Alternate Realities.* New York: M. Evans; 1976.

62. Breci S. Fire walking has its pitfalls. *Fate.* October 1982:67–69.

# PK on the PC—A Macintosh PK Event-Generator Based on the Princeton Engineering Anomalies Research Experiments

*William J. Croft*

This chapter describes *Intent,* a Macintosh version of the random event generators (REGs) used to study psychokinesis (PK) effects by the Princeton Engineering Anomalies Research (PEAR) group.[1] Some background material also is presented on PK theory and the Princeton REG methodology. The Macintosh program is public domain and available from the address given at the end of the chapter. The distribution disk includes both the executable program and complete C source code for the program. This allows examination of the algorithms and customization for laboratory environments.

## PSYCHOKINESIS

Psychokinesis is the term used in parapsychology to refer to the possibility that consciousness can influence the physical position or motion of objects in the real world without touching them. Somehow, even for parapsychologists, this is a bigger stretch of the imagination than, say, telepathy, in which thoughts or image information can be transferred between minds. One might explain telepathy as the transfer of consciousness waves between one person and another, but how could an inanimate object be affected by the thoughts of a person?

The fact is that these PK effects do exist; a major portion of the PEAR work is devoted to PK. Because the PK effects are certainly weak in most of the population, one way to study the phenomena is by running experiments that involve an operator trying to influence an object over thousands of trials. This way, if a weak effect exists, statistical theory can be used to bring it "out of the noise" so that the nature and magnitude of the PK are more measurable.

The PEAR approach to PK has been quite ingenious. Influenced by the early work of Helmut Schmidt, PEAR quickly developed a methodology using computer sampling and large operator databases with robust statistical analyses.[2,3]

The PEAR experiments initially focused on the REG, described in more detail in the next section. This device uses electronics to simulate the random process involved in flipping a coin. The operator uses his conscious *intention* to influence the device to produce more heads than tails or vice versa.

After success with the REG device, PEAR wanted to discover if operators could influence the motion of real physical objects, rather than just electrons in an REG machine. They built a device called the random mechanical cascade.[4] This device consists of a matrix of pegs and 9,000 polystyrene balls that drop down through the center of the matrix to form a Gaussian distribution in the bins below. Over thousands of trials, when the operators intend more balls to fall in the right bins than in the left bins (or vice versa), there is indeed a statistically significant effect corresponding to the intent.

If psychokinesis exists, what does it imply about the nature and structure of the universe in which we live? For one thing, one would have to argue that things are certainly more interconnected and interdependent than pure physical models of reality would admit. One also could speculate that if consciousness is the interconnecting element, all objects, whether animate or inanimate, possess some degree of this universal consciousness. This would certainly agree with ancient philosophies accepted by such peoples as the Native Americans, Hindus, and Taoists.

One also could hypothesize that we have a profound ability to create and structure our own reality, even beyond what we consider possible by the consensus reality in which we live. We can venture that as our human species evolves and matures, more such paranormal abilities will emerge and become accepted as normal. One way to use these PK devices and experiments would be to discover correlations and effects of various technologies on the PK performance:

- Psychological history or state
- Body and mind therapies
- Spiritual and meditative disciplines
- PK machine design improvements

## REG MACHINES

A random event generator is basically an electronic coin-flipper. It can be either a custom hardware box or a general purpose computer (e.g., the Macintosh program described later). On the computer, one *trial* of the program consists of 200 flips of an electronic "coin." In a computer, this is represented as a collection (a *sample*) of 200 random bits *(binary digits)*. Each bit can randomly assume the values of either one (1) or zero (0).

The *sample count* of a single trial is simply the addition of these 200 random ones and zeros. In experimental trials with perfectly random ones and zeros, one can expect to get a sum of around 100, since about one-half of the bits will be one and one-half, zero. Indeed, one can run a great number of these trials and plot a histogram with the *x* axis showing the sample count (e.g., 96, 97, 98, 99, 100, 101, 102, 103, 104). Then on the *y* axis, we would plot the number of trials that produced the sample count.

This histogram would be fit and predicted by a bell-shaped curve called a *Gaussian distribution*. The highest number of trials would be at sample count 100, with lesser values at 99 and 101, lower still at 98 and 102, and so forth. Now, what happens during this random process if the operator directs his conscious *intention* to seek, for example, more ones than zeros (higher sample counts)? There is an extremely slight shift of the bell curve in the direction intended. This histogram, however, is a poor way of looking at the data, and it makes statistical interpretation difficult.

Instead, we construct a graph called a *cumulative deviation plot*. On the *x* axis, we plot the trial number, and on the *y* axis, we show cumulatively how much the sample count has deviated from the expected mean value of 100. For example, if on trial 1 our sample count is 105, then that is 5 more than the expected mean of 100, so the graph goes up 5 ticks. We would plot a point at $x = 1$, $y = 5$. If on trial 2 we get a count of 94, that is 6 less than 100, so the graph goes down 6 ticks. We plot the point at $x = 2$, $y = -1$. Figure 18.1 shows a small plot of 50 trials (not the *x* and *y* points mentioned above). X is the trial number, and Y is the number of bits of cumulative deviation from the expected mean value (plus or minus).

If we have a truly random process, then the cumulative deviation plot of that process after thousands of trials should look like a jagged line (a random walk) that never gets very far from the *x* axis ($y = 0$, no effective cumulative deviation). If the operator's consciousness is influencing the process, then the plot should go up if he is intending for more ones, and down if intending for less ones. But how much up or down does it need to go to be statistically significant?

The cumulative deviation plots drawn by *Intent* (and the PEAR group) show a gently curving gray line on both sides of the *x* axis. This line corresponds to the *z* score for 5% significance. If the operator manages to influence the process such that his plot line crosses outside the dotted line, then this is significant at the 5% level. In other words, such a deviation has only a 5% probability of being produced by chance. In Figure 18.1, the deviation plot stays within the 5% lines; therefore, the operator influence is not significant.

To have statistical confidence that you are seeing a real effect, there must be

**Figure 18.1**
**Cumulative Deviation Plot Showing Random (Non-Significant) PK Series**

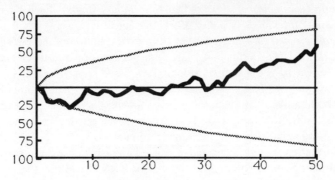

The black line of operator trials is within the 5% chance deviation envelope (grey parabola). *x*-axis = number of trials. *y*-axis-deviation from chance.

more than simply an isolated crossing of this dotted line. Rather, the plot must stay outside the dotted line for large numbers of trials, say, 5,000 to 10,000 trials at a minimum.

A collection of trials (50 to 50,000 trials) is called a series. Each series is recorded in a separate data file on the computer. To investigate the phenomena, you will want to record multiple series of data and count the number of series that achieved significance. For any arbitrary statistical significance criterion, a certain number of results exceeding that criterion are to be expected by chance. For example, if you run 20 series, 5% of those (one series) would be expected to exceed the 5% criterion for each direction of intention. Thus you would need several series out of the 20 to exceed the 5% line to claim significance.

**Figure 18.2**
**Tripolar Series in PK Trial**

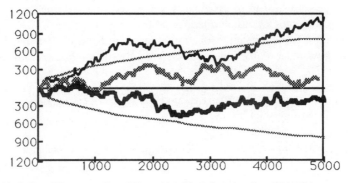

Thin black line, PK +; gray line, PK −; thick black line, baseline (BL). This operator shows "inverted" intention pattern of PK −, which goes in the PK + direction.

**Figure 18.3**
**Operator Variance in PK Trials**

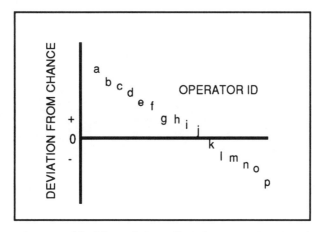

Operators at the extreme left of the *x*-axis (zero effect) show greater than chance ability for PK. Operators at far right show "psi missing" effect.

## TRIPOLAR SERIES

Another unit, the "run," of 50 trials was chosen to break up the data collection into chunks that might correspond to the operator's attention span.

A single series of data is composed of three parts, which the operator records in separate "runs" of data. The three components correspond to the operator

**Figure 18.4**
**Macintosh Screen Shot of *Intent* Program**

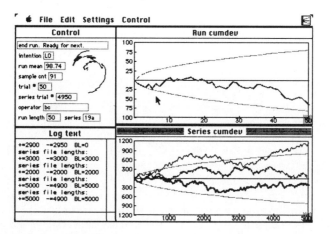

Menu bar items show at top of screen.

directing his intention in one of three directions: (1) plus, or higher sample counts; (2) minus, or lower sample counts; and (3) baseline, the operator trying to keep the deviation as close to zero as possible. The operator can collect the data in any order he chooses. Before recording a particular run or group of runs, the operator selects a menu item on the computer screen showing which direction he *intends* to record.

This menu selection controls (1) the appearance of the series graph (each of the three intentions is shown in a different "color") and (2) how each intention will be recorded in a separate subfile for later graphing. Figure 18.2 shows a complete (small) series of about 5,000 trials in each intention (15,000 trials total). Plus intention is shown as a thin black line, minus intention as a gray line, and baseline as a heavy black line. In this example, the plus intention has achieved significance.

Figure 18.2 also shows the idea of an operator's "signature"—a pattern that tends to be operator-specific. This particular operator frequently records series with the plus intention high, as you might expect, but with minus intention inverted, that is, opposite to the direction of intention. Some operators will be able to move both lines in the direction intended; other operators will have one or both of the lines inverted. Some operators will have high or low baselines.

In judging the significance of a particular series, one can look at the individual deviations of the plus and minus intentions. One can also look at *delta,* or the spread between the plus and minus intentions.[5]

## OPERATOR'S CONSCIOUSNESS

Certainly, with a phenomenon such as this, the operator state of mind is crucial. The PEAR experiments are performed in a quiet room with home-like furniture and decorations to calm the operators. If the basis for the phenomenon is a kind of resonance with the environment and the objects in the environment, operators would not want to be worrying about a recent argument with a spouse or come to the experiment after having just performed some detailed, analytical, "left-brain" activity such as balancing a budget or debugging a computer program.

The laboratory staff maintain a minimal presence during the actual operation, but openly discuss the experimental goals, gear, and protocols prior or subsequent to the session in as much detail as requested. They display cheerful, albeit professional, attitudes of openness to any results or lack thereof, and encourage the operators to take a playful approach to the task, rather than being overly concerned about the outcome.

On the basis of informal discussions with our operators, casual observations of their styles, occasional remarks that they record in the experimental logbooks, and our own experiences as operators, it is clear that individual strategies vary widely. . . . If there is any unity in this diversity of strategy, it would be that most effective operators seem to associate successful performance with the attainment of some sense of "resonance" with the device. This has been variously described in such terms as: "a state of immersion in the process which leads to a loss of awareness of myself and the immediate surroundings, similar to the experience of being absorbed in a game, book, theatrical performance, or some creative occupation. I don't feel any direct control over the device, more like a marginal influence when I'm in resonance with the machine. It's like being in a canoe; when it goes where I want, I flow with it. When it doesn't, I try to break the flow and give it a chance to get back in resonance with me." (p. 142)[6]

## OPERATOR VARIANCE

As would be expected, PEAR reports that a wide spectrum of ability exists among their 33 operators.[7] There does not seem to be clustering of ability into those who can and "those who cannot; the ability exists to some degree in almost every operator. Figure 18.3 shows the spread of operator ability typical of PEAR's operators.

The operators on the left side of graph (operators a through f, above the midline) are facile in influencing the process with their intention. This ability gradually decreases with subsequent operators. A few operators (g through l) are close to the $x$ axis, meaning that their intention had no effect on the process. Operators below the $x$ axis affected the REG in a manner *opposite* to their intention. Operator $p$, at the far right, was best at influencing the process in the opposite direction to intention, an effect known in parapsychology as *psi-missing*.

What magnitude of effect can be expected in working with a REG device? PEAR's largest collection of data for which sample size and run length were held constant consists of efforts by 33 operators completing 87 series, totaling more than 250,000 trials per intention.

With this group of operators, 10 achieved significant series (.05 criterion) in PK+, 8 operators achieved significance in PK−, and 0 scored at baseline (as expected).[5] For any arbitrary statistical significance criterion, a certain number of results exceeding that criterion are to be expected by chance. For the .05 criterion, 5% of 87 series, or roughly 4, would be expected to achieve significance by chance.

## SECONDARY PARAMETERS

In the gathering of the experimental data, a number of secondary parameters are held fixed for the duration of one or more series. Experience with a large number of series and operators at PEAR has shown that these parameters are important to operator performance. Unfortunately the parameters seem to be operator-specific, so that the set of parameters that works well with one operator may work poorly with another operator. One way to deal with this may be to gather a sufficient number of series with a given operator, changing the secondary parameters between series or groups of series until the best combination is found. The variables are as follows.

1. *Number of bits per trial and the number of trials per run.* In the Macintosh version, these are held fixed at 200 bits per trial and 50 trials per run. This corresponds to the most commonly used settings at PEAR and seems to be somewhat of a standard.

2. *Real-time feedback to the operator.* If feedback is enabled, the operator sees a real-time graph of his cumulative deviation performance. For some operators, this may increase their nervousness if the graph moves opposite to intention. On the Macintosh, a menu item can be used to disable feedback if desired.

3. *Manual versus automatic sequencing of trials within the run.* In *Intent,* another menu item controls this setting. In manual mode, the operator presses a button to begin each trial. In automatic mode, only one button is pressed, at the beginning of the run; after this, the 50 trials are automatically sequenced.

4. *Instructed versus volitional assignment of intention.* As mentioned above, the operator may select by menu item which intention of data he will be collecting (high, low, or baseline). Some operators perform better if this assignment is decided by the computer instead of by themselves. Accordingly, a menu item is provided (called randomize intention) that selects the direction of intention randomly. The operator then directs his intention as instructed.

## PSEUDORANDOMNESS

Computer scientists may now be asking, "But how can a computer program be random? Isn't it totally deterministic?" This is partly true. The random numbers generated by a computer program are called pseudorandom because they are generated by an algorithm, not a truly random process of nature.

The original PEAR experiments were performed with an analog electronic noise source, a noise diode, that was amplified, clipped, and digitally sampled to produce a stream of random ones and zeros. This type of randomness is nondeterministic in that the sequence of bits has no pattern and never repeats itself.

Later PEAR experiments used several types of pseudorandom bit generators, based both on hardware shift registers and on computer algorithms. In both cases, one can think of the bit generator as free-running and continuously generating the random stream of bits, just as the analog source is free-running. Only when the operator presses the button to start the trial is actual sampling of the random stream initiated. With the algorithm-based generator, when the operator presses the button to start the trial, the computer time-of-day and tick-count (sixtieth of a second) clocks are interrogated. These values are then used to seed the random-number generation algorithm, and the user enters the pseudorandom bit stream at that point in time. Because the random bit stream is 128 billion bits long before it repeats, sampling 200 bits at random from this total stream is assumed to be a fair approximation of a natural, nondeterministic random source.

The PEAR experiments performed with the original REGs versus the pseudo-REGs are virtually identical. Both machines are influenced by the operator's intention and produce similar cumulative deviation graphs. This naturally leads to the question, Where, then, does consciousness enter the system? With the noise diode, one might imagine that the operator has some quantum-level effect on the electrons or processes in the electronic device. With the computer, things are more insidious, and one must conclude that consciousness has an effect at some sort of systemic informational level (pp. 120–123).[6]

The random-number algorithm used in the Macintosh program is the best 32 bit linear congruential generator given by Professor Donald Knuth in his *Art of Computer Programming*.[8]

## PROGRAM OPERATION

The following sections briefly describe the Macintosh program *Intent,* which operates as a pseudo-REG device. A more detailed manual is included with the program disk. The program name is derived from the fact that the operator's *intention* is the primary focus in the experiments. Figure 18.3 shows a snapshot of the computer screen during operation.

### Windows

*Intent* places four windows on the screen that may be repositioned or resized as desired: (1) series cumulative deviation graph, as shown earlier in Figure 18.2 (each intention is shown as a different line-type); (2) run cumulative deviation graph, which is similar to the series window but only shows the results of the current run of 50 trials; (3) a control window with readouts showing the various program counters and status messages. In this control window, a box at the top gives status messages that indicate what is expected of you next, for example, "End run. Ready for next." or "Please open a series data file." The intention box shows which intention is currently being collected, and this can be altered by a menu item. Other boxes show the run mean, the sample count, and the number of the trial within the current run and series. Boxes also show the operator name or code number and the series identification number. These correspond to where the data is being stored on disk.

The final item in the control window is a circular object, visible underneath the top status box. This is a circular representation of the run cumulative deviation graph. The graph moves clockwise for positive deviation and counter-clockwise for negative deviation. Finally, each trial moves the graph one dot closer to the center. Thus if the deviation is moving in a consistent direction, this graph will have a spiral appearance. The idea for this display was taken from Helmut Schmidt's circular array of light bulbs.[2]

The fourth window is a log text area used for general messages. This can be moved backward (scrolled) to see older messages.

## Files

The program stores the data in series data files. The file structure is simple: If the operator name is Smith and the series name is 123, the program creates three data files for that series: smith.123.pl, smith.123.mi, and smith.123.bl. These files hold the data points for each direction of intention: plus, minus, and baseline. The data in the files is also simple: There is just one byte per trial, and that byte holds the sample count of that trial. This simple file structure allows easy export of the experimental data to a program that can run statistical tests.

## Startup and Option Selection

On the Macintosh, programs are controlled by means of their menus. In Figure 18.3, the menu titles are shown across the top of the screen: File, Edit, Settings, and Control.

A new series is opened by selecting New in the File menu. This brings up a dialog box in which to enter the operator name and the series name. Filling in the names and pressing OK causes a new series to be opened up, and the data files mentioned above are initialized.

After opening the series, you next indicate option and parameter settings before starting the data collection. These settings are selected with the Settings menu. Looking inside this menu, you see the information grouped in three categories: Intention, Sequencing, and Misc.

Under Intention, you see the items High, Low, Baseline, and ·Randomize·. The currently selected intention is shown inside the menu with a check mark. You can pick any other intention simply by selecting it. To allow the option of instructed intention, mentioned in the Secondary Parameters section above, the Randomize item is used. If you select this item, the computer will randomly select an intention among the three possibilities.

Under Sequencing, the default is Auto, which performs an entire run on each button press. You can also select Manual, which requires a button press for each trial. A check mark is shown on the menu next to the currently selected mode.

Under Misc. we see Feedback. This controls the real-time feedback mentioned in the Secondary Parameters section. Each time you select this item, it toggles the state of the operator feedback. A check mark in the menu means feedback is enabled, which is the case by default. If feedback is turned off, no information is shown in the graph windows and the control window only shows the status and series number items. All other feedback is disabled.

## Data Collection

After a series has been opened and the intention and other settings selected, you may then begin to collect data. The operator directs his intention as desired and then presses a keyboard key for either next run or next trial. (Keyboard definitions are available online in the About Intent . . . help screen.) Typically, the operator will collect a number of runs in one intention and then switch intentions and collect data in the new intention.

At the end of the session, selecting Quit or Close from the File menu will close and save the active data files. Open in the File menu can be used to append data to an existing session rather than beginning a new set of data files.

## Program Availability

The *Intent* program distribution disk includes both the executable program and the complete C source code *(Lightspeed C)* for the program. This allows examination of the algorithms and customization for laboratory environments. The disk, including program, source, and documentation, is available for a nominal handling fee ($5) from William Croft, 327 Waverley St., Menlo Park, CA 94025, e-mail: croft@igc.org, (415) 322-8306.

### NOTES

Assistance from the staff at the Princeton PEAR project is gratefully acknowledged. Roger Nelson, Brenda Dunne, and Robert Jahn were supportive in sending reports, answering questions, and analyzing calibration runs. In particular, Nelson answered all my e-mail questions and did the calibration analysis.

1. The Princeton work is fully documented in a series of technical reports from PEAR Publications and Technical Reports, Princeton Engineering Anomalies Research, C131, School of Engineering and Applied Science, Princeton University, Princeton, NJ 08544-5263, 1991.

2. Schmidt H. *Anomalous Prediction of Quantum Processes by Some Human Subjects*. Boeing Scientific Research Laboratories Document #D1-82-0821, February 1969. (See also Schmidt H. A PK test with electronic equipment. *Journal of Parapsychology*. 1970;34(3):175–181.)

3. Technical Note PEAR 84003. Nelson RD, Dunne B, Jahn R. An REG experiment with large data-base capability, ILL: Operator related anomalies. September 1984.

4. Dunne B, Nelson R, Jahn R. Operator-related anomalies in a random mechanical cascade. *Journal of Scientific Exploration*. 1987;2(2):155–179.

5. In the PEAR literature, the three intentions are sometimes referred to with this terminology: plus intention is called PK+, minus intention is called PK−, and the baseline intention is called BL. The delta spread is called ΔPK.

6. Jahn R, Dunne B. *Margins of Reality: The Role of Consciousness in the Physical World*. Harcourt Brace Jovanovich; 1988. The PEAR group has been in operation since 1979. *Margins of Reality* is a popularized version of technical reports on PEAR's results in the primary areas of man-machine anomalies (PK) and remote perception (telepathy and clairvoyance). There are also excellent sections on the background paradigm shifts and progress in theoretical modeling of these phenomena.

7. PEAR Technical Note 85001. Variance effects in REG series score distributions. July 1985.

8. Knuth DE. *The Art of Computer Programming. Vol 2: Fundamental Algorithms.* Reading, MA: Addison-Wesley; 1969. Knuth devotes some 170 pages in this volume to the theory and testing of random number generators. See the comments in the program source for more information on the generator.

# 19

# Brainwave Synchronization: Report on a Pilot Study

*James R. Johnston*

In 1980, Dr. Jean Millay and I did a pilot study in brainwave phase synchronization at the Washington Research Center in San Francisco and the Langley Porter Neuropsychiatric Institute, University of California San Francisco.[1] This was continuation of work that Dr. Millay had done on her Ph.D. thesis.[2] (She discusses visual processing of subtle information in Chapter 6.) We were looking for the possibility that there might be some kind of brainwave resonance that corresponded to states of deep rapport between people. Dr. Millay had experimented personally and with associates using equipment made especially for her by Tim Sculley of Aquarius Electronics,[3] based on her requests for signal analysis features and including her thoughtful and artistic design of visual and auditory feedback, and had found correspondences between phase synchronization feedback and the experience of rapport.

My own motivation comes from contemplation of issues in physics, particularly concerning macroscopic (large-scale) quantum coherence or correlation. There has never been any significant disagreement between quantum theory and experience in this regard, but there has been continual discussion and experimentation with respect to issues of our understanding or interpretation of these unique quantum phenomena (e.g., wave-particle duality; quantum coherence in superconductors, superfluids, and lasers; and quantum correlated behavior in remote [spatially separated] members of correlated [Einstein-Podolsky-Rosen or EPR] pair-states). It has become clear that these issues in understanding are related to our strong conceptual and perceptual bias toward perspectives of reality based on *separate individual objects* that interact. The quantum phenomena listed above and the quantum theory that predicts and describes this behavior indicate that reality is fundamentally a *wholeness* that manifests in discrete individualistic events. The events of experience (or measurements) by which reality becomes sensed and known are discrete and individualistic. The fundamental lawfulness that gives rise to order or pattern in the individualistic events or sensings (their "underlying cause") is in essence a single wholeness. The issues of understanding arise when we describe quantum phenomena in terms of interaction and correlation among individual objects that already exist, rather than considering our sensings as discrete and individualistic events of a quantum wholeness that already exists. The fundamental quality of wholeness is *ontologically prior* to the individualistic events (or a seeming continuum thereof) that make up our experience of reality. In this perspective, the paradoxes of quantum physics disappear, and the sense of mystery deepens.

This perspective of individuality and wholeness, based entirely on consideration of quantum physics, is consistent with perennial wisdom that through the ages has described our beingness or consciousness similarly, particularly by those who believed that the nature of our consciousness could be ascertained from direct experience of it and who participated in such practice. It is not unreasonable, then, to carry into the mental domain a perspective arrived at in the physical domain and to treat the issue of individuality and wholeness as being fundamentally relevant to both domains. Thus we are led to explore scientifically areas of experience that will inform and enhance our understanding of the relation between individuality and wholeness, in physical reality and in our being.

This pilot project was aimed at exploring possible relationships between mental and social rapport and physiological rapport between the members of several pairs (teams) of people. It was based on some "romantic notions" that were not validated but led to some interesting and statistically significant results. Those notions are best described perhaps by paraphrasing a couple of introductory paragraphs from the report submitted to the Institute of Noetic Sciences:

This work is motivated by the belief that an increased awareness of self and our relationship to environment is crucial to our evolution, even becoming a matter of survival. There is a common thread in the problems presented to us by life on this planet, and in the perplexities of modern science as well: we are not just individuals, but also an inseparable part of the whole. The pretense that we are ever separate from the whole is at best an approximation. (This is as true for a hydrogen atom as it is for a sentient being.) Because it has served our industrialization, technology and science, the qualities of separateness and individuality have predominated our perspective of reality.

Knowing is a process, not simply a collection of facts in a deductive logic. Knowing in its deepest sense involves a state of awareness in which there is a "resonance": there is no separation between "knower" and "known." This essential knowing (without separation) is somehow enhanced, or perhaps completed, by that part of awareness that pretends to "stand apart from" for the sake of an "outside" view. The latter has become so important in our technological evolution (it is the basis of our sense of scientific objectivity) that we seem to have forgotten the former. Special qualities of resonance in various arts (music, healing, dance, martial, etc.) have always been appreciated by practitioners of those arts, but are commonly relegated to the "esoteric." As a technological culture, we have developed little language and have very little consensus regarding those aspects of our being. It seems to us the problems we now face as a civilization are calling for a deeper knowing of our interconnectedness: with each other and with Earth. Thus, we find ourselves very interested in the possibility that resonance in physical or biological dimensions may help tag and enhance resonance in more subtle, subjective dimensions.[1]

The romantic notion here was that we would find a resonance in electroencephalograph (EEG; brainwave) alpha patterns between pairs of individuals while they were in rapport during telepathic activity. Telepathic activities seemed particularly appropriate to me: I seldom consider access to subtle information to be a special communication between individuals, but rather an opening of awareness to our nonindividualistic or wholeness aspect.

In this pilot project, we intentionally avoided issues of proof of the reality of telepathic phenomena. Given the limitations of a pilot project, we preferred to explore the possibility of relationship between physiological rapport and mental rapport represented by telepathic phenomena, which we assume to be real.[4,5] If a correlation between telepathic performance and physiology does exist, then any accounting of the telepathic performance must account for the physiological correlation as well.

We did not find evidence to support the idea that telepathic rapport would be accompanied by EEG phase synchrony, but we did find a solid correlation ($.74p < .001$) between team-average interpersonal brainwave (EEG) phase synchronization (IP phase sync) scores and team-average telepathy scores. Our intent had been for each team (1) to compare learning trends in IP phase sync scores with variations in telepathy scores across training and testing sessions and (2) to compare telepathy scores with IP phase sync scores taken during telepathy trials in the three testing sessions. Learning across sessions was not significant, and there was little interpersonal phase sync during testing-session telepathy tests. Thus we looked instead at team averages, telepathy scores versus IP phase sync scores, across teams and found the correlated averages indicated above.

## PILOT STUDY

The pilot project involved five male-female teams that we considered to have good rapport between the two members.[6] To reduce the traditional separation between subject and researcher-observer, Dr. Millay and I were one of the teams. We considered random sampling of a general population of subjects to be inferior to the use of a sample of adepts and used our own judgment for subject selection.

The physiological resonance explored in this project was alpha phase synchronization. Here, *alpha* refers to a brainwave rhythm of 7 to 12 oscillations per second (Hertz), which is found to be strongest for most people when they close their eyes and relax and are attentive with a wide or "soft" focus with minimal visual or mental processing of their perceptions. Phase synchronization refers to a kind of resonance between two brainwave signals: Both signals are at nearly the same frequency, with electrical oscillations moving nearly in unison. Each team member was given feedback training for alpha phase synchronization between his or her left and right hemispheres (IH phase sync, or IH sync), and each team was given training in IP phase sync (or IP sync). (As one might expect, allowing one's own brainwaves to resonate with another's is a delicate and subtle task.) Personal rapport was represented by scores from free-response telepathy tests.

In the following, the phrase *two brainwave signals* refers to two situations: (1) left and right hemispheric EEG for a single subject (IH sync), or (2) one EEG signal from each member of a team (IP sync). The phase coherence (synchronization) analysis is the same for both situations.

The feedback training sessions used Aquarius Electronics' (AE) brainwave analyzers and an AE phase comparator. A special feedback tone generated a pleasant *om* sound[7] when the two brainwave signals were simultaneously producing alpha waves above a preset threshold. A gentle, harmonious buzz was added to the tone when, in addition, the two signals were in phase with each other to within ¼ wavelength (+ or −45 degrees). For each one-minute scoring period, the percent time of simultaneous alpha and the percent time of phase-synchronized simultaneous alpha were each measured. The numeric scores for phase synchronization were based on the ratio of the two (alpha phase sync ratio, APSR):

$$\text{APSR} = \frac{\% \text{ time of two-channel alpha phase synchronization}}{\% \text{ time of two-channel (simultaneous) alpha}}$$

It is the fraction of the time of simultaneous alpha that is also phase-synchronized. This provides a measure that allows comparison of phase synchronization among low and high alpha producers.[8]

Each team participated in several feedback training sessions at the Washington Research Center. Each session consisted of training to increase or control IH phase sync for each team member followed by training in IP phase sync for the team, using the AE brainwave analyzers and phase comparator. The total time in each mode of training was typically 1 to 1.5 hours for each person.

In addition, special testing runs were done on the laboratory computer programmed to analyze each of the team's four EEG signals (left and right hemisphere for each subject) and to generate phase-synchronization measures on each of the six pairs of EEG signals (two interhemispheric, four interpersonal combinations), using the same analysis techniques as the AE training equipment. The testing data obtained on the laboratory computer could not be combined with the training data as had been originally planned, but it provided us with data not previously available and generated a puzzle regarding the connection between EEG phase synchrony and telepathic performance.

Each team was given 10 to 15 extrasensory perception (ESP) test sessions, usually at the end of a training or testing session, each of which consisted of five free-response telepathy trials. The targets were pictures of many disparate subjects cut from magazines and pasted on $3 \times 5$ cards (e.g., an astronaut landing on the moon, a black-and-white picture of a little girl sitting hungry in a ghetto, Batman hitting a villain, a colorful clown). One member of the team, the *sender,* concentrated on the target for a moment and then drew his or her own rendition of it with colored pencils and wrote comments about it—mood, central focus, and so on. The other member of the team, the *receiver,* in a remote room, at the same time drew his or her perceptions or guesses and comments on a $3 \times 5$ card. The original picture and the sender's rendition of it were combined as a *target* to be matched by the receiver's $3 \times 5$ card. Each set of five trials (five targets and five receiver's cards) was subjected to five independent forced-match blind judgings by people otherwise not involved in the experiment. The average of the separate judging scores was used as a single score.

It may be useful to note some of the differences between IH and IP feedback. Almost everyone who produces a significant amount of alpha simultaneously in both hemispheres also produces a significant amount of phase synchronization between the hemispheres. This is probably due to entrainment between the hemispheres. As a result, once one learns to produce simultaneous alpha, there is a significant amount of feedback signal from the naturally occurring phase synchronization, so that learning to increase and to control IH phase sync is aided by sufficient variation in the signal. However, the naturally occurring phase sync between participants is insignificant. As a result, in IP phase sync training, there is very little feedback signal, and the learning process is much more difficult.

The amount of learning in either IH or IP phase sync was not as high as we had hoped for. Thus it was not possible to correlate changes in telepathy scores with changes in IP phase sync scores. To make the data more robust, we combined the data for the five teams in this study with the 11 teams Dr. Millay used in her Ph.D. thesis, using only data obtained in similar training sessions on the same AE equipment with the same procedure for telepathy testing. The correlation between the average over all AE training sessions for each of the 16 teams of IP sync with the corresponding average of all telepathy scores of each team was .74 ($p < .001$). The correlation between the team-average IH sync and telepathy scores was lower and also significant ($r = .54, p < .0015$). The average IP phase sync scores varied from 10.8% to 30.6%. The average telepathy scores ranged from 10% to 36%, where 20% represents chance. Vi-

**Figure 19.1**
**Interpersonal Alpha Phase Sync Ratio (APSR) Versus Telepathy Scores**

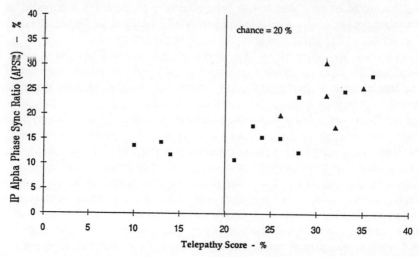

The triangles represent team averages from the current study. The boxes represent team averages from the previous study (see Text Reference 3). Note the three telepathy scores below chance: one might look for a different slope in that region.

sual inspection of a scatter plot of the data indicates a good correlation, with the major skew being due to the cluster of three subjects that scored significantly below chance on the telepathy scores (see Figure 19.1). We expect that the significant correlation would be replicable in a more formal experiment.

EEG patterns recorded during telepathy in the laboratory test sessions were quite different from those recorded in training sessions. After strenuous testing of the two sets of equipment and testing for possible electromagnetic interference at both sites, we can only surmise that the differences were due to the change in environment and to anxiety in a laboratory testing situation. IH and IP phase sync data on all possible pairs of channels were recorded during the session. We calculated IH and IP phase sync scores during a few minutes of quiet time during the telepathy test (in which there was no eye/body movement or muscle tension artifact). Those data indicated that there were strong left-right asymmetries in the alpha production of almost all subjects during that time and little IH or IP phase sync. That created a puzzle. (But not a new one. In a small follow-up study using eight of the teams from her dissertation experiment, Dr. Millay failed to find any correlation between telepathic performance and IP phase sync scores taken during telepathy.) The telepathy scores at the laboratory were more or less typical for each team, but there was little IH phase sync and no IP phase sync in the quiet interval during telepathy. The correlation between EEG phase synchronization and telepathy scores combined with the lack of evidence for a direct connection between the two was quite puzzling: If EEG phase synchronization did not accompany telepathic activity, what was the explanation for the correlation between the two sets of performance scores?

We are inclined to attribute the left-right alpha asymmetries to "extra efforting": activity associated with trying to do telepathy but not necessarily with telepathy itself. As an analogy, one can imagine trying to learn to wiggle one's ears while measuring muscle tension in the near vicinity. There would be a lot of activity (e.g., facial contortions) that had to do with the trying but not with the doing. That is, it is possible that extra efforting during the telepathy process may introduce left-right asymmetries and possibly mask out EEG patterns, if any, related to the telepathic process. Because no appreciable IP phase sync was recorded during the telepathy trials in the testing sessions, we believe that the correlation between IP phase sync and telepathy scores was not due to a direct relationship between them, but that they were both related to another factor: a skill at focus of attention. That is, a team that was good at one task would be good at the other because both tasks require similar attentional skills. We believe that important attentional skills, including immunity from distraction, can be learned and studied by the process of holding a subtle focus, as is required in these kinds of EEG tasks. (And perhaps in such tasks we may learn more of the repertoire of choice that is available to our awareness and perception.)

In summary, we believe this to be a plausible and important consideration: Volitional maintenance of EEG phase synchronization and telepathic performance both involve skill in cognitive and attentional processes. Skill in one activity would imply skill in the other. This perspective shifts the emphasis, appropriately, from consideration of states of being to skills in attention and awareness.

## OBSERVATIONS ON EEG FEEDBACK

Having been both a researcher and an occasional subject at Joe Kamiya's EEG psychophysiological research laboratory at Langley Porter Institute for a number of years, I have had some experience with less complex single-channel alpha feedback. The more complex task of generating alpha in both hemispheres was more difficult at first, but after a while it became much easier than I had experienced with the single-channel task at Langley Porter. I believe there are two reasons for this. First, and it is debatable, the more pleasant tone, rich in harmonics (as compared with a pure sine wave), was more conducive to success. Second, and more important, the presence of a second, subtler and more difficult task (phase synchronization) allowed skills in the first task to be integrated at a more automatic level. Although it was an attentional skill, it felt somewhat like training a muscle.

I believe there is an important message here. Although many of the generalizations of the experience of enhanced alpha have some truth and definitely exceptions, much of what each feedback participant attributes to the so-called *alpha state* are really concomitants of an early strategy for achieving the feedback task. Once a strategy begins to work, one naturally returns to that strategy and refines it. Thus my description of early single-channel alpha feedback would include subtle aspects of attending, whereas my description of the more complex task involving enhancement in both hemispheres would be more in terms of training an "attentional muscle" to hold a new kind of focus automatically. I probably would not have discovered the easier strategy if I had not tried the more complex task. (In later sessions, I experimented with a few other strategies that were quite different, and they also worked.) Some meditation experience has suggested that we often define a state of consciousness by a particular "doorway" that we have found in which to enter it. The experiential aspects of the doorway provide something to which we can align in order to find it again. And, if not careful, we find ourselves aligning to a doorway rather than to the state or experience to which it is an entrance. Thus it takes a wide range of exploration, passing through many doorways, to construct a map of mental process.

An incident in this project was particularly instructive. In one session, I *reduced* the amount of IH phase synchronization while maintaining a reasonably high level of simultaneous alpha. While doing so, I noticed something in the feedback that gave me an insight regarding a correction needed in the computer program I was writing to simulate the AE equipment on the laboratory computer. There was some thought about the changes needed in a subroutine and then a picture of the flowchart in my mind. All during this time the simultaneous alpha feedback tone was on. Whenever I tried to direct the process (e.g., volitionally going back to review something in the flowchart), the simultaneous alpha dropped out. Letting go of directing while attending to the thoughts that did emerge regarding the program allowed the simultaneous alpha to return. Whether or not the association of simultaneous left and right alpha with *nondirected* attending to intellectual activity would be replicable, it brought into awareness one of the dimensions of attention: directed versus undirected focus, likely to be independent of content and other dimensions, such as wide versus narrow and inner versus outer focus. The use of physiological feedback to aid in direct observation of mental process, done systematically, could increase our abilities of discernment and discrimination[9] in the study of attention, intention, and so forth, even though it would present methodological challenges.[10,11]

## SUMMARY

We did not find evidence that interpersonal EEG phase synchronization accompanies telepathic rapport at the time of testing the latter. However, among 16 pairs of subjects, those pairs with higher average interpersonal phase synchrony scores tended strongly to have higher-average telepathic performance scores ($r = .74$, $p < .001$). I believe this correlation indicates a similarity in the attentional skills required for the two tasks.

This project was supported in part by the Institute of Noetic Sciences, San Francisco; the Holmes Center, Los Angeles; the Washington Research Center, San Francisco; Paul and Diane Temple, and Joe and Joanne Kamiya.

## NOTES

1. Johnston JR, Millay J. A pilot study in brainwave synchrony. Submitted to the Institute of Noetic Sciences, October 1983. Copies may be obtained from IONS, Sausalito, California. A preliminary version was published in *Psi Research*. March 1983;2:1.

2. Millay J. *The Relationship Between Phase Synchronization of Brainwaves and Success in Attempts to Communicate Telepathically: A Pilot Study.* San Francisco: Saybrook Institute; 1978. Dissertation. Also published in Millay J. Brainwave synchronization: a study of subtle forms of communication. *The Humanistic Psychology Institute Review.* Spring 1981:3.

3. Now Mendocino Microcomputers, Albion, California.

4. Jahn RG, Dunne BJ, Nelson RD. Engineering anomalies research. *Journal of Scientific Exploration.* 1987;1:21–50.

5. Targ R, Puthoff H. Information transmission under conditions of sensory shielding. *Nature* 1974;252:602–607.

6. Anecdotal observations and technical details for this project, beyond that described below, examples of some EEG records showing examples of both interhemispheric phase sync and interpersonal phase sync, and some observations of a few sessions with healers are included in the report available from the Institute of Noetic Sciences, Sausalito, California.

7. Designed, built, and contributed by Tom Etter, Mill Valley, California.

8. For those wanting more detail, the EEG signals were measured from occiput to frontal, which is typical of much of the commercial home equipment. The specific hemisphere for each member during IP feedback was chosen arbitrarily, after some "getting-acquainted" runs, at the beginning of the project. The AE equipment used zero-cross analysis for dominant frequency determination and for cross comparisons for phase synchronization analysis. The zero-cross analysis is quite reasonable in the alpha band, since the EEG usually shows a dominant rhythm in that frequency range.

9. The original work leading to research in operant conditioning of EEG was in fact a discrimination study asking the question, Could subjects, if given feedback on their answers, learn to discriminate two physiological states defined as high alpha production and low alpha production? (Kamiya J. Conditioned discrimination of the EEG alpha rhythm in humans. In *Biofeedback and Self-Control,* edited by Kamiya J, Barber TX, Di Cara LV. New York: Aldine; 1969:279). The important original consideration of ability to discriminate was forgotten in the subsequent enthusiasm over ability to control.

10. Stoyva J, Kamiya J. Electrophysiological studies of dreaming as the prototype of a new strategy in the study of consciousness. *Psychological Review.* 1968;75:192–205.

11. Kamiya J. On the relationships among subjective experience, behavior, and physiological activity in biofeedback learning. In *Self Regulation of the Brain and Behavior,* edited by Elbert T, Rockstroh B, Lutzenberger W, and Birbaumer N. New York: Springer-Verlag; 1984:245–254.

# Near-Death Experiences: Implications for Human Evolution and Planetary Transformation

*Kenneth Ring*

About a decade ago, the world began to hear about a curious but irresistibly intriguing phenomenon. Called the *near-death experience* (NDE) by its chief popularizer, psychiatrist Raymond Moody,[1] whose books proved to be international best-sellers, this moment of transcendental radiance that occurs when individuals reach the apparent threshold of imminent death somehow fascinated and captured the attention of millions of people around the world. Indeed, one wonders whether, aside from sexual orgasm, there has ever been an experience whose duration is so brief—many NDEs appear to last less than a minute—that has stimulated so much reflection and commentary.

In this connection and in the wake of this pioneering work,[2] many books and articles examining NDEs and their implications have been published both in the United States and elsewhere. Numerous professional conferences in the United States, Europe, and Asia have likewise dealt with this experience, and an international organization—the International Association for Near Death Studies (IANDS)[3]—has emerged as a vehicle for disseminating the findings of NDE research around the world. Such attention appears to have triggered a deep and growing absorption with this tiny sliver of life—its apparent last moments—on a wide scale.

So pervasive is this interest that, at least in the United States, the near-death experience has achieved the status of a *cultural* and not just a clinical phenomenon. Not only have hundreds of radio and television talk shows featured discussions on the subject in addition to countless articles about it in the print media, but also one can scarcely find anyone who has not encountered such an experience in a Hollywood film, television soap, short story, or novel or even in a cartoon of a fashionable magazine. If one is sensitized to their existence, they seem to be as ubiquitous as convenience stores and just about as well known. In the United States alone, literally millions of people are now known to have had NDEs; this means that many millions of us are directly acquainted with one or more persons to whom this kind of experience has happened.

Consequently the NDE hardly appears to be a passing fad[4] but is a salient fact of our time and one that continues to exert a powerful hold on our collective consciousness. In addition to its popular appeal, in recent years, it has begun to be appreciated as a phenomenon with the potential for affecting human consciousness, and thus life on earth, in a profound way. Some have speculated that it is already beginning to do so.[5-9] But before we can meaningfully explore the deeper implications of NDEs, specifically those concerned with human evolution and planetary transformation, we must first examine the experience itself more closely, for it is the foundation stone on which our conclusions must rest.

## CONTENT AND PATTERNING OF THE NDE

What is it exactly that someone experiences who reports having survived an NDE? Perhaps the best way to grasp this (through the written word) is for you to imagine that this is something that is happening to you. There are two important qualifications. First, although they tend to follow a single common pattern, NDEs vary greatly in terms of the number of experiential elements that serve to define the prototypic pattern. In short, some are more complete than others. Second, as one gets deeper into the experience, there are several "branches" one may follow after experiencing the basic NDE "stem." For our purposes, you should imagine a fairly full NDE, which will progress along one of the most common branches.

Suppose you are driving in your automobile at a high rate of speed along a crowded highway when suddenly a truck pulls in front of your car, forcing you to jam on the brakes—but too late. In the next instant, there is a terrible, sickening collision and then. . . . If you are typical of the thousands of people researchers have interviewed who have reported NDEs, what would you experience?

Probably the first sensation you would be aware of would be a feeling of extreme peace and tremendous well-being. You would feel no pain—nor indeed any bodily sensation of any kind. You might be aware of a kind of crystalline, pure silence unlike anything you have ever experienced before. You would probably have the direct awareness that whatever this was, you were absolutely safe and secure in this all-pervading atmosphere of peace.

Then you would begin to have a kind of visual awareness of your environment. The first thing you would notice is that while you—the real you—appear

to be watching everything from above, your *body* is "down there" surrounded
by a knot of concerned people. You are watching all the frenetic activity below
you with a feeling of detached objectivity, perhaps even with a sense of slight
amusement. "Why are they making such a fuss about that body?" You might
think, *"I'm* perfectly fine." Indeed, you have never felt better in your life—
your perception is extremely vivid and clear, your mind seems to be functioning in a hyperlucid manner, and you are feeling more fully alive than you can
ever remember. You watch the scene below you, noting your crumpled car
flipped over on its belly by the side of the road, and you observe that off in
the distance an ambulance is trying to weave its way through the stalled traffic.

Suddenly your attention is drawn to an inviting, velvety blackness, and you
find yourself moving through this blackness—without a body but with an un-
mistakable sense of motion—and as you do, you are aware that this blackness
has the configuration of a tunnel. That is, the black space is bounded (although
vast) and cylindrical, and you seem to be propelled through it as if you are
headed for a definite but still unknown destination. Although you are traveling
through this tunnel with a sense of increasing, indeed extraordinary, speed, you
do not feel afraid. You just accept what is happening to you, knowing that
everything will be all right.

As you approach what appears to be the end of the tunnel, you become
aware of what is at first a pinpoint of light. This light quickly grows bigger
and brighter and becomes more effulgent. It is an extremely brilliant light—
golden-white—but it does not hurt your eyes. You have never experienced a
light like this—it seems to be sourceless and to cover the entire vista before
you. As you move closer to the light, you begin to be overwhelmed with the
most powerful waves of what can only be described as pure love, which seem
to penetrate to the very core of your being. There are no thoughts now, only
total immersion in this light. All time stops; this is eternity, this is perfection—
you are home again in the light.

In the midst of this timeless perfection, you become aware that somehow
associated with this light there is a definite *presence*. It is not a person, but it
is a *being* of some kind, a form you cannot see but to whose consciousness
your own mind seems now to be linked. A telepathic dialogue ensues. The
presence informs you that you must make a decision whether to remain here or
go back. Even as this thought is communicated to you, you are suddenly seeing,
as though a million simultaneous yet precise and sharp images, everything that
has ever happened to you in your life. There is no sense of judgment—you are
watching all this like a spectator—but as this patterned fabric of your life un-
ravels before you, you grasp the essential meaning of your life, and in the
moment of that realization, you see with absolute clarity that you must go back,
that your family, especially your children, need you.

That is the last bit of transcendental awareness you have. The next thing you
know is that you are in excruciating pain in what is clearly an altogether different and heart-breaking human environment that you eventually recognize to

be a hospital room. It is three days later, you are enmeshed in tubes and intravenous lines in an intensive care unit, unable to talk but able to remember every detail of what happened to you when your body lay on the roadside and you hung suspended between life and death.

In reflecting on your near-death experience—although you would probably not label it thus—what is clear to you is that this was no dream or hallucination. Nor was it something you imagined. This was compellingly real and objective: It was more real than life itself. You wish you could talk to somebody about it, but who could understand, even if you found words adequate to describe it? All you know is that this is the most profound thing that has ever happened to you and that your life—and your understanding of life—will never again be the same.

So much for a fairly common *deep* near-death experience and its immediate aftermath. In any event, this is what many people have said "it is like to die." The bare recital of such an experience only raises a multitude of empirical and interpretative questions; it does not provide any firm answers (except, possibly, to those who have the experience) concerning what occurs at death, much less what, if anything, takes place *after* biological death. Considerable research has recently been conducted into these experiences, and we now know a great deal more about them.

## PARAMETERS AND INTERPRETATIONS OF THE NDE

Among the first questions usually asked about this phenomenon is, How often does it occur?[10] If one were to take 100 consecutive cases of patients who clinically died,[11] how many of the survivors would relate NDEs?

Early research[12,13] suggested that the answer might be about 40%, and this estimate has also been supported by the results of a Gallup poll[14] based on a much larger and more representative sample of people who have been close to death.[15] The body of research on NDEs is consistent in showing that most people remember nothing as a result of a near-death crisis, but that a high percentage of those who claim to have some conscious recall report experiences that conform, at least in part, to the prototypic NDE we have considered. A scattered number will report idiosyncratic experiences that usually seem to be hallucinatory in character; likewise, a tiny fraction of all cases appear to be negative experiences.

If one extrapolates from Gallup's sample base to the population from which it was designed to be representative (160 million adult Americans), it is possible to estimate how many people living in the United States have already had an NDE—about 8 million! This number has astonished many people (including some researchers) and should be carefully noted, since it plays a key role in the thesis to be advanced later in this chapter.

Another question that often is asked is, Does the way one nearly dies affect the experience? Investigators have examined a diverse array of conditions associated with the onset of death: combat situations, attempted rape and murder, electrocutions, near-fatal falls, near-drownings, vehicular crashes, freezings, hangings, and a great range of strictly medical and surgical conditions. Overall, the pattern seems quite clear-cut: By whatever means a person comes close to death, once the NDE begins to unfold, it is essentially invariant and has the form described earlier. In addition, research on suicide-related NDEs [16,17] has shown that these experiences likewise tend to conform to the prototypic pattern. In short, so far as is now known, situations that cover a wide gamut of near-death conditions appear to have a negligible effect on the experience itself.

If situational variables do not significantly influence the experience, what about personal characteristics? Are certain people more likely to have such an experience because of social background, personality, prior beliefs, or even prior knowledge of NDEs? Once again, the research to date is consistent in finding that individual and social factors appear to play a minimal role. Demographic variables such as gender, race, social class, and education, for example, have been shown not to be connected with NDE incidence and form. Similarly, it is evident that there is no particular kind of person—defined by psychological attributes—who is especially likely to have an NDE. It might be thought that people who have a preexisting or strong religious orientation or who already believe in some form of postmortem existence would be more prone than others, but this is not so. Atheists and agnostics are no less likely to recount prototypic NDEs than religious people, although the interpretation of the experience is apt to be different. Finally, prior knowledge does not seem to increase the probability of having an NDE.

Thus, despite persistent inquiry and recently renewed interest in the question, we are obliged to conclude that the NDE seems to select its recipients in a random manner. At any rate, if there is any type of person who is an especially good candidate, we have not yet succeeded in identifying the characteristics.

When we come to the question—and it is an all-important one—of *universality*, we must admit that this is an area of research that is still lamentably underdeveloped. [18] Nevertheless, we do at least have a fair amount of data from various cultures that afford us some tentative answers concerning the extent to which the NDE is a culture-free phenomenon.

We already have enough information to assert confidently that in England and continental Europe, NDEs take the same form as those in the United States. [6,19,20] This is hardly surprising, since these countries share a Judeo-Christian heritage. In the IANDS archives and in a few scattered articles, [21-23] there are fragmentary data from a diverse number of cultures whose traditional beliefs are quite different from those of the West. Included here are cases from India, Japan, South America, Melanesia, and Micronesia, among others. These cases show some obvious parallels to the classic pattern but often involve elements that deviate in specific ways, especially in the deeper stages, where more archetypal imagery comes into play. At this point, then, the prudent conclusion must be that in Western cultures, our data are simply too fragmentary to permit any firm judgment concerning the universality of the prototypic NDE model.

From the body of cross-cultural data that we do have, it seems plausible to infer that despite some degree of cultural variation, there may be certain universal constants, such as the out-of-body experience, the passage through a realm of darkness toward a brilliantly illuminated area, and the encounter with "celestial" beings. Only further research can substantiate this hypothesis as well as settle the question of the universality of the prototypic NDE as a thanatological phenomenon.

Finally, we must address the issue of the general interpretation of the NDE. Because many considerations of this formidable matter have already been established,[1,6,12,13,24,25] there exist a plethora of theories and a minimum of consensus about them. The interested reader is advised to consult the literature in near-death studies for the specifics of the theory, over which debate continues to be heated. These theories tend to fall into three broad classes—biological, psychological, and transcendental—although many interpretations do not confine themselves to a single perspective. The biological theories tend to be reductionistic and antisurvival in tone, whereas those with transcendental emphases tend to be empirically untestable but compatible with a survivalistic interpretation. Naturally, the psychological theories are intermediate in most respects.

We must emphasize that a decade of research on the NDE has failed to produce any kind of generally accepted interpretation, even among those who have spent years carefully examining it. Moreover, I have recently tried to show[8] that the surrounding interpretative issues are even more complex than many theorists have appreciated. The question of how such an experience can be explained—or indeed whether it even can be—remains shrouded in a cloud of obscurity and contentiousness. The irony is that this entire question may well prove to be irrelevant to the issue of its importance to humanity at large.

The larger significance of the NDE turns not so much on either the phenomenology or the parameters of the experience, but on its *transformative* effects. For it is precisely these effects that afford us a means of merging it with certain broad evolutionary currents that seem to be propelling humanity toward the next stage of its collective development. To understand the basis of this linkage, we must now explore the ways in which an NDE changes the lives, conduct, and character of those who survive it.

## TRANSFORMATIVE EFFECTS OF NDES

The most recent work in near-death studies[5,6,8,26] has increasingly been focused on the aftereffects of the NDE, and it is concordant in revealing a provocative set of findings. First, it appears that just as the NDE itself seems to adhere to a common pattern of transcendental elements, so also there seems to be a consistent pattern of transformative aftereffects. Second, this pattern of changes tends to be so highly positive and specific in its effects that it is possible to interpret it as indicative of a *generalized awakening of higher human potential*. To see how this could be so and to lay the groundwork for its possible evolutionary significance, let us now review the findings of my own study of aftereffects, described in my last book, *Heading Toward Omega*.[8]

This investigation, whose findings rest on the statistical analysis of specially designed questionnaires as well as qualitative data from personal interviews, examined three broad categories of aftereffects: (1) changes in self-concept and personal values, (2) changes in religious or spiritual orientation, and (3) changes in psychic awareness. Wherever possible, the self-reports of respondents were compared with assessments provided by such people as close friends or family members who had known the experiencer well both before and after his or her NDE. For most statistical analyses, data from appropriate control groups also were available for comparative purposes. What, then, is the psychological portrait that can be drawn from this study?

First, in the realm of personal values, people emerge from this experience with a heightened *appreciation of life,* which often takes the form not only of a greater responsiveness to its natural beauty, but also of a pronounced tendency to be focused intently on the present moment. Concern over past grievances and worries about future problems diminish. As a result, these people are able to be more fully present to life now, in the moment, so that an enhanced attentiveness to their environment and a freshness of perception follow naturally. They also possess a greater appreciation of themselves in the sense that they have greater *feelings of self-worth.* In most cases, it is not that they show signs of ego inflation, but rather that they are able to come to a kind of acceptance of themselves as they are, which sometimes they will attribute to the tremendous sense of affirmation they received "from the Light."

Perhaps one of the most evident changes that follows an NDE is an *increased concern for the welfare of others.* This is a broad and important domain with many aspects to it. Here I will only be able to briefly summarize its principal modes of expression—increased tolerance, patience, and compassion for others and especially an increased ability to express love. Indeed, after an NDE, people tend to emphasize the importance of sharing love as the primary value in life. In addition, they seem to feel a stronger desire to help others and claim to have more insight into human problems and more understanding of other human beings. Finally, they seem to demonstrate an unconditional acceptance of others, possibly because they have been able to accept themselves in this way. In a sense, one might characterize all these changes as exemplifying a *greater appreciation of others,* and as such, it may represent still another facet of what appears to be a general appreciation factor that the NDE itself serves to intensify.

Because there is an overall increase in the aforementioned values, other values show a clear and consistent decline. For example, the importance placed on material things, on success for its own sake, and on the need to make a good impression on others all diminish after people undergo an NDE. People-oriented values rise, whereas concern over material success plummets.

One more change in the realm of personal values should be noted. These people tend to seek a deeper understanding of life, especially its spiritual or religious aspects. They often become involved in a search for increased self-understanding as well and appear more inclined to join organizations or engage in reading or other activities that will be conducive to achieving these ends.

Incidentally, with respect to these value changes—as well as to other categories of aftereffects—it appears that these self-reports may well reflect changes in behavior. Although we clearly need more corroborative evidence than is available in *Heading Toward Omega,* statements by close friends and family members provide support for the behavioral changes that these people describe in themselves.

Moving to the area of religious and spiritual changes, it will come as no surprise to learn that there are far-reaching aftereffects here too. Such changes characteristically follow a particular form to which the term universalistic might most appropriately be applied. In characterizing this universalistic orientation, it will be helpful to distinguish a number of components that together make up the model spiritual worldview of those who have experienced a near-death crisis.

First, there is a tendency to describe themselves as more spiritual, not necessarily more religious. By this they appear to signify that they have experienced a deep inward change in their spiritual awareness, but not one that made them more outwardly religious in their behavior. They claim to feel, for example, much closer to God than they had before, but the formal, more external aspects of religious worship often appear to have weakened in importance. They also are more likely to express an unconditional belief in life after death for everyone and to endorse the conviction that not only will there be some form of postmortem existence, but that "the Light" will be there for everyone at death, regardless of one's beliefs (or lack of them) about what happens at death.

Interestingly—and this is a finding also suggested by my earlier research in *Life at Death*[12] as well as Gallup's survey—a greater openness to the idea of reincarnation often is expressed. It is not that they find themselves ready to subscribe to a formal belief in reincarnation, but rather that it is a doctrine that makes more sense to them than it did before their NDE. My impression is that this increased receptivity to reincarnational ideas is part of a more general friendliness to and acquaintance with Eastern religions and with some of the more esoteric and mystical variants of Christianity and Judaism.

Finally, the NDE draws people to a belief in the idea known to students of comparative religion as the "transcendent unity of religions," the notion that underlying all the world's greatest religious traditions, there is a single and shared transcendent vision of the Divine. In espousing this view, some people will aver or imply that they came to this realization directly through their own NDEs. Similarly, they are more inclined than others to admit to a desire for a form of universal spirituality that by embracing everyone would exclude no one. This is not a naive hope or wish that the multitudinous and incredibly diverse religious traditions throughout the world might somehow meld into a single "universal religion," but only that people of different and seemingly divisive religious faiths might one day truly realize their unity with one another.

The last domain of aftereffect explored in *Heading Toward Omega* deals with changes in psychic awareness. Not only my finding, but also those of others [27,28] support the hypothesis that the NDE serves to trigger an increase in psychic sensitivity and development—that after their experience, subjects become aware of many more psychic phenomena than had previously been the case. For example, they claim to have had more telepathic and clairvoyant experiences, more precognitive experiences (especially in dreams), greater awareness of synchronicities, more out-of-body experiences, and a generally increased susceptibility to what parapsychologists call "psi-conducive states of consciousness," that is, psychological states that seem to facilitate the occurrence of psychic phenomena. Although the data on apparent increases in psychic awareness lend themselves to various interpretations, it does seem clear that a heightened sensitivity to psychic phenomena follows an NDE (which may well include subjectively convincing paranormal features in its own right).

Having now reviewed the findings on some of the major aftereffects of NDEs, we must seek a coherent framework to place them in so that their implicit patterning may be brought into relief. It is possible and plausible to regard the NDE as playing a critical catalytic role in personal development. Specifically, it seems to serve as a catalyst to promote the spiritual awakening and growth of the individual because of its power to thrust one into a transcendental state of consciousness whose impact is to trigger a release of a universal inner programming of higher human potentials. There may be in each of us a latent spiritual core that is set to manifest in a particular form if only it can be activated by a powerful enough stimulus. [29] In the NDE, it appears that the stimulus is the light, and the similarity and consistency of the spiritual changes after an NDE point to what may be a common "spiritual DNA" of the human species. In these people, the pattern of changes in the consciousness and conduct bears a marked similarity to what Bucke [30] long ago claimed for his examples of "cosmic consciousness" and to which the modern psychiatrist Stanley Dean, [31] has more recently called our attention. An NDE often stimulates a radical spiritual transformation in the life of the individual, which affects his self-concept, his relations to others, his view of the world, *and* his worldview as well as his mode of psychological and psychic functioning. But how does any of this— profound as these changes may be—speak to the weighty issues of human evolution and planetary transformation?

## IMPLICATIONS OF THE NDE FOR HUMAN EVOLUTION AND PLANETARY TRANSFORMATION

Only a partial understanding of the significance of the NDE can be attained from a strictly psychological perspective, that is, one that concentrates on the *individual's* experience and its effects on him. A more complete appreciation is available if we shift the level of analysis from the individual plane to the sociological, where the meaning of the transformative pattern will be more apparent. We must look at the NDE from this broader perspective to discern the possible deeper significance for humanity at large.

Recall, first of all, that it has already been projected that perhaps as many as 8 million adult Americans have experienced this phenomenon—and we know that American children also report such experiences.[32-35] Although we do not have even a crude estimate of how many people worldwide may have had this experience, it certainly does not seem unreasonable to assume that additional millions outside the United States must also have had them. But the point is not simply that many millions will know this experience for themselves, but also *how the NDE will transform them afterward.* We have already examined how people's lives and consciousness are affected and what values come to guide their behavior. To begin to appreciate the possible planetary impact of these changes, we must imagine these same effects occurring in millions of lives throughout the world, regardless of race, religion, nationality, or culture.

From various studies of transcendental experiences,[30,31,36-39] we know that the radical spiritual transformation that often follows a NDE is by no means unique to that experience. Rather, as Grof[38] has recently implied, transcendental experiences, however they may come about, tend to induce similar patterns of spiritual change in people who undergo them. In short, the NDE is only *one* means to catalyze a spiritual transformation, but many others, which seem to reflect the same underlying spiritual archetype, have unquestionably been triggered by something other than a near-death crisis.

Is there any way to estimate the extent of such transcendental experiences in general? Probably not with any real hope for acceptable accuracy, but we do have at least a basis for a rough sort of guess for English-speaking countries. In national surveys in the United States, England, and Canada, for example, up to one-third of those polled admit that they have had some kind of powerful spiritual experience.[37] From these data only, it is impossible to claim that such experiences necessarily induce the kind of transformative pattern I have previously delineated. Nevertheless, it does seem warranted to infer that many more people must undergo these transformations by means other than an NDE. Thus, if these other transformations are added to the presumed millions of NDEs, we immediately see that we are dealing with a far more pervasive phenomenon than one might have first assumed.

A third consideration in this argument pertains not simply to the number of people in the world who may have experienced a major transformative awakening, however it may have been occasioned, but to the rate of increase in such transformations. In the case of NDEs, it is mainly modern resuscitation technology that is responsible for creating such a large pool of survivors. Before the advent of cardiopulmonary resuscitation, for example, most would have died; now many not only are saved, but go on to live drastically changed lives because of their close encounter with death. With resuscitation technology likely to improve and spread in use around the globe, it appears inevitable that many more millions will undergo and survive NDEs and thus be transformed according to this archetypal pattern.

Similarly, although there are not, as I have indicated, any systematic studies of the incidence of transcendental experiences in general, various students of higher consciousness[38,40-42] have speculated that such experiences are widespread, at least in the Western world, and that their number may be growing exponentially.

Such intriguing possibilities fit neatly with the next observation needed to complete the foundation for my argument based on recent theories concerning the spread of behavioral properties throughout a population. I am thinking here particularly of the theory of a young English biologist, Rupert Sheldrake, whose book *A New Science of Life*[43] has fanned widespread interest and controversy in scientific circles ever since its publication. In his book, Sheldrake propounds a hypothesis of what he calls "formative causation," which states that the characteristic forms and behavior of physical, chemical, and biological systems are determined by invisible organizing fields—*morphogenetic fields*, in Sheldrake's phrase. Although I cannot review here the author's evidence in support of his hypothesis,[44] Sheldrake's basic idea is that once such fields do become established through some initial behavior, that behavior is then facilitated in others through a process called *morphic resonance*. Thus, for example, once an *evolutionary variant* occurs in a species, it is likely to spread throughout the entire species.

Sheldrake's ideas are similar to (but certainly not identical with) the theme of the currently popular "hundredth monkey effect," whose empirical authenticity now appears entirely without foundation, but whose appeal as a framework for conceiving social contagion phenomena is almost irresistible. This seemingly apocryphal tale describes how a new behavior, potato washing by monkeys, spread to all monkeys on a certain Japanese island as well as to monkeys on adjacent islands when an imaginary "hundredth monkey" indulged in the new ritual. In principle, once the hundredth monkey engaged in this new behavior, that was all that was needed to create a strong enough field for morphic resonance to occur, thus turning innovation into custom. In this case, the hundredth monkey presumably established the critical mass necessary to transform the eating habits of the entire colony.

What is the relevance of all this to the NDE and to the issues of the evolution of consciousness and planetary transformation? There is a possible connection stemming from the following observation, which has previously been made by a number of others besides myself. We do not know the limits of Sheldrake's hypothesis. If it is correct—and it is the subject of much excited interest and experimental work—it is distinctly possible that it may apply to states of consciousness as well. This extrapolation has in fact been made by science writer Peter Russell, whose commentary will make explicit the connection between our concerns here and Sheldrake's work.

Applying Sheldrake's theory to the development of higher states of consciousness, we might predict that the more individuals begin to raise their own levels of consciousness, the stronger the morphogenetic field for higher states would become, and the easier it would be for others to move in that direction. Society would gather momentum toward enlightenment. Since the rate of growth would not be dependent on the achievements of those who had gone before, we would enter a phase of super-exponential growth. Ultimately, this could lead to a chain reaction, in which everyone suddenly started making the transition to a higher level of consciousness (p. 129).[41]

Although Russell's own formulation may seem somewhat hyperbolic and simplistic, it does have the virtue of suggesting both a hopeful and a larger vision of the inherent potential of the NDE and similar transcendental experiences. If we now consider the high base rate of all transcendental experiences generally throughout the world, the likelihood of their increasing incidence, and the possible mechanism by which the effects of such states may spread across a population, we may finally discern the possible global significance of the NDE.

May it be that this high rate of transcendental experience *collectively represents an evolutionary thrust toward higher consciousness for humanity at large?* Could it be that the NDE is itself an *evolutionary mechanism* that has the effect of jump-stepping people into the next stage of human development by unlocking previously dormant spiritual potentials? Indeed, are we seeing in these people, as they mutate from their former personalities into more loving and compassionate people, the prototype of a new, more spiritually advanced strain of the human species striving to come into being? Do these people represent the early maturers of a new breed of humanity emerging in our time—an evolutionary bridge to the next shore in our progression as a species, a missing link in our midst?

These are heady and provocative questions, but they are not entirely speculative ones. Many thinkers before me have dreamed and written of the coming to earth of a higher humanity and have attempted to describe the attributes of such people. Although these visions of a higher humanity are subjective, the transformations outlined in this chapter have happened to real people, and they are among us now. And we can at least ask, How well do these visions of a new humanity match the characteristics of these people?

For one representative portrait of this new humanity,[45] let me draw on the views of the well-known author John White, who has helped to popularize the term *Homo noeticus* in this connection. In reading his description, bear in mind that it was not intended as a characterization of someone who had experienced a near-death crisis and that it is similar to accounts provided by other evolutionary thinkers who have addressed the same issue.

*Homo noeticus* is the name I give to the emerging form of humanity. "Noetics" is a term meaning the study of consciousness, and that activity is a primary characteristic of members of the new breed. Because of their deepened awareness and self-understanding, they do not allow the traditionally imposed forms, controls, and institutions of society to be barriers to their full development. Their changed psychology is based on expression of feeling, not suppression. Their motivation is cooperative and loving, not competitive and aggressive. Their logic is multi-level/integrated/simultaneous, not linear/sequential/either-or. Their sense of identity is embracing-collective, not isolated-individual. Their psychic abilities are used for benevolent and ethical purposes, not harmful and immoral ones. The conventional ways of society do not satisfy them. The search for new ways of living and new institutions concerns them. They seek a culture founded in higher consciousness, a culture whose institutions are based on love and wisdom, a culture that fulfills the perennial philosophy (p. 14).[42]

Although this is an idealized description, the transformative process that the NDE sets into motion certainly appears to lead to the development of people who approximate the ideal type White posits as the prototype of the new humanity.

Even if my own ideas about the seeding of a new humanity through the spread of NDEs and other transcendental experiences are found to have some plausibility,[46] their implications for planetary transformation admittedly allow for a variety of short-term scenarios. I am not the one who foresees the emergence of a new, cooperative planetary culture as a necessary consequence of the kind of evolutionary shift in consciousness I detect. Rather, I see that shift as a potential of the human species that is beginning to manifest, but whether it takes hold and transforms the earth depends on many factors; not the least is the extent to which many of us consciously align with these trends and seek to awaken.[47] Clearly, nothing in the collective human potential emerging from the spawning grounds of transcendental experiences precludes the possibility of our planet's self-destructing. Nothing is assured or inevitable. No one living in the last years of the twentieth century—inarguably the most horrific in history—could deny for a moment that our prospects for surviving intact into the next millennium are shrouded in black uncertainty.

At the same time, human beings live in hope as well as fear, and this recent curious phenomenon—the NDE—seems to be holding out a powerful message of hope to humanity that even, and perhaps especially, in its darkest moments, the Light comes to show us the way onward. It is up to each of us whether we shall have the courage and the wisdom to follow where it beckons.

## NOTES

1. Moody R, Jr. *Life After Life*. New York: Bantam; 1975.

2. To be sure, others had researched the phenomenon long before Moody—and another physician, Elizabeth Kübler-Ross, was already a highly visible international figure who spoke compellingly about the NDE—but it was really Moody's book that, by *labeling* the phenomenon, rooted it in the soil of contemporary Western culture.

3. IANDS' address is Box U-20, University of Connecticut, Storrs, CT 06268.

4. Raymond Moody has said that after his first book, *Life After Life,* came out, he expected that the interest in the NDE that it generated would run its course within a few months (personal communication, 1981).

5. Flynn C. *After the Beyond*. Englewood Cliffs, NJ: Prentice-Hall; 1986.

6. Grey M. *Return from Death*. London: Routledge & Kegan Paul; 1985.

7. Grosso M. *The Final Choice*. Walpole, NH: Stillpoint; 1986.

8. Ring K. *Heading Toward Omega*. New York: William Morrow; 1984.

9. Ring K. From alpha to omega: ancient mysteries and the near-death experience. *Anabiosis*. 1985;5(2):3–16.

10. A more detailed consideration of these issues is found in my recent book, *Heading Toward Omega* (1984), especially in ch. 2.

11. In fact, many people who have only been close to death but seemingly not clinically dead (i.e., without vital signs such as heartbeat and respiration for a short time) have related that they, too, have had NDEs. A broader consideration of the conditions under which people may undergo NDEs or similar experiences is broached later in this chapter.

12. Ring K. *Life at Death*. New York: Coward, McCann & Geoghegan; 1980.

13. Sabom M. *Recollections of Death*. New York: Harper & Row; 1982.

14. Gallup G, Jr. *Adventures in Immortality*. New York: McGraw-Hill; 1982.

15. Actually, Gallup's figure is about 35 percent, but there are methodological reasons for thinking that this may be a slight underestimation of the population parameter.

16. Greyson B. Near-death experiences and attempted suicide. *Suicide and Life Threatening Behavior*. 1981;11:1016.

17. Ring K, Franklin S. Do suicide survivors report near-death experiences? *Omega*. 1981–1982;12:191–208.

18. Near-death studies is that branch of thanatology that is especially concerned with the study and understanding of the NDE.

19. Giovetti P. Near-death and deathbed experiences: an Italian survey. *Theta*. 1982;10:10–13.

20. Hampe J. *To Die Is Gain*. Atlanta: John Knox Press; 1979.

21. Counts D. Near-death and out-of-body experiences in a Melanesian society. *Anabiosis*. 1983;3:115–135.

22. Green J. Near-death experiences in a Chammorro culture. *Vital Signs*. 1984;4:6–7.

23. Trpas S, Richa TAS, Stevenson I. Near-death experience in India: a preliminary report. *Journal of Nervous and Mental Diseases* 1986;174:165–170. press).

24. Greyson B, Flynn C, eds. *The Near Death Experience*. Springfield, IL: Charles C Thomas; 1984.

25. Grosso M. Toward an explanation of near-death phenomena. *Journal of the American Society for Psychical Research*. 1981;75:37–60.

26. Bauer M. Near-death experiences and attitude change. *Anabiosis.* 1985;5:39–47.

27. Greyson B. Increase in psychic phenomena following near-death experiences. *Theta.* 1983;11:26–29.

28. Kohr R. Near-death experiences, altered states and psi sensitivity. *Anabiosis.* 1983;3:157–174.

29. In preparing this paper for publication, I discovered that Stanislav Grof, in his most recent book, *Beyond the Brain,* had independently arrived at a similar conclusion based on his work of nearly three decades with psychedelic therapy and other forms of deep experiential work. In this connection, he writes that "according to the new data, spirituality is an *intrinsic* property of the psyche that emerges quite spontaneously when the process of self-exploration reaches sufficient depth. Direct experimental confrontation with the [deep] levels of the unconscious is *always* associated with a spontaneous awakening of a spirituality that is quite *independent* of the individual's childhood experiences, religious programming church affiliation, and even cultural and racial background. The individual who connects with these levels of his or her psyche automatically develops a world-view within which spirituality represents a natural, essential and absolutely vital element of existence" (p. 368; my italics).

30. Bucke R. *Cosmic Consciousness.* New York: E.P. Dutton; 1969.

31. Dean S. Metapsychiatry: the confluence of psychiatry and mysticism. In: Dean S, ed. *Psychiatry and Mysticism.* Chicago: Nelson Hall; 1975:3–18.

32. Bush N. The near-death experience in children: shades of the prisonhouse reopening. *Anabiosis.* 1983;3:115–135.

33. Gabbard G, Twemlow S. *With the Eyes of the Mind.* New York: Praeger; 1984.

34. Morse M. A near-death experience in a 7-year-old child. *American Journal of Diseases in Children.* 1983;137:959–961.

35. Morse M, Conner D, Tyler D. Near-death experiences in a pediatric population. *American Journal of Diseases in Children.* 1985;139:595–599.

36. Hardy A. *The Spiritual Nature of Man.* New York: Oxford University Press; 1979.

37. Hay D. *Exploring Inner Space.* Middlesex, England: Penguin Books; 1982.

38. Grof S. *Beyond the Brain.* Albany: State University New York Press; 1985.

39. James W. *The Varieties of Religious Experience.* New York: Mentor; 1958.

40. Ferguson M. *The Aquarian Conspiracy.* Los Angeles: JP Tarcher; 1980.

41. Russell P. *The Global Brain.* Los Angeles: JP Tarcher; 1983.

42. White J. Jesus, evolution and the future of humanity. Part I. *Science of the Mind.* September 1981;8–17.

43. Sheldrake R. *A New Science of Life.* Los Angeles: JP Tarcher; 1981.

44. I have discussed some of it briefly elsewhere; see note 12, pp. 261–262.

45. By using this phrase, I do not mean to imply that NDErs and others who have undergone similar transformations represent a new biological species—that would be absurd. Rather, I am suggesting that such people may be signaling a rapid shift in the overall level of spiritual awareness in *Homo sapiens;* that is, that humanity at large may be about to move into a higher stage of its inherent evolutionary capacity. The extent to which there may be actual changes in human biological parameters is an open question that will need to be addressed empirically.

46. Interestingly enough, another near-death researcher, Margot Grey, has recently independently arrived at conclusions almost identical to mine on the basis of her own research on NDEs. In addition, Rupert Sheldrake, without having had an opportunity to

review my work in detail, has told me (Sheldrake, private communication, 1985) that my extrapolation of his ideas seems legitimate to him.

47. Toward that end, a colleague, Alise Agar, and I are establishing a new foundation, to be called the Omega Foundation, to further scholarly inquiry, professional research, and public involvement through the arts and media concerning the ways in which people may better align with and help to realize our collective evolutionary potential.

# 21

# Channeling

*Jon Klimo*

Today we are hearing increasingly about something called channeling. It is a phenomenon in which otherwise normal people seem to let themselves be taken over by or in other ways receive messages from another personality, who uses them as a conduit, medium, or channel for the communication—hence the term *medium* or *channel*. Such personalities usually purport to be from some other dimension or level of reality, and claim to be more highly evolved than we on earth. Much of their information seems intended to hasten personal and planetary growth.

Cases of channeling have become pervasive. An increasing number of people are now seeking and following the guidance provided through channeling. Millions of readers have been introduced to the phenomenon through actress Shirley MacLaines's recent best-selling books that feature her own dramatic experiences with channels. All this activity and visibility points to the fact that something interesting and unusual is happening on a wide scale. Exactly *what* is going on remains open to question.

Often the channeled personalities have names such as "Seth," "Ramtha," the "Invisibles," "Jesus," and "Archangel Michael," imparting a mythic quality complete with biblical, Egyptian, and other ancient overtones or an otherworldly flavor. Does this mean that channeling is simply the stuff of fantasy and wishful thinking, of myth devoid of objective reality? Or, as with spiritual practice throughout history, might something real, although transcending our normal reality, be involved?

Other questions arise: questions regarding the honesty of the channels; questions regarding whether currently understood mechanisms of the brain and mind can adequately account for the phenomenon. And given how many people are allowing themselves to be guided by channeled material with an almost religious fervor, we also must inquire into the benefits or dangers of this phenomenon.

Let me begin with my definition of channeling: *Channeling is the communication of information to or through a physically embodied human being from a source that is said to exist on some other level or dimension of reality than the physical as we know it, and that is not from the normal mind (or self) of the channel.* Jeffrey Mishlove, author of *The Roots of Consciousness*, points out that a great deal rests on the phrase "is said to" in this definition.[1] Clearly it is the channels, their alleged sources, and the various followers of the phenomenon who compose the rapidly growing worldwide channeling subculture, who say that the sources being channeled come from another level of reality.

I want to rule out by my definition not only communication from one's own normal mind as its source, but also communication from fellow physically embodied minds. Additionally, I make a distinction between energy and information, and so I do not include "channeling" energy without information as part of my definition.

This description of channeling contains three basic presuppositions: (1) that there exists a multidimensional or multileveled universe only one subset of which is the three- or four-dimensional objective reality with which we are familiar; (2) that other levels or dimensions of this universe are inhabited by conscious forms that are capable of communication with us on our level of reality; and (3) that the traditional insular concept of the self—"the skin-encapsulated ego"—is in actuality part of something far more open with extremely ambiguous boundaries.

Although channeling as just defined may seem far out, I would proffer that it is a spectrum that includes not only spirits of the deceased, alien disembodied intelligences, the Higher Self, and the Universal Mind, but also such familiar concepts as intuition, inspiration, and creativity. These phenomena are as various as current information-processing models in cognitive science, recent interest in multiple-personality disorder, and the age-old mysteries of spiritual, religious, and artistic experience.

Clearly a great many people are experiencing a hunger for personal meaning in their lives, for deeper—some say spiritual—connectedness and fulfillment. Add to this the fact that recent attempts by scientific inquiry to understand the universe are beginning to lose their traditional objectivity and precision. Many of us find ourselves, like many of the scientists, in a shadowland where inarguable public evidence is no longer possible; unprovable, often unshareable private experience and belief are all that remain in its place. Channeling lies at the heart of this territory.

## WHAT IS CHANNELING?

The mind of the ordinary self includes conscious and assorted altered states like the daydream and dream as well as memories and the personal unconscious. We need to exclude such ordinary, embodied mind from being a channeling source if we are to separate the study of channeling from disciplines already established to investigate versions of simply talking to oneself (clinical and cognitive psychology), and telepathy and extrasensory perception (ESP) communication between minds of embodied people (parapsychology).

### Definition of Terms

Several terms will help to build a conceptual framework: *entities*, *planes*, *states*, and *stages* are at the heart of the beliefs of most channels and claims of their sources.

An *entity* is the core identity of any individual living being said to exist. The concept especially refers to a being that exists on a level of reality other than the physical and that operates as a source in the channeling process. By this definition, you and I are entities, and we would remain entities if we were to survive our own physical deaths. Entities also can be beings said not to be human—for example, extraterrestrials and angels. Philosopher Huston Smith prefers to use the term *psychic centers*, rather than entities, to cover various kinds of possible living, individual beings that could function as communicators by way of the channeling process.[2] My own preference is the term *source*, which I define as *the generic term for anyone or anything occupying the transmitting end or comprising the informational origin in the channeling process*.

Although there is no unanimity among researchers on key terms, there is fairly good consensus throughout the channeling literature that there are levels, dimensions, or planes of reality, the physical plane being only one of them, and the lowest at that. Depending on one's viewpoint, there are a number of ever more spiritual planes beyond the causal involving will, wisdom, power, and love, approaching the source of All That Is. We are told that all these planes operate and interact in a superimposed, coherent manner, with causal succession flowing from "higher" to "lower" planes.

One thing left unresolved is what physical means, since only the lowest plane of this hierarchy is said to be physical. Again, there is lack of consensus among those writing, teaching, and doing research in the broad areas of the occult, paranormal, and mystic. A strict, although somewhat vernacular, definition is "the realm of matter and energy that is agreed on as objectively real by a consensus of contemporary physicists." Even this definition falters from the interconversion between energy and matter, given by Einstein's famous $E = mc^2$, and from speculation in mathematics, physics, and cosmology about physical and non-local[3] properties of higher dimensional spaces.[4]

Also central to the phenomenon of channeling is the concept of a spectrum of discrete *states of consciousness*. This is an ancient notion—as old as the Indian Vedas and Plato. Normal waking consciousness, sleep, hypnosis, dreams, psychedelic drug states, alcoholic inebriation, general anesthesia, and coma are only a few possibilities. There may be as many separate realities that can be experienced as there are states of consciousness. The real or true reality, then, may be simply the one being consensually experienced by the most similar entities. To argue the merits of one reality over another may be as specious as a New Yorker debating with a Californian whether it is "really" twelve o'clock or nine.

Consider the following analogy: *Lucid dreaming* occurs when the dreamer becomes aware that he or she is dreaming and then is able to continue dreaming consciously. Lucid-dream researchers, such as Stephen LaBerge at Stanford University, tell us that a normal dreamer usually becomes lucid when something anomalous takes place within the dream that alerts the dreamer to the fact that it *is* a dream and not reality that he or she is experiencing. Perhaps some aspects of channeling are the anomalies that could awaken us to a kind of lucidity within the waking dream of earthly existence, resulting in conscious wakefulness of a kind higher than normal waking.

To entities, planes, and states must be added a fourth concept: *stages* of consciousness. Is channeling a discrete passing *state* of consciousness, or is it a *stage* in the development or evolution of consciousness for the individual or the species in the same way opposable thumbs were in animal evolution? Are channels the avant-garde of human behavior and experience that lie ahead for the rest of us? Michael Murphy offers a metaphor for what may be occurring: "We are amphibians coming ashore in a multidimensional world."[5]

## EXPLANATIONS FOR CHANNELING: MODELS OF CONSCIOUSNESS

In my book *Channeling,* I discuss the historical and phenomenological aspects of channeling and review theories and research from the four major disciplines used to explain channeling: psychology (experimental, cognitive, and clinical), parapsychology, neurophysiology, and physics.[6]

### Psychological Models

Psychology is probably in the best position to provide a relevant and reasonable contemporary explanation for channeling. It is the chief discipline through which the scientific analytical mind can attempt to come to terms with subjective, idiosyncratic material.

To examine channeling within the context of psychology triggers questions such as, What is the nature of the individual? Where do we draw the line between the self and the not-self? Once we draw it, what kind of interaction can take place across it? How open or closed is the individual system in this interaction? And what is the conscious versus unconscious mind?

The larger model of consciousness must account for how an individual consciousness, manifesting as a uniquely differentiated form, comes to be in the first place. A multicausal model of channeling must reflect a number of kinds of possible processes at work. The model needs to accommodate the prospect of endless individuated seats of conscious systems spread across many kinds of reality, differently limited and enabled in how they can communicate with one another.

Orthodox psychological explanations agree that we each have a conscious part and an unconscious part that are held to be correlated with the physical brain. Interactions between mind and brain occur in the venue of the physical individual, in a self-contained system to which all stimuli become physically and biochemically internal. In the traditional view, imaginational, memory, and dream imagery are all generated from within the brain.

The mainstream psychological, psychiatric, and neurobiological explanations of channeling are built on concepts of pathological processes of ego dissociation, often lumped together as multiple-personality disorder (MPD). According to this view, people who claim to be channeling, rather than being in communication with an entity external to themselves, are actually operating in a *dissociated* state. Within this state, fragments of their own psyches operate autonomously with respect to the usual waking center of control, or ego.

What becomes dissociated from the ''main'' person is variously termed subpersonalities, alter personalities, or secondary personalities and is construed as hallucinated, projected, delusional, or repressed material amounting to hysterical conversions and other official conditions of psychopathological nomenclature.

Yet there are differences between MPD and channeling. Seventy-five percent of MPD subjects report having personalities who are under twelve years old, whereas virtually no reported channeled sources are children. Also, most multiples have more than one alter personality, whereas most contemporary channels appear to have only one source. Channels almost always claim to possess a normal sense of their own identity while experiencing themselves mediating expressions from other identities or to have their own identity replaced by another temporarily and usually intentionally. The dissociated state is pathological when it is involuntary or unchecked, for example, when a person is unable to reclaim control of the executive or ego function from unwanted, spontaneously appearing alter personalities.

Professionals mostly use two criteria to establish the existence of a mental disorder: a painful symptom (distress) and impairment in functioning (disability). By this definition, it would be difficult to describe channels as suffering from a mental disorder, for they do not typically report suffering, nor are they witnessed as suffering such distress or disability.

## Parapsychological Theories

Parapsychology has as its focus three basic areas: ESP, which includes all kinds of anomalous information *reception:* telepathy, clairvoyance, precognition, and psychometry; *psychokinesis* (PK), including mind-affecting-matter (e.g., spoon-bending) teleportation, materialization, psychic surgery and healing, levitation, and out-of-body experiences; and *survival phenomena,* including channeling, possession, ghosts and hauntings, reincarnation, and afterlife evidence.[7]

Although the category of survival research would seem most dedicated to investigating channeling, parapsychology pioneer J. B. Rhine called for an abandonment of survival research in 1960. Rhine claimed that channeling and related information could not be sufficiently distinguished from information that can be obtained by ESP from living people.

Extending the ESP concept, researchers speculate that the mind of the channel may roam other realms to telepathically receive information. In a computer metaphor, the channel's mind "logs on" to some vast database composed of all living—and possibly previously living or not yet living—minds. Perhaps the database includes the entire evolutionary mental envelope that surrounds the earth, which Jesuit scientist-philosopher Pierre Teilhard de Chardin called the noosphere. Or perhaps it includes Jung's collective unconscious or the ancients' Akashic Records. In any case, the adherence of some parapsychologists to such a "grand unified ESP" explanation for channeling seems to display an inability to make the conceptual leap to the possibility of nonphysical intelligent beings.

Other parapsychologists choose to explain channeling in terms of an extended notion of PK, which holds that there is some nonordinary way mind can affect matter. The PK argument for channeling is based on a dualistic notion that mind and matter are different, that all minds are basically of the same nature whether they are embodied or not, and therefore would have to interact with brain matter in the same way.

Underlying this view is the fundamental wonderment of how the mind can affect even normal motor activity by way of the brain, such as lifting a pen. This is no less miraculous than the idea of moving a pen at a distance, without physical contact. So the reasoning goes, if your own mind can affect your own brain, then the similar nonphysical nature of *another* mind also might be able to affect your brain.

## Physical Models

The correlates of physics, paraphysics or "new physics," consciousness, and psi activity have been covered elsewhere in this book. A key concept for our consideration is that of the multidimensionality of spacetime and the inconceivability to most of us of how a five-, six-, or infinite-dimensional realm might be experienced in and of itself or projected into our dimensions.

We can draw an analogy from the theme in the classic *Flatland,* by Edward Abbott,[8] and continued in the *Planiverse,* by A. K. Dewdney.[9] Flatland and the Planiverse are two-dimensional worlds populated by beings who are points and lines and planar (two-dimensional) figures. For these entities, the third dimension is not only nonexistent, but it is inconceivable to most inhabitants. Imagine that a three-dimensional being such as ourselves were to introduce a solid object into Flatland by bouncing a ball in that world. The Flatlander would experience the bouncing ball as a point on the plane of their universe, suddenly appearing and disappearing—a miracle. Their mainstream science might have no theory to postulate the third dimension, and the event would be debunked.

Our current theoretical physics necessitates at least an 11-dimensional universe to account for the behavior of the four fundamental forces: gravity, electromagnetism, and the strong and weak nuclear forces.[4] Yet in our three-dimensional world, *events* from higher dimensions also appear miraculous and inconceivable.

### A Personal Theory/Metaphor

My own ten years of research on channeling has led me to conclude that some people said to be channeling are indeed essentially making up their supposedly transpersonal sources out of the activity of their internal psychodynamic systems, in keeping with the reigning skeptical view. Others fail to fall into any recognized category such as MPD, schizophrenia, delusional and hallucinatory states, and hysterical conversion. I believe that these people are in informational and energetic contact with consciousness-possessing beings of a higher dimensional nature. In this sense, I accept a multicausal approach toward the phenomenon, which in any one case may be either self-generated material or the result of genuine otherworldly communication.

Even in cases where psychopathology is not evident, self-generation as the mainstream scientific community's explanation for channeling may not be as simple or traditional as it sounds. Those who appear to be generating messages out of their own intrapsychic activity may in fact be generating offspring subpersonalities in something like the manner in which they themselves were generated by and out of their Creator.

Given the fact that many consider the mind to be nonphysical, imagine that our own respective minds are part of some vast sea of mind (or energy) with which we interact to give birth to further seemingly separate minds or personalities or energy systems that are the entities being channeled. Looked at another way, we are buds off the main branch of this mind.

This model moves the concept of dissociation from the realm of psychopathology into the realm of cosmology and metaphysics. My central hypothesis is that Universal Consciousness, the Source, God, or All-That-Is approximates a dissociated or multiple personality that experiences itself from the perspective of its own subpersonalities, our individual human and nonhuman consciousnesses. Each of us is thus a subpersonality of the whole interacting with one another as seemingly independent divisions with diverse experiential repertoires drawing from and feeding back to the Source.[10]

Because of this kind of dissociation, humans and perhaps other conscious entities experience isolation, ignorance, and states of unconsciousness. Put another way, we experience limitations of consciousness commensurate with a failure to access and manipulate conscious and subconscious information within ourselves and with regard to one another. Instances of channeling and other extrasensory experiences are examples of how some of us are able to at least temporarily transcend the usual limitations to information processing. (Elsewhere I have tried to speculate on why the Universe or God has given us, and/ or why we have given ourselves, this dissociated condition in the first place.[11]) In more or less practical terms, God's own fulfillment and self-understanding occur by way of us, God's agents. Within this context, what we call channeling is the way in which some of this being's own cosmological subpersonalities at one level of embodiment are able to communicate with subpersonalities that exist at another level.

One thing seems clear: The various phenomena collected under the general rubric of channeling take us to the edge of human experience and understanding. They involve a variety of as yet largely unexplored fields as well as processes, including consciousness itself.

We cannot afford to either ignore or perfunctorily explain away the chief anomalies that remain for us in science today. These unknowns exist to stimulate us individually and as a species into the restructuring of thought and action that inevitably accompanies scientific revolutions. Channeling is one of the most visible and perplexing of these anomalies and implicates most others in its possible nature. As such, channeling should be treated as an expanded type of information-processing capacity potentially available to us all and amenable to scientific investigation as well as soul-searching.

## NOTES

1. Jeffrey Mishlove, interview with the author, August 26, 1986.

2. Huston Smith, interview with the author, October 9, 1986.

3. For a definition of nonlocal, see Chapter 8 in this volume.

4. Freedman DZ, Nieuwenhuizen P. The hidden dimensions of spacetime. *Scientific American.* May 1985:74–82.

5. Michael Murphy, interview with author, September 13, 1986.

6. Klimo Jon. *Channeling: Investigations on Receiving Information from Paranormal Sources.* Los Angeles: Tarcher; 1987.

7. Psychic Research at a Glance. In: Mitchell E, White J, eds. *Psychic Explorations.* New York: Putnam/Capricorn; 1974.

8. Abbott EA. *Flatland*. New York: New American Library; 1984.

9. Dewdney AK. *The Planiverse: Computer Contact with a Two-Dimensional World.* New York: Poseidon Press; 1984.

10. Jane Roberts elaborates a similar theory, and diagrams a theoretical structure for this scheme in *Adventures in Consciousness: An Introduction to Aspect Psychology.* Englewood Cliffs, NJ: Prentice-Hall; 1975.

11. Klimo J. Cosmological dissociation: toward an understanding of how we create our own reality. *Paranormal Research '89*. Proceedings of the Second International Conference on Paranormal Research, Colorado State University Fort Collins. Fort Collins: Rocky Mountain Research Institute; June 1–4, 1989:78–82.

# Implications of Consciousness Research for Psychotherapy and Self-Exploration

*Stanislav Grof*

Nonordinary states of consciousness have long been of interest to me both for their extraordinary therapeutic applications and for their evolutionary potential. It is my firm belief that the new knowledge of the psyche brought by research into nonordinary states has the potential to drastically change not only the future of psychiatry and psychotherapy, but also the basic philosophical assumptions of Western science.

When I began my research into psychedelic use in psychiatry, I was deeply influenced by my orthodox Freudian training and the fact that I was convinced of the value of psychoanalysis as a conceptual framework. I hoped that the use of LSD (lysergic acid diethylamide) as a catalyst would help to improve the highly disappointing therapeutic efficacy and practical results of this otherwise fascinating analytic approach.

The therapeutic modality combining analytically oriented psychotherapy with the administration of psychedelic drugs has become known as *psycholytic treatment*. Records from early research sessions are a rich source of information about the nature of the psychedelic state, the dynamics of psychopathological symptoms and syndromes, and the dimensions of the human psyche.

LSD and related substances can best be understood as catalysts and amplifiers of mental processes. They do not produce any specific contents in the psyche, but make its deep unconscious dynamics available for conscious experience and direct observation. It is, therefore, appropriate to compare the potential role of psychedelics in psychiatry and psychology to the role that the microscope has in medicine or the telescope in astronomy.

Research with these fascinating substances, shunned since the widespread nonmedical use of psychedelics made the continuation of this work difficult, is one of the most promising approaches to the study of the human mind. People who take LSD do not experience "toxic psychosis," but undertake a fantastic journey into the realms of their own unconscious that are not experientially accessible under normal conditions.

Knowledge about the psyche acquired in psychedelic sessions is directly applicable to a variety of situations in which nonordinary states of consciousness occur spontaneously or are induced by different nondrug techniques. Such situations include aboriginal healing ceremonies and rites of passage, shamanic rituals, laboratory mind-altering techniques, traditional methods of spiritual practice and self-exploration, different forms of experiential psychotherapy, death and near-death experiences, and spontaneous evolutionary crises.

Since the 1980s my wife Christina and I have been developing what we call *holotropic therapy*. (The term *holotropic* is derived from the Greek *holos* meaning "whole" and *trepein*, "to move toward"; it suggests aiming for totality and wholeness.) This is a technique of self-exploration that uses activation of the unconscious through a combination of controlled breathing, evocative music, and focused body work. Holotropic therapy mediates access to the entire spectrum of experiences that are available in psychedelic sessions and to powerful therapeutic mechanisms on the perinatal and transpersonal levels.

Traditional schools of psychotherapy see biography as the only source of psychogenic disorders. Modern consciousness research, however, has revealed beyond a doubt that emotional, psychosomatic, and interpersonal disorders also have important roots in the perinatal and transpersonal domains of the psyche. In this context, psychopathology represents as much an opportunity as a problem for the person involved.

Verbal (and sometimes even experiential) work limited to biography typically requires months or years to produce noticeable change. Yet deep experiences of death and rebirth, mystical and transcendental states, reliving of past-incarnation sequences, or encounters with powerful archetypal figures, themes, and energies can result in significant emotional and psychosomatic healing, personality transformation, and consciousness evolution within a matter of hours or days.

The model that I had to construct to include the entire spectrum of experiences available to an average person with the use of psychedelics or powerful nondrug experiential techniques has four major levels or realms.

1. *Sensory experiences.* In the initial phase, techniques that activate the unconscious stimulate the sensory organs. This results in visions of geometrical and architectural patterns and kaleidoscopic displays, hearing of various elementary sounds, and unusual body sensations and, sometimes, tastes or smells.

2. *Recollective-analytical experiences.* This is the only aspect of the new

cartography of the psyche acknowledged and recognized by traditional psychiatry and psychotherapy. In therapy that is limited to verbal exchange, one may merely *remember* or *reconstruct* repressed material. In experiential therapy, it is possible not only to fully reexperience the emotions and physical sensations from the past, but also to relive complex memories in complete age regression.

Experiential therapy also reveals the importance of physical traumas that are all but neglected in mainstream psychotherapeutic work. When the unconscious is activated, it will quite spontaneously disclose repressed memories, with all the emotions and physical sensations involved. While reliving these experiences, many clients are surprised to discover that these past events had a direct impact on their psychological development and played an important role in the genesis of the problems that they brought into therapy.

3. *Perinatal experiences.* The activation of the next level of the unconscious leads to powerful experiences that combine an authentic encounter with death and biological birth with elements of ego death and psychological and spiritual rebirth. The profound existential crisis that often accompanies sequences of dying and being (re)born leads to a spontaneous opening of intrinsic spiritual and mystical domains in the psyche, since the only way to resolve the crisis is through transcendence.

The phenomenology of the positive aspects of this process typically involves oceanic and cosmic experiences, a sense of mystical union, and radiant white or golden light. Negatively, one may have encounters with insidious demonic appearances, existential despair, and selective access to archetypal images of hells from the repertoire of the collective unconscious.

4. *Transpersonal experiences.* This domain of the new cartography of the unconscious contains a rich spectrum of experiences for which I coined the term transpersonal. They are characterized by transcendence of the person's usual ego boundaries (body image) and of the limitations of the Newtonian space and time. Here belong experiences of unity with other people, groups of people, or all humanity; authentic identification with animals, plants, or inorganic nature; and ancestral, phylogenetic, racial, and past-incarnation experiences. An important subgroup of transpersonal phenomena involves mythological sequences, archetypal figures and themes, and identification with the Universal Mind and the Supracosmic and Metacosmic Void.

## A NEW STRATEGY OF PSYCHOTHERAPY AND SELF-EXPLORATION

Experiential therapy has revealed the far-reaching, self-healing potential of the psyche. As I have stated, the emergence of symptoms is seen in the new context not as the onset of disease, but as the beginning of a radical and powerful healing process—if properly understood and approached. The new therapeutic strategy based on this insight consists of using techniques that directly activate the unconscious (psychedelic drugs, various nondrug techniques of experiential psychotherapy, trance-inducing technology) and facilitate the emergence of biographical, perinatal, and transpersonal material. An essential part of this approach is deep trust in the autonomy and spontaneity of the healing process and willingness to encourage and support it, even if at times one must transcend rational understanding. This approach has its precedent in Carl Gustav Jung's shift of emphasis from the efforts of the therapist to change the dynamics of the psyche according to a particular conceptual system, to reliance on the intrinsic wisdom of the collective unconscious.

## INSIGHTS INTO THE NATURE OF REALITY AND THE NEED FOR A NEW PARADIGM

Observations from psychedelic sessions and holotropic therapy represent a serious challenge to current psychiatric theory and to the worldview of mechanistic science. This is particularly true with regard to the spectrum of transpersonal experiences whose existence is irreconcilable with philosophical materialism and with the Cartesian-Newtonian paradigm that has dominated Western science for the past 300 years.

In my book *Beyond the Brain,* I provide a detailed exploration of this fascinating aspect of modern consciousness research. The revolutionary data range from the various forms of extrasensory perception to the frequent occurrence of extraordinary synchronicities in Jung's sense. I offer the possibility of using intuitive channels to acquire new information about different domains of nature and the universe—by experiential identification with them.

Observations of this kind banish to the historical archives the myths of mechanistic science that portrays consciousness, life, and creative intelligence as epiphenomena of matter and as insignificant accidents in the evolution of the universe. In light of the new data, consciousness appears to be an equal partner of matter or even a principle supraordinated to it.

## REFERENCES

Grof S. *Realms of the Human Unconscious: Observations from LSD Research.* New York: EP Dutton; 1976.
———, Grof C. *Beyond Death: The Gates of Consciousness.* London: Thames & Hudson, 1980.
———. *LSD Psychotherapy.* Pomona, CA: Hunter House; 1980.
———. *The Adventures of Self-Discovery.* Albany: State University New York Press; 1985.
———. *Beyond the Brain.* Albany: State University New York Press; 1985.

# VII ——————————————————

## REFLECTIONS

# 23

# The Dilemma of Parapsychology

*William H. Kautz*

## THE GRASS ROOTS

We are living at a time of increasing public openness to inner experiences, the mind, consciousness, and the paranormal. Surveys show that more than one-half the people in the United States have had some kind of inner or psychic experience. Publishers and the media have produced countless books, articles, reports, and movies on UFOs, ghosts, fantasy, poltergeists, ancient wisdom, crystals, and so on. Psychics, astrologers, channels, and other latter-day practitioners of the intuitive arts are having a heyday (and not just in California). Beyond, and perhaps behind, all this activity there has been a renewed and less conspicuous public interest in spiritual matters, raising again the old questions about the purpose of human existence, the limits on human capacities, and the mysteries of the mind and how it works.

On the practical side, one can certainly identify an urgent social need for the kind of skills that are traditionally the province of parapsychologists: precognition, clairvoyance, and psychometry. Most of the institutions of our society would like to be able to access information that cannot be obtained by "normal" means. For example, scientists and economists alike need to be able to make accurate predictions about the future, something parapsychology subjects are supposed to be able to do.

On the other hand, where is parapsychology in the midst of all this activity? It is no secret that the discipline is seriously ill. Many parapsychology magazines, including the time-honored *Parapsychology Review,* have stopped publication. Ten years ago doors were beginning to open at a few universities, but now college programs in parapsychology, most notably the program at John F. Kennedy University in Orinda, California, are no longer being offered. For a while there was even government support for parapsychological research, with relatively few strings attached. Research funds have all but dried up now, and a number of laboratories have closed.

After decades of struggle against prejudice, ridicule, and criticism from various quarters, parapsychology ought now to be a vital and thriving field. Instead, it seems to be dying. Why is this so?

Before offering my own answer to this question, it will be interesting to review the interpretations others have given.[1]

- It is a fear of the phenomenon, particularly among experimenters who confine themselves to doing tiny, safe, boring experiments.
- Scientists sense a danger because they feel that they have to shift their paradigms, and they are not ready yet.
- Studying things that by nature are epiphenomenal is truly hard to do. Parapsychology hasn't yet found everyday experiences that can be studied closely and repetitively.
- The skeptics have been active and aggressive.
- Parapsychology is trying to apply methods developed for studying statistically based phenomena to an area that is precisely the complement of that—individual events.
- Consciousness functions with a kind of ego structure, which is threatened by anything beyond itself. When something goes beyond it, the ego almost wants to go to war.
- It's the Christians—they take this seriously. It's Old Testament logic that parapsychologists are in the same league as astrologers and devil worshipers.

These alleged reasons certainly vary from the substantial to the specious. Some are not fundamental, not the underlying reasons. For example, we can say that parapsychology hasn't moved ahead because of a lack of funding, criticisms from skeptics, or a lack of good subjects, but these reasons just beg the questions, Why isn't there more funding? Why should the criticism be so restrictive? Why cannot suitable subjects be located?

After all, we are dealing here with a powerful human capacity. A little opposition from the skeptics, the Christians, or the government should not be holding us back! In truth, some of the explanations offered are feeble excuses: It is so easy to blame the difficulty on external obstacles instead of ourselves. But we humans are much more resourceful than that. If something we hold dear is felt to be at stake, we soon enough find solutions to problems such as lack of funding, inadequate subjects, raving skeptics, judgmental Christians, and the various difficulties of conducting meaningful experiments.

When we face these matters honestly, we in parapsychology must ourselves accept responsibility for the lack of success. This doesn't mean that these statements about the outer world are false. There are certainly valid obstacles to be overcome, and they may be substantial, but they are not valid reasons for failure. (Sometimes we forget that a true *fact* is not of itself a true *reason*.)

We need to look to our own house for the real reason (or reasons) for failure. We need to examine how we have been selecting and defining the problems we work on; how we have been developing our strategies, approaches, and procedures; and particularly the motivations, assumptions, and attitudes we have adopted in coming into this work.

Let us take a closer look at the origins of the possible imminent collapse of our discipline.

## THE ROOTS OF THE ILLNESS

Broadly speaking, we humans are afraid of the unknown and, particularly, the unconscious mind. When new or buried material comes to the surface, the resulting experience can be exhilarating, but more often it is uncomfortable or even painful. It behooves us to face these barriers to effective functioning, to try to understand them better and weed them out. We will not address here techniques for dealing with disturbing unconscious information, but only make the point (elaborated in Chapter 1) that the resolution of personal fears is an issue central to parapsychology, one that merits deeper examination.

From a fundamental perspective, then, the issue behind stagnancy in any discipline is one of the fear of having to confront information or experience that seems to contradict an already accepted model or hypothesis. These personal fears manifest as distrust, inappropriate beliefs, and closed minds. Moreover, they affect collective attitudes, motivations, and subsequent decisions within the entire professional field. Parapsychology is no exception. As with most fears, their origins are not conspicuous. It is not always clear that they are present or that they are affecting us to so great an extent. But also, like most fears, they are inherently a misinterpretation of a situation. They are not substantial, and they vaporize on honest confrontation (which may be difficult to do).

Restated from a less psychological perspective, the problem may be that as parapsychologists, we have adopted the wrong posture toward the phenomena being studied. Our research strategy and attitude may be inappropriate for the particular subject matter we are trying to understand.

## THE LESSONS FOR PSI

In Chapter 1, we examined the inquiry process in science from a broader perspective than the traditional one. We looked first at science—how it works and how it doesn't work—and then at the subject of intuition: what it is, how it functions, what it is able to do, and what is our experience with it. Finally, we looked at the place of intuition in science and then in parapsychology and examined the consequences.

We noted that intuitive functioning, which underlies psi ability, is dulled by mechanistic attempts to perceive information that is already available by usual sensory and rational means. Yet such "already known" inquiries are typical in parapsychological experiments, since one ordinarily asks only for information that can be confirmed. Such information is not needed for any purpose other than to prove something to someone who is probably reluctant to believe it anyway. When any reasonable and beneficial human motive is provided, the intuitive inquiry process proceeds smoothly and effectively.

In the past 100 years, it has been proved countless times that psi exists and is a valid human experience. However, we are still repeating these same experiments, over and over with new variations, as if we are still not sure.

One of the lessons we can learn by looking at psi as a manifestation of intuition is that psi is a natural process, not a weird and rare phenomenon. It is interesting that this observation has been emerging gradually over the decades from parapsychological research itself, most recently from remote-viewing experiments.[2]

Another important realization is that psi needs to be experienced to be understood. The old image of the experimenter who refuses, in the interests of objectivity, to become involved in the process he is studying is simply not correct. The most successful psi researchers have had a good experiential understanding of the object of their study, and they did not obtain it from textbooks.

Still another lesson was referred to earlier: Success in psi is closely tied to the motivation for carrying out the experiment. Again, asking questions for which the answer is already known or could easily be found is less likely to be successful than if the answer cannot be easily obtained. It is no wonder that the results of so many psi experiments are so weak. A preferred research procedure is to collect the needed data as a by-product of using psi/intuition to solve a real human problem. For example, instead of secretly burying objects for the "subject" to find, let the intuitive assist people who have lost actual personal objects important to them. A pragmatic, human reason for finding the objects is then present, so better results can be expected. This revised approach not only works, but it works well.

In scientific studies, the intuitive inquiry process slows down somewhat, probably because the path from obtaining the information to its ultimate application typically is long and subject to uncertainties. Consider the earthquake application cited in Chapter 1, for example. After learning about earthquake mechanisms through an intuitive inquiry, one must then conduct validation studies to make the information credible to the scientists and technologists who would utilize it. (This must be done for any scientific advance, but it normally is dwarfed by the trial-and-error effort required to obtain the searched-for result in the first place.) This step involves designing experiments, setting out instrumentation, collecting data, analyzing it, and reporting on it. Only then can one begin to arrange funding to establish a novel earthquake-prediction system.

Also, just as for any major research endeavor, the motivation for carrying out the entire procedure must be clear and strong if it is to succeed. Fortunately, if the motivation for conducting an enterprise is weak, it tends to reveal itself early in an intuitive inquiry.

When providing intuitive counseling for individuals and intuitive consulting for businesses, the path is shorter. In fact, the client is the direct recipient and principal user of the intuitive information, which may be tried out immediately. The main point here, again, is that the inquiry process is facilitated when the topic has keen human interest and the requested information is directly applicable.

A fourth lesson from intuition experience is that psi appears to function with the whole mind—that is, holistically—and not out of a separable portion of the mind. If an intuitive is tired, emotionally upset, or preoccupied with a personal issue, this background condition can block or distort the flow of information. If one is going to practice the intuitive arts successfully, then it is important to maintain a fairly balanced life. Also, intuitive performance cannot be willed into action with the cognitive mind; it must be allowed. To this end, the only proper use of will (in the ordinary sense) is for becoming clear about one's purpose and for establishing a firm determination to confront and remove obstacles from the path of clear intuitive flow.

## A NEW PATH FOR PARAPSYCHOLOGY?

What action, then, can psi researchers take in respect of these observations?

First and foremost, they need to examine their methodology of inquiry. Because the scientific method that we were taught and on which we lean so heavily rests so firmly on assumptions—objectivity, reductionism, positivism, and replicability—described in Chapter 1, we must ask, Can we accomplish our task effectively under these assumptions? It may turn out, as we suspect, that they are neither necessary nor appropriate for parapsychological work.

A second item to be questioned is, What constitutes acceptable proof, explanations, and evidence? Outside of science, one person's notion of what is an adequate explanation of a process or proof of an assertion is not necessarily another's. The popular concept of adequate evidence serves for many human purposes, but it is unfortunately an expedient one and sometimes completely wrong. In all walks of life, we humans often fool ourselves as we create an argument for something we *believe* to be true or *want* to be true. Even within science, scientists are not free from the game of justifying action on the basis of insufficient or irrelevant "reasons." Even though science purports to use a rigorous criterion of "sufficient evidence," the criterion is not universally applied. In any case, it is based on the questionable assumptions discussed previously. The new parapsychology must deal with this fuzzy "evidence" issue.

If we choose not to accept the traditional assumptions of science, then, how will it be possible to make progress in parapsychology? This is a prime question that needs to be answered. Here are a few starting points.

First, we need to honor and encourage subjective reports of our so-called subjects. When they say that they sense something, we must value that statement and regard it as data. This approach is surely one of the reasons why remote viewing has worked so well: It relies on subjective reports and utilizes a protocol that involves independent judges to compare these reports with the record of what actually transpired during the experiment.[2]

Second, we must encourage the experimenter to become more personally involved in the experiment and to utilize means other than the traditional ones to maintain a sufficient level of objectivity. For example, automatic means of data collection (such as computers) can be used to free the experimenter to use his own intuition freely without biasing the results. When objective decisions are to be made, they can be carried out by individuals far removed from the experiment and not otherwise connected with it. One can make a good case that an experimenter should never ask his subject to do something he cannot do himself, although presumably not so well.

Third, the models set up to "explain" psi phenomena and from which further experiments are designed need not be so reductionistic, assuming, as they usually do, that the human subject is functioning pretty much as a simple machine (input and output, stimulus and response, all variables but one tightly controlled). The researcher stands to gain by being more respectful of the complex and highly interconnected way in which the parts of the human mind and body are functioning together. Mechanistic models must give way to a more intuitively based gestalt of human activity in which the knowledge derived from experience is more internal, not necessarily expoundable in rational terms. The new experiments are more likely to be total-being experiences, with less distinction between the researcher and the researched and with the goal of overall comprehension rather than fragmentary understanding.

There are signs that science itself is beginning to change along these lines, without the gracious help of parapsychologists. However, 300 years of history creates quite a bit of inertia, so it may be a long time before such changes become dominant. It is probably not wise for parapsychology to wait for conservative science to take the lead. Indeed, it is now time for parapsychologists to grab the reins themselves and restore this centrally important discipline to full vitality and health.

## NOTES

1. These responses were offered by members of the audience to which the material in this chapter was presented at a Parapsychology Research Group meeting in June 1990.

2. Targ R, Puthoff H. *Mind-Reach: Scientists Look at Psychic Ability.* New York: Dell Publishing; 1977.

# 24

# Truth and Science: The Ethical Dimensions of Psi Research

*Shelley Thomson*

As yet, our society has no standard way to refer to people who use "paranormal" abilities. The terms we use are largely borrowed from other cultures. The profusion of labels—witch, warlock, shaman, sorcerer, wise woman, psychic, seer—and their various connotations mirror the current state of confusion. For purposes of this discussion, therefore, the term "psi" will be used to refer to actions any of these individuals may take in their special roles. In time, "psi" may come to denote an expanded realm of normal human behavior.

## TRUTH

Human societies place strong emphasis on understanding reality. In practice, this means that each society has a preferred belief system that concerns itself with the interpretation of observed events. Observations that conflict with the belief system may be denied, and individuals who persistently profess different views may be identified as evil, subversive, or insane. The system of explanation itself commonly is regarded as self-evidently true and as the unique and previous discovery of one's forebears.

By a historical accident, Western scientific materialism has become the dominant philosophy on large portions of the earth. It is regarded both as self-evidently true and as scientifically proven beyond doubt. The conquest of other peoples by white Europeans and the significant cultural changes brought about by technological progress are viewed as evidence for the superiority of the Western belief system.

This is not the first time that the military prowess of individual tribes has been advanced as proof that their philosophy is the one true way. It is not even the first time that the dominant people thought that their uniquely valuable belief system was a recent invention by themselves. Some conquerors have acknowledged a cultural heritage from ancient times; others preferred a fresh start, ordering the destruction of monuments and written records to erase evidence of the past. Some groups maintained a theory about the origin of human life in which they themselves were the only real humans and all other peoples were explained as flawed, lesser, or nonhuman beings—sometimes as the result of intercourse with animals![1]

The quest for the one correct belief system is an important cultural activity here and now because it is an element of our current belief system that there must be one such explanation—just as there is one true God, and so on.

Perhaps the idea that there is a single truth has not received the examination it deserves. In some sense, a single truth would represent a single state of the universe, in which the value of each element is known. The value is a "truth" value and not necessarily equivalent to a physical value such as velocity or mass. On the other hand, every statement about a particle should have a "truth" value, thus making truth a coordinate system of a type that current mathematics identifies as nonunique. If we assume that truth exists independent of measurable facts but as a reality unto itself, we have a scheme that performs mathematical or aesthetic judgments but is not true in the usual sense; that is, it is not materially verifiable.

Absolute truth, therefore, is knowable in the abstract as a mathematical property. Materially verifiable truth must be known differently, as one of an unlimited number of possible explanations for a given set of experimental data.

## SCIENCE

The creative experimenter begins with an idea about the nature of the universe. Often the idea seems to come out of nowhere: "as if it fell off the truck," one said, "and I just happened to be there." Experimental design is a discipline by which the abstract essence of reality may be encouraged to take tangible form. As the alternative interpretations that obscure the central truth are excluded, the intuited principle emerges into view. A sophisticated reader may see it for himself and perhaps even duplicate the experiment, thus having the "Aha!" experience enjoyed by the discoverer.

Experimentation is a creative process. Because it is not possible to test all hypotheses, even all those that occur within a relatively limited frame of reference, the experimenter must structure the research to evoke what he believes to be the quintessential abstractions. The criterion of quality in experimental design is aesthetic. Therefore, the outcome of an experiment can satisfy the intellectual demand for truth.

Significantly, the result of the experiment cannot be separated from its context. A finding is meaningful only with reference to the conditions under which it was obtained. The result may be convincing in a syllogistic sense, but it is never the only possible explanation for the data. Science, in the sense of empirically verifiable knowledge, inhabits the world of multiple truths.

## PSI

The foregoing suggests that there is no single truth to be known about reality. The impact of this idea on the study of psi is enormous. Western society is committed to the view that psi events are qualitatively different from non-psi events.

Many scientific studies of psi have dealt with phenomena of high strangeness. The participant may be asked to levitate an object without touching it, to bend a piece of metal by merely thinking about it, to "read" a closed book, to interfere in someone else's dream, and so forth. The proofs of psi most readily accepted by the public are of this type. These demonstrations are persuasive because they support the belief that psi operates independent of, and contrary to, the operations of natural law.

In popular culture, psi experience commonly is thought of as belonging to the spiritual domain, specifically, the domain of God and the Devil. These supremely powerful figures of Judeo-Christian mythology are closely associated with psi events, often in a negative context. A respectable proportion of the public and not a few experimenters have a thinly veiled fear and loathing of psi. They perceive it as immoral and dangerous behavior practiced by flawed individuals.

I suggest that this attitude is derived from the mistaken belief that unambiguous distinctions can be drawn between mental and material causes of events. In fact, it is exceedingly difficult to distinguish psi events from non-psi events.

Experimenters normally have addressed the issue by exclusion: The protocol eliminates the material causes of the phenomenon. If the phenomenon continues to take place, psi can be offered as a plausible explanation. This is not entirely satisfactory. Even a tight experimental design necessarily leaves unanswered (and unanswerable) questions, such as, What if the experimenter was mistaken about what he or she observed?

Further, this approach assumes that psi events are ontologically distinct—differently caused—from ordinary events. It is difficult to use a lawful process, such as an experiment, to elucidate a nonlawful phenomenon. One cannot know at what point psi, conceived as an extracausal influence, entered into the experiment. An experiment in which classical causality is assumed cannot prove anything one way or another about a noncausal process.

All we really know about psi events, in the categorical sense, is that they are in some way connected with human attention. Except for this factor, a coincidence of ordinary causes is a perfectly satisfactory explanation for most experimental data.

Anomalous experimental events that are not viewed as connected with human attention—for example, anomalous events that occur in the course of research in other fields of science—normally are attributed without hesitation to unverifiable ordinary causes: chance uneven heating of the apparatus, temporary interference, and so forth. These attributions should not be taken for granted. The concept of causality itself is in need of refinement.

The actions of the mind are no more amenable to psi/non-psi distinctions than are material events. Normal mentation operates independent of space and time; for example, one may plan a future task or ruminate on a past action without needing to do so in any particular order. It is difficult to think of a single feature of normal mentation that is not shared by psi. When a scientist conceives the design for a successful experiment, how does his act of imagination differ from a precognitive remote viewing of the experimental result? What influence does the physicist's wish to observe a $Z_0$ particle exert on its detection? How does the visual image of a past event (normal memory) differ from the visual image of an event that has not yet occurred (precognition)?

The wish to distinguish psi from non-psi mentation may be a motive for the emphasis on altered states and trance as psi-generating conditions. Philosophically, there is a strong desire on the part of conservative scientists to argue that psi acts, if they occur at all, must be qualitatively different from ordinary acts and, therefore, committed in a distinctive state of mind.

Experimental findings, however, offer little support for this belief. Psi action has been associated with both normal and altered states and has been observed under a wide variety of conditions. Objectively, psi and "ordinary" mentation appear to follow the same laws: If it is possible to pay attention to some past, future, or distant event (or object), it is possible to have a psi interaction with it.

Much time has been spent on the mind-matter and psi-ordinary distinction because the belief that it exists is responsible for much public prejudice and is a common source of experimenter error, as will be shown.

## Psi in the Scientific Environment

Research is a highly valued activity in our society, despite the long hours and low pay. The experimenter gains knowledge (if the experiment is well planned), prestige (if the findings are important), and some measure of fame (if he publishes). What does the participant gain? Approval, validation of his abilities, and the pleasure of helping science? Would he still go through with the experiment if he knew that he would be labeled a "so-called psychic" in the published article? Would he contribute his time if he knew that the experiment was a hoax and his efforts were intended to be futile? Would the experimenter have done so in his place?

Scientific research currently reflects some of the confusion our society suffers over values and ethics, ends and means, and old and new truths. Scientists possess belief systems that have direct impact on the conduct of research. To complicate matters, there is a widespread belief that the ethics used in research especially in the behavioral sciences should be different than those applied in daily life.

Clearly the task of experimental design in psi research is directly affected by the designer's belief about the nature of reality. In the classical world of definable events and objects separable from their surroundings, the neat experimenter/psi agent/target paradigm was the obvious way to proceed. In the world as seen by new physics, it is much more difficult to isolate "causes" from "effects."

To some, this signals the disintegration of the scientific method. Scientific research has long been identified with the task of finding causal chains. In reality, the scientific method is merely a means of making certain observations meaningful. A change in philosophy signals a change in experimental design. The concept of performing experiments to acquire knowledge is by no means invalidated.

For example, the separability of psi into its various categories need not be taken for granted. Psi action was initially categorized with reference to the object of the action: psi between individuals was defined as telepathy, psi contact with a future event was classed as precognition, and psi contact that affected the condition of a physical object was labeled psychokinesis (PK). It ultimately may be difficult to defend this distinction. Existing research may be taken to show a relationship between remote viewing and PK, for example.[2] Psi action itself may be worth investigating; perhaps it will be found to have complexity apart from its objects, much as languages have grammar apart from their content.

Does the watched pot take longer to boil? In the Newtonian world, we *knew* that the answer was no. In the world of new physics, where it is much more difficult to take the measured one-way flow of time for granted, perhaps someone should look to see.

Many ethical problems in psi research, as in examples shortly to be cited, result directly from attempting to handle psi phenomena as if they obeyed classical concepts of causality. These problems generally manifest as conflicts of intention between participant and experimenter and as intellectual problems with the design (e.g., providing false feedback in a clairvoyance experiment).

Evidence is accumulating to the effect that the ostensible psi agent cannot be isolated from other elements in the experiment, including the attitudes of the experimenter. An experimenter may not believe that psi skills can be learned in the sense that we deliberately learn other skills like typing and foreign languages. He may take the position that performance is strictly a matter of the emotional state of the subject.[3] During a "psi training session," he may attempt to manipulate the subject's state of mind so that psi hitting will occur. There might be little formal difference between this type of session and a session conducted by someone who thought that psi could be consciously learned. The differences would lie in attitudes toward the psi agent: whether he or she is thought capable of conscious, intelligent use of psi. (The subject as helpless tool of the all-powerful experimenter is a popular scenario with strong emotional appeal on both sides.)

Does intention matter in psi? Does it make a difference whether the experimenter intends the participant to succeed freely, or intends to assert control of the participant's psi performance? Is it reasonable to assume that the participant will be unaware of the experimenter's attitude?

There is some basis for considering psi behavior to be intentionally motivated, that is, "goal-directed." If the participant happens not to wish his performance controlled by the experimenter, their intentions are in conflict. There is no reason to assume that the experimenter's influence on the outcome of the experiment will be less important than the participant's. For scientific as well as ethical reasons, conflicts of intention should be minimized in research.

The problem of composing experiments is made somewhat more difficult by the attitude of our society toward mental acts. We conventionally regard gestures of mind as void of consequences. In fact, we set aside the realm of the imagination as a mode wherein socially unacceptable desires may be harmlessly enjoyed. Scientists have difficulty making the transition from this attitude to an experimental setting in which the mental acts of everyone concerned must be taken into account.

Experimenters' beliefs have an important influence on the ethics of psi research. To the extent that experimenters believe that psi is "not real," they may regard normal ethical standards as unnecessary. To the extent that experimenters believe that psi-capable individuals are sick or morally inferior, they may treat these "subjects" in a demeaning way.

Examples of these attitudes are found in the literature. "Cultist," "alleged healer," and "so-called psychic" are terms used by scientists to describe individuals who participated in good faith in their experiments, in some cases scoring impressive and statistically significant results.[4] Nowhere in these accounts do the authors refer to themselves as "so-called scientists." These labels are clearly inappropriate.

A second type of ethical problem occurs with respect to feedback and general honesty with the research participant. Certainly, in some cases, it is impossible to do the research if the experimental plan is revealed beforehand to participants. Where, then, are the limits?

This question deserves careful study. For example, some approaches to research in PK involve deliberately providing false/positive feedback. The rationale is that this encourages the subject to put forward his best efforts. A second justification that has been offered is that PK agents cheat—consciously or unconsciously—and should be encouraged in this at the start of the experimental work. Controls can be introduced later to separate the real from the fraudulent results.[3]

Oddly enough, the experimenters do not see the provision of false feedback as fraud on their part, and they do not see this process as an extinction paradigm, which in fact it resembles.[5]

Inviting people to participate in a psi experiment and then frustrating them when they attempt to perform their task has been the basis of a number of experiments. The existence of experimenter effect has been well documented.[6] Advising the participant afterward that his difficulties were part of the experiment may not compensate for his disappointment and loss of self-esteem.

What if the same procedure were used in another discipline? Suppose the experimenter invited a group of physicists to participate in a study, telling them that the purpose of the research was to learn something about how they performed their experiments, with the end purpose of improving their scientific ability. The experimenter then subjects the physicists to stressful conditions and checks to see whether this affects their ability to do research. The stressful conditions would include defective equipment, rudely critical observers, bad lighting conditions, and falsified data from their experiments.

The above suggests a useful test for ethics in psi research: If an element is deemed unethical in other situations, it should not be tolerated in psi studies. The waste of the physicists' time in the hypothetical example above is improper; the waste of any person's honestly given time and effort is unacceptable.

Generally speaking, if the concept of ethics is to have any relevance, the experimenter-participant relationship must include an expectation of good faith and fair dealing on both sides. The same ethical considerations should apply in the research as in daily life. In normal circumstances, any action that deceptively deprives a person of something of value, such as his time and reputation, or deliberately inflicts emotional harm is not only unethical, but also may form the basis for legal action.

Actions taken that are embarrassing or hurtful to the participant, or that damage his psi capability should be considered unethical. Abuses of any person's time and trust should not be tolerated in the experimental environment. If a problem cannot be explored scientifically in an ethical manner, it should be addressed in another way.

The majority of this discussion so far refers to conditions that affect participants. The reason is that a good experimental design, by definition, removes fraud by participants as a believable explanation for the data. The experimenter should not be at risk. An ethically conducted experiment is not a fraud contest between experimenter and participant.

What the participant is asked to do in the experiment also needs to be examined. Obviously, experiments that involve the intention to harm others should be avoided, regardless of whether the experimenter himself believes that actual damage will result. (This is precisely the objection to the famous electric shock experiment.[7] The fact that the victim actually received no shocks does not excuse the scenario.)

Ethically speaking, a person may not be made the subject of hostile intention unless there is some real grievance at issue, or controlled (even if he wants to be), or "helped" beyond his level of consent. Experimenters who undertake to be ethical must think through these issues.

Ethical concerns apply to the control as well as the treatment parts of the research design. Sometimes this point is overlooked. For example, one research plan involves asking the participant to view, heal, or psychokinetically affect a target in a given location. During the control sessions, no target is placed at the location.

This design has several flaws. First, it assumes that the participant will not know the target is missing or that if he does know, it will not affect his actions on the occasions when a target is present. Second, it assumes (if the same target is repeatedly monitored) that psi phenomena are separable in a timewise and spacewise fashion. Most psi experiments show that space and time offer no barrier to psi effects. Finally, it assumes that asking the participant to expend effort in a context where the experimenter *believes and intends* that effort to have no effect, creates a neutral ground against which a psi effect can be measured.

A more sophisticated approach to experimental design seems to be in order. The idea of a control should have some logical connection with the model of effect that is used. If the participant is expected to have an effect on the target by intending to do so, the appropriate control is to measure the target while he is not intending. In many cases, the cure is simple: Tell the participant not to exert effort during the control periods.

It is interesting to note that in this instance, as in others, removing the intellectual problems in the design incidentally removes a conflict of intention that had constituted an ethical problem.

The usual reason experimenters give false information to their participants is the assumption that the participants will believe that it is genuine. Studies of telepathy and remote viewing call this assumption into question. Ethically speaking, the provision of false information is wrong; here, too, is a situation in which ethics and good experimental design work together.

This reasoning may be applied in other fields as well. In medical research, the efficacy of a treatment may be evaluated in a placebo study. Half of the participants will receive the drug; the other half receive an inert substitute (the placebo). The study is arranged so that no one knows to which group a given participant belongs until the conclusion of the experiment. The participants normally are informed beforehand of the risks and conditions of the study, including the fact that they may not receive the experimental drug. This information cures the ethical objections in a manner consistent with good scientific research. It would seem both simple and desirable to adopt the same standards in psi research.

The suggestion is that ordinary standards in use by other disciplines can be adapted to psi research without great difficulty.

How well does the ordinary standards argument apply to psi action itself?

Unless some "psi particle" or "psi field" can be identified, we will continue to lack a reliable means for distinguishing psi behavior from ordinary behavior. The existing test, actions contrary to nature and/or actions accomplished at a distance, does not distinguish psi from other acts of mentation.

What if all acts of mentation are considered action at a distance? Ethically speaking, this implies that psi action should be judged by the same standards that apply to other behavior.[8] For example, psychokinetically interfering with someone's computer should be considered no more and no less ethical than physically sabotaging it in some fashion. If a physical action is improper, its accomplishment by psi means also should be deemed improper.

It follows, then, that treatments that would be deemed deceitful and hurtful in ordinary social interaction should be avoided in scientific experimentation. An experiment should be viewed as an agreement between individuals in which mutual honesty and good faith are essential elements.

It is my belief that these simple standards, which are largely borrowed from other disciplines, from common sense, and from what is already known about psi, can be used to create better scientific experiments and to allow more powerful and varied expressions of psi in the laboratory.

## NOTES

Acknowledgments to Richard F. Haines, Ph.D., and George R. Gilmour, Ph.D. for helpful suggestions with this manuscript.

1. "The local natives told us an old folk tale about a girl who had refused to marry. Her father then married her to a dog and put them on an island together. There she gave birth to eight children whom she placed in a boat made from the sole of her kamik. The children sailed away and eventually became the terrors of the world, namely, the white men and Indians." Freuchen P. *Arctic Adventure*. New York: Farrar & Rhinehart, Inc; 1935:434.

2. Osis K, McCormick D. Kinetic effects at the ostensible location of an out-of-body projection during perceptual testing. *Journal of the American Society for Psychical Research*. 1980;74:319–329.

3. Isaacs J. The Batcheldor approach: some strengths and weaknesses. *Journal of the American Society for Psychical Research*. 1984;78:123–132.

4. Krippner S, Solfvin G. Psychic healing: a research survey. *Psi Research*. 1984;3:16–28.

5. The contribution of Jon Klimo, Ph.D., to this portion of the argument is gratefully acknowledged.

6. See "The Influence of Experimenter Motivation, Attitudes, and Methods of Handling Subjects on Psi Test Results," by Rhea A. White, in *Handbook of Parapsychol-*

*ogy,* edited by Benjamin B. Wolman. New York: Van Nostrand Reinhold Co; 1977:273–301.

Note that for adverse stimuli, as described on page 291, "the experimenter behaved in an abrupt, authoritarian manner . . . the treatment of the negatives was so unfriendly, so stereotyped and boring that most of the subjects were very close to the 'breaking point' at the end of the experiment." This experiment (Johnson & Johannesson, 1972) was designed to explore a sheep-and-goats effect wherein subjects who had positive attitudes toward psi at the start of the experiment were well treated and subjects with negative attitudes toward psi were badly treated in the course of the experiment.

In the same vein, see "Effects of Belief in ESP and Distorted Feedback on a Computerized Clairvoyance Task," by Kristinn R. Thorisson, Fridrik Skulason, and Erlendur Haraldsson in the *Journal of Parapsychology.* 1991;55(1):45–58.

ABSTRACT: In a fully computerized experiment 220 University of Iceland students were administered a 12-item questionnaire on attitudes toward ESP and related phenomena, and a 40-trial clairvoyance computer game (probability of a hit, 1 in 4). A test of the effect of belief and interest in psychic phenomena on the clairvoyance task revealed a significant reversal of the sheep-goat effect ($p = .002$, two-tailed). To test the hypothesis that feedback about their success, or lack of it, would affect their scores, we randomly divided subjects into three groups, each group getting different play-by-play feedback for their guesses in the game by having displayed to them either a reduced, correct, or increased number of hits. The hypothesis, that different amounts of distorted feedback would affect the number of correct guesses, was not confirmed.

In fact, subjects who had positive attitudes toward extrasensory perception (ESP) made lower scores in this experiment than the subjects with negative attitudes. The overall level of psi hitting was not impressive, yielding no significant differences between feedback groups. The experimenters could not account for these results but speculated in part, "could the deception of subjects by the experimenters regarding the distortion of the feedback have reversed the sheep-goat effect?" (p. 55).

An experiment in which false feedback is deliberately offered to the participants is an adverse environment. Could it reasonably be assumed that individuals who might score above chance on a clairvoyance test would remain ignorant of the experimenters' lack of good faith? Would these subjects have remained entirely cooperative and trusting? Might the "goats" have felt more comfortable with false feedback than the "sheep?"

This study is cited as an example to show that the provision of false feedback is not widely recognized as an ethical problem. Efforts to deceive subjects in psi experiments are not unusual. Surveying the literature, it is easy to form at least the casual impression that the deliberate provision of false feedback reduces the overall expression of psi in the experiment.

7. Milgram S. Behavioral study of obedience. *Journal of Abnormal and Social Psychology.* 1963;67(4):371–378. In the course of this experiment, a naive subject was ordered by the experimenter to administer increasingly severer punishment to a victim in the context of a "learning experiment." The "victim" was a confederate of the experimenter and exhibited prerehearsed responses. "Punishment" was administered by a shock generator with thirty graded switches ranging from "Slight Shock" to "Danger: Severe Shock." Twenty-six subjects fully obeyed the experimental commands and administered the highest shock on the generator. Fourteen subjects broke off the experiment at some point after the victim protested and refused to provide further answers.

There is perhaps some point at which each of us would abandon his most dearly loved friend or steal from or torture an innocent human being. Who among us cares to be provided with this type of indelible self-knowledge? The anguish of the situation is not relieved by the information, presumably offered after the experiment, that the shocks were not real and no one was actually harmed. All of the participants in this experiment were harmed in a way that cannot be redressed by the experimenter or erased by time.

Milgram notes that "there is, at best, ambiguity with regard to the prerogatives of a psychologist and the corresponding rights of his subject. There is a vagueness of expectation concerning what a psychologist may require of his subject, and when he is overstepping acceptable limits. . . . There are few standards that seem directly applicable to the situation" (p. 377).

Indeed.

8. Thomson S. Ethical dimensions of psi capability. *Applied Psi.* 1985;(4) 3:3–10;4:6–14;(5)1:8–16.

# 25

# Increasing Psychic Reliability

*Russell Targ, William Braud, Marilyn Schlitz,*
*and Charles Honorton*

**Russell Targ:** In 1955, the CIBA Foundation held a meeting called a "CIBA Symposium on the Nature of Extrasensory Perception." At that international conference there was a strong consensus that if parapsychologists were going to achieve any further progress in the field of psi research, it would be essential to find repeatable experiments.[1] Now in 1990 I believe the data indicate that we have accomplished that goal. We have seen the meta-analysis of hundreds of experiments in both paranormal perception and random-number PK [psychokinesis] that overwhelmingly support the existence of robust phenomena. We on this panel have been conducting free-response experiments for many years and have seen percipients give amazingly accurate descriptions of hidden target material in both remote viewing and ganzfeld protocols. The subjects which this panel will discuss are the techniques we can use to increase the reliability of psi functioning while maintaining its accuracy.

We have analyses from laboratories all over the world showing great statistical significance from the ganzfeld, random number generator PK, and other manifestations of psychic functioning. Today we are not going to be talking about the significance levels of psychic functioning, but rather why psychic functioning isn't 100% reliable under laboratory conditions. In experiments that

A panel discussion at the Thirty-Third Annual Conference of the Parapsychological Association, Chevy Chase, Maryland, August 16–20, 1990. Reprinted with permission from the *Journal of Parapsychology*, 1991;(55):59–83.

Honorton has described in the ganzfeld[2] and in experiments that we've seen at SRI over a decade,[3] we have frequently carried out what we thought of as experimental series to find out whether some functional psychic relationship exists. To determine whether this factor is true, we would do six experimental trials with the assumption that if what we were trying to do was correct, we would get statistical significance from a half a dozen trials. This implies an effect size very close to unity. So, our question this evening is why shouldn't all of our experiments come out that way? Can we bring psychic functioning to a level of consciousness so that the person doing the psychic functioning, the viewer or the percipient, can tell you after a remote viewing trial or after a ganzfeld experience, "I saw all these different things I described, but I don't think that was a very good description. I would take a pass." Our task as experimenters is to help the subject learn to separate the psychic signal from the mental noise.

Gertrude Schmeidler yesterday expressed doubts about whether psychic functioning could be brought to consciousness. She felt that it was a preconscious or nonconscious or precognitive ability and I think one of the things that we will do this evening is examine that. I agree, for example, that during a psychic perception experiment you should not ask a viewer to tell you at the time whether the data he's giving you is excellent data. It would be like asking a singer during a concert to keep track of her intonation and how she is doing. I think she would sing herself into the floor very quickly. However, after the concert you can ask her, "During these half-dozen songs you sang, how did you do?" and the singer would be able to tell you, I'm certain, note for note, which notes were hit incorrectly and which songs were sung perfectly. During the largely automatic, somewhat nonanalytic act of singing or remote viewing, I would argue that you cannot keep track of the quality of your functioning. But I would propose that *after* the functioning, it would be possible and certainly desirable if we could teach people how to reflect back on what they've done and give some assessment of the quality.

The other aspect that I'll suggest very briefly for increasing the reliability of psychic functioning is to try and carry out the experiment in what I am thinking of these days as a state of grace. That is to say, the experimenters, the judges, the subjects, everybody in the environment has reached some kind of harmonious agreement. And, really, by a state of grace, I mean agreement with the universe, or some kind of affirmation or acceptance that what we are doing makes sense, can be done, and nobody in particular is going to be responsible for it. In the SRI work, we did trials at the rate of one trial per day. We recognized, as physicists carrying out ESP [extrasensory perception] research that we had no idea whatsoever of the physical mechanisms behind the experiments we were doing. But, after a decade of work, we learned a great deal about the psychology of the phenomenon. That's a great disappointment for us physicists. But, in our day-to-day activity doing these trials at one trial per day, it is almost as though we had carried out a sacrament to the factors (powers) controlling the psychic functioning that we were asking to manifest. The sacrament might involve lunch and ice cream, general play and great light-heartedness, with the assumption that when the scheduled experiment time came, we would do the experiment, and we could accept success. As a remarkable outcome of this acceptance, outstanding success is what we often found. In our most foolish days, for example, just before we published a paper in the *Proceedings of the IEEE*, we noticed that precognition seemed to be creeping un-asked for into our experiments.[4] We asked ourselves, since we were running short of time, how many experimental trials would be necessary to generate significance so that we could demonstrate precognition in some kind of accept-able way? If you do four successful trials, and they're all judged perfectly, the probability of that a priori outcome is ¼ factorial or ¹⁄₂₄. In these four trials, they were all judged successfully (first place matches), and we had a very small experiment, significant at about the .04 level with an effect size very close to unity. I think, looking back, that it shows incredible naiveté or stupidity to think that we could demonstrate a scientific principle with four trials, let alone achieve success. But we did our four trials, we invited Hella Hammid back from Los Angeles to Palo Alto, and said we'd like to do four more trials "a different way." They were all equally successful with a significant outcome.

What we would like to reexplore this evening is what it takes in order to get that level of psychic functioning. And one last word: I'll remind you that al-though we did a great deal of work with Hella during the decade at SRI, she was brought in as a *control* subject to compare with the other two experienced psychics we had worked with. So, can you shed some light on that for us, William?

**William Braud:** I've been frantically scribbling notes over the last two days, so what I'm about to say is just coalescing and it may or may not come together as I'd hoped. Russell introduced a spiritual metaphor of "grace" and "sacra-ment." Grace could mean harmony or comfort or total agreement on success, and the absence of resistance. And sacrament, perhaps, is a reminder that all of this is going on. I'd like to continue that metaphor. A few years ago, Bill Roll asked me to make a presentation at one of his conferences to summarize a lot of the psi-conducive and psi-interfering literature.[5] Before my eyes, the idea fell into place that much of this literature could be described rather well by three factors. Those three factors turned out to be faith, hope and love. Ordinarily I wouldn't use those terms, but Russell has given me permission to do so, so I have some confidence in introducing them. We can translate faith into belief: filling ourselves with a strong belief that what we want to accom-plish can come about and banishing doubt as completely as possible. The late Kenneth Batcheldor emphasized that belief may be critical to macro-PK and not just plain belief, but a real thoroughgoing belief, complete belief.[6] By hope we mean an expectation of that which is very likely. This could be translated, perhaps, into multiple visualizing, or imaging an outcome in its myriad forms:

all possible outcomes that are associated with success in the experiment, from what's happening in the trial to jumping up and down at the successful writing of a very positive article. Finally, love could translate into strong, positive emotions, into caring, connectedness, and meaning, perhaps.

Interestingly, Matthew Manning described three ingredients in his successful PK performances.[7] In order to make things happen, Matthew says that he *believes* very strongly that they will happen, he *expects* them to happen, and he *desires* that they happen. Perhaps these are three different words for the same three concepts. I'll mention concepts, procedures, and ideas that might allow these three things to be more fully realized.

One is to conduct experiments that are very meaningful, that are practical, that meet some important goals, or use a method of investigation in which everyone can see the connection between what you're doing (although it is simplified, abstract, and analogical) and something that is truly meaningful. The late Jan Ehrenwald made a very useful distinction between what he called "need-determined" psi and "flaw-determined" psi.[8] Need-determined psi is something that happens across the board and something that would work regardless of conditions. It has to do with some very ethologically relevant or very immediately relevant need. Crisis telepathy could be a prototypical example. He also talks about flaw-determined psi and would view most of what we study in our laboratories as flaw-determined. These are tiny cracks in the cosmic egg—tiny cracks in the inhibitory or filtering function of the brain, perhaps. If the brain is very delicately balanced, if conditions are just right, then the filtering that the brain or the individual aspect of my mind might normally do is broken down and some trivial psi comes through. One could work with need-determined psi by using processes that are obviously meaningful, such as healing-related studies, using archetypal material, or using psi to solve real, practical problems. Or, one could artificially introduce need into an experiment. You can create need by making an experiment meaningful to the participant in an individual way, or you can generate need or meaning through excitement, challenge, or novelties of an experiment.

The agreement Russell mentioned involves the ambiance of an experiment. This includes the extent to which everyone involved in the experiment, and especially the experimenter, is focused on or in agreement with what is to be accomplished. Small groups could be used to facilitate that agreement—groups with the same interests and the same world views. In some of our early experiments, we worked under such conditions with a small group that met weekly, and I think our very best results were obtained under those conditions.[9] We have since gone on through the years and matched those results statistically, but I haven't really seen the abundance of very strong qualitative correspondences that we found in those more intimate group meetings. The people in that group were very familiar with one another, comfortable with each other, shared a common world view, and were not very defensive about anything that was going on.

Something that hasn't been discussed has to do with presenting an experiment to a subject. You can tailor any experiment to match the subject, or to match the subject's interests and goals. That is what is nice about bio-PK (Chuck Honorton last night suggested *bio-psi* perhaps is a better term): there are so many possible psi channels in that paradigm. It could be presented as an almost physicalistic influence of electromagnetic waves from my brain upon someone else's physiology, at one extreme. We can talk about psychokinetic influences on someone's body, about telepathic communications, or about merging or blending with another person which initiates some self-regulation.[10] What I do automatically and sometimes intentionally is to "scan" a subject when I'm introducing an experiment to find the language and the world view of that person and try to speak to that person on that level and make the experiment meaningful to him or her. It is very easy to do that in almost any experiment. In the case of a stereotyped technique, the technique is standardized, but not the message that reaches the person. I would strongly emphasize tailoring the details of the experiment, and the reason for doing it, to make it meaningful to that individual or participant.

Now for a few comments on attention. Russell and I were discussing a couple of hours ago that what might be critical in understanding attention (in a model that is useful to me and has been through the years) is to treat attention as a quantity. It is as though there is only so much, and to the degree that we rob that attention away from some goal, we are reducing our likelihood of bringing about the goal. In reducing various conditions of noise we are eliminating certain kinds of distractions. There are, however, other noise sources in the background: irritating or unsettling matters of a personal, social, or ethical nature, of a consequential type—such as might follow from the success of the experiment. If all of those matters can somehow be understood and all participants become comfortable with them, then a lot of attention is freed and that attention can be directed to the task at hand. As I was writing that, it occurred to me that an interesting way to determine the extent to which this had been accomplished might be to use an automatism. We might have every member of the group using a pendulum, for example, and have them ask the pendulum if there are any matters that should be settled before we begin this experiment. Are the conditions appropriate? Let the part of you that knows tell the other part of you automatically, through some ideomotor activity. Perhaps one could even ask the pendulum when to begin the experiment, when is the time right.

**Russell Targ:** Is that the opposite of running an experiment?

**William Braud:** Yes, it is setting the stage for the experiment and wishing gently for whatever-it-is to cooperate with you.

We emphasize *conscious* psychic functioning a lot (in remote viewing certainly almost exclusively)—using images and words to know when a person is having a psi experience and letting the participant communicate that to the experimenter. In a way, it is almost a historical accident that we use that technique. In the olden days this was all we had. The only way I could let it be known that I was having a psychic experience was to put it into words, to translate it into an analytical left-hemispheric mode. Today that is not necessary. Today, due to concepts such as Rex Stanford's PMIR [psi-mediated instrumental response], we can make use of unintentional, unconscious behaviors to know when psi is happening.[11,12] We can use physiological detectors. It could well be that a lot of the problems that we experience with psi replicability have to do with the *expression* of psi. Attention might be critical, and distractions might be critical, in dealing with conscious left-hemispheric material. We could perhaps bypass a lot of difficulties by assessing what Gertrude Schmeidler called "ante-cognitive" activity happening at a physiological level.[13] Perhaps attention of the sort that could be problematical is not as important here, or at least there are fewer translations or transformations of information from one mode to another, and certainly there is less opportunity for cognitive distortion.

I have one final comment: This is a trivial thing which may or may not have any substance. It may be helpful for us to pay attention to *subtle physical variables* that could interact with our results. We tend to discount most physical variables; we tend to assume that psi is independent of spatial constraints, distance, time, physical variables of most sorts. There is a growing literature that living organisms are sensitive to subtle energies, to extremely weak electromagnetic frequencies and intensities. That evidence is building. There are frequency and intensity windows at which very strange things happen, and it could well be that a lot of the variability of our experiments could be attributed to, or at least modulated by, some of these ongoing changes. The geomagnetic fluctuations that Michael Persinger and others have pointed out could be one aspect of that.[14] A silly one occurred to me: Assume in the golden days at Duke University, that experiments were being conducted in a room that happened to have an overhead fan, a fan that happened to have a motor that was going at a certain frequency in the ELF range, and perhaps the brains of participants were being influenced by that fan either in a positive way or a negative way. And suppose individuals attempt to replicate that study in the absence of such a fan. That very simple factor could have profound effects. It is just another possibility people would overlook because it is so silly, but it is something we can actually test and explore.

**Russell Targ:** Thank you, William. Marilyn, will you carry on?

**Marilyn Schlitz:** The reason Russell asked me to participate in this panel is that I have been involved in a lot of experiments in the form of replication studies. I have been involved in successfully replicating remote viewing.[15-17] When I was at the Institute for Parapsychology we replicated the Watkins and Watkins bio-PK work with mice.[18] Working with William Braud at Mind Science Foundation, we have been successfully replicating the bio-PK work.[19,20] Chuck Honorton and I have just finished a very successful replication involving ganzfeld.[21] Having said that I have all this experience with replication, I want to add that I feel I don't know anything about how to make psi more reliable. I may, however, have a couple of clues. But you know, honestly, I don't want to say that I know anything other than what my own experience leads me to believe. Another caveat I want to make before I get going on this is that my background is really in the humanities. I am an anthropologist by training and therefore I have to question the very premise that reliability is the central issue here. If we are interested in studying psi, perhaps the question isn't replicability but understanding psi on its own terms. And if it is something that is somewhat capricious, then more power to it. It is our responsibility to accept psi on its own terms. We should understand those kinds of environments, personalities, and social situations that are conducive to psi processes, and perhaps not try to force it into a physics kind of model.[22]

Having made these disclaimers, I have made some observations from doing experimental research that lead me to have some intuitions about what makes it more likely to get a successful result in a laboratory setting. There is not much I can say that hasn't already been said. William emphasized the importance of need. I would say that intellectually it is important, when starting out to do a psi experiment, to feel that you are on a mission. If you approach the task itself as mundane, as though it is something that is just perfectly meaningless, then you are very likely to get nothing in response. I think it's very important that we empower ourselves as experimenters with the knowledge that we have an important task here and therefore carry it out with that sense of enthusiasm.

[A previous speaker at the conference] mentioned the psychological notion of ego attachment. I think it is also important to work with people, both experimenters and participants in psi studies, that don't have a tremendous amount of ego invested in success or failure. For years Russell has been talking about the model subject. This is somebody who hasn't necessarily had psi experiences. Rather it is somebody who is confident of himself in everyday life, accustomed to being successful in some area of endeavor, and who really is willing to take a risk but isn't risking his reputation by failing in the experiment. Also, when you have people who are generally successful in life, their confidence allows them to approach the task with a lot of fun and a joking temperament.

Something I have learned from the Julliard study that Chuck and I did last year, as well as some of the other works that I have done in the past, is the importance of conveying enthusiasm. Again, when I mention the intellectual task of need, I am talking about something that comes into a social kind of context. I think it is necessary that when our subjects come in, or when we are working with ourselves as subjects, that we make the task exciting. We should not sit our participants down with the ESP cards and just say, "Okay go to it."

If we are not excited about the task ourselves, it is very likely we will not be able to impart enthusiasm to others. So, in order to facilitate that kind of success in the laboratory, I think it is important to convey enthusiasm.

When somebody comes into the laboratory, the operation should be smooth. If the person comes in and you are fumbling over the equipment or fumbling over the procedure or fumbling over your explanation, then you are not representing the positive image that I think is necessary to convey encouragement and support to your participant. I think it is really necessary to set the stage for psi to happen so that things are operating fluently. One thing we learn from the cross-cultural literature relating to psi-types of experiences is that ritual is an important component, especially working with unselected subjects. When I say ritual, I don't necessarily mean some exotic tribal dance. What I mean here is that, for example in a ganzfeld situation, where you bring somebody in and you use the ping-pong balls and other sensory deprivation techniques, the effect may have nothing directly to do with that procedure. I mean, I'm willing to accept the idea that it may be a purely psychological effect, providing the participant with a positive expectation of success. It provides the subject with a view that at least the experimenter believes this is a psi-conducive procedure. The responsibility is no longer on the individual. It has been transferred to the situation, so that our subjects are not ego laden with guilt or the burden of responsibility. I think that is very important.

From the experimenter's perspective I think it is vital to keep the situation novel. Just doing exact replications is not the ticket. Conceptual replications, however, may be enough to keep the situation intriguing and interesting for the experimenter. Furthermore, I think we have to acknowledge the experimenter effect. There is no way, in dealing with the social or psychological aspects of psi, to ignore the fact that if the experimenter is at all important, it's not just for psychological reasons, but probably for psychic reasons as well. Having said that, both about the experimenters and about the subjects, I suggest a couple of possible areas that I think are worthy of research. One is to continue something that I started a couple of years ago, which is to look at the phenomenology of the experimenter.[23] We have some experimenters in the field who do well and we have some who don't do so well. That tendency seems to be fairly reliable. If we have a reliable effect it's that you can look at some people and see a fairly consistent success rate which others do not show. So I think that we have a lot to learn from these successful experimenters about their implicit assumptions. And here I think that anthropological research can be very useful. It allows us to get at some of those preconceived notions that a researcher has about what is successful and what is helpful, but that may not be fully conscious in his or her awareness. So I think some detailed, probing examinations of what goes on in the minds and bodies of successful experimenters, as well as focusing on the phenomenology of successful subjects, may lead us to more reliable effects in the future.

Second, I think there is a lot to be learned from ritual in terms of the social and cultural aspects of the psi elicitation process.[18] There are important things to be learned about the social context. Taken from a cross-cultural perspective, most healing rituals, for example, are not done on a diadic basis where, for example, you go to the doctor as an individual. Rather, you go with your family or members of your community and the community itself is often healed. If it is not the community being healed, at least it is the individual in the context of the community—the broader framework. So if we are going to design experiments, it is probably good to maximize that sort of social support and cohesiveness.

Third: This leads me to the idea of studying psi in a field setting. And again, looking at psi through an anthropological framework, we see cross-culturally that every society has beliefs in the supernatural, magical practices, and what we call psi phenomena. Every culture has these beliefs. Whether it is mere superstition or whether it is based on some kind of experiential knowledge or reference is what is open to empirical investigation. I think one of the things we need to do is incorporate our experimental rigor within a natural setting and explore psi as it occurs naturally, rather than trying to force it into these experimental paradigms all the time. Finally it is important that we don't take ourselves too seriously. I think that once that starts happening we can get awfully burdened and then it takes away from all our enthusiasm and our ability to be successful in our mission. That's about it for me; I will now pass it on to Chuck.

**Charles Honorton:** Marilyn did very well here and I don't know what is left to say. Take two ping-pong balls and call me in the morning. Or it is all done with magnets and mirrors. Just about everything has been said except what you can do going back to your own setting and doing an experiment that is going to have a chance of success. There certainly are many important clues that we have learned this evening. I will talk a little bit about the language we use with participants. There is something very different in the attitude of a participant when you tell him, "We are going to do a session together," rather than, "I'm going to run you in an experiment."

Imagine that you treated your house guests the way you treat your subjects. I think you would not have very many house guests after a time because we have been trained to view the experimental, scientific enterprise in a way that simply is not conducive to the occurrence of the phenomena that we are interested in. Nor is it necessary for scientific rigor. We need to differentiate between rigor and rigidity, a distinction that is frequently confused. The white lab coat has really no place in parapsychology except when you are cleaning your equipment. We learned this very early at Maimonides. We had white lab coats at Maimonides and we wore them to have our picture taken for the media and to clean the inkwells of the EEG, but we certainly didn't want our subjects to see us in white lab coats.[2] Human beings are vulnerable. They are particularly vulnerable in situations such as the ganzfeld or a dream experiment where you are removing their normal anchors to reality. Unless they feel safe and comfortable with you, and unless you give them some reason to want to do whatever it is you brought them there to do, there is really no reason why you should expect success.[24-26]

The main thing that I disagree with tonight—and I think Marilyn threw this out specifically for this purpose—is this whole notion of experimenter effects which I think has paralyzed us for many years without adequate justification.[21] There is no controversy whatsoever over the fact that different investigators have obtained different patterns of results. It also is impossible to interpret this, given the difference in research styles across experimenters. One of the most interesting things to emerge from the various meta-analyses is how variations in research style are related to differences in psi performance. There are so many variables that are probably unrelated to the experimenter as a human being. These have to do with choices that are made, sampling parameters, the kinds of participants that are selected for the experiments and so on and so forth. I really wish it were as simple as: Take two ping-pong balls, go into the room, and do this. But it obviously is not; there is a lot more that goes into it. The technique may be very important, whether it is ganzfeld, progressive re-laxation, bio-psi, or whatever other paradigm we have that has been successful. But there is a lot more that goes into it.[27,28]

**Russell Targ:** Thank you, Chuck. And I want to thank all the panelists. Let me say again, the thing that is new about this panel is that you have four people who have a lot of experience doing successful psi experiments over several decades. The focus of the emerging recipe for success seems to involve love and trust and faith. I think this is new stuff for the Parapsychological Association. Now I have to put in one other question, for Marilyn, which is just a technical question. Marilyn was saying that perhaps psi in these perception tasks is inherently intermittent or unreliable. And I think that is a completely fair assessment. In the note that I had made for myself, here was the question: Is there a psi uncertainty principle? After we have nine successful trials in a row, do we then owe them some? And that is really not known. One of the things that made me want to convene this panel is that we did a series of trials sometime ago where we had nine successes in a row forecasting silver futures changes, and then I tried to replicate that a few years later. We used a computer generated protocol, very sanitary computer scoring, with an outside group of subjects who mailed in responses, and we got eight out of nine hits. That was very exciting for me, because there were hundreds of people involved in that automated experiment. I then sought for replication, to take advantage of this mechanical psi machine that we had created, and I got eight out of nine fail-ures. That really stopped my personal psi investigation now for a couple of years while I tried to meditate on what the problem was there. It is as though the universe is clearly telling me that psi is a powerful machine and there is a loose screw, and that I should really think about how to tighten that screw before I go and run more experiments or even waste the time of people with whom I am working. So I would accept it if it turns out that there is a psi uncertainty principle that says I can't count on the universe giving me nine successful trials in a row, or replicating it. But it remains to be seen whether that lack of replication is in the experimenters or is in the phenomenon. I believe that is an essential principle for us to find out—which leads me to a question for Marilyn. You did a series of ten trials in remote viewing, an early replication.[15] Everyone was very interested in that, and a lot of attention was focused on your success. Then you were able to replicate that.[17] How were you able to do again what you had done before and make it a new successful experiment?

**Marilyn Schlitz:** I talked about the enthusiasm issue, and I think that during the time of those experiments I was on a mission. At that point I was really convinced that parapsychology was paradigmatic, that we were on the verge of a major revolution, and that I could have a principal role in that process. I think that was probably enough to drive me in feeling the confidence to go ahead and do the successful replication. One thing in listening to your description of your study, and again contemplating the field setting and how psi manifests itself cross-culturally, is that maybe we are a little too greedy in expecting that we should always be able to manifest psi at our whim. If you look at other cultures, psychic phenomena are experiences that are highly valued. They are put in the hands of certain specialized practitioners and only brought out at certain specialized times. It is not something that is used on a daily basis, nine to five. In our culture we attempt to turn it on and at five o'clock we punch out and go home. Maybe we're too greedy in expecting that we should always be able to do it on demand. If we look at the way it's manifested cross-culturally and in terms of my own personal experience with that successful replication, I would just say that it goes back to that enthusiasm, that sense of need, and the sense of importance that is really vital.

**William Braud:** Before we open this to the audience, could I add something to this issue of capriciousness in psi? Let's look at the misses. There are these very interesting misses. Russell does an experiment in which there are four out of four remarkable correspondences. The next two don't work. What is happening in those misses, what kind of information is occurring? An image just occurred to me that psi might have a default mode that is other than the sensory mode. We try to force psi into a sensory mode and say psi is present to the extent that it replicates or duplicates our conventional senses. Why would nature be so redundant? Maybe psi is playing in another arena. And maybe by motivation, by some of these factors that we spoke of, we can force psi. Imagine psi is like a rubber band. We can stretch it to an extent and it will mimic a sensory mode for a while. But maybe that cannot be maintained and psi will snap back like a rubber band into its default mode, which may have to do with something very unlike sensory processing. So the challenge would be to learn what is happening of a non-trivial sort during those misses. If there is some kind of commonality there, can we develop a technology or "state-specific science," to use Charley Tart's terminology,[29] that will allow us to explore some of these not-evident-to-the-senses aspects of psi?[30]

**Charles Honorton:** I agree with that. Although we are trying to make psi serve a perceptual- or motor-analogous function, it may in fact be something very different. One possibility suggested by Eccles, for example, is that the fundamental function of psi is to serve as a liaison between brain and mind.[31] If that is the case, the kind of perceptual things that we are trying to do in our experiments are really not very closely related to what psi might be in terms of its fundamental nature. But I think also that we have to always be aware of the fact that things are more complicated than is convenient; I mean we would like them to be very simple, but maybe, for example, those next two trials involve targets that were poor targets. Evidence is increasing, I think, that there is systematic variability in free response success in relation to qualities of targets. There is a sense in which I despair of free-response, process-oriented research in that it is so time-intensive for each trial that if there are systematic target effects, we could very easily obscure a small but real relationship with some other variable because each participant only does a very limited number of trials and some of those trials inevitably are going to be with poor targets. Now obviously we must learn a lot more about that so that we can specify these kinds of things in greater detail. And although I very much resonate with and appreciate a lot of the poetry that we have heard tonight, I think that there is a lot more that can be done at the analytical level in terms of delineating specific characteristics of successful and unsuccessful experiments that will improve our success rate.

**Russell Targ:** I just want to agree with William and Chuck. And one of the things that we've observed, and I think Marilyn has reflected on also, is that very often, the more challenging or impossible the task seems, the more likely the percipient is to be successful. So the idea of not doing tasks that mimic ordinary perception may be one of the clues to get a good result. At SRI, one of our most experienced viewers, Ingo Swann, often would say that he didn't want to take part in a particular experiment, because he considered it to be a "trivialization" of the ability.

**William Roll:**[32] First of all let me say that to me this is really a remarkable evening and a remarkable series of contributions. I find that the whole mood of parapsychology lightened, and by the way I like the poetry. I think that it helps to lighten the mood and make it more evocative, more suggestive. I hope that these contributions will appear in published form; I think you should seriously consider that possibility. They should be available to people who ask for suggestions on how to do experiments in this field. I think there has been a change. The yoke of responding to critics has sort of fallen away and the speakers are now orienting yourselves to psi.

Let me make one additional suggestion that has to do with failure, psi missing. I think part of that story lies in your own explorations or aspirations, particularly in the Delphi project. You remember how Keith and Russell and some others were predicting silver futures. You were going to be of some use to the world, particularly to parapsychology; we were going to get rich. And then as you were moving forward, the gears suddenly shifted and you were moving in reverse as vigorously as you had moved forward. Now you were having significant psi missing in this crucial situation and the effort sort of subsided.[33] Well, imagine that you had succeeded and imagine that you and we now have total ESP. Imagine the world we would be living in. It wouldn't be this world; it would be some other world. Would it be a better world? I don't know, I'm somewhat skeptical about that.

So, I think there is another principle that we need to bring out: the principle of *homeostasis*. We may be dealing with something like an organism, or a body. Psi may operate within some sort of organism-like structure, and just as with our bodies, there is this principle of balance. The organism can't function in the sympathetic mode; the nervous system can't function in that mode too much or too long, nor too much in the parasympathetic mode either. It can go for a while in one and then it has to swing back. I think that's a principle that is very worth looking into. Psi-missing is not a failure, it offers an insight into how the thing operates, an insight into the psi process.

**Russell Targ:** Do you feel that the experimenters sense that the world isn't ready for perfect ESP and conduct their experiments to demonstrate that?

**William Roll:** Well I think we have to give up the idea of experimenters and subjects. It is a configuration, it's a group, it's an organism. There isn't any experimenter as such and there isn't a subject as such when they enter into a psi relationship. The group may have a purpose that is quite different from the purposes of the experimenter, the subject, and the others that make it up. Here, perfect ESP may be imperfect ESP, psi-missing.

### NOTES

1. Wolstenholme GEW, Millar ECP, eds. *Ciba Foundation Symposium on Extrasensory Perception*. Boston: Little Brown; 1956.

2. Honorton C. Meta-analysis of psi ganzfeld research: a response to Hyman. *Journal of Parapsychology,* 1985;49:511–591.

3. Targ R, Harary K. *The Mind Race: Understanding and Using Psychic Abilities*. New York: Villard (Random House); 1984.

4. Puthoff H, Targ R. A perceptual channel for information transfer over kilometer

distances: historical perspective and recent research. *Proceedings of the IEEE*. 1976;64:3239–3383.

5. Braud WG. Implications and applications of laboratory psi findings. Invited address to the national conference on parapsychology: From Lab to Life. West Georgia College, Carrollton, Georgia, April 22–24, 1988.

6. Batcheldor KJ. Contributions to the theory of PK induction from sitter group work. Proceedings of the Presented Papers of the Society for Psychical Research and the Parapsychological Association Centenary-Jubilee Conference, Trinity College, Cambridge, 1982.

7. Manning M. The subject's report. *Proceedings of the Society for Psychical Research*. 1982;56(212):353–361.

8. Ehrenwald J. Psi phenomena, hemispheric dominance and the existential shift. In: Shapin B, Coly L, eds. *Psi and States of Awareness*. New York: Parapsychology Foundation; 1978:211–220.

9. Braud WG, Braud LW. Preliminary investigation of psi-conducive states: progressive muscular relaxation. *Journal of the American Society for Psychical Research*. 1973;67:26–46.

10. Braud WG. On the use of living target systems in distant mental influence research. In: Shapin B, Coly L, eds. *Psi Research Methodology: a Re-examination*. New York: Parapsychology Foundation; 1991.

11. Stanford RG. An experimentally testable model for spontaneous psi events. I. Extrasensory events. *Journal of the American Society of Psychical Research*. 1974;68:34–57.

12. Stanford RG. An experimentally testable model for spontaneous psi events. II. Psychokinetic events. *Journal of the American Society for Psychical Research*. 1974;68:321–356.

13. Schmeidler GR. Is psi an anti-cognitive process? Invited address to the Thirty-Third Annual Convention of the Parapsychology Association. Chevy Chase, Maryland, August 16–20, 1990.

14. Persinger M. Psi phenomena and temporal lobe activity: the geomagnetic factor. In: Henkel L, Berger R, eds. *Research in Parapsychology*. Metuchen, NJ: Scarecrow Press; 1988:121–156.

15. Schlitz M, Dacon S. Remote viewing: a conceptual replication. In Roll W, ed. *Research in Parapsychology*. Metuchen, NJ: Scarecrow Press; 1979:124–126.

16. Schlitz M, Gruber E. Transcontinental remote viewing. *Journal of Parapsychology*. 1980;44:305–317.

17. Schlitz M, Haight JM. Remote viewing revisited: an intrasubject replication. *Journal of Psychology*. 1984;48:39–49.

18. Schlitz M. Psi induction rituals: their role in experimental parapsychology. In: White R, ed. *Research in Parapsychology 1981*. Metuchen, NJ: Scarecrow Press; 1982:39–40.

19. Braud WG, Schlitz M. Psychokinetic influence on electrodermal activity. *Journal of Parapsychology*. 1983;47:95–119.

20. Braud WG, Schlitz M. A methodology for the objective study of transpersonal imagery. *Journal of Scientific Exploration*. 1989;3:43–63.

21. Schlitz MJ, Honorton C. ESP and creativity in an exceptional population. *Research in Parapsychology 1990* Metuchen, NJ: Scarecrow Press; 1992:45–49.

22. Schlitz M. The phenomenology of replication. In: Shapin B, Coly L, eds. *The*

*Repeatability Problem in Parapsychology.* New York: Parapsychology Foundation Press; 1985:73–97.

23. Schlitz M. An ethnographic approach to the study of psi: methodology and preliminary data. In: Weiner D, Nelson R, eds. *Research in Parapsychology.* Metuchen, NJ: Scarecrow Press; 1987:103–106.

24. Honorton C, Ferrari DC. Future telling: a meta-analysis of forced choice precognition experiments, 1925–1987. *Journal of Parapsychology.* 1989;53:281–308.

25. Honorton C, Berger RB, Varvoglis MP, Quant M, Derr P, Schechter EI, Ferrari DC. Psi communication in the ganzfeld: experiments with an automated testing system and a comparison with meta-analysis of earlier studies. *Journal of Parapsychology.* 1990;54:99–139.

26. Honorton C, Ferrari DC, Bem DJ. Extroversion and ESP performance: a meta-analysis and a new confirmation. *Research in Parapsychology 1990* Metuchen, NJ: Scarecrow Press; 1992:35–38.

27. Radin DI, Ferrari DC. Effects of consciousness on the fall of dice: a meta-analysis. *Research in Parapsychology 1990* Metuchen, NJ: Scarecrow Press; 1992:39–44.

28. Radin DI, Nelson RD. Consciousness related effects in random physical systems. *Foundations of Physics* 1989;19:1499–1514.

29. Tart C. States of consciousness and state-specific sciences. *Science.* 1972;176:1203–1210.

30. Braud WG. Nonevident psi. *Parapsychology Review.* 1982;13:16–18.

31. Eccles J. *The Neurophysiological Basis of Mind.* Oxford: Oxford University Press; 1953.

32. These comments are included here because they seem to bring an additional and very thoughtful point of view to the discussion.

33. Harary K, Targ R. A new approach to forecasting commodity futures. *Psi Research.* 1985;4:79–88.

# Reflections on 25 Years and 25 Chapters

*Charles T. Tart*

Charles T. Tart, Ph.D. (psychology, University of North Carolina Chapel Hill) is professor of psychology at University of California Davis. Dr. Tart is an internationally recognized authority on altered states of consciousness as well as parapsychology. Over the past thirty years, he has published ten books and numerous research studies on parapsychology, the nature of sleep and dreaming, hypnosis, and marijuana intoxication. He is past president of the Parapsychological Association, the professional group in the field.

At a "fireside chat," we asked Dr. Tart, "What have we learned in the past twenty-five years of studying parapsychology?"

There's one sense in which we've learned nothing. Nothing in the sense that there isn't any drastically new information that was never thought of before. But there have been a few exciting developments.

We have remote viewing as clearly one of the most successful ways to elicit extrasensory perception (ESP) from a wide variety of people. Although the psi is ancient, the fact that it can be done so well and work so consistently in the remote method is new.

Another new development is the information-processing mechanism I accidentally discovered in my research on improving telepathy through feedback, a mechanism I call transtemporal inhibition. That was entirely unanticipated, except, once discovered, it turned out to be analogous to certain aspects of sensory processing in biological systems. Advances in neurophysiology that identified lateral (transspatial) inhibition among neurons provided a good model for transtemporal inhibition as a noise filter in ESP.

The computer age has given us psychokinesis (PK) and ESP on microsystems, such as the protocols developed by Helmut Schmidt and at the Princeton Engineering Anomalies Research Lab and by Dave Hurt and Russell Targ. You can probably find a few forerunners, such as attempts to influence radioactive decay, if you go back before 1963, but very little. Microelectronic PK has really taken off since then. In doing PK to influence the innards of an electronic machine, what are you doing? Which "electron" do you "push"? What is an electron anyway? We're far afield from a commonsense view of the world here, and yet the stuff works.

We know more about the psychophysiological correlates of psi then we did twenty-five or more years ago. We know that in some cases, you can receive a message by psychic means that will influence your body, even though the signal doesn't necessarily get through to your consciousness. "You" can be unconsciously reacting to psychic information by producing measurable changes in the body. This leads into another area of psychology that has always interested me: If you can learn to tune into your body (which is not a major priority in this culture), you will open up another information channel. Much important and specific information is expressed by feelings and sensations in the body. If you never pay attention to your body, you have no chance of receiving the messages—like a telephone that rings with no one to answer.

What I've also learned in twenty-five to thirty years is how rich are the foundations, the reality of psychic stuff, and how psychic functioning begins to correlate with the nature of consciousness. When I was sixteen, I read Rhine's books. In a certain sense, there's been nothing fundamentally new since then, except for the few exceptions I mentioned. But on the other hand, I certainly understand psi in a much more sophisticated manner than I ever did before. I've watched it and worked with it in the laboratory and I've also had a lot more experience of the paranormal in everyday life to give me a personal feel for it. A lifetime of research has made me willing as a scientist—I am not speaking just from my personal belief system, but as a scientist—to propound a testable transpersonal model of human beings.

We are spiritual beings in some sense. There is a part of the mind that transcends what we know about ordinary matter and that has to be studied with nonphysical methods. As interesting as some of the ideas in quantum physics are, we can't sit around waiting for quantum physicists to explain psi some day. There are parts of the mind that have to be looked at on their own terms.

Because of the reliability of several kinds of psychic phenomena, I now know that the spiritual or transpersonal is not just an imaginary realm. You could take a conventional view of transpersonal psychology as the study of illusions about spiritual things that weak-minded people need to comfort themselves. It is not unreasonable to look at it that way because some ideas about the spiritual and transpersonal *are* illusory things that are being used by people to comfort themselves. But I would now argue very strongly that an orthodox view is insufficient. We know that in telepathy two minds can reach each other through barriers of space. We know that sometimes the mind can directly know the state of matter or, with PK, affect the state of matter. We know that sometimes the mind can predict the future in ways that are logically and physically impossible.

When someone has a transpersonal experience and he speaks of union, it could be a metaphor. Sometimes it could just be a description of how his own psychological boundaries get so fuzzy that he sort of stupidly can't distinguish between himself and something else. But sometimes when people speak of an experience of union they may be talking about some literal kind of interdigitation—of "minds," of "souls," of whatever you want to call these sorts of things. I see laboratory parapsychology as forming a technical basis for what is fundamentally possible in transpersonal psychology.

If I didn't have parapsychology to draw on, I might see transpersonal psychology primarily as the study of daydreams, illusions, pathological sorts of visions, and drug-induced hallucinations. But because of the reality of parapsychological research, I see that we have to take the transpersonal much more seriously. The spiritual, the transpersonal, is important to human beings. It's become clear to me that we have a *need* for values, high-level values, spiritual values, in the same way we have a need for vitamins in our food. If we don't get them, we get sick and go crazy.

I can recommend spiritual activities to people now with a clear conscience as a scientist, not just as me personally. I tell them that there's a lot of nonsense out there in the name of the spiritual, but there's also something real and vital going on that tells us about our place in the universe, about higher levels of meaning. Sure there's a risk of running into nonsense, but there's also a very real risk of dying of these "value-deficiency diseases" if we don't look for the spiritual.

I want to balance this conceptual discussion by also noting that for all the exotic spiritual stuff I've looked at and practices I've done, I've begun to think more and more that being kind and considerate to someone else is really the major theme in what it's all about. Really, all the other stuff is just fancy window-dressing.

# Epilogue

*Dean Brown*

The contributions to this retrospective volume have taken us far afield, to topics as varied as medicine, physics, perception, and communication. But there is a pattern, an underlying common landscape that emerges from these seemingly diverse perspectives.

Are there other research groups with parallel interests in other cities, in other countries, in other cultures? Is there a commonality in seeing the world in this way? We believe that there is, and that this collection of insights matches up with those of other inquiring minds viewing the world from various centers. In a sense, our research is intensely intimate, based on personal interests, direct experience, and disciplined observation. It is expressed and shared by hammering out research designs and results within the group, in accord with our mutual concepts and vocabularies. It is reflected and shaped by our conviviality. It is to say what is going on here among thoughtful people.

Remote viewing has always been the main core of our group's thrust throughout the past quarter century. Perhaps that is the area in which results are easier to get. Or is it that remote viewing is closer to the substrate of objective reality than the other domains of parapsychological research? Or could it be merely an expression of the zeitgeist of this particular place and time? Whatever the reason, I believe that a profound understanding of remote viewing can be the foundation on which the other so-called psychic phenomena ultimately will be mapped.

The dimensions of parapsychological research, as brought out in this compendium are as follows:

- Viewing and otherwise experiencing remotely—in space, time, and states of consciousness (thought forms, precognition, clairvoyance, telepathy)
- Healing (shamanism, psychoneuroimmunology)
- Deep sharing, including perception of archetypes
- Channeling (spirit guides, artistic inspiration)
- Causation, including psychokinesis
- States of consciousness (hypnosis, near-death experiences)
- Possession and exorcism, poltergeists
- Intentionality (synchronicity and providential events, supply and demand)
- Innate intelligence (instinct, migration, plant and animal wisdom, genius, talent, savants)

Parapsychological research is fundamentally based on mind processes. We can make good use of the 16-dimensional classification analyzed in the Aitareya Upanishad:

Consciousness
Instinct
Discrimination
Intelligence
Wisdom
Insight
Perseverance
Reason
Genius
Impulse
Memory
Conception
Will
Vitality
Desire
Drive

All these faculties combine and blend in the processes of perception, experience, and expression.

Parapsychology is the cutting edge of science, where experience is yet barely cognized, patterned, repeatable, subject to consensus—the horizon where the known meets the unknown. The unknown can mean that which is not yet understood or that which is not yet experienced. What is now the dead heartwood of science, holding up the tree of knowledge, was once parascience.

The etymology of the word science derives from the root *skei,* meaning to cut, to separate one thing from another (as in the words discern, conscience, conscious, prescient, schism, scissors)—to know by the process of making critical distinctions. Science is based on observation and critical reasoning, first personal and then consensual. Science is obliged to accept all data unless and until they can be invalidated by experiment. Data must be triangulated and cross-checked from every possible perspective.

Hypotheses come and go as matters of convenience. Theories arise from inductive insights and are tentatively accepted (as intellectual scaffolding) until they can be rejected by contradicting data or by the principle of beauty or by the principle of economy (Occam's razor). The quality of a theory is superior if it is more comprehensive and more concise. The dynamic of science is to gather and confirm data, to infer theories, and then proceed with diligence to find ways to reject them.

We are living in an epoch of convergence between the physical and personal sciences, between external and internal, between observer and observed, between manifest and unmanifest. Quantum physics has become the most quantitative branch of science, able to compute states with 12-digit precision, yet it is centrally based on probabilities and intrinsically unmanifest realities such as virtual states, vacuum excitations, and indeterminancies.

Science is not necessarily expressed in mathematics, and it is rarely predictive. Its highest successes have been descriptive (as in geology and astronomy) or comprehensive (as in medicine and economics).

We understand the laws of nature as distillations of reality. There are two coexistent definitions of reality. They are polar opposites:

• Reality is the pattern that is invariant and eternal, that remains fixed in a flux of change, that never varies under transformations to other situations.
• Reality is the pattern (gestalt) that you experience at this very instant.

Examples of the invariant kind of reality are fixed-point theorems in topology and standards of aesthetics in art. Examples of the now-and-here kind of reality are being in love and having a life-changing dream. Laws of nature are of the invariant kind.

Physics and psychology have many elemental laws in common. For example, they share the principle of least action, principles that involve energy, entropy, and chaos, symmetry and symmetry breaking, and principles that involve discrete states and state transitions.

Mihaly Csikszentmihalyi, in his recent book *Flow* (1990), identifies a set of parameters that can be used directly in formulating laws of psychology: purpose, quest, center, entropy and negentropy, chaos, control, goal, skill, mood, order, sensation, harmony, rules, game, intention, joy, play, rhythm, challenge, grace, effort, meaning, event, feedback, shaping experience, order, states of mind, concentration, motive, attention, ecstasy, faith, expectation, and the experience of time. And he goes on to derive algorithms using these parameters to achieve practical outcomes. Other modern psychologies are isomorphic to his. We are well on our way to enunciating laws that will provide a framework for designing experiments, obtaining verifiable and consensually acceptable data, and organizing the results in elegant formulations.

Perhaps the richest domain for future research in parapsychology is emerging from the classic boundary between the brain and the mind, at the interfaces between neuroscience, psychology, and immunology. Here is where our contributions on shamanism, healing, and body chemistry come to bear.

In an article, "Organization of the Human Brain," published in *Science* (1989;245), Michael Gazzanaga, professor of psychiatry at Dartmouth, correlates discrete modules of brain activity with cognitive functions. For example, visual areas, the receptive language area (Wernicke's area), and the expressive motor language area (Broca's area) are distinguished. Gazzanaga has located a module in the dominant left verbal hemisphere that he terms the interpreter. The interpreter harmonizes and unifies discontinuities between internal and external reality. Gazzanaga's insight is shared by William Blake in his beautiful engraving on pewter, "The Man Sweeping the Interpreter's Parlour" (1822). Each of us is compelled by our biological circuitry to be a theoretician! A driving thrust of intelligence, of life itself, is to explain experience. The domain of parapsychology has an abundance of solid facts to work with and a drive to explain them.

The work presented here and similar work elsewhere have established the setting for the future. We can expect new understanding of the nature of space and time (which depend so much on biological and subjective considerations), the interconnectedness of observer and the observed, intelligence of plants and animals, and the influence of chemicals, set and setting on psychic processes.

Not only will the external universe be more understood as a projection of Mind, but also more of the personal universe will become clear. The cycle of conception→perception→sensation→cognition will become the basis for all science. The processes of intention, knowing, expression, and causation and the interplay of states of consciousness will come more within our grasp.

With the new understanding, a richer lifestyle will emerge with the goals of health (wholeness), joy of living, radiance, wealth, harmony within self and with nature, energy (action), purpose, and fulfillment. And (by one of the laws of the universe) the capabilities for evil will increase in lockstep. A profound understanding of ethics, as treated in Chapter 24 by Shelley Thomson, becomes urgent for us to cope responsibly with these new powers.

And so we arrive at the summation of our work, at the frontier of science, where we possess that most precious asset of humankind, the body of experience that cannot yet be honestly invalidated nor can it yet be explained—the zest and the life blood of true sciences. Its value? Remember that what you believe sculpts what you perceive. What we believe together forms what we perceive together. Let us proceed to broaden our horizons and expand our aliveness.

# Milestones in the History of the Parapsychology Research Group: 1963–1992

1963    Jeffrey Smith, professor of religion and philosophy at Stanford, gives a talk at the university about his own psychic experiences.

1964    Charles Tart, Arthur Hastings, Russell Targ, David Hurt, and others meet in Jeffrey Smith's home to begin discussions of parapsychology.

1965    The political and cultural climate in northern California—characterized by the civil rights, free speech, and peace movements, and the psychedelic subculture—provides a legendary milieu for revolutionary and creative thinking.

1966    The Parapsychology Research Group (PRG) is founded in January. The first board of directors consists of Frederick Domeyer, David Hurt, Walter Neumeyer, Jeffrey Smith, Russell Targ, and Charles Tart. Also present at that time were Charles Schulz and Anthony White. Russell Targ was elected president at the first official meeting in February.

1966    Charles Tart, assistant professor of psychology at University of California Davis, publishes "Models for the Explanation of Extrasensory Perception" in the *International Journal of Neuropsychiatry*.

1968    Joe Kamiya reports that subjects can gain voluntary control of their brainwaves. This work stimulates research among parapsychologists as well as medical scientists. The biofeedback societies evolve from this work, and the operant conditioning models that follow reach into the new field of psychoneuroimmunology.

1969    Charles Tart publishes the influential book *Altered States of Consciousness: A Book of Readings*.

1969    Stanley Krippner and Montague Ullman begin their ground-breaking work in dream telepathy at Maimonides Medical Center in Brooklyn, New York.

1970    *Psychic Discoveries Behind the Iron Curtain* by Shelley Ostrander and Lynn Schroeder stirs up new interest in psychic research. Limited funding for research gradually becomes available in some areas.

1971    Tim Scully and Jean Millay develop the brainwave biofeedback light sculpture with a grant from Stanley Krippner.

1971    David Hurt and Russell Targ create the multiple-choice extrasensory perception (ESP) teaching machine.

1972    With a grant from the U.S. government, Targ and Puthoff establish a parapsychology research lab at SRI International in Menlo Park, California, and carry out successful experiments in remote viewing. Ten years of research follows.

1972    Charles Tart organizes a major conference on ESP at the University of California Davis, repeated at the University of California Berkeley.

1972    Stanley Krippner and James Hickman travel to the USSR to meet Soviet parapsychologists.

1973    Astronaut Edgar Mitchell founds the Institute of Noetic Sciences. Later, Willis Harman becomes president.

1974    Stanley Krippner and James Hickman return to the USSR for a conference and lay the groundwork for the Soviet-American exchange program to be sponsored by Esalen Institute, Big Sur, California.

1974    Eleanor Criswell initiates a special studies program in parapsychology at California State University at Sonoma, attracting students from all over the country.

1974    Criswell, as president of the Association for Humanistic Psychology, establishes an educational arm called the Humanistic Psychology Institute, renamed Saybrook Institute in 1976. Stanley Krippner joins the faculty as professor of psychology. The institute becomes a center for students interested in parapsychology and alternative healing.

1975    Henry Dakin establishes the Washington Research Institute, which sponsors activities that play a major role in opening communications between the United States and the USSR.

1975    Elizabeth Rauscher convenes the Fundamental Fysiks Group at Lawrence Berkeley Laboratory with forty physicists to discuss quantum theory and Bell's remote-connectedness theorem. They also perform remote-viewing experiments and continue to meet regularly until 1979.

1975    Jeffrey Mishlove receives the first and only Ph.D. in parapsychology from the University of California Berkeley.

1975    William Kautz founds the Center for Applied Intuition in San Francisco.

1975    A successful intercontinental remote-viewing session is conducted among participants at four locations: the Congress of Sorcery in Bogota, Colombia (led by Jean Millay); the Association for Humanistic Psychology in Estes Park, Colorado (led by Stanley Krippner); the Metatantay Foundation in Carlin, Nevada (led by Rolling Thunder); and a studio in Santa Rosa, California, where artist Jim Dowlin accurately drew the images of the target that he received telepathically.

1978    Henry Dakin publishes *High-Voltage Photography* to aid researchers in understanding Kirlian photography as well as other methods for showing physiological and psychophysical energy interactions as visible images.

1979    Barbara Honegger becomes president of the PRG for one year while earning the first accredited graduate degree in parapsychology at John F. Kennedy University. Two years later, she becomes a policy analyst in the Reagan White House Office of Policy Development.

1979    Arthur Hastings becomes dean of the Institute of Transpersonal Psychology, and becomes president from 1983 to 1984.

1980    Elizabeth Rauscher becomes president of the PRG until 1986.

1980    Willis Harman becomes a member of the board of regents of the University of California until 1990. His 1988 book, *Global Mind Change,* is an important influence.

1981    Larissa Vilenskaya, sponsored by Henry Dakin and the Washington Research Institute, emigrates from USSR to the United States. She translates papers smuggled out of the USSR for the Voice of America and becomes editor of the *Psi Research Review.*

1984    Ruth-Inge Heinze inaugurates the annual International Conference on the Study of Shamanism and Alternative Healing.

1986    Jean Millay becomes president of the PRG until 1988 and conceives of publishing a book, to be called *Mind Matters,* to celebrate the PRG's twentieth anniversary. Dean Brown is enlisted as coeditor.

1988    Saul-Paul Sirag becomes president of the PRG.

1988    Beverly Rubik becomes director of the Center for Frontier Sciences at Temple University, Philadelphia.

1989    Shelley Thomson becomes president of the San Francisco Tesla Society.

1989    Jean Millay returns as president of the PRG. The idea of a PRG book is revived, now to be a twenty-fifth anniversary volume.

1990    Beverley Kane assumes production of the PRG book, to be called *Silver Threads: 25 Years of Explorations in Parapsychology.*

1990    Jean Burns cofounds the Consciousness and Science Discussion Group at University of California San Francisco with Ravi Gomatam of the Bhaktivedanta Institute.

1992    The PRG board of directors consists of Jean Millay, Ph.D., president; Bryan McRae, secretary; Henry S. Dakin, treasurer; Dean Brown, Ph.D.; Jean Burns, Ph.D.; Ruth-Inge Heinze, Ph.D.; Beverley Kane, M.D.; Elizabeth Rauscher, Ph.D.; Russell Targ; Shelley Thomson.

1992    Elizabeth Targ, M.D., becomes president of the PRG.

# Appendix: PRG Belief Survey

The Parapsychology Research Group (PRG) is composed of a diverse group of people—diverse in personalities, in backgrounds, in interests, and, most important, in beliefs. As discussed in Chapter 2, most of us are largely unconscious of the rules we have established for deciding what to believe. In entertaining beliefs about parapsychology, many of these internalized rules do not suffice to decide among our self-inconsistent interpretations of reality. Yet when asked to give a spontaneous opinion based on our beliefs, we can do so with little hesitation.

The thread of consensus that runs through as PRG members is an open-mindedness that permits us great flexibility in the belief formation process. The most important function of the PRG has been to provide a lively forum for discussion of controversial ideas in a spirit of tolerance that celebrates the diversity of our views and allows us to play with new beliefs.

For our own interest, we conducted a poll to evaluate the prevalence of certain beliefs and experiences among our members. The survey was printed on the monthly meeting notice that was sent out, as is customary, to the active member mailing list about two weeks before the July 1987 meeting. Other copies were distributed at the July meeting. Although the replies were optionally anonymous, most respondents supplied their names. Many of the authors in this book are represented in the survey.

The questionnaire asked respondents to mark an $x$ beside each of ten types of phenomena he or she believed to occur and to mark two $x$s beside those that he or she had experienced (Figure A.1). Respondents also were asked about the general frequency of their psi experiences and were invited to share anecdotes. The categories were not meant to be exhaustive, and many paranormal experiences are difficult to assign to any of the given categories.

Twenty-five questionnaires were returned, a few apparently from nonmember visitors

**Figure A.1**
**Belief Survey of PRG Members**

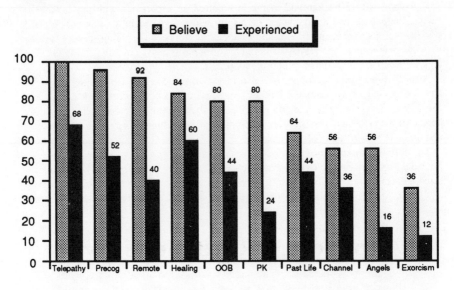

Numbers represent percentage of sample. N = 26. Labels refer to surveyed categories of telepathy, precognition, remote viewing, psychic healing, out-of-body experience, psychokinesis, past-life experience, channeling, visions of saints or angels, exorcism.

attending the meeting. Not surprisingly, the survey reveals that more than three-quarters of the respondents believe in telepathy (100%), remote viewing (92%), precognition (96%), psychokinesis (80%), psychic healing (84%), or out-of-body experiences (80%). (What is not evident in the tables is that the patterns of belief were quite variable, with some people accepting all ten types of phenomena and some accepting only two or three types.) With the exception of exorcism (36%), more than half the respondents subscribe to the existence of each phenomenon listed. The survey additionally reveals that one-half or more of the respondents believe that they have *experienced* telepathy, precognition, or psychic healing. One-third or more of the respondents believe that they have experienced remote viewing, out-of-body travel, channeling, or past-life memory. For each type of phenomenon surveyed, at least 12% report having experienced it. All respondents reported having had at least one psi experience. Thirty-three percent have such experiences once a month or more; 46% have such experiences several times per year; and 21% have had only one or two experiences in their lifetimes. What is most significant, as evident in the graph, is that, on the whole, people *believe* in more things than they have *experienced*. From this we conclude that we accept as evidence for reality material that is neither logical, in a strict sense, nor received from direct personal experience.

Several respondents provided reports of personal experiences. For example, a woman with a professional background in physical science described her own informal telepathy experiment: "The sender thought of three wavy lines and of ocean waves; I saw two wavy lines and thought of ocean waves. Then the sender visualized a triangle inscribed in a circle, plus an eye in a pyramid; I thought of a triangle and a circle (separately, not together), and an eye in a pyramid.''

A woman with a background in music reported an experience with psychokinesis: ''My grandparents had a huge house on a farm which I visited in the summer. When I was twelve or thirteen, my friends and I dabbled in the occult, holding seances and the like. At one seance, the leg of an upright card table jumped out from the table. The legs were *not* loose; you had to pull them out.''

A professional anthropologist who also is a shaman described her healing work: ''I have conducted many shamanic journeys and sealed psychotic breaks before they became final. I tune in to people and gently guide them out of their confusion. I use my hands for diagnosis and healing—not touching but transmitting energy from a distance— and am able to shift and balance energy.''

The following experience was related by a paralegal appeals officer who has done graduate work in psychology and who characterizes herself as being ''picky [about] scientific credibility.'' The event happened three years before the night of the survey and illustrates the problem of labeling paranormal events. It does not seem to fit into any of the ten survey categories.

> I am a working, single parent who leads a rather quiet, but busy, life. I had been asleep and woke up from a rather ordinary dream. I felt slightly odd on waking up, as though ''someone'' were present. I simply thought I was groggy; I started to get up and felt the need to urinate. A feeling of ''presence'' threatened me—was someone was breaking [into] the house? I thought about my teenage son sleeping in the other room and wondered what to do.
>
> Then I thought perhaps I was dreaming or having a [hypnogogic] response while still half asleep. I pinched myself hard—it hurt—to assure myself that I was awake; looked back on my pillow to see that my head was *not* there (as in an out-of-body experience), that is, I was sitting up. All seemed to be in order.
>
> Then I became aware of something on the wall at the foot of my bed about three feet tall and one foot wide. It was a silver cylinder–type thing with blue, lavender, and silver flowing from it. The motion seemed viscous, and the object was quite lovely. I had *no* reference for it. I was both astonished and uptight and thought, ''Is this a psychotic break?''
>
> To document that I was fully awake, I pinched myself again, then I pulled off the socks I was wearing, threw them to the side, and reached into the drawer under the bed to *change* socks (in order to document in my own mind later that in fact I *was* fully awake). I then noted the time on my digital clock—it was 1:10 A.M. The phenomenon remained on the wall by my clock until 1:50 A.M. I felt too freaked out to get up or call out.
>
> About 1:50 A.M., an ''inner'' voice pressed me strongly to ''Get up and reassure yourself that the house is in order.'' I felt argumentative: ''No way!'' It *gently* pressed me once again.
>
> I got up and did *not* turn on the lights; everything seemed fine. I urinated; went back to my room. ''It'' was still there. I could *not* believe this episode. I was again gently pressed to return to sleep and informed that I was OK.
>
> This whole event took almost an hour. I had not been drinking or using

drugs. I am not into "religion," though I presume there are those who have visions, etc. I do not consider myself either a mystic or a kook. I do not know what the phenomenon was.

Most psi experiences are less striking—a small coincidence, a precognitive dream. This latter story illustrates several features of the more dramatic psi experiences: The person may initially feel a bit frightened but soon realizes that there is no danger. A reality testing repertoire seems to be in order, such as pinching oneself, seeing if one's body is "left behind" in the bed, and doing something ordinary that can be corroborated later, like changing socks. Fleeting doubts about one's psychological condition—"Am I going crazy?"—may arise. In addition, this event was extremely powerful and detailed in the person's mind, even three years after the occurrence.

Like the person who contributed this story, some who come to the PRG are otherwise rational people who have had a single anomalous experience that is vivid, undeniable, and perplexing. The individual typically has no context in common sense, religion, or science in which to interpret the event. Many people attempt to assimilate their experience by further experimentation, such as the first woman describes. Unfortunately many others opt to exorcise such experiences from their memories rather than face the awkward cognitive dissonances that would arise from exploring the nature and implications of these occurrences. Once the status quo is defended blindly, once the path of denial is taken, it becomes difficult for the person to open his perceptions to the more subtle paranormal or extrasensory stimuli that occur on a daily basis.

Yet all thoughtful, perceptive people must be alert for new data. It is likely that as a society, our collectively pooled samples of elusive daily events, small episodes colored by faint hues of the vaguely extraordinary, will yield the most important clues to paranormal functioning.

Parapsychology is still in its infancy. Our ad hoc experiments, like those in the stories above, await perhaps our analogous Benjamin Franklin and his kite. Our formal experiments, although definitive at this point in time, are still crude and empirical. We have little in the way of testable models for how psi phenomena operate. We have much disagreement about even the definition of psi categories and no clue whatever as to the limits of what we can accomplish with our current human faculties. We in the PRG, however, share a most ardent belief: that psi, through expanded scientific exploration, will be understood and utilized in a practical, physical way to benefit humanity, the earth, and the universe.

# Selected Bibliography

**GENERAL PARAPSYCHOLOGY**

Broughton RS. *Parapsychology the Controversial Science*. New York: Ballantine; 1991.

Edge HL, Morris RL, Rush JH, Palmer J. *Foundations of Parapsychology*. Boston: Routledge & Kegan Paul; 1986.

Eysenk HJ, Sargent C. *Explaining the Unexplained: Mysteries of the Paranormal*. London: Weidenfeld & Nicolson; 1982.

Gauld A. *The Founders of Psychical Research*. New York: Schocken, 1968.

Gurney E, Myers FWH, Podmore F. *Phantasms of the Living* (2 vols). London: Tribner; 1886.

James W. *Essays in Psychical Research*. In *The Works of William James*. Cambridge, MA: Harvard University Press; 1986.

Koestler A. *The Roots of Coincidence*. New York: Vintage Books; 1973.

Krippner S, ed. *Advances in Parapsychology* (6 vols). Vols 1–3: New York: Plenum; 1977, 1978, 1982. Vols 4–6: Jefferson, NC: McFarland; 1984, 1987, 1990.

LeShan L. *Alternate Realities*. New York: Ballantine Books; 1976.

Murphy M. *The Future of the Body*. Los Angeles: Tarcher; 1992.

Persinger MA. *The Paranormal* (2 vols). New York: MSS Information; 1974.

Price H. *Fifty Years of Psychical Research*. London: Longmans, Green; 1939.

Rhine JB. *The Reach of the Mind*. New York: Sloane; 1947.

Wolman BB, ed. *Handbook of Parapsychology*. Jefferson, NC: McFarland; 1986.

**GENERAL CONSCIOUSNESS, PSYCHOLOGY, AND PHILOSOPHY**

Abbott EA. *Flatland*. New York: New American Library; 1984.

Blakemore C. *Mechanics of the Mind*. New York: Cambridge University Press; 1977.

Bohm D. *Wholeness and the Implicate Order*. London: Routledge & Kegan Paul; 1980.

Broad CD. *The Mind and Its Place in Nature*. London: Routledge & Kegan Paul; 1927.

d'Espagnat B. *In Search of Reality*. New York: Springer-Verlag; 1983.

Ferguson M. *The Aquarian Conspiracy*. Los Angeles: Tarcher; 1980.

Garfield CA, with Bennett HZ. *Peak Performance. Mental Training Techniques of the World's Greatest Athletes*. New York: Warner Books; 1984.

Gregory RL. *Mind in Science: A History of Explanations in Psychology and Physics*. New York: Cambridge University Press; 1981.

Grim P, ed. *Philosophy of Science and the Occult*. Albany: State University of New York Press; 1982.

Grof S. *Realms of the Human Unconscious: Observations from LSD Research*. New York: E. P. Dutton; 1976.

———. *Beyond Death: The Gates of Consciousness*. London: Thames & Hudson, 1980.

———. *The Adventures of Self-Discovery*. Albany: State University New York Press; 1985.

———. *Beyond the Brain: Birth, Death and Transcendence in Psychotherapy*. Albany: State University of New York; 1985.

Harman W. *Global Mind Change: The Promise of the Last Years of the Twentieth Century*. Indianapolis: Knowledge Systems, Inc; 1988.

Heinze R-I. *Shamans of the Twentieth Century*. New York: Irvington Publ; 1991.

Hilgard E. *Divided Consciousness, Multiple Controls in Human Thought and Action*. New York: Wiley & Sons; 1986.

James W. *The Varieties of Religious Experience*. New York: Mentor; 1958.

Kautz WH, Branon M. *Intuiting the Future: A New Age Vision of the 1990s*. San Francisco: Harper & Row; 1989:37–39.

Krippner S. *Human Possibilities: Mind Exploration in the USSR and Eastern Europe*. Garden City, NY: Doubleday, Anchor Press; 1980.

LeShan L. *The Medium, the Mystic and the Physicist*. New York: Ballantine Books; 1975.

Maslow A. *Toward a Psychology of Being*. Princeton, NJ: Van Nostrand; 1962.

Nadel L. *Sixth Sense: The Whole-Brain Book of Intuition, Hunches, Gut Feelings, and Their Place in Your Everyday Life*. New York: Prentice-Hall; 1990.

Pearce JC. *The Crack in the Cosmic Egg*. New York: Pocket Books; 1973.

Peat FD. *Synchronicity: The Bridge Between Matter and Mind*. New York: Bantam; 1987.

Roberts J. *The Nature of Personal Reality*. Englewood Cliffs, NJ: Prentice-Hall; 1974.

Tart CT. *Altered States of Consciousness*. New York: John Wiley & Sons; 1969.

———. *Waking Up: Overcoming the Obstacles of Human Potential*. Boston: Shambhala, New Science Library; 1986.

Warcollier R. *Mind to Mind*. New York: Farrar, Strauss and Strauss & Co.; 1948, 1963.

## PHENOMENOLOGICAL PARAPSYCHOLOGY

Bardens D. *Psychic Animals: A Fascinating Investigation of Paranormal Behavior*. New York: Henry Holt & Co; 1987.

Braude SE. *ESP and Psychokinesis: A Philosophical Examination*. Philadelphia: Temple University Press; 1979.

Hastings A. *With the Tongues of Men and Angels: A Study of Channeling.* Fort Worth, TX: Holt, Rinehart & Winston; 1991.

Heinze R-I. *Trance and Healing in Southeast Asia Today.* Berkeley/Bangkok: Independent Scholars of Asia, Inc. White Lotus; 1988.

Jahn RG, Dunne BJ. *Margins of Reality.* New York: Harcourt Brace Jovanovich; 1987.

Kautz W, Branon M. *Channeling: The Intuitive Connection.* San Francisco: Harper & Row; 1987.

Klimo J. *Channeling: Investigations on Receiving Information from Paranormal Sources.* Los Angeles: Tarcher; 1987.

Kübler-Ross E. *On Death and Dying.* New York: Macmillan; 1969.

Monroe RA. *Journeys Out of the Body.* Garden City, NY: Anchor/Doubleday; 1977.

Moody R, Jr. *Life After Life.* New York: Bantam; 1975.

Murphy M, White R. *The Psychic Side of Sports.* Reading, MA: Addison-Wesley; 1978.

Rhine JB. *Extrasensory Perception.* Boston: Bruce Humphries, 1973 (originally published 1934).

Ring K. *Heading Toward Omega.* New York: William Morrow; 1984.

———. *Life at Death.* New York: Coward, McCann & Geoghegan; 1980.

Smythies JR, ed. *Science and ESP.* London: Routledge & Kegan Paul; 1967.

Targ R, Harary K. *The Mind Race. Understanding and Using Psychic Abilities.* New York: Villard Books; 1984.

Targ R, Puthoff HE. *Mind Reach: Scientists Look at Psychic Ability.* New York: Delacorte; 1977.

Tart CT, Puthoff HE, Targ R, eds. *Mind at Large.* New York: Praeger; 1979.

Ullman M, Krippner S. *Dream Studies and Telepathy: An Experimental Approach* (Parapsychological Monographs No. 12). New York: Parapsychology Foundation; 1970.

Vilenskaya L, Steffy J. *Firewalking: A New Look at an Old Enigma.* Falls Village, CT: Bramble Co; 1991.


## GENERAL SCIENCE AND BIOSCIENCE

Achterberg J, Lawlis F. *Bridges of the Bodymind.* Champaign, IL: Institute for Personality and Ability Testing; 1980.

Achterberg J. *Imagery and Healing, Shamanism and Modern Medicine.* Boston: Shambhala, New Science Library; 1985.

Ader R, ed. *Psychoneuroimmunology.* New York: Academic Press; 1981.

Becker RO, Selden G. *The Body Electric: Electromagnetism and the Foundation of Life.* New York: William Morrow; 1985.

Benson H, with Klipper MZ. *The Relaxation Response.* New York: William Morrow; 1975.

Broad W, Wade N. *Betrayers of the Truth.* New York: Simon & Schuster; 1982.

Dewdney AK. *The Planiverse: Computer Contact with a Two-Dimensional World.* New York: Poseidon Press; 1984.

Dossey L. *Meaning and Medicine.* New York: Bantam Books; 1991.

Eccles J. *The Neurophysiological Basis of Mind.* Oxford: Oxford University Press; 1953.

Hartmann F. *Occult Science in Medicine.* New York: Samuel Weiser, Inc; 1975 (originally published 1893).

Herbert N. *Faster Than Light: Superluminal Loopholes in Physics*. New York: New American Library; 1988.

Herbert N. *Quantum Reality: Beyond the New Physics*. New York: Doubleday; 1985.

Justice B. *Who Gets Sick*. Los Angeles: Tarcher; 1988.

Kohn A. *False Prophets: Fraud and Error in Science and Medicine*. Oxford: Basil Blackwell; 1986.

Kuhn TS. *The Structure of Scientific Revolutions*, 2nd ed. Chicago: University of Chicago Press; 1970.

Seligman MEP. *Helplessness: On Depression, Development and Death*. San Francisco: W. H. Freeman; 1975.

Selye H. *The Stress of Life*. New York: McGraw-Hill; 1956.

Shulgin A, Shulgin A. *Pihkal: A Chemical Love Story*. Berkeley, CA: Transform Press; 1991.

Worrall A, Worrall O. *The Healing-Touch*. New York: Harper & Row; 1970.

# Index

# About the Contributors

SONDRA BARRETT, Ph.D. (Biochemistry, University of Illinois) is associate professor in clinical psychology (adjunct) and co-director of the Integral Health Studies program at the California Institute for Integral Studies. As former assistant professor at University of California San Francisco Medical School's Cancer Research Institute, her research was in human lymphocyte receptors and the diagnosis and treatment of human leukemias. Dr. Barrett uses psychoneuroimmonology techniques in clinical private practice in Marin County, California.

WILLIAM BRAUD, Ph.D. (Psychology, University of Iowa) is the director of research for the Institute of Transpersonal Psychology in Palo Alto, California. He worked for more than a decade in psychoenergetic (bio-PK) research at Mind Science Foundation in San Antonio, Texas. Braud is a pioneering researcher in ganzfeld and bio-PK investigations.

DEAN BROWN, Ph.D. (Physics, University of Kansas) is founder and president of Picodyne Corporation, Menlo park, California, an educational software company. Previous to that, he was a founder of Zilog Inc. and pioneered the use of computers in education at Stanford Research Institute, now SRI International, where he worked with the United Nations Educational Scientific and Cultural Organization (UNESCO) on international education projects. In the 1950s he worked on nuclear power projects for the United Nations and for the

International Atomic Energy Agency. A physicist, a metaphysicist, and a Vedic scholar, Dr. Brown has recently completed a translation of the Upanishads from Sanskrit.

JEAN E. BURNS, Ph.D. (Physics, University of Hawaii) is a physicist now doing research in consciousness from a multidisciplinary standpoint. She is the author of a recent review of models of consciousness and of various other papers about consciousness. Together with Ravi Gomatam of the Bhaktivedanta Institute, Dr. Burns formed the Consciousness and Science Discussion Group, which meets in San Francisco. Dr. Burns has a long-standing interest in psychic techniques, has taught numerous classes in these, and is author of a book on the subject, *Your Innate Psychic Powers.*

WILLIAM J. CROFT, E.E./C.S. (Electrical engineering/Computer Science, Purdue University) is a telecommunications engineer at the Institute for Global Communications, home of the Account and PeaceNet international networks. He previously held research positions at Stanford University, SRI International (formerly Stanford Research Institute), and Sun Microsystems, where he was founding staff engineer. He was a research staff member at Purdue University for ten years in the computer center and electrical engineering departments.

STANISLAV GROF, M.D. (Charles University, Prague, Czechoslovakia) is a psychiatrist with more than thirty years experience researching nonordinary states of consciousness. He is one of the founders and chief theoreticians of transpersonal psychology and founding president of the International Transpersonal Psychology Association. His professional career includes seven years as assistant professor at The Johns Hopkins University and chief of psychiatric research at the Maryland Psychiatric Research Center.

WILLIS HARMAN, Ph.D. (Electrical Engineering, Stanford) is president of the Institute of Noetic Sciences, Sausalito, California, a nonprofit organization founded by astronaut Edgar Mitchell to expand knowledge of the nature and potentials of the mind. Dr. Harman was previously senior social scientist at SRI International of Menlo Park, California, where he initiated a program on futures research and worked on long-term strategic planning and policy analysis. He is emeritus professor of engineering-economic systems at Stanford University, author of *Global Mind Change,* and coauthor of *Creative Work, Paths to Peace, Higher Creativity,* and *Changing Images of Man.*

RUTH-INGE HEINZE, Ph.D. (Asian studies, University of California, Berkeley) trained in anthropology at the University of Berlin in her native Germany. During the past thirty years, she has lived and worked with shamans in South, Southeast, and East Asia. Since 1984, Dr. Heinze has produced the annual International Conference on the Study of Shamans and Alternative Modes of

Healing. Her books include *Shamans of the 20th Century* and *Trance and Healing in Southeast Asia Today*. She is on the board of directors of the Parapsychology Research Group.

NICK HERBERT, Ph.D. (Physics, Stanford University) is an experimental physicist in northern California. In addition to his counseling work, Dr. Herbert conducts seminars at the Esalen Institute. His books include *Quantum Reality, Faster-Than-Light,* the upcoming *Elemental Mind,* and the shortest proof of Bell's theorem to date.

CHARLES HONORTON was pursuing his doctorate in the Department of Psychology at the University of Edinburgh under the auspices of the Arthur Koestler Chair of Parapsychology at the time of his death in 1992. Previously, he was the Director of Psychophysical Research Labs in Princeton, New Jersey.

JAMES R. JOHNSTON, Ph.D. (Physics, University of California, Riverside) helped to develop a theoretical framework showing the similarity of coherence in lasers and macroscopic quantum coherence in superfluid helium at the University of California, Riverside. He taught graduate physics at Dalhousie University in Halifax, Nova Scotia, and at California State University, San Diego, before entering into electroencephalographic (EEG) biofeedback research with Joe Kamiya at Langley Porter Neuropsychiatric Institute, University of California, San Francisco. He is now working on commercial applications of EEG technology at SAM Technology Inc., San Francisco.

BEVERLEY KANE, M.D. (University of California, San Francisco) specializes in preventive medicine and medical informatics at Apple Computer, Inc., Cupertino, California. After completing a residency in family practice (San Francisco General Hospital) and a fellowship in sports and preventive medicine (University of London), she joined the staff at the Stanford University Center for Research in Disease Prevention, where she was involved in research in coronary artery disease. Having studied computer science (Massachusetts Institute of Technology, Columbia University) and having majored in art as an undergraduate (Barnard College), Dr. Kane combines art, medicine, computer technology, and consciousness studies by creating computer-human interfaces for medical and other applications.

WILLIAM H. KAUTZ, Sc.D. (Massachusetts Institute of Technology) is founder and director of the Center for Applied Intuition, P.O. Box 218, Fairfax, CA, 94978, (415) 453-2130. Previously he was staff scientist at the Stanford Research Institute, where he formed a basic research group (now a laboratory) in computer science. For thirty-five years, Kautz participated in research projects in computer science and technology and in geophysics. His book in progress deals with the origins of knowledge and the role of science in society.

JON KLIMO, Ph.D. (Psychology, Rosebridge Graduate School) is director of research and director of alternative programs at Rosebridge Graduate School, Concord, California. He received his master's degree from Brown University in interdisciplinary studies and was professor of education at Rutgers University for eight years.

STANLEY KRIPPNER, Ph.D. (Educational Psychology, Northwestern University) is professor of psychology at Saybrook Institute, San Francisco, and distinguished professor of psychology at the California Institute of Integral Studies, San Francisco.

JEAN MILLAY, Ph.D. (Human Science, Saybrook Institute) is the art director for the development of interactive educational software at DynEd International, Foster City, California. She is the author of various publications on the subject of brain wave synchronization, telepathy, and visionary experience. She has taught numerous college classes in biofeedback and parapsychology. In 1971, Dr. Millay co-invented (with Tim Scully) the stereo brain wave biofeedback light sculpture, a device that compares brain waves between two persons or between one's own cerebral hemispheres and feeds that information back as aesthetic patterns of light and sound. This was demonstrated at the Metropolitan Museum of Art in New York in May 1972. Dr. Millay is past president of the Parapsychology Research Group.

MICHAEL A. PERSINGER, Ph.D. (Physiological Psychology, University of Manitoba) is professor of psychology and neuroscience at Laurentian University, Sudbury, Ontario, Canada.

CHERI QUINCY, D.O. (Texas College of Osteopathic Medicine) did a residency in internal medicine at the Fort Worth Osteopathic Hospital and a fellowship in geriatrics at New York Medical College. She is founder and co-owner of the Santa Rosa (California) Medical Group and medical director of the Health Information Network, a computerized information retrieval service for traditional and nontraditional medical databases.

ELIZABETH A. RAUSCHER, Ph.D. (Nuclear Engineering, University of California, Berkeley) is founder and president of Tecnic Research Laboratories, a biomedical engineering company in Reno, Nevada, where she is coinventor of the pulsed magnetic field pacemaker. For nineteen years, Dr. Rauscher has been associated with the Lawrence Berkeley Laboratory and has taught at Stanford and John F. Kennedy University, Orinda, California. From 1980 to 1986 she was president of the Parapsychology Research Group.

KENNETH RING, Ph.D. (Social Psychology, University of Minnesota) is professor of psychology at the University of Connecticut, Storrs. In 1980, he published *Life at Death,* the first scientific study of the near-death experience (NDE). The next year he helped found the International Association of Near-Death Studies, which has branches in ten countries around the world. The *Journal of Near-Death Studies,* which he established, is in its tenth year of publication. In 1984, Dr. Ring introduced his second book, *Healing Toward Omega,* which was concerned mainly with the after effects and evolutionary implications of NDEs. In 1992, he published his book, *The Omega Project,* which examines the NDE-prone personality.

BEVERLY RUBIK, Ph.D. (Biophysics, University of California, Berkeley) is director of the Center for Frontier Sciences at Temple University, Philadelphia. The center facilitates global information exchange, networking, and education in frontier areas of science, including parapsychology, technology, and medicine. She previously was a faculty member in physics, chemistry, the Center for Interdisplinary Sciences, and NEXA, a program devoted to examining the convergence of science and the humanities at San Francisco State University. Until 1990, Dr. Rubik was on the board of directors of the Parapsychology Research Group.

MARILYN SCHLITZ, Ph.D. (Anthropology, University of Texas, Austin) is a research fellow in the Department of Psychology, Stanford University, Palo Alto, California. She has published extensively in the areas of remote viewing, ganzfeld, and psychic healing.

SAUL-PAUL SIRAG was born in 1939 of missionary parents in Dutch Borneo and spent three years in Japanese concentration camps in Java. His higher education in Prairie Bible Institute, Alberta, Canada, and the University of California, Berkeley emphasized theology, philosophy, mathematics, and physics. Sirag was a research associate to Arthur Young at the Institute for the Study of Consciousness in Berkeley (1973–1977). With Nick Herbert, he co-led the annual Esalen Physics Conferences (1978–1988) and led the monthly seminars of the Consciousness Theory Group in Berkeley and San Francisco (1977–1979). Sirag has published papers on cosmology and unified field theory in *Nature* and *The International Journal of Theoretical Physics.* He is working on a book on the mathematics of unified field theory and consciousness to be published by World Scientific, Singapore, in 1993. From 1988 to 1989, he was president of the Parapsychology Research Group.

RUSSELL TARG is senior staff scientist at Lockheed Research and Development Laboratories in Palo Alto, California. A physicist who has conducted pioneering research on the development of the laser, Targ was codirector of the psychic research program at SRI International (formerly Stanford Research Institute). He has published numerous articles on plasma physics, microwaves, lasers, and remote-viewing research in *Nature,* the *IEEE Proceedings,* and the

*AAAS* (American Association for the Advancement of Science) *Proceedings.* In 1982, Targ carried out the first remote-viewing experiments between Moscow and San Francisco. Targ was a founder and the first president of the Parapsychology Research Group.

SHELLEY THOMSON conducts research in the new paradigm physics. Sponsers of the project include Cotati Research Foundation and the Foundation for Mind-Being Research. She is president of the San Francisco Tesla Society and resides in Berkeley, California. She is on the board of directors of the Parapsychology Research Group.

LARISSA VILENSKAYA, L.H.D. (College of Spiritual and Psychic Sciences, Montreal) is a researcher in parapsychology. She received her master's degree in engineering in the former Soviet Union, her country of birth, and worked with many psychics, healers, and researchers in that country. In 1980, Vilenskaya moved to Israel, where she became an active member of the Israeli Parapsychology Society. In 1981, she emigrated to the United States, where she founded *Psi Research,* a journal devoted to parapsychology research in the Soviet Union and Eastern Europe. Since learning how to firewalk in 1983, she has conducted numerous seminars teaching others how to accomplish the feat. She is a past member of the board of directors of the Parapsychology Research Group.